ANNUAL EDITIONS

International Business
Sixteenth Edition

EDITOR
Fred H. Maidment
Western Connecticut State University

Dr. Fred Maidment is a Professor in the Department of Management of the Ancell School of Business at Western Connecticut State University in Danbury, Connecticut. He received his Bachelors from the Stern School of Business of New York University, his MBA from the Zicklin School of Business of the Baruch College of the City University of New York, and his Doctorate from the University of South Carolina. In addition, he did post-graduate work at the Warrington College of Business of the University of Florida where he was a Resident Fellow. He and his wife reside in Connecticut and have four grown children, one granddaughter, and two grandsons.

McGraw-Hill
Connect
Learn
Succeed™

The McGraw·Hill Companies

Connect
Learn
Succeed™

ANNUAL EDITIONS: INTERNATIONAL BUSINESS, SIXTEENTH EDITION

Published by McGraw-Hill, a business unit of The McGraw-Hill Companies, Inc., 1221 Avenue of the Americas, New York, NY 10020. Copyright © 2011 by The McGraw-Hill Companies, Inc. All rights reserved. Previous editions © 2009, 2007, and 2005. No part of this publication may be reproduced or distributed in any form or by any means, or stored in a database or retrieval system, without the prior written consent of The McGraw-Hill Companies, Inc., including, but not limited to, in any network or other electronic storage or transmission, or broadcast for distance learning.

Some ancillaries, including electronic and print components, may not be available to customers outside the United States.

Annual Editions® is a registered trademark of The McGraw-Hill Companies, Inc.

Annual Editions is published by the **Contemporary Learning Series** group within the McGraw-Hill Higher Education division.

1 2 3 4 5 6 7 8 9 0 QDB/QDB 1 0 9 8 7 6 5 4 3 2 1 0

ISBN 978–0–07–352862–5
MHID 0–07–352862–5
ISSN 1091–1731

Managing Editor: *Larry Loeppke*
Developmental Editor: *Dave Welsh*
Senior Permissions Coordinator: *Shirley Lanners*
Senior Marketing Communications Specialist: *Mary Klein*
Project Manager: *Robin A. Reed*
Design Coordinator: *Margarite Reynolds*
Buyer: *Sandy Ludovissy*
Media Project Manager: *Sridevi Palani*

Compositor: Laserwords Private Limited
Cover Images: Keith Brofsky/Getty Images (inset); IMS Communications Ltd./Capstone Design/FlatEarth Images (background)

Library in Congress Cataloging-in-Publication Data
Main entry under title: Annual Editions: International Business, 16/e.
1. Management—Periodicals. I. Maidment, Fred H., *comp*. II. Title: International Business.
658'.05

www.mhhe.com

Editors/Academic Advisory Board

Members of the Advisory Board are instrumental in the final selection of articles for each edition of ANNUAL EDITIONS. Their review of articles for content, level, currentness, and appropriateness provides critical direction to the editor and staff. We think that you will find their careful consideration well reflected in this volume.

ANNUAL EDITIONS: International Business
16th Edition

EDITOR

Fred H. Maidment
Western Connecticut State University

ACADEMIC ADVISORY BOARD MEMBERS

Preface

In publishing ANNUAL EDITIONS we recognize the enormous role played by the magazines, newspapers, and journals of the public press in providing current, first-rate educational information in a broad spectrum of interest areas. Many of these articles are appropriate for students, researchers, and professionals seeking accurate, current material to help bridge the gap between principles and theories and the real world. These articles, however, become more useful for study when those of lasting value are carefully collected, organized, indexed, and reproduced in a low-cost format, which provides easy and permanent access when the material is needed. That is the role played by ANNUAL EDITIONS.

The theme of *Annual Editions: International Business Sixteenth Edition* is change. In September of 2008, the global economy changed. It entered into the most severe economic recession since the Great Depression of the 1930's. Some people even labeled this period the "Great Recession." Actual unemployment in the United States reached levels that had not been seen since the last half of the Great Depression; the housing crisis was not just an American phenomenon, but a global one; and a small, western country, Iceland, for all intents and purposes, actually declared bankruptcy.

Governments the world over rushed to save their respective financial systems and the entire global economy, was, for a time, in danger of collapsing. For now, the imminent danger that the world economy will collapse has passed, but the changes the economic crisis brought to the global economy and world trade have yet to be fully understood or realized.

The relative positions and importance of various national economies have changed. China has become much more important as have the economies of the rest of the developing world. In the United States, the debt the country has accumulated since the end of World War II is now beginning to impair the ability of the nation to grow and support the demands of its citizenry and its obligations. In Japan and Europe, the economic ramifications of population decline and stagnation are beginning to be realized as more people retire and fewer workers enter the workforce to take their place and support the social contract that provides many of the social services including medical and retirement benefits for an ageing population. While these problems are also present in the United States, they are much greater in Europe and Japan than in the United States.

The world is changing and the financial crisis of 2008 was the first trumpet alerting the world to the changes occuring in the global economy. These changes, like any great societal change, will not come overnight. But they are coming. September 2008 was only the first of many financial, political, technological, and social changes that await the global economy in the future.

The 40 articles that have been chosen for *Annual Editions: International Business Sixteenth Edition,* represent an outstanding cross-section of current articles in the field. This volume addresses various component parts of international business including financial management, international trade theory, international marketing, foreign direct investment, the global corporation, as well as others. Articles have been chosen from leading business magazines such as *Forbes, Business Week,* and *The Journal of Business Strategy,* to provide a wide sampling of the latest thinking in the field of international business.

Annual Editions: International Business Sixteenth Edition contains a number of features designed to be useful for people interested in international business. These features include a Table of Contents with abstracts that summarize each article using bold, italicized key ideas and a Topic Guide to locate articles on specific subjects. The volume is organized into five units, each dealing with specific interrelated topics in international business. Every unit begins with an overview that provides background information for the articles in the section. This will enable the reader to place the selection in the context of the larger issues concerning international business. Important topics are emphasized and key points that address major themes are presented.

With this sixteenth edition of *Annual Editions: International Business,* it is hoped that more will follow addressing these important issues. I believe that the collection is the most complete and useful compilation of current material available to the international business student that is possible in a printed edition. We would like to have your response to this volume, for we are interested in your opinions and recommendations. Please take a few minutes to complete and return the postage-paid Article Rating Form at the back of the volume. Any book can be improved and we need your help to continue to improve *Annual Editions: International Business.*

Fred H. Maidment
Editor

Contents

UNIT 1
Overview of International Business

The concepts in bold italics are developed in the article. For further expansion, please refer to the Topic Guide.

UNIT 2
International Finance

The concepts in bold italics are developed in the article. For further expansion, please refer to the Topic Guide.

16. The Global Financial Crisis: What Went Wrong?, Richard Mallett and Victor Smart, *Financial Management (UK),* July/August 2009
How did the global financial crisis happen? What were the events that preceded the crisis and could they be avoided in the future? It began from a series of events that led to the largest world financial crisis since at least the Great Depression. — 81

UNIT 3
International Organizations and Operations

Unit Overview — 84

Part A. The Global Corporation

17. The Work Left Undone: Perspectives on Small Business Opportunities in International Trade, Matthew Carr, *Business Credit,* January 2010
There is great opportunity for small businesses in global businesses, especially in the import/export sector. The government has recently stepped-up with new programs to assist small businesses and the opportunities for assistance remain great. — 87

Part B. Global Corporate Strategy

18. Brazil's Iron Giant Reaches for the Top, Joshua Schneyer, *Business Week,* March 3, 2008
Multinational firms do not just come from developed countries. Some of the largest and most powerful ones come from the developing world, such as Vale, which is on the brink of becoming the world's largest mining company. — 90

19. NanoTech Firm Takes Passage to India, Peter Gwynne, *Research Technology Management,* May–June 2009
Small high tech firms are going to developing countries to develop, manufacture, test and market their products before they do so in the United States and the rest of the developed world. Here is one company from Massachusetts that is doing it. — 92

20. Tata: Master of the Gentle Approach, Manjeet Kripalani, *Business Week,* February 25, 2008
India's Tata Motors recently acquired the truck division of the failing Korean conglomerate Daewoo. This was one of just a number of overseas acquisitions Tata corporate has recently made, totaling US$18 billion, including well known names like Tetley Tea and operations in the UK, US and Europe. Tata now employs over 300,000 people. — 94

Part C. Global Marketing

21. Rethinking Globalization: Does "Think Global, Act Local" Still Apply?, Nigel Hollis, *Marketing Research,* Spring 2009
One of the axioms of international business has been to "Think global, act local," but does that still apply in today's world? The fact is that there are few strong global brands. One of the keys to success is being part of the local culture. — 96

22. Expanding Opportunity at the Base of the Pyramid, David G. Altman, Lyndon Rego, and Peg Ross, *People and Strategy,* June 2009
There are 4 billion people living on US$2 a day or less, a group that represents trillions of potential sales in basic necessities in the developing world. Strategies for reaching these potential consumers are discussed. — 102

23. Hailun Piano and the Quest for Quality, *Music Trades,* February 2010
Hailun Piano of China manufactures high quality pianos, primarily for the export market, but is now also selling them in China. The obstacles and opportunities that this company faces are outlined here. — 107

The concepts in bold italics are developed in the article. For further expansion, please refer to the Topic Guide.

UNIT 4
Issues in International Business

The concepts in bold italics are developed in the article. For further expansion, please refer to the Topic Guide.

UNIT 5
The Future and International Business

The concepts in bold italics are developed in the article. For further expansion, please refer to the Topic Guide.

Correlation Guide

The *Annual Editions* series provides students with convenient, inexpensive access to current, carefully selected articles from the public press. **Annual Editions: International Business, 16/e** is an easy-to-use reader that presents articles on important topics such as *international trade policy, financial markets and exchanges, the monetary system* and many more. For more information on *Annual Editions* and other *McGraw-Hill Contemporary Learning Series titles,* visit www.mhhe.com/cls.

This convenient guide matches the units in **Annual Editions: International Business, 16/e** with the corresponding chapters in two of our best-selling McGraw-Hill International Business textbooks by Hill.

Annual Editions: International Business, 16/e	International Business: Competing in the Global Marketplace, 8/e by Hill	Global Business Today, 7/e by Hill
Unit 1: Overview of International Business	**Chapter 1:** Globalization **Chapter 5:** International Trade Theory	**Chapter 1:** Globalization **Chapter 5:** International Trade Theory
Unit 2: International Finance	**Chapter 8:** Regional Economic Integration **Chapter 9:** The Foreign Exchange Market **Chapter 11:** Global Capital Markets	**Chapter 2:** National Differences in Political Economy **Chapter 7:** Foreign Direct Investment **Chapter 10:** The International Monetary System
Unit 3: International Organizations and Operations	**Chapter 2:** National Differences in Political Economy **Chapter 3:** Differences in Culture **Chapter 5:** International Trade Theory **Chapter 6:** The Political Economy of International Trade **Chapter 7:** The Political Economy of Foreign Direct Investment **Chapter 8:** Regional Economic Integration **Chapter 14:** Entry Strategy and Strategic Alliances **Chapter 15:** Exporting, Importing, and Countertrade **Chapter 16:** Global Production, Outsourcing, and Logistics	**Chapter 3:** National Differences in Culture **Chapter 5:** International Trade Theory **Chapter 6:** The Political Economy of International Trade **Chapter 7:** Foreign Direct Investment **Chapter 8:** Regional Economic Integration **Chapter 11:** The Strategy of International Business **Chapter 12:** Entering Foreign Markets **Chapter 13:** Exporting, Importing, and Countertrade **Chapter 14:** Global Production, Outsourcing, and Logistics
Unit 4: Issues in International Business	**Chapter 7:** The Political Economy of Foreign Direct Investment **Chapter 11:** Global Capital Markets **Chapter 15:** Exporting, Importing, and Countertrade **Chapter 16:** Global Production, Outsourcing, and Logistics **Chapter 17:** Global Marketing and R&D **Chapter 18:** Global Human Resource Management **Chapter 19:** Accounting in the International Business **Chapter 20:** Financial Management in the International Business	**Chapter 7:** Foreign Direct Investment **Chapter 14:** Global Production, Outsourcing, and Logistics **Chapter 15:** Global Marketing and R&D **Chapter 16:** Global Human Resource Management
Unit 5: The Future and International Business	**Chapter 1:** Globalization	**Chapter 1:** Globalization

Topic Guide

This topic guide suggests how the selections in this book relate to the subjects covered in your course. You may want to use the topics listed on these pages to search the Web more easily.

On the following pages, a number of websites have been gathered specifically for this book. They are arranged to reflect the units of this Annual Editions reader. You can link to these sites by going to www.mhhe.com/cls.

All the articles that relate to each topic are listed below the bold-faced term.

Accounting

7. The Global Debt Bomb
8. The World Economy: The Global Financial Crisis and Collapse in World Trade
11. The Balance of Payments: Office for National Statistics
15. Planning Ahead for IFRS 1: Initial Adoption of IFRS by U.S. Companies
16. The Global Financial Crisis: What Went Wrong?
28. Keynote Panel Session 1: Whose Income Is It? How Business Is Caught in the Global Competition and Controversy for Tax Revenues

Consumer behavior

9. International Special Report: A Financial Crisis to the West—a Fundamental Crisis to the East
14. Engaging China: Strategies for the Small Internationalizing Firm
17. The Work Left Undone: Perspectives on Small Business Opportunities in International Trade
21. Rethinking Globalization: Does "Think Global, Act Local" Still Apply?
22. Expanding Opportunity at the Base of the Pyramid
23. Hailun Piano and the Quest for Quality

Corporate culture

16. The Global Financial Crisis: What Went Wrong?
18. Brazil's Iron Giant Reaches for the Top
20. Tata: Master of the Gentle Approach
21. Rethinking Globalization: Does "Think Global, Act Local" Still Apply?
22. Expanding Opportunity at the Base of the Pyramid
23. Hailun Piano and the Quest for Quality
24. Distant Dilemmas
33. International OHS: Through the Looking Glass of the Global Economy
35. Global Corporate Citizenship: Working with Governments and Civil Society
36. Going Green: The Challenges and the Solution

Developing countries

1. Globalization: Where Do We Go from Here?
2. China Must Carry the World
3. The World Is Not Flat
4. Is Global Trade a Threat or Opportunity?
5. Economists Rethink Free Trade
6. Globalization with a Human Face
7. The Global Debt Bomb
8. The World Economy: The Global Financial Crisis and Collapse in World Trade
9. International Special Report: A Financial Crisis to the West—a Fundamental Crisis to the East
11. The Balance of Payments: Office for National Statistics
12. Potential Future Functions of the World Trade Organization
14. Engaging China: Strategies for the Small Internationalizing Firm
18. Brazil's Iron Giant Reaches for the Top
19. NanoTech Firm Takes Passage to India
20. Tata: Master of the Gentle Approach
22. Expanding Opportunity at the Base of the Pyramid
23. Hailun Piano and the Quest for Quality
24. Distant Dilemmas
25. Jobs on Another Shore
27. A Material World
30. What One Hand Gives, the Other Takes: Industrial Countries' Policy Coherence for Development

31. Unequal Access
32. China and India Go to Africa: New Deals in the Developing World
33. International OHS: Through the Looking Glass of the Global Economy
34. Deadly Business in Moscow
35. Global Corporate Citizenship: Working with Governments and Civil Society
37. The New Population Bomb: The Four Megatrends That Will Change the World
38. The Man Who Named the Future
40. Finding a Job in the 21st Century

Economic organizations

1. Globalization: Where Do We Go from Here?
4. Is Global Trade a Threat or Opportunity?
5. Economists Rethink Free Trade
6. Globalization with a Human Face
7. The Global Debt Bomb
8. The World Economy: The Global Financial Crisis and Collapse in World Trade
9. International Special Report: A Financial Crisis to the West—a Fundamental Crisis to the East
10. "Everyone Needs to Rethink Everything": Reflections from the IMF's Former Chief Economist
12. Potential Future Functions of the World Trade Organization
13. The Wicked Problem of Good Financial Markets
16. The Global Financial Crisis: What Went Wrong?
17. The Work Left Undone: Perspectives on Small Business Opportunities in International Trade
39. The Enterprise of the Future

Ethics and international business

4. Is Global Trade a Threat or Opportunity?
5. Economists Rethink Free Trade
6. Globalization with a Human Face
7. The Global Debt Bomb
8. The World Economy: The Global Financial Crisis and Collapse in World Trade
9. International Special Report: A Financial Crisis to the West—a Fundamental Crisis to the East
10. "Everyone Needs to Rethink Everything": Reflections from the IMF's Former Chief Economist
13. The Wicked Problem of Good Financial Markets
16. The Global Financial Crisis: What Went Wrong?
20. Tata: Master of the Gentle Approach
22. Expanding Opportunity at the Base of the Pyramid
24. Distant Dilemmas
25. Jobs on Another Shore
28. Keynote Panel Session 1: Whose Income Is It? How Business Is Caught in the Global Competion and Controversy for Tax Revenues
30. What One Hand Gives, the Other Takes: Industrial Countries' Policy Coherence for Development
31. Unequal Access
32. China and India Go to Africa: New Deals in the Developing World
33. International OHS: Through the Looking Glass of the Global Economy
34. Deadly Business in Moscow
35. Global Corporate Citizenship: Working with Governments and Civil Society
36. Going Green: The challenges and the Solution
37. The New Population Bomb: The Four Megatrends That Will Change the World

Internet References

The following internet sites have been selected to support the articles found in this reader. These sites were available at the time of publication. However, because websites often change their structure and content, the information listed may no longer be available. We invite you to visit www.mhhe.com/cls for easy access to these sites.

Annual Editions: International Business 16/e

General Sources

Chambers of Commerce, World Network
www.worldchambers.com

This site of the World Chamber Network and Industry describes itself as "the world's first, oldest and largest business network." Access a global index of Chambers of Commerce & Industry and Chambers for International Business, as well as information on "Strategic Alliance Partners" such as G-7.

International Business Times
http://ibtimes.com

"The mission of the International Business Times is to empower readers by bringing clarity and simplicity to global markets."

International Economic Law Website
www.law.georgetown.edu/ilel

This site of the International Economic Law Group of the American Society of International Law contains valuable research tools and links to Web resources regarding international law.

WashLaw
www.washlaw.edu

This site from the Washburn University School of Law Library Reference Desk can direct you to primary documents related to GATT and other information about the agreement. It also reproduces world constitutions and the text of NAFTA and other major treaties.

World Trade Centers Association (WTCA)
www.wtca.org

WTCA ON-Line presents this site as a news and information service. Members can access the *Dun & Bradstreet* Exporters *Encyclopedia* and other valuable sources, and guests to the site can also gain entry to interesting trade-related information.

UNIT 1: Overview of International Business

Information Institute: Law About . . . Pages
www.law.cornell.edu/topics/index.html

Explore this site's searchable index to learn about myriad of international legal subjects. Organized by topic, it provides useful summaries with links to key primary source material and off-Net references.

STAT-USA
www.stat-usa.gov/stat-usa.html

A service of the U.S. Department of Commerce, this essential site presents daily economic news; a myriad of links to databases, statistical releases, and selected publications; and general information on export and international trade as well as business leads and procurement opportunities.

United Nations
www.un.org

The website of the United Nations.

Unit 2: International Finance

Foreign Direct Investment Is on the Rise Around the World
www.neweconomyindex.org

FDI data are a clear indicator of the trend toward globalization, as this report demonstrates.

India Finance and Investment Guide
www.finance.indiamart.com/

This site is a guide to investing in India, one of the largest markets in the world. It discusses taxation, organizations, capital market investment, and other topics.

Institute of International Bankers (IIB)
www.iib.org

Examine this site for information on the Institute of International Bankers (IIB), IIB Events, and publications in order to become familiar with trends in international banking. The site also features regulatory compliance issues relating to the Year 2000 date change.

International Monetary Fund (IMF)
http://imf.org

The International Monetary Fund was founded by the Breton Woods Agreement at the end of World War II and is designed to help and assist the global economy and to bring stability to the international marketplace.

Lex Mercatoria: International Trade Law Monitor
http://lexmercatoria.net

Access a number of resources related to international trade from this site, including data on the European Union and the International Monetary Fund. Among its many links, it addresses such topics as Principles of International Commercial Contracts and UN Arbitration Laws.

North American Free Trade Association (NAFTA)
www.nafta-sec-alena.org

NAFTA's stated objective is "to provide accurate and timely information to U. S. exporters experiencing market assess barriers in Canada or Mexico."

Resources for Economists on the Internet
http://rfe.org

This site and its links are essential reading for those interested in learning about the Organization for Economic Cooperation and Development, the World Bank, the International Monetary Fund, and other important international organizations.

World Bank
www.worldbank.org

Like its sister organization, the IMF, the World Bank was also founded as a result of the Breton Woods Agreement. It is often the lender of last resort when countries are in financial difficulty and need funds.

World Trade Organization (WTO)
www.wto.org

The World Trade Organization is the successor to the GATT agreements and is the organization that handles trade disputes between nations, often involving tariffs and quotas.

Internet References

UNIT 3: International Organizations and Operations

CIA Home Page
http://cia.gov

The CIA covers news and events inside the intelligence community from the War on Terror to all aspects of intelligence.

European Union
www.europa.eu

The website of the European Union.

Harvard Business School
www.hbs.edu

Harvard Business School's West Site provides useful links to library and research resources relating to the *Harvard Business Review* and to information regarding executive education opportunities.

International Business Resources on the WWW
http://globaledge.msu.edu/ibrd/ibrd.asp

Michigan State University's Center for International Business Education and Research provides this site that allows a keyword search and points you to a great deal of trade information and leads, government resources, and related periodicals. It also provides general and specific country and regional information.

International Labor Organization (ILO)
www.ilo.org

ILO's home page leads to links that describe the goals of the organization and summarizes international labor standards and human rights. The site's official UN website locator can point you to many other useful resources.

Outsourcing Center
www.outsourcingcenter.com

An internet portal on methods for creating competitive advantages, the Outsourcing Center is part of the Everest Group.

Sales & Marketing Executive International (SME)
www.smei.org

Visit this home page of the worldwide association SME. Through the "Digital Resource Mall" you can access research and useful articles on sales and management. You can even listen in as marketing leaders discuss their latest strategies and ideas.

United States Trade Representative (USTR)
www.ustr.gov

The home page of the U. S. Trade Representative provides links to many other U. S. government resources of value to those interested in international business. It notes important trade-related speeches and agreements and describes the mission of the USTR.

UNIT 4: Issues in International Business

China.org
www.china.org.cn/english/index.htm

The official website of China.

Ethics Link
www.ethicsandbusiness.eng/links

The Center for Business Ethics maintains this site of alphabetical listings of business ethics sources.

Green Peace
www.greenpeace.org/usa/

Green Peace is a conservation organization that believes in direct action in protecting the environment and endangered species. It has been particularly successful in drawing the world's attention to the practice of whaling.

Private Sector Development Blog of the World Bank
www.psdblog.worldbank.org

"The private sector development blog gathers together news, resources and ideas about the role of private enterprise in fighting poverty. The blog is informal and represents the opinions of the bloggers, not the World Bank."

The Development Gateway
www.developmentgateway.org/

The Development Gateway is an interactive portal for information and knowledge sharing on sustainable development and poverty reduction around the world. It includes analysis of business opportunities.

The Economic Times
www.theeconomictimes.com

An online publication focusing on business in India.

UNIT 5: The Future and International Business

Commission on the Future of the Worker-Management Relations
www.dol.gov

This report was issued by the US Federal Commission on the Future of Worker-Management Relations. Issues addressed include enhanced productivity and changes in collective bargaining.

The Economist
www.theeconomist.com

The *Economist* is a news publication that deals with global events both inside and outside the United States. It gives extensive coverage to events outside North America.

The Futurist
www.wfs.org/futurist.htm

A publication of the World Future Society, *The Futurist,* is a magazine devoted to analyzing the likelihood of future events.

Virtual Library Demography & Population Studies
www.einet.net/review/18183-838592/Demographic_Population_Studies_ANU.htm

Through this internet guide to demography and population studies, learn about leading information facilities of value and/or significance to researchers in the field of demography. The site is provided by the Australian National University.

UNIT 1

Overview of International Business

Unit Selections

Key Points to Consider

• In the fall of 2008, the world experienced the worst financial crisis since the Great Depression. How do you think that effected world trade?

• The role of China has become far more important over the past couple of years. What do you think that means?

• Neo-liberal attitudes about globalization have been challenged since the financial crisis. The ideas espoused by such people as Thomas Friedman in books like *The World is Flat* are now being challenged. What do you think about this? With whom do you agree?

• Globalization is now being challenged on many fronts. It is recognized that there are some winners and some losers in the global economy. How do you propose to address these issues? Do you think they should be addressed or is it up to the individual?

Student Website
www.mhhe.com/cls

Internet References

Information Institute About Law . . . pages
www.law.cornell.edu/topics/index.html
STAT-USA
www.STAT-USA.gov/stat-usa.html
United Nations
www.un.org
Further information regarding these websites may be found in the book's preface or online.

The world has changed. In October of 2008 the financial markets in the United States and the rest of the world suffered the most significant reversal since the crash of the Great Depression of 1929 and what some have called the "Great Recession" began.

This collapse in the financial markets affected all of the economies of the world. Everywhere, at least the growth in the gross domestic product (GDP) declined from where it had been the year before; banks failed; insurance companies failed; corporations could not get financing for their operations. Commerce on both the domestic and global levels started to come to a halt. It was a financial and economic crisis of epic proportions.

In the United States, the government came to the rescue of the private sector with the TARP funds designed to rescue the banks and to shore-up their balance sheets so that they could weather the financial storm that, in many cases, they had brought upon themselves. If the U.S. Treasury had failed to do this, there would have been many more failures of financial institutions in the United States that most certainly would have led to the failure of financial institutions all over the world. A financial panic on that scale would certainly have made the recession much worse and what other consequences may have been produced by such massive global failures of financial institutions could only be imagined. The failure of Lehman Brothers was only a small taste of the kinds of consequences that could be brought on by a massive global financial failure.

But, this brush with catastrophe has brought many changes. The giant financial institutions that were considered to be too big to be allowed to fail and were therefore rescued in the financial bailout are being examined. Should an organization be allowed to grow to the point where it is so big and so important to the economy that it cannot be allowed to fail no matter how poorly run it may be? Is the management of that organization then given a license by the society to operate with impunity in the marketplace, free of the discipline of the market because it is too important to the society and too big to fail? Is the current understanding of the economic environment, sometimes called neo-liberalism, really valid in light of recent events? Perhaps, "The World Is Not Flat," and "Globalization: Where Do We Go from Here?"

One of the facts that emerged from the "Great Recession" is the ascendance of China as an important global, economic power. China has become a great creditor nation, holding much of the debt of the United States. It is one of the fastest growing economies in the world and was one of the first economies to come out of the recession caused by the financial crisis of 2008, while the developed world of Europe, Japan and the United States are not expected to truly come out of the recession for a few more years. China has a middle class of between 200 to 300 million people, at least as large as the middle class in the United States and is now the largest market for automobiles in the world. It also is the largest market for cell phones with more cell phone users than there are people in the United States and its economy continues to outpace the growth of every industrialized country. "The Great Recession" has made China a new pole in what was once a tri-polar economic world consisting of the United States, Europe, and Japan. In this new "quad-polar" global economy "China Must Carry the World," out of the global economic recession. It is a new role for the Chinese and one that they must learn to use not only to their benefit, but to the benefit of the global economy. Taking the role of one of the major economies of the world carries with it certain responsibilities. It is simply no longer in the interests of China to ignore the trading

concerns of other countries whether they are large or small. Intellectual property rights, something that has been an issue with China for some years, are now really important, and the Chinese government must take them seriously. Counterfeit goods must be curtailed, and contracts must be enforced. The Chinese economy may not be fully mature, but it is now large enough so that it must take on the role of a leading economic power because it is one, and that role carries with it certain privileges and responsibilities.

For centuries, economists believed that the rationale for international trade was the law of comparative advantage. The law of comparative advantage can be explained most simply as one country has the ability to make lots of product "X" but little of product "Y." Another country has the ability to make lots of product "Y" but little of product "X." Each has a comparative advantage in a product. The two countries should trade "X" for "Y" and "Y" for "X" respectively to maximize their benefits so that their citizens get the most X's and Y's.

This may sound fine in theory, but in practice it does not necessarily work out that way. Cost structures in the various countries may be different. Price purchase parity may be different (In country A, a potato may cost $.25; in country B, only $.05). Given the nature of the global economy and the ability to access global workforces, it is much easier, today, to off-shore work to much lower cost venues than was the case 20 years ago. There will always be winners and losers in any economic equation, but now many of those losers would seem to be in the developed world as organizations seek to cut their costs in a hyper-competitive global economy and there would seem to be few winners in the developing world, especially among those in low skilled positions.

A question being asked in many quarters is "Is Global Trade a Threat or Opportunity?" Traditionally, it has always been viewed as an opportunity, but now, with the "Great Recession," some aspects of global trade are starting to be questioned. Questioning is healthy and nothing should be taken for granted or etched in stone so having "Economists Rethink Free Trade," is probably a good thing. The issue is still out and it is important that when they do rethink free trade they develop the right answers.

Globalization: Where Do We Go from Here?

ABBAS J. ALI

Current global business events and the severity of the credit crisis prove without doubt that the invisible hand, the market mechanism, is not as beneficial as it was once thought. Adam Smith, who coined the term "invisible hand," assumed that when an owner or an entrepreneur pursues "his own interest he frequently promotes that of the society more effectually than when he really intends to promote it." This implies that in a capitalistic society, economic activities which are driven by self-interest by necessity are those which are most efficient and most beneficial to the society.

In a globalized world and under certain conditions, this principle is impossible to defend. To begin with, the market does not operate independent of its actors. Marketing actors, due to their varying motives, directions, and interests, logically intend to operate in ways which either further their benefits or minimize damages to their interests. In the process, they may engage in activities which either jeopardize the interest of others or that of the society as a whole. The actions of Enron's senior executives harmed the company's employees and resulted in consequences which adversely affected many other stakeholders. Similarly, the crisis of the mortgage giants, Fannie Mae and Freddie Mac, has created hardships for their stockholders, the majority of their employees, and most likely, also, the American taxpayers.

The seizing of these two mortgage giants by the US government evidences that the invisible hand can be manipulated or influenced directly by market actors and that the forces of invisibility, if left without proper monitoring, can lead to undesired consequences. Indeed, the intervention by the federal government has purposefully sought to create conditions necessary for containing damages which could engulf various players in the market. This might be the very reason which also motivated the US Federal government to summon the executives of major Wall Street firms to a meeting in Lower Manhattan on September 12, 2008 to address the financial crisis at Lehman Brothers and other major institutions, including Merrill Lynch. The federal government insisted that the industry, as a whole, must come up with a rescue plan for the stricken investment bank and that, in the meantime, the executives must collectively consider plans to stabilize the financial markets. In Europe, major central banks announced (September 15, 2008) plans to inject billions into global money markets to limit the spread of US financial crisis to the rest of the world's financial systems.

The intervention of the US and other governments in the market, while intended to ensure confidence in the financial market and limit the spread of the financial and credit crises, demonstrates that market actors are not solely confined to suppliers and customers but include governments, super-national organizations, and NGOs. While the last three players may enter the market as customers or suppliers, they have increasingly assumed significant roles in intentionally or unintentionally shaping market mechanisms. The invisible hand principle assumes that market actors act independently. But in today's business world, all players attempt to predict or at best have reasonable knowledge of what other actors might do in the market. Under these conditions, the market mechanism may lose its unique characteristics as an unguided and instantaneous process.

Globalization has altered many economic assumptions. Chief among them is the ability of the market to regain its balance, recover its health, and optimally create wealth for its participants. Perry (2008) in the *Wall Street Journal* reported that Nobel Laureates in economics have argued that governments should intervene to help those at the bottom. It quoted Robert Fogel stating, "Governments in wealthy countries like the US are obligated to improve conditions of life for the poor." Likewise, Finn Kydland, underscored the disruptive nature of economic globalization when he highlighted that the benefits of economic globalization is not shared responsibly across the globe and that "globalization ought to be good for all countries."

There is no question that globalization has been responsible for the flourishing of international trade and foreign direct investment (FDI) and subsequently for delivering benefits to areas which were until recently untouched by economic prosperity. Likewise, globalization has contributed significantly to economic growth in countries like China, Brazil, India, and Turkey, to name a few. But globalization, as a process, has generated imbalances in the market and has resulted in disastrous consequences both in developing and developed worlds.

The rapid integration of many countries in the global economy and the emergence of MNCs as unrivaled wealth-generating global actors have redrawn the economic landscape on a global scale. In developing countries, politicians, newly emerging entrepreneurs, and established business classes and bureaucrats have rushed to take advantage of opportunities resulting from liberalization, privatization, and openness. Many of them, motivated by selfish interests and operating where legal guidelines and institutions are either weak or do not exist, engage in questionable practices and have, occasionally, opted for fraud and bribery to accumulate wealth at any expense. This has not only undermined government institutions but has become a destabilizing force which poses a threat to market functions and to an otherwise normal integration of the world economy. Likewise, the gap between the rich and poor has become even wider, feeding popular resentments and inciting political and social unrest.

In the developed world, liberalization and deregulation have put pressure on executives to deliver quick returns on investments and to focus on short-term performance. Faced with mounting pressures to make profits and take advantage of relaxed regulations, some executives have had difficulty in resisting temptations to engage in or tolerate corrupt practices. This has resulted in major corporate scandals and court indictments of leading executives. Likewise, the offshoring of production activities is blamed for deteriorated living standards for a large segment of workers.

Whether in developing or developed countries, critics of globalization point to the fact that unbridled market mechanisms and rapid globalization have led to disastrous outcomes. Furthermore, there has been a growing concern among activists and people from developing nations that developed countries are not pursuing globalization for the sake of sharing economic prosperity and providing greater benefits for people across the world. Rather, the leading developed nations are accused of being motivated by purely nationalistic interests and the quest to recolonize poor countries.

The collapse of the WTO's negotiations in Geneva in July 2008 to open world markets, the phenomenal worldwide increase in food and basic commodities prices, the spread of financial and credit crises, and the unfolding revelations of major corporate scandals, along with rising militaristic attitudes among the world's powerful nations, give credence to the voices which call for rethinking globalization and market mechanisms. The proposition by *Wall Street Journal* (August 25, 2008) that free markets aren't always fair and the call by the *New York Times* (2008) for the need for better regulations underscore the urgency to rethink globalization and how to proceed into a better future.

Critics and supporters of globalization, whether they are in developed or developing nations, understand that in today's world, no country can achieve economic prosperity by barricading itself from the rest. World interdependence and connectivity have become the hallmarks of the last and this new century. This reality offers hope that the future will be better for all citizens, and that human ingenuity will creatively address the shortcomings of globalization.

There are certain conditions for sustaining global economic integration and substantially minimizing its negative consequences. These conditions are:

- Developing countries must be assured that their concerns and needs are incorporated into any global framework or trade regime.

- Developing nations should be an integral part of the world system and that neither their resources nor national sovereignty are taken advantage of.

- Developing nations, in their search for healthy integration into the world economy, should independently design their own growth strategies by focusing primarily on upgrading and enhancing their domestic institutions capabilities.

- Super-national institutions have to be apolitical actors and transparent in their operations and management.

- Global economic and political challenges are interdependent. Both should be addressed collectively. That is, the actions must be perceived as legitimate by all concerned parties.

- WTO and other super-national institutions should be instrumental in broadening global benefits and should be concerned with the creation of tangible and intangible wealth on a global basis.

- Super-national institutions, in cooperation with NGOs, should set general guidelines and rules for governing business conduct and that of MNCs.

- Rules and regulations might be important for minimizing frauds and preventing corruptions. Nevertheless, in the absence of a business culture which sanctions and reinforces ethical conduct and the virtue of pursuing self-interest within the context of corporate and societal interest, corruptions and scandals may find fertile soil in which to multiply.

- Super-national institutions, governments and MNCs have to promote and observe social and economic justice, basic human rights, and non-discriminatory conduct.

In their rush for globalization in the 1980s and early 1990s, MNCs and their respective home-country governments ignored two facts: business and societal issues are highly interwoven and neither should be treated separately, and globalization benefits and responsibilities go hand in hand. The negligence of these two facts has hindered the ability of many societies and actors to optimally develop the capacity to deal with globalization and reap its benefits. It will undoubtedly take prudent and ethical discipline to behave responsibly in an open and dynamic global marketplace.

References

New York Times (2008), "The bailout's big lessons", Editorial, September 9, *New York Times*, available at: www.nytimes.com.

Perry, J. (2008), "Nobel Laureates say globalization's winners should aid poor", *Wall Street Journal*, Vol. A2, August 25.

China Must Carry the World

ANDREW B. BUSCH

In December, the Chinese had a 30-year anniversary of an event that changed the nation. In 1978, Deng Xiaoping and his "capitalist roaders" managed to gain political control from the Maoists and embarked on a path of economic reform. The powerful black cat-white cat principle—it doesn't matter what kind as long as it catches mice—embodied what was sorely needed in a nation that ranked No. 175 in the annual income statistics.

The concept allowed individuals to make production decisions instead of the state. This unleashed the productive and creative energies of the private sector that were tethered during the previous 29 years of the Great Leap Forward and Cultural Revolution. The miracle that occurred has been stunning and reaffirms how critical economic liberty is to increasing growth.

Essentially, a middle class of 200 million people was created since 1990. To put this in perspective, this middle class is larger than the entire working population of the United States. During a 30-year period, China has grown by nearly double digits and is now the fourth-largest world economy (No. 2, if you use purchasing power parity). More important, it is the third-largest trading nation and runs the largest trade surplus with the United States. It also holds the largest U.S. dollar reserves of any nation, which are more than $2 trillion.

As an exclamation point, China hosted the Olympics last summer and wowed the world with its opening ceremonies that were a technological extravaganza. Without question, China's economic transformation is unparalleled and not likely to ever be repeated in our lifetime.

However, there are risks. The retrofitting of a capitalist economic system onto a communist/socialist political system may be inherently unstable. One system asks for individual decision making, risk taking and entrepreneurship; the other system asks the individuals to turn over decision making to a central body. With China, this is a great experiment, and so far, it has been extremely successful. (To be honest, the United States' capitalist economic system and representative government do not function very well together at times, either.)

The retrofitting of a capitalist economic system onto a communist/socialist political system may be inherently unstable.

A Challenge for China

Last year for SFO magazine, I interviewed the head of Eurasia, Ian Bremmer, and asked him about the risks for China. He said, "The longer-term issues are a greater concern. If the growing wealth gaps between the coast and the country's interior, between urban and rural Chinese, between those with connections and those without them get wider, we may see a backlash in the form of greater social instability. The confiscation of land for development projects without much compensation, the risk of public health crises and environmental catastrophes fuel the fire. So far, the party has managed to open China's economy without surrendering its monopoly on the country's political power. There is no guarantee they can pull that off indefinitely."

This strain increases when the structure is challenged by an unforeseen crisis like the current global recession.

For the first time in 30 years, Chinese political leaders are faced with a challenge to their economic reform from outside their country—and that is going to test the economic leadership. During the height of the U.S. credit crisis in the fall, Chinese exports shrank 2 percent, imports collapsed 18 percent and power generation fell 7 percent. The World Bank and other forecasters are now predicting Chinese GDP to shrink to 7.5 percent for 2009, which is a level that could bring "a reactive situation of mass-scale social turmoil" according to a senior party researcher. It's estimated that China needs to grow at 8 percent per year just to keep employment steady for the 7 million members of its workforce that join each year.

The Economist states, "Indeed, demonstrations and protests, always common in China, are proliferating, as laid-off factory-workers join dispossessed farmers, environmental campaigners and victims of police harassment in taking to the streets." Although this is an extreme view, 2009 is also the 20th anniversary of the Tiananmen Square uprising, or the June Fourth Incident as the Chinese call it. As an example of more aggressive and public action occurring, the Financial Times reported in December: "More than 300 Chinese intellectuals have called for the creation of a new democracy movement in a sign of growing dissatisfaction with the Chinese Communist party's strategy of encouraging economic reform without meaningful political liberalisation."

Perhaps the greatest challenge comes from the United States. The U.S. has had a credit-nuclear bomb explode with the failure of Lehman Brothers as the detonator. The ensuing shock waves have extracted credit from an economy that has been basing itself on credit to grow. What does this mean for a $14 trillion economy? Does it drop to $12 trillion or even $10 trillion from credit demand destruction before it stabilizes?

The U.S. has had a credit-nuclear bomb explode with the failure of Lehman Brothers as the detonator.

The U.S. consumer is also likely to cut back on spending from the mounting job losses that are occurring and are predicted to extend throughout 2009. Already 12 months old, the U.S. recession is forecasted to extend well into this year. As the top destination for Chinese exports, the United States recession is going to severely crimp Chinese economic growth. From the trade and current account data, the Chinese dependence on the U.S. consumer is strong.

Picking up the Slack

The Chinese leaders are not simply going to ignore what is happening. They have already announced an extremely large stimulus program of 4 trillion yuan ($600 billion) and indicated that they want to spur domestic demand to help pick up the slack from the drop in exports. Chinese consumers are increasing their spending, and domestic retail sales continue to be a bright spot. Some experts predict that BRIC (Brazil, Russia, India and China) consumers will be the stabilizing force for the global economy.

The problem is that these countries are much smaller in their contribution to global consumption: The United States, Japan and Europe account for 68 percent, while BRIC only represents 10 percent. The scale of the increase in domestic consumption by China would need to be enormous. Peking University Professor of Finance, Michael Pettis writes, "A decline in U.S. consumption equal to 5 percent of U.S. GDP, for example (which is a low estimate), would require an increase in Chinese consumption equal to 17 percent of Chinese GDP—or a nearly 40 percent growth in consumption. This is clearly unlikely."

There are two more major risks with China as the global economy remains in recession: deflation and trade wars. Think of the Chinese economy like an oil rig. You have a massive piece of productive capabilities that needs to be run by several crews of workers going around the clock to pump oil out of the ground. If the price of crude goes down below your operating costs, you don't shut down the rig. Why? The shut-down costs are extremely high with unemployment benefits, lost ability to generate revenue to pay for debts and the cost of moth-balling the rig someplace. This means you continue to run the rig even as you lose money in the hope of keeping the operation going until the market turns around.

This is the dilemma facing Chinese business leaders and the government—with a twist. They will keep producing goods as the goals of businesses and the government are intently focused on keeping workers employed at all costs. This means that potentially the Chinese keep producing goods when the world's demand does not exist to absorb them. Instead of global production dropping to meet lower levels of global demand, output remains at elevated levels putting downward pressure on prices.

This also means that there is potential for producers from other nations to lose market share to the Chinese. Without serious government subsidies, how can foreign private-sector manufacturers keep producing goods with prices dropping and supply remaining unchanged? This could create a serious trade backlash against the Chinese as nations take actions to limit the amount of Chinese exports entering their economies.

A Democratic administration has come to power in Washington that is unlikely to be as tolerant of China's trade or currency policies. The textile quota agreement between the United States and China signed in 2005 is up for renewal soon, and that will be a test case for the rest of the world.

China's extraordinary economic growth during the past 30 years is truly a modern miracle that is unlikely to be repeated any time soon. The country has managed to balance economic growth with the challenges of one-party political rule. This delicate balance is under duress with a global recession putting pressure on growth and employment. This will challenge the Chinese leadership to act aggressively and to find creative solutions.

Thirty years ago, Deng began the economic reform and described it as "crossing the river by feeling for the stones." Now, the economic rocks are slippery and the current is strong. The world needs China to stay upright, or we will all get wet.

ANDREW B. BUSCH is a keynote speaker, author of *World Event Trading* and CNBC contributor and guest host of "Man Vs. Market." He also writes the daily financial/political newsletter The Busch Update. He can be reached at his website AndrewBusch.com

The World Is Not Flat

How Thomas Friedman gets it wrong about globalization.

MARK ENGLER

Turn on the TV and flip to a C-SPAN or CNN discussion of the global economy and you are likely to spot the square head and mustachioed face of *New York Times* columnist Thomas Friedman, who will probably be expressing enthusiasm for the business world's newest high-tech innovations. With his best-selling book *The Lexus and the Olive Tree,* Friedman stepped forward in the late 1990s as a leading cheerleader of neoliberal globalization. Then, in the wake of 9/11, he made common cause with White House militarists. He became a high-profile "liberal hawk" and supported the war in Iraq—only to distance himself later in the Bush era and return to championing corporate expansion with a second widely read book on globalization, *The World Is Flat.* For better or for worse, his punditry provides an indispensable guide to how mainstream commentators have tried to defend neoliberalism in the face of challenges from worldwide social movements. Moreover, Friedman's renewed emphasis on corporate globalization in the wake of the botched war in Iraq may also be a significant bellwether for how the Democratic Party— especially the more conservative "New Democrat" wing of the party—crafts a vision for international relations after Bush.

You Can't Stop the Dawn

In Friedman's view, the end of the Cold War left the world with a single, unassailable ideology. "Globalization," he wrote in *The Lexus and the Olive Tree,* "means the spread of free market capitalism to every country in the world." He saw this as an unmitigated good: "[T]he more you open your economy to free trade and competition, the more efficient and flourishing your economy will be." He marveled that "computerization, miniaturization, digitization, satellite communications, fiber optics, and the Internet" were bringing about untold wonders.

Friedman's conversion into the church of corporate expansion took place over many years. His academic training is not in economics, but in Middle Eastern studies. During the 1980s, Friedman was a respected *New York Times* correspondent in Israel and Lebanon, winning two Pulitzer Prizes for his reporting from the region. In 1994, just at the beginning of the Internet boom, he switched to a beat covering the intersection of politics and economics, and his excitement for globalization began to mount in earnest. By the time he became the *Times'* foreign affairs columnist the following year, he was perfectly positioned to evangelize about how unregulated markets and new technology were reshaping global affairs.

Aware that many people saw him as a modern-day Pangloss extolling the best of all possible worlds, Friedman contended in *The Lexus and the Olive Tree* that he was "not a salesman for globalization." But this is precisely what he was. More than any other public personality, he was responsible for portraying neoliberalism as an inevitable and laudable march of progress. "I feel about globalization a lot like I feel about the dawn," he wrote. "[E]ven if I didn't care much for the dawn there isn't much I could do about it. I didn't start globalization, I can't stop it—except at a huge cost to human development." By defining "globalization" as a broad, sweeping phenomenon—political, economic, technological, and cultural— he saw resistance as ridiculous. So when massive protests erupted at the World Trade Organization meetings in Seattle in late 1999, he disgustedly derided the demonstrators as "a Noah's ark of flat-earth advocates, protectionist trade unions and yuppies looking for their 1960s fix."

More than any other public personality, Friedman was responsible for portraying neoliberalism as an inevitable and laudable march of progress.

You might think that the deflating of the dot-com bubble that began in March 2000 would have quelled Friedman's fervor, but you would be wrong. In Friedman's view, the end of the 1990s boom only led to more advancement. "[T]he dot-com bust," he later wrote, "actually drove globalization into hypermode by forcing companies to outsource and offshore more and more functions in order to save on scarce capital." Friedman's cheerleading, too, would go into "hypermode," but not before the columnist took a detour to become one of the country's most prominent liberal hawks in the wake of 9/11. When Friedman did return to the subject of economic globalization with his 2005 book, *The World Is Flat,* he was once again wowed. Over the course of just a few years, he concluded, "we entered a whole new era: Globalization 3.0."

Fueled now by wireless technology and ever-smaller microchips, this wave of capitalism was "shrinking the world from a size small to a size tiny and flattening the playing field at the same time." Hospitals in the United States were sending CT scans to India for analysis; other corporations opened bustling call centers there to handle customer service calls, training their new South Asian employees to speak in American accents; globetrotting columnists could file their stories from the middle of a golf course in China by using their Blackberries. The march of progress was back on.

Friedman is known for conveying complicated ideas through the use of colorful metaphors. Yet his metaphors consistently get so mixed and muddled as to require delicate linguistic untangling. In the course of his two books on globalization, Friedman goes from seeing the world in 3-D to, remarkably enough, seeing it in at least six dimensions. Technological advance, he tells us, has now accelerated so much that we have gone through Globalization versions 1 .0 and 2.0 and entered version 3.0. Friedman presents ten "flatteners," four "steroids," and a "triple convergence," plus at least seven releases of "DOScapital." Various steroids and flatteners are meant to have multiplied globalization's effects exponentially. Journalist Matt Taibbi, who has written the most cutting analysis of Friedman's peculiar language, notes, "Friedman's book is the first I have encountered, anywhere, in which the reader needs a calculator to figure the value of the author's metaphors."

If ever Orwell's warnings that "the slovenliness of our language makes it easier for us to have foolish thoughts" and that the world's "present political chaos is connected with the decay of language" apply to anyone, they apply to Friedman. The connection between Friedman's hazy writing and his suspect conclusions about the global economy shows up in the very premise of his second book on globalization. During a meeting between Friedman and Nandan Nilekani in Bangalore, the Infosys CEO offers that "the playing field is being leveled." For Friedman, the tired cliché is a revelation. He mulls it over for hours and then, suddenly, decides: "My God, he's telling me the world is flat!"

Now, it is quite a stretch to take a routine sports metaphor and superimpose it on the globe; there could be few worse metaphors for talking about a global system that is more integrated and networked than ever before. "Friedman is a person who not only speaks in malapropisms, he also hears malapropisms," Taibbi argues. Nilekani off-handedly mentions a level field and Friedman attributes to him the radical idea of a flat world. "This is the intellectual version of Far Out Space Nuts, when NASA repairman Bob Denver sets a whole sitcom in motion by pressing 'launch' instead of 'lunch' in a space capsule. And once he hits that button, the rocket takes off."

It would all be funny if it didn't mask a deeper political problem: For the world's poor, the playing field is far from level. Our world is not flat.

Putting on Reagan's Jacket

With the ideology of neoliberalism steadily losing ground in international discussion, it is important to see how a leading apologist mounts a defense. In Friedman's case, he does so by holding on to dogmatic assumptions, training his sights on high technology, conducting his interviews largely within the insular world of jet-setting corporate elites, and ignoring a world of evidence that would contradict his selective viewpoint.

With the ideology of neoliberalism steadily losing ground in international discussion, it is important to see how a leading apologist mounts a defense.

Some reviewers have applauded Friedman for acknowledging negative aspects of globalization in his books. But for Friedman, this does not mean looking at the realities of exploitation or environmental destruction that have resulted from corporate expansion. Instead, his caveats boil down to two points: that terrorists, too, can use the Internet, and that many countries, especially in "unflat" Africa, are too backward to read the signs that would put them on the high tech, "free trade" superhighway to prosperity. With regard to the latter, it's not that anything is wrong really, only that the process has not gone far enough and fast enough for everyone to benefit yet.

Needless to say, Friedman's is hardly a biting exposé. In fact, it is virtually impossible to find any evidence that might make him skeptical about the fundamental greatness of corporate globalization. In 1999, even *BusinessWeek* argued "The Asian financial crisis of 1997–99 shows that unfettered liberalization of capital markets without proper regulation can lead the world to the brink of disaster." But for Friedman this crisis, too, was all for the best. He writes, "I believe globalization did us all a favor by melting down the economies of Thailand, Korea, Malaysia, Indonesia, Mexico, Russia and Brazil in the 1990s, because it laid bare a lot of the rotten practices and institutions in countries that had prematurely globalized." He slams the countries for corruption and cronyism, suggesting that they deserved their fates. But by "prematurely globalized" he does not mean that mese countries should have been more cautious about linking their fates to speculative international markets. Rather, he believes that they had not done enough to "reduce the role of government" and "let markets more freely allocate resources." Friedman's solution to the dangers of unregulated markets is more deregulation, the remedy for the excesses of unfettered capitalism is even more excess. The argument is airtight.

Missing from this account, of course, is any sense of the social impact of the Asian crisis. In the end, wealthy foreign investors were bailed out by the International Monetary Fund and lost little. The real losers were an untold number of middle-class families in places like Thailand and Korea whose savings were wiped out overnight, as well as the poor in places like Indonesia who went hungry when the government cut food subsidies. It takes a very twisted viewpoint to say that the Asian financial crisis did these people a favor.

Friedman holds that the Internet age has created a "flat" world with opportunity for all. Yet he freely admits that the system he describes is founded on the Reagan-Thatcher model of extreme, "trickle down" neoliberalism—one of the most unequal methods of distributing social goods ever devised. Friedman writes: "Thatcher and Reagan combined to strip huge chunks of economic decision-making power from the state, from the advocates of the Great Society and from traditional Keynesian economics, and hand them over to the free market." Countries now have one choice for economic policy: neoliberalism. They must radically deregulate and privatize their economies. Friedman calls this the "Golden Straitjacket." It's "golden" because the model supposedly creates widespread affluence. But it's a "straitjacket" because it radically constricts democracy. Sounding a lot like Ralph Nader, Friedman writes:

Once your country puts [the Golden Straitjacket] on, its political choices get reduced to Pepsi or Coke—to slight nuances of taste, slight nuances of policy, slight alterations in design . . . but never any major deviation from the core golden rules. Governments—be

they led by Democrats or Republicans, Conservatives or Labourites, Gaullists or Socialists, Christian Democrats or Social Democrats—that deviate too far away from the core rules will see their investors stampede away, interest rates rise, and stock market valuations fall.

The difference between Friedman and Nader is that the *New York Times* columnist approves of this situation. He does not condemn it as an assault on democracy; he says it's just the way things are. Of the Democrats, he writes, "Mr. Clinton effectively kidnapped the Democratic Party . . . moved it into the Republican economic agenda—including free trade, NAFTA and the WTO for China—while holding onto much of the Democrats' social agenda." Any Democrat who would try to move it back meets Friedman's wrath. In the new global age, all those to the left of Ronald Reagan on economic policy are simply out of luck.

Sitting on Top of the World

Friedman's contention that everyone benefits when countries bind themselves into market fundamentalism is based less on a careful review of the evidence than on blind faith. In July of 2006, he made a startling admission during a CNBC interview with Tim Russert. He said:

We got this free market, and I admit, I was speaking out in Minnesota—my hometown, in fact, and a guy stood up in the audience, said, "Mr. Friedman, is there any free trade agreement you'd oppose?" I said, "No, absolutely not." I said, "You know what, sir? I wrote a column supporting the CAFTA, the Caribbean Free Trade initiative. I didn't even know what was in it. I just knew two words: free trade."

That a nationally prominent columnist would gloat about such ignorance is a sad statement about the health of our political debate. "Free trade" is an incredibly politicized phrase, with little concrete meaning. For instance, CAFTA (which actually stands for the *Central American Free Trade Agreement*) includes provisions designed to protect the monopoly rights of giant pharmaceutical companies rather than to create "free" commerce.

But the larger point is that neoliberal globalization does not make winners of everyone. Its global track record for producing GDP growth is dismal. In fact, its main accomplishment may be to produce inequality. And Friedman's own position amid this global divide is telling. He regularly represents himself as just an average guy from Minnesota trying to make sense of the world. The real picture is far from average. In July 2006, *Washingtonian* magazine reported that in the 1970s Friedman married into one of the 100 richest families in the United States—the Bucksbaums—who have amassed a fortune worth some $2.7 billion, with origins in real estate development. The magazine noted that he lives in "a palatial 11,400-square-foot house, now valued at $9.3 million, on a 7.5-acre parcel just blocks from 1-495 and the Bethesda Country Club." Given that the über-rich, those with huge stock portfolios and investments in multinational corporations, have benefited tremendously from corporate globalization, commentators like David Sirota have suggested that Friedman's vast wealth represents an undisclosed conflict of interest in his journalism. It is as if multimillionaire Richard Mellon Scaife were to write about the repeal of the estate tax without disclosing that he stands to profit handsomely from such a policy change.

Whether or not that is the case, Friedman's position at the very pinnacle of global prosperity is certainly reflected in his view of the world. In a telling admission, he relates in *The Lexus and the Olive Tree* that his "best intellectual sources" about globalization are hedge fund managers. Hedge funds are elite, largely unregulated investment pools that handle money for individuals of extremely high net worth. Their managers are among the highest paid individuals in the United States. In 2006, the top 25 hedge fund managers in the country made in excess of $240 million each. This means they each pulled in $27,000 per hour, 24 hours per day, whether waking or sleeping, whether at the office or teeing off on the ninth hole. Corporate CEOs and hedge fund managers may indeed be well informed about certain aspects of the global economy. But if that is where you get your information, you end up with a very partial view of the world. You get the winner's view.

In an eloquent critique of *The World Is Flat,* Indian ecofeminist Vandana Shiva writes:

> Friedman has reduced the world to the friends he visits, the CEOs he knows, and the golf courses he plays at. From this microcosm of privilege, exclusion, blindness, he shuts out both the beauty of diversity and the brutality of exploitation and inequality . . .

> That is why he talks of 550 million Indian youth overtaking Americans in a flat world, when the entire information technology/outsourcing sector in India employs only a million out of 1.2 billion people. Food and farming, textiles and clothing, health and education are nowhere in Friedman's monoculture of mind locked into IT. Friedman presents a 0.1% picture and hides 99.9%. . . . In the eclipsed 99.9% are the 25 million women who disappeared in high growth areas of India because a commodified world has rendered women a dispensable sex. In the hidden 99.9% . . . are thousands of tribal children

in Orissa, Maharashtra, Rajasthan who died of hunger because the public distribution system for food has been dismantled to create markets for agribusiness.

A Race to the Top?

The corporate globalization that Friedman champions has alarming changes in store not just for the poor of the global South, but also for working people in the United States and Europe. One of the things that Friedman particularly lauds about Reagan and Thatcher is their success in breaking unions. He writes: "it may turn out that one of the key turning points in American history, going into the millennium, was Ronald Reagan's decision to fire all the striking air traffic controllers in 1981." "No single event," he notes with satisfaction, "did more to alter the balance of power between management and workers." Everyone wins from this, he argues, since "[t]he easier it is to fire workers, the more incentive employers have to hire them." Because America busted its unions and Western European countries did not, he contends, the United States developed a more dynamic economy.

Because America busted its unions and Western European countries did not, Friedman contends, the United States developed a more dynamic economy.

What Friedman fails to note is that real wages for working people in the United States have been largely stagnant since the early 1970s, while working hours have skyrocketed. When compared with workers in Western Europe, the average American works 350 hours more per year, the equivalent of nine extra weeks. A study by the International Labor Organization reported that in 2000 the average U.S. worker put in 199 more hours than in 1973. Dramatizing such realities, a group of union and nonprofit activists now observe "Take Back Your Time Day" every October 24. On that day, if the U.S. workload were on par with the rest of the industrialized world, Americans would have the rest of the year off.

Friedman utters not a word of protest about the trend toward more work; in fact, he celebrates it. He argues that European social democracies are obsolete, even though they are successful capitalist countries. These nations are running on the wrong version of "DOScapital," Friedman contends, and need to shift to U.S. standards. Never mind that economies like Sweden's have performed very well over the past decade, all while maintaining a much higher quality of life for their citizens.

He has a special hatred for the French, who, he writes, "are trying to preserve a 35-hour work week in a world where Indian engineers are ready to work a 35-hour day." In what he calls a "race to the top," Friedman predicts a turbulent decade for Western Europe, as

> aging, inflexible economies—which have grown used to six-week vacations and unemployment insurance that is almost as good as having a job—become more intimately integrated with Eastern Europe, India and China in a flattening world. . . . The dirty little secret is that India is taking work from Europe or America not simply because of low wages. It is also because Indians are ready to work harder and can do anything from answering your phone to designing your next airplane or car. They are not racing us to the bottom. They are racing us to the top. . . . Yes, this is a bad time for France and friends to lose their appetite for hard work—just when India, China and Poland are rediscovering theirs.

It is unclear what Friedman sees as getting to the "top" if paid vacations, unemployment insurance, and retirement—benefits traditionally regarded as signs of a civilized economy—must be sacrificed. But, Friedman tells us, that is the new reality.

Ultimately, the "race to the top" is another of Friedman's botched metaphors. In the long-standing progressive argument that corporate globalization creates a "race to the bottom," it is not Indian or Chinese workers who are doing the racing at all. It's capital. Deregulation allows corporations to wander the globe in search of ever lower wages and laxer environmental standards. The moment workers stand up for their rights, refusing to tolerate a "35-hour day," a company can pick up and move elsewhere. The governments that might curb such abuses are in straitjackets. The unions that workers might have organized themselves into have been busted. All Friedman can offer is this cryptic and seemingly masochistic advice: "When the world goes flat—and you are feeling flattened—reach for a shovel and dig into yourself. Don't try to build walls."

Globalization from Below

An interesting aspect of Friedman's renewed focus on corporate globalization at the end of the Bush era is that governments and international financial institutions have faded from his picture of the integrating world. Even corporations are becoming less relevant. In his view, the new era of "Globalization 3.0" is all about *individuals.* Today, it is up to all people to pull themselves up by their bootstraps. He writes, "every person now must, and can, ask: Where do *I* as an individual fit into the global competition and opportunities of the day, and how can *I*, on my own, collaborate with others globally?"

Conveniently enough, accepting this idea makes it impossible to oppose neoliberalism. In a world of extreme individualism, no one in particular is responsible for setting the rules of the world order. It is pointless to protest governments or international financial institutions. Globalization is unstoppable because people want it.

These arguments are not new. With scant evidence, Friedman has long claimed that there is a "groundswell" of people throughout the developing world demanding corporate globalization. Of course, the massive protests of the past decade would seem to contradict his assertion. But he does not see this as a problem. He dismisses global justice activism by arguing, "from its origins, the movement that emerged in Seattle was primarily a Western-driven phenomenon." The backlash that does exist in poorer countries, he argues, is not rational politics but simple lawlessness: "what we have been seeing in many countries, instead of popular mass opposition to globalization, is wave after wave of crime—people just grabbing what they need, weaving their own social safety nets and not worrying about the theory or the ideology." In the end, Friedman seems ideologically incapable of accepting that people in the global South could organize their own movements or articulate a coherent politics of resistance.

Today, with much of the world in open rebellion against neoliberalism, this fiction is getting harder and harder to maintain. That Friedman has perpetually failed to spot the vibrant network of grassroots organizations that has built a worldwide campaign against the Washington Consensus is not a sign of widespread support for corporate globalization. It is an indictment of his reporting. Well before Seattle, there had been protests of millions of people throughout the global South against the "Golden Straitjacket."

These have continued into the new millennium. In their book *Globalization from Below,* Jeremy Brecher, Tim Costello, and Brendan Smith note that in just a two-month period, in May and June of 2000, there were six general strikes against the impact of neoliberalism. In India, as many as 20 million farmers and workers struck, protesting their government's involvement with the WTO and the IMF. Twelve million Argentineans went on strike in response to fiscal austerity policies imposed by the IMF. Nigeria was paralyzed by strikes against neoliberal price hikes on fuel. South Koreans demanded a shorter workweek and the full protection of part-time and temporary employees by the country's labor laws. Finally, general strikes in South Africa and Uruguay protested increasing unemployment rates, which resulted from IMF austerity policies. All of these escaped Friedman's notice.

In truth, they are only suggestions of wider resistance. The people of Latin America have certainly not joined the groundswell of support for neoliberal ideology. In country after country they have ousted conservative governments since 2000 and elected more progressive leaders, redrawing the region's political map. The columnist has yet to comment.

There is a way in which Friedman perfectly matches the politics of our times. "Like George Bush, he's in the reality-making business," Matt Taibbi argues. "You no longer have to worry about actually convincing anyone; the process ends when you make the case. Things are true because you say they are. The only thing that matters is how sure you sound when you say it."

As much as he might resemble Bush in this respect, however, Friedman also tells us something important about the post-Bush moment. As a new administration takes over, an increasing number of politicians will seek to move the United States away from the aggressive militarism of imperial globalization and back toward a softer approach to ruling the world. Following Friedman, many will look to revitalize corporate globalization as a model for international affairs. These "New Democrats" will promise a fresh approach to foreign affairs. But really, they will return to something old: a Clintonian model of corporate globalization. Like Friedman, many will proclaim it as the best of all possible worlds, a global order both exciting and unavoidable. It will be up to the world's citizens to demand something better.

MARK ENGLER is an analyst with Foreign Policy In Focus. This article is adapted from his book *How to Rule the World: The Coming Battle Over the Global Economy* (Nation Books, 2008). He can be reached via the website www.DemocracyUprising.com

Sources—By Thomas Friedman: *The Lexus and the Olive Tree: Understanding Globalization* (Anchor Books, 2000); *The World Is Flat* (Farrar, Straus & Giroux, 2005); "Senseless in Seattle," *New York Times,* December 1, 1999; "Senseless in Seattle II," *New York Times,* December 8, 1999; "A Race To The Top," *New York Times,* June 3, 2005. Other sources: Matt Taibbi, "Flathead: The peculiar genius of Thomas L. Friedman," *New York Press,* April 27, 2005; "The Lessons of Seattle," *Business Week,* December 13, 1999; Robin Broad and John Cavanagh, "The Hijacking of the Development Debate: How Friedman and Sachs Got It Wrong," *World Policy Journal,* Summer 2006; David Sirota, "Caught on Tape: Tom Friedman's Truly Shocking Admission," SirotaBlog, July 24, 2006; Garrett M. Graff, "Thomas Friedman is On Top of the World," *The Washingtonian,* July 2006; David Sirota, "Billionaire Scion Tom Friedman," DailyKos, July 31, 2006; Roger Lowenstein, "The Inequality Conundrum," *New York Times Magazine,* June 10, 2007; Vandana Shiva, "The Polarised World Of Globalisation," ZNet, May 27, 2005; Jeremy Brecher et al., *Globalization from Below* (South End Press, 2000).

Is Global Trade a Threat or Opportunity?

JIM CHAMPY

The age-old argument resurfaces 21st century-style, as modern developments and technology spawn new sources for materials and customers on a scale never before possible. Along with the golden opportunity for expanding open trade among companies and countries, however, many see the other, darker side.

Globalization of life and trade in the 21st century and beyond is upon us. And, like the Chinese philosophical concept of yin and yang—which describes two opposing but complimentary principles or global forces—open global trade among nations and companies is often viewed from two perspectives: opportunity and threat.

Regardless of which view is held, however, the time and pace of events and developments are driving change in the essence of trade among nations and companies. Instead of fighting or avoiding the inevitable, smart companies—and countries—are rapidly expanding their capabilities and know-how to embrace the opportunities and overcome potential threats.

When the National Academies (of Science, Engineering and Medicine) published its 2005 report on U.S. global competitiveness, open global trade certainly looked like a threat to U.S.-based companies and the U.S. economy. The title of the report, *Rising Above the Gathering Storm,* signaled what's ahead.

A follow-up essay published by Norm Augustine, chair of the committee that developed the *Rising Storm* report, noted (among others) the following alarming conditions:

- The U.S. share in the world's leading-edge semiconductor manufacturing capacity dropped from 36 percent to 11 percent in the past 7 years;
- The U.S. "Big Three" automakers announced the closing of 26 plants in the U.S. over the next several years, while Japan-based companies are opening four new plants in the U.S. between 2006 and 2008;
- Only one of the 25 largest initial public offerings in 2006 took place on American exchanges;
- American companies spend three times on litigation what they do on research; and
- The U.S. ranks 17th among nations in high-school graduation rate and 14th in college graduation rate.

In another reference to the threat of open global trade, Augustine titled his essay, "Is America Falling off the Flat World?", a nod to Thomas Friedman's blockbuster book, The World is Flat. Friedman fairly assesses the impact of open global trade: access to new sources of supply, talent and customers. But the flat world also means new competitors that will change the structure of industries and the basis of competition.

Examples already abound of the force of such new competitors: Nokia Corp., of Finland, in cellphones; Infosys Technologies Ltd., of India, in information services; Lenovo Group Ltd., in China, in personal computing. These companies, and others like them, are providing quality products and services at highly competitive prices.

Many U.S. Companies Are Strong

Not all prognoses for U.S. competitiveness, however, are gloomy. The World Economic Forum has just published its annual assessment of the competitiveness of countries. It ranks the U.S. as the world's most competitive country, up from sixth place a year ago. The good news is that most U.S. companies continue to be highly innovative, both in the products and services they provide, as well as how those products and services are delivered.

However, the study's author, strategist Michael Porter, warns that the larger economic condition of the U.S.—balance of payments and dependencies on foreign sources of energy, along with a weakening dollar—puts the U.S. and its companies at risk.

Global conditions aside, a look at individual U.S. companies shows that they can and do compete. The Boeing Co., for examples, continues to write orders for its jumbo jets—in spite of the competition from Airbus. Multiple European governments have helped Airbus grow, while U.S.-based Boeing flies solo.

Boeing is applying highly innovative engineering and manufacturing capabilities to building its jumbo jets. It's reengineered how it sources globally, and its planes utilize the most advanced carbon fiber technologies. These innovations will eventually change how all airliners are manufactured.

For Boeing, global trade means access to more markets and customers. From its position of innovation and competitive strength, it's clear that global trade presents no threat, but rather a big opportunity.

The Opportunity

For companies that embrace global trade and build the capabilities to operate globally, open markets will be the key to growth. The U.S. economy alone may no longer support the growth of many companies.

For companies that embrace global trade and build the capabilities to operate globally, open markets will be the key to growth. The U.S. economy alone may no longer support the growth of many companies.

How will global trade support growth? Information technology now enables access to millions of additional highly skilled and motivated workers. Companies in the information services business are all adopting a global delivery model, a way of operating that puts work on-shore, offshore or near-shore—wherever it can best be performed at the best price. And work is moving not only because of price, but because of talent and skills.

Companies like IBM Corp. and Accenture, for example, would find it almost impossible today to deliver their services solely with a U.S.-based workforce. There are just not enough U.S.-based information technology professionals. The key to growth in the services industry is being "global," both in terms of sourcing talent and in finding customers in new markets.

On the product front, the wonders of modern-day logistics enable products to be manufactured wherever quality and price dictate. Some countries support the export of manufactured goods with purposefully lax controls—even at the cost of product safety, as the U.S. has recently experienced with some "made in China" goods.

These lax controls may first appear as a threat, giving offshore competitors an unfair advantage. But consumer rejection of faulty products gives hope to the proposition that product quality means something—and that the manufacture of all goods will not leave the U.S. shores, and that U.S. companies will step up their diligence over suppliers for their products manufactured abroad.

Indeed, U.S. manufacturers have proven that they can export products—high-tech machine tools are a good example—and operate globally, from General Motors Corp. making cars in Asia to Kellogg Co. making cereal in Germany.

Global trade also opens up new markets with new customers. The flat world has 3 billion people waiting to become new consumers. As countries like India develop, new classes of customers with buying power are emerging. New consumers quickly acquire new appetites to buy—and U.S. companies just have to develop an appetite to sell into these markets.

Tata Motors of India is developing an automobile that will sell for $3,000 to a new class of consumer. Why won't GM, Ford Motor Co. or Chrysler LLC do the same? These "Big Three" U.S. manufacturers certainly possess the engineering capabilities. What they each sorely need, however, is a new operating model and the state of mind that sees the opportunity—for their business and, thus, their customers, employees and shareholders—instead of seeing the situation as a threat.

The Specter of Protectionism

Unfortunately, there are those who see global trade only as a threat to U.S. jobs. The response is a call to government for policies that protect jobs. Some companies also fear the fierce price competition that open global trade often produces. These companies, too, seek government help in establishing trade barriers and leveling tariffs on imported goods and taxing companies for certain offshore business operations.

With changes likely on the horizon in Washington, there is the prospect that these protectionist voices will be heard more forcefully and that the U.S. government will, indeed, take action to create laws and regulations that favor U.S. labor and U.S. companies at the expense of open trade and competition.

Such policies could prove to be a big mistake and create additional problems. It is appropriate to lobby other countries—and even to apply some subtle economic pressure—to assure fair trade practices and global monetary policies that give all companies a fair chance to compete on the proverbial "level playing field." But strict protectionist measures always result in creating weak country economies and weak corporate competitors.

It was not too long ago that a college student in the U.S. shopping for a first car chose either a Volkswagen or Renault. More prosperous buyers might have shopped for a sleek Citroen or Peugeot. But, unfortunately, there are no longer Renaults, Citroens or Peugeots to be seen on U.S. highways. That's because French protectionist policies have bred companies that are weak global competitors. Companies that do not have to compete on open markets simply become lazy and workers who do not have to compete for jobs ask—and get—more and more until their companies can no longer afford them.

Now, this policy works for some, as some innovative and quality companies do thrive, even in a protectionist environment. For example, luxury goods manufacturers in France are surviving, although an economy cannot live on $2,000 handbags and good cognac alone!

Longer term, the U.S. may be saved from any protectionist movement by the strength of consumerism. Consumers and their economic clout rule in the U.S.—even over labor. The fact that much of what Wal-Mart Stores Inc. sells is made in China does not seem to disturb consumers—but if consumers had to pay twice as much for those goods because of protectionism, Congress would likely hear about it.

How Companies can Seize the Opportunity

Global trade clearly presents enormous opportunity for strong and innovative companies. But companies must embrace global trade in order to not become its victim. The following are

Box 1
Innovating to Drive Differentiation, Competitive Advantage

Cargill Inc.'s concept of infusing modern technology into its logistics system has enabled it to deliver fresh food to thousands of customers in four Central American countries. It's also making doing business with Cargill more dependable for owners of *"tiendas"* (comparable to "mom and pop" stores in the U.S.).

When Cargill's Sun Valley Foods business acquired Perry Foods in 1999, it looked at the business as a supply chain challenge, says Greg Good, who leads the Supply Chain practice for Cargill's Strategy and Business Development. Sun Valley handles retail-branded, processed meats and cheeses in four countries—Guatemala, Nicaragua, Costa Rica and Honduras—the "heart and soul" of which is delivering to its thousands of customers in remote locations, and ensuring freshness of mostly perishable goods.

Looking at its acquisition, Good says, there were three principal issues to deal with: food safety (upgrading where necessary), general plant operations (including employee safety and making sure they were up to Cargill's standards) and the distribution itself.

The Perry Foods business (like much of Sun Valley's business in the region) was serving customers who didn't have freezers or large refrigerators to stack with food, and who shopped daily to purchase fresh ingredients that were needed for that day's meal. In turn, the 30,000 tiny stores serving these customers had little refrigerated storage space and, thus, little room to stock inventory.

The challenge, says Good, was "how do you distribute fresh food—within our product line—so the stores can have the right inventory at the right time for customers?"

They selected a "high-service, high-touch customer solution" for improving the delivery system, says Good. For the Guatemalan market, they used a GPS system to map out all 30,000 locations their trucks and motorcycles would service—aiming to find the best routing and best time-frame for getting from store to store.

"We found this approach allowed us to differentiate from competitors in several ways," says Good. First, they became very efficient at laying out paths so that drivers were making the stops that needed to be made in the right order. As a result, Sun Valley became well-recognized for being extremely accurate in timing deliveries. "A shop-owner knew that the Sun Valley truck or motorcycles would arrive with that day's distribution at, say, 9:00 am on delivery day," says Good.

Second, through the use of handheld computers by drivers, Sun Valley was better able to manage inventories and invoices to its customers.

Another advantage is that the system allowed Sun Valley to make deliveries twice a week, whereas competitors were only delivering once a week. This additional delivery has served to build confidence and trust with the *tienda* owners, and more business has come to Sun Valley because of it.

Routing was set up so drivers could leave one of the several plant locations where the product was made. The project started with a fleet of refrigerated trucks, pickup trucks and motorcycles equipped with coolers. Due to concern for the safety of the drivers, the motorcycles have been upgraded to small delivery trucks.

Since the initial launch, the sales and delivery program has been started in all four Central American countries. Cargill continues to work on improvements—in the areas of enterprise resource planning (ERP) systems and standardizing the back end. The approach of using handheld computers and the GPS modeled-system to deliver on a very tight schedule to *tienda* locations continues to be improved and expanded across the region. The process was touted in print and TV ads for Cargill.

While Cargill hasn't rolled this model out to its business in countries other than Central America, Good says some customers are asking about using the process in places like Thailand, Vietnam and others.

—Ellen M. Heffes

some steps that companies and their financial executives can consider:

- *Develop a Global Business Model.* A company must look at its operations and ask hard questions about where work can best be performed, in terms of both quality and cost. The company must then develop a set of business processes that enables it to operate globally.

  Today, for example, a U.S.-based manufacturer of automotive components might engineer its products in Germany, close to its customer; might produce the component in Taiwan; ship it to the Philippines to be tested; then ship the component to the customer to be installed in a vehicle. That vehicle will end up in a driveway in Atlanta. A company today must have processes and systems to manage that kind of work flow.

  A real global delivery model also includes the ability to understand offshore markets and how to sell into those markets. This is not the old "hub and spoke" model with "foreign" branches. This is about operating in offshore locations, and living the business and culture of that country.

Having low costs is a requirement to compete globally. Even for those that are now industry leaders, pricing power will not be guaranteed in the long term. Customers will continue to ask for more—and for less.

- *Be a Low-Cost Producer.* Global trade means new competitors. Some will have the advantage of lower labor costs. Others will have achieved new levels of efficiency through better processes or improved technology. Whatever the case, having low costs is a requirement to compete globally. Even for those that are now industry leaders, pricing power will not be guaranteed in the long term. Transparency and access to multiple markets make customers very conscious of price. Customers will continue to ask for more—and for less.

- *Also Focus on Value.* On the "more" side, customers will want value, not just a lower price. A global business model has to deliver both. That's why companies like Nokia are able to compete globally. Each generation of a Nokia phone delivers more value for less cost—more functionality, better design, improved quality.

  Also, the Huggies brand disposable diaper you purchase today, made by Kimberly-Clark Corp., is a far superior product to the one originally introduced in the 1950s—in quality, strength, ease of use, etc. And, due to innovation and technology, the cost is about the same inflation-adjusted price for a superior product as it was a decade ago.

  A company's value proposition also determines its competitive distinctiveness in global markets. Competing on price alone means that a company's products or services have become commoditized—a very unattractive position.

- *Find the Right Partners.* A company is not likely to have all of the capabilities to operate globally. Finding the right partners is critical, especially if a company for selling or sourcing in unfamiliar markets. But a partner should not be chosen on the basis of cost and capability alone. Business partners must share the same business values—especially across oceans. Global partners must be chosen very carefully.

  How will a partner respond to a crisis, an operational breakdown, an unusual customer need? A company must be able to trust how its business partners will behave.

- *Hire the Best.* In whatever markets a company operates, it must hire the best "athletes." In the competitive global marketplace, talent is critical, and a company's workforce must have good international sensibilities. A company that is too American in its work style will not be effective in global trade. In Asia, for example, simply knowing how to exchange a business card with a Japanese partner or customer demonstrates international sensibilities—or the lack thereof.

- *Maintain One Culture.* A company needs to have a set of consistent internal business values that are shared by all its people—in all its locations. Ethics and behaviors must be consistent. Otherwise, trust breaks down between workers and a company experiences difficulties in global operations.

- *Dramatically Strengthen Finance Capabilities.* Operating globally requires considerable change in the finance processes of a company. Many more questions need to be answered:

The Realities of Global Trade

- Politics and technology have widely opened the world to global trade
- Global trade means access to new sources of supply and new customers
- Global trade also means fierce new competitors
- Protectionists will make noise and create fear
- The economic benefits of global trade are too great to reverse
- Competing in global trade requires a global operating model
- Countries must also provide a supportive fiscal and educational infrastructure
- Companies that fail to embrace global trade will become its victims

- Where and how should assets and profits be accounted for—and reported?
- What are the accounting and tax ramifications and choices of operating globally?
- What markets are best for raising capital? Are there advantages in borrowing in non-U.S. dollar currencies?
- How do profits get consolidated and repatriated, or do they?

Bottom line, finance requires much more muscle in global markets.

What's a Country to Do?

Companies that follow the steps outlined above will experience vast opportunity in global trade. However, if their home countries fail to support them with sound infrastructure policies, companies could find themselves at a competitive disadvantage. Competing globally requires a home country infrastructure that aggressively supports education—especially in science and engineering—and research that engenders innovation.

That's what the National Academies' *Rising Storm* report aggressively recommends for the U.S. Indeed, the *Rising Storm* report cited the following alarming facts:

- Almost twice as many bachelor's degrees were awarded in physics the year before Sputnik, deemed a time of dangerous educational neglect, as last year.
- The number of engineering doctorates awarded by U.S. universities to U.S. citizens dropped by 23 percent in the past decade.
- In 2002, Asian countries as a whole awarded 636,000 first engineering degrees; European countries awarded 370,000; North America awarded 122,000.
- Fewer than 15 percent of U.S. high-school graduates have sufficient mathematics and science credentials to even begin pursuing engineering degrees.
- The U.S. is graduating more visual-arts and performing-arts majors than engineers.

From the facts above, it appears that U.S. citizens are assured they will be well entertained, but the question remains as to how they will live and compete in global markets.

To truly compete worldwide, the U.S. must undertake aggressive programs to encourage and support students entering technology-related careers. U.S.-based companies are struggling to find the onshore science and engineering talent that they need to compete. IT jobs can no longer be filled just onshore, as the U.S. doesn't have sufficient skills. Educational reform and investment is required at all levels and grades.

Further, the U.S. government must expand its support of basic research—and not shrink it, as it has been doing. There is substantial evidence that basic research leads to innovation and economic profit. The growth of Silicon Valley around the Internet and Cambridge, Mass., around human health and sciences are examples of how research and education fuels economic growth and opportunity.

Companies must also adopt cultures of innovation that seriously support the development of new products and services. The U.S. has demonstrated consistently that it can produce highly innovative companies, but the country is at risk of falling behind.

Hard choices and substantial private and public investment are required so that global trade remains an opportunity. The move to open markets is not reversing, and while we speak of the world getting smaller, its very "smallness" is actually fueling its growth. The benefits of the global economy are just too strong, and the progress and opportunity worldwide are too compelling to go in any other direction.

JIM CHAMPY is chairman of Consulting for Perot Systems. He is the co-author of the best-selling book, *Reengineering the Corporation.* His new book, *OUTSMART: How To Do What Your Competitors Can't,* will be published in April 2008.

From *Financial Executive,* January/February 2008, pp. 36, 38–41. Copyright © 2008 by Financial Executives International (FEI). Reprinted by permission from Financial Executives International; 1750 Headquarters Plaza, West Tower, 7th Floor, Morristown, NJ 07960; 973.765.1000; www.financialexecutives.org

Economists Rethink Free Trade

It's no wholesale repudiation, to be sure, but something momentous is happening as doubts begin to creep in.

Jane Sasseen

Many ordinary Americans have long been suspicious of free trade, seeing it as a destroyer of good-paying jobs. American economists, though, have told a different story. For them, free trade has been the great unmitigated good, the force that drives a country to shed unproductive industries, focus on what it does best, and create new, higher-skilled jobs that offer better pay than those that are lost. This support of free trade by the academic Establishment is a big reason why Presidents, be they Democrat or Republican, have for years pursued a free-trade agenda. The experts they consult have always told them that free trade was the best route to ever higher living standards.

But something momentous is happening inside the church of free trade: Doubts are creeping in. We're not talking wholesale, dramatic repudiation of the theory. Economists are, however, noting that their ideas can't explain the disturbing stagnation in income that much of the middle class is experiencing. They also fear a protectionist backlash unless more is done to help those who are losing out. "Previously, you just had extremists making extravagant claims against trade," says Gary C. Hufbauer, a senior fellow at the Peterson Institute for International Economics. "Now there are broader questions being raised that would not have been asked 10 or 15 years ago."

So the next President may be consulting on trade with experts who feel a lot less confident of the old certainties than they did just a few years ago. From Alan S. Blinder, a former vice-chairman of the Federal Reserve and member of the Council of Economic Advisers in the Clinton Administration, to Dartmouth's Matthew J. Slaughter, an international economist who served on President George W. Bush's CEA, many in the profession are reevaluating the impact of globalization. They have studied the growth of low-wage work abroad and seen how high-speed telecommunications make it possible to handle more jobs offshore. Now they fear these factors are more menacing than they first thought.

Gains Only for a Tiny Slice

No one is suggesting that trade is bad for the U.S. overall. According to estimates by the Peterson Institute and others, trade and investment liberalization over the past decades have added $500 billion to $1 trillion to annual income in the U.S.

Yet concern is rising that the gains from free trade may increasingly be going to a small group at the top. For the vast majority of Americans, Dartmouth's Slaughter points out, income growth has all but disappeared in recent years. And it's not just the low-skilled who are getting slammed. Inflation-adjusted earnings have fallen in every educational category other than the 4% who hold doctorates or professional degrees. Such numbers, Slaughter argues, suggest the share of Americans who aren't included in the gains from trade may be very big. "[That's] a very important change from earlier generations, and it should give pause to people who say they know what's going on," he says.

Dartmouth's Slaughter notes that income is down for every educational level except those with PhDs or professional degrees.

Blinder warns the pain may just be starting. He estimates that eventually up to 40 million service jobs in the U.S. could face competition from workers in India and other low-wage nations. That's more than a quarter of the 140 million employed in the U.S. today. Many of the newly vulnerable will be in skilled fields, such as accounting or research—jobs U.S. companies will be able to move offshore in ever greater numbers. "It will be a messy process of adjustment, with a lot of victims along the way," Blinder says.

The rumble of academic debate is already having an effect on the Presidential campaign. In an interview with the *Financial Times* late last year, Hillary Clinton agreed with economist Paul A. Samuelson's argument that traditional notions of comparative advantage may no longer apply. "The question of whether spreading globalization and information technology are strengthening or hollowing out our middle class may be the most paramount economic issue of our time," her chief economic adviser, Gene Sperling, recently wrote. Barack Obama's adviser, the University of Chicago's Austan D. Goolsbee, is not convinced free trade is the culprit behind the squeeze on incomes. But he believes many U.S. workers aren't sharing in the gains from open markets and fears a political blowback unless something is done.

A Call to Action

What to do? Blinder argues for a big expansion of unemployment insurance and a major overhaul of the poorly performing Trade Adjustment Assistance program (TAA), which retrains manufacturing workers whose jobs disappeared. More vocational training and wage insurance, which would partially reimburse displaced workers who take new jobs at lower pay, also figure in his proposals. Both Clinton and Obama—and even Republican Senator John McCain—have similar ideas.

That's not enough, says Slaughter. He sees a need for some form of income redistribution to spread the gains from free trade to more workers. In a controversial article Slaughter co-wrote last summer for *Foreign Affairs,* he proposed "A New Deal for Globalization" in which payroll taxes for all workers earning below the national median income level would be eliminated. Slaughter has talked with campaign advisers in both parties. So far, he has no takers. But it's one more sign of how far the trade debate has moved.

From *BusinessWeek,* February 11, 2008, pp. 32–33. Copyright © 2008 by Bloomberg BusinessWeek. Reprinted by permission of Bloomberg LP.

Globalization with a Human Face

Jagdish Bhagwati on the trouble with protectionism, how to deal with climate change, and why NAFTA was bad for free trade.

SHIKHA DALMIA

Free trade is never more necessary—or vulnerable—than in times of economic distress. The current global downturn is no exception. Protectionist barriers have shot up all over the world, including the United States. Earlier this year, Congress killed a pilot program allowing Mexican trucks to transport goods across America and included "Buy America" provisions in the stimulus bill banning foreign steel and iron from infrastructure projects funded by the legislation. More disturbingly, President Barack Obama, after chiding the Congress for flirting with protectionism, initiated his own ill-advised affair by imposing a 35 percent tariff on cheap Chinese tires.

If the world manages to avoid an all-out trade war of the kind that helped trigger the Great Depression after the U.S. imposed the Smoot-Hawley tariffs in 1930, it will be in no small part due to the efforts of one man: Jagdish N. Bhagwati, an ebullient and irreverent 76-year-old professor of economics at Columbia University. Bhagwati has done more than perhaps any other person alive to advance the cause of unfettered global trade.

A native of India, Bhagwati immigrated to the United States in the late '60s after a brief stint on the Indian Planning Commission, where he learned first-hand the insanity of an economic approach that tried to modernize a country by cutting it off from world trade. Since then, he has devoted his efforts, both in academia and in the popular press, to showing that there is no better way of improving the lot of both advanced countries and the developing world than through free trade. His path-breaking contributions to trade theory have put him on the short list for a Nobel Prize in economics.

Though a dogged trade advocate, Bhagwati is anything but dogmatic. He is a free spirit who draws intellectual inspiration from many disparate ideological camps. A self-avowed liberal, he is also something of a Gandhian social progressive, though Gandhi himself supported economic autarky. Bhagwati works with numerous Third World NGOs on a host of human rights issues. Yet he has no problem taking on these groups—or his famous student, Nobel laureate Paul Krugman—when they question the benefits of trade. In fact, he devoted his 2004 magnum opus, *In Defense of Globalization,* to a point-by-point rebuttal of these critics. Although he doesn't vote Republican because he dislikes the party's nationalistic jingoism, he readily declares that Democrats pose a far bigger threat to international exchange than Republicans.

This summer Shikha Dalmia, a senior analyst at the Reason Foundation, interviewed Bhagwati in his New York office.

reason: You have been on the short list for a Nobel Prize in economics for your contribution to trade theory. Could you explain what your main contribution is?

Jagdish Bhagwati: My breakthrough in trade theory was very simple, as all breakthroughs are. Back in the 1950s, when the case for free trade was widely regarded as less compelling analytically than today, protectionists had one very powerful argument on their side. They noted that a country necessarily benefits from free trade only when markets are perfect—that is to say, only when market prices reflect true social costs can we expect these prices to guide allocation correctly. Take pollution. Say your production process makes you spew things into the air and water but you do not have to pay for this pollution. Then the social cost of harming others is not being taken into account by you and hence your production costs are less than the "correct" social costs.

So you could take two points of view. The time-honored view was that when there is such "market failure," or what might be better called a "missing market," the case for free trade was compromised and any form of protectionism was justified. I argued that if you had a market failure, fix that, and you are back to perfect markets and the legitimacy of free trade. So, for example, you can have a polluter-pay principle on the environment. If you do that, then there's no damaging spillover which has not been taken into account.

The proper policy response then is not to abandon free trade but rather to fix the market failure and then to embrace free trade. This was a revolutionary thought. For 200 years, serious economists had abandoned free trade in the presence of market failures of one kind or another.

reason: *In Defense of Globalization* was addressed to non-academic critics of free trade and globalization who claim that globalization does not have a human face. What was your argument?

Bhagwati: When I was in Seattle in 1999, when everything went haywire as far as trying to get a new round of trade negotiations, I realized that the young people who were agitating, and some of the older folks also, were not interested in whether trade was good for national income and prosperity. They were claiming that globalization has an adverse impact on a whole lot of social issues—gender equity issues, environmental issues, the effects of globalization on the polity and democratic rights. In short, to use the fetching phrase, they were concerned that economic globalization lacked a human face.

My book addressed precisely such issues. I found that, contrary to the fears of the critics, most social agendas were advanced rather than handicapped by globalization. Globalization, I concluded, *had* a human face.

Take women's issues, for example: If you look at what happens to the gender gap on pay inequality, it turns out that you can make a perfectly solid argument that in fact it's narrowed rather than widened as a result of international trade. The reason is very simple: If a man is paid twice as much as a woman, when they are both equally competent, that is inefficient. So when you are engaged in international competition, you're really not going to be able to indulge your prejudice in this way. This will lead to more demand for women and less for men, bringing pressure to bear on their relative wages in the direction of greater pay equality.

Two brilliant young women, Sandra Black and Elizabeth Brainerd, did their dissertation at Harvard on this hypothesis. They found that in two decades in internationally traded industries in the United States, the gender wage gap narrowed faster than in non-traded industries. Trade had thus been good for an important social objective, not a drag on it.

reason: You still hear the argument—President Obama made it during his campaign—that we want fair trade, not free trade.

Bhagwati: In the United States the phrase "fair trade" holds a lot of sway, because fairness is an important issue here. In the United States it's the equality of opportunity, not of outcome, that matters. We have a fairness-oriented culture. The Europeans, who are actually more stratified—they're more into equality of outcome. The social mobility of people is much less, so they want the state to intervene and redistribute. They're more into justice and we're more into fairness.

So if you want to be a protectionist in the U.S., you've got to say that these Japanese or these Indians are trading unfairly. People will much more readily give you protection if they think the other guy is a wicked unfair trader.

President Obama hasn't really understood the case for free trade because I don't think he's been too interested in trade. His background is as an activist working with the poor people, so he hasn't thought about these issues. So he ends up listening to other people, and a lot of people who are protectionist are around him, particularly the unions, who are afraid of international competition. But they dress up the fair trade argument in altruism, that they're doing it to raise the labor standards and wages of workers in India and Brazil and so on and so forth, when in fact, they're doing it to protect their own workers from competition. The president doesn't seem to realize that this is something which other people, whom you pretend you're trying to help, actually see as a naked, cynical ploy.

Instead of pandering to union fear, Obama has got to engage them. You have got to help these doubting Thomases confront their fears. He's got to say that trade with the poor countries is actually helping, not hurting, you. The unions' main fear is that unskilled jobs are disappearing. They see these jobs being taken up elsewhere where the labor is cheap. But they can't hold onto these jobs anyway. What they get in return from trade are cheap products that they need as consumers. So free trade moderates the downward pressure on their real wages.

Big portions of the wages of poor workers go toward low quality textiles, for instance. That is well-established. But if you look at the structure of protectionism, if you go and buy something from Anne Klein that's going to be expensive, but it carries no tariff at all because these high-end designers compete on variety. Tariffs matter where the competition is on prices. So the low-quality items which poor people buy end up carrying higher tariffs than high-end items that rich people buy.

reason: So free trade's harm to union workers as producers is minimal, but the harm to them as consumers would be very great if we didn't have free trade?

Bhagwati: Yes. So what President Obama has to do is basically change the ethos in this country so that it understands that the United States has profited enormously from free trade. Free trade has rescued India and China from poverty, yes. But the U.S. working class has also profited from international trade.

He's got to make an eloquent case like that. He's got to see that this is something that needs as much attention and as much of his eloquence as the speech he made on race after he got into trouble over his pastor.

But then to move the case of free trade forward, the Obama administration has to show global leadership, because the U.S. is the biggest trading country. He has got to make sure that the stimulus package and everything that he does is completely consistent with openness. I think he's got to understand this is not something he can keep postponing and postponing.

When President Clinton came in the first year, he was into Japan bashing and he hadn't made up his mind on whether he wanted trade or not, because he had advisors on both sides. So his first year was extremely tentative. Then he made up his mind and was fiercely pro-trade after that. President Bush, the junior, he too gave into steel tariffs when he first came in, but after the first year, when he found his feet, he was very pro-trade.

President Obama doesn't have that luxury because the weaknesses are showing in the way the stimulus is being designed and played out. So someone has to tell him very clearly that he doesn't have the luxury of most presidents, which is to use a first year to find your feet on trade. He's got to be out there and he's got to provide the leadership. He's got to bring in the people who waiver and dither, the AFL-CIO, the Democrats who are indebted to the AFL-CIO, and say: "Look, you're wrong. Here, let's have a debate." There are lots of Democratic economists who'd be able to engage these guys in a proper debate.

reason: In recent years, the opposition to free trade hasn't just come from left-wing unions, but also people on the right who fear that outsourcing will cause the U.S. to lose its economic edge as it imports high-value-added products and exports low-value-added ones. How do you respond to that?

Bhagwati: It's an irrelevant argument. To say that the United States should be exporting high-value items rather than low-value items is itself a fallacy. But America's great comparative advantage lies in innovation. For someone like me who has come from India it is very obvious that this country is full of innovators. When I was a student I read about Britain's Industrial Revolution. And it was powered by all kinds of people, inventing the spinning jenny and so on. They were like little Americans, you know, thinking of new ways of doing things and making a buck. Almost every other American I know is thinking about something, some way to do something. We are a highly inventive people, and technology therefore is our driving force. It's not savings and investments which are driving our productivity. It's technology and innovation and immigrants like me—not me in particular—lots of people who come here and by the second generation go through the mill and become Colin Powell or Orlando Patterson at Harvard.

Almost every other American I know is thinking about something, some way to do something. We are a highly inventive people, and technology therefore is our driving force. It's not savings and investments which are driving our productivity. It's technology and innovation and immigrants.

Nobody can compete with us in the long run, in my view, because these are not advantages which people in traditional societies can reproduce. So we're always going to be doing high value. We'll lose the high value we generate to others quickly because now technology diffuses very fast. But then we'll have new ideas, new technologies.

reason: Which side poses the bigger threat to free trade, conservatives on sovereignty, neo-mercantilist grounds, or liberals on equity and environmental grounds?

Bhagwati: In the U.S., I think the Democrats are the biggest threat to free trade. I don't see the right-wing threat to globalization in terms of sovereignty as being a major one, frankly.

Conservatives are principled people, so they have Edmund Burke type of reservations about continuous change and so on. But they are not people who are going to undermine the rule of law when it comes to trade. Even their arguments against immigration are rule-of-law arguments. Anti-globalization noises saying we've lost our sovereignty and so on and so forth, it's not going to get very far in the U.S. system.

The threat from the left, on the other hand, is much more serious because they oppose free trade on equity grounds. I love America. I have settled in it. But there is a tendency, particularly on the part of the Democrats, to become totally self-righteous on everything and this is the way it has to be and if you disagree, then you're a Republican. I mean, that's the way they argue it. It's unbelievable. They don't want to argue the merits of the case.

The threat from the left . . . is much more serious because they oppose free trade on equity grounds. . . . There is a tendency, particularly on the part of the Democrats, to become totally self-righteous on everything. . . . They don't want to argue the merits of the case.

reason: Why do you think Republicans are better on free trade than Democrats?

Bhagwati: Both the last Bush and Ronald Reagan believed in America. They thought that their own people could win. That made them more prone to accept international competition and trade.

They carried that attitude over into politics, of course. For instance, President Reagan won the Cold War by pushing Gorbachev to the limit. But he was lucky. President Bush went into Iraq with the same attitude, and that was unfortunate.

But since they both believed that Americans would win, they were good on international trade, although maybe for the wrong reasons. Democrats don't believe that America can remain number one, and hence they cannot bring themselves to be completely in favor of open markets.

reason: You are a big believer in multilateral trade agreements over bilateral trade agreements. What's wrong with bilateral trade agreements?

Bhagwati: Free trade agreements and protectionism are two sides of the same coin. When I have free trade just with you, I'm freeing trade with you but I handicap those who are not members of our free trade area. They have to keep paying the duties to get into our markets. So that becomes a de facto way of increasing protection against outsiders. Multilateral free trade would be a closer thing to pure free trade.

Free trade agreements and protectionism are two sides of the same coin. When I have free trade just with you, I'm freeing trade with you but I handicap those who are not members of our free trade area. They have to keep paying the duties to get into our markets.

But there are two additional worries about bilateral trade agreements: One, we don't just have two or three free trade agreements. Today there are close to 500, and every week there's another new one being constructed. As a result, you're getting all kinds of special tariffs, rules of origin, and other things multiplying in the system, something which I've called the spaghetti bowl. Exporters rightly get upset by the large numbers of tariffs they face depending on where you're coming from.

Two, how do you enforce these agreements in a globalized world? It's very chaotic. Parts are coming from everywhere. For a country to have to then decide which product is my partner country's product rather than an outside country's product becomes completely arbitrary. A car produced in Canada with Japanese steel and German chemicals, where 80 or 90 percent of the parts may come from elsewhere—is that a Canadian car or is it really something else? Does it qualify for the zero tariff under the North American Free Trade Agreement or not?

reason: Was NAFTA a mistake?

Bhagwati: I think in retrospect, yes. It's not a slam dunk argument because it did bring in Mexico. Otherwise, they were talking about CAFTA which included just Canada and the U.S. But when you brought in Mexico, it made it a much bigger thing.

President Clinton was carrying on the multilateral negotiations in tandem with NAFTA. But NAFTA created worries on the part of the unions here, because this is a poor country and they were worried that Mexican competition would really hurt their wages. So even though the multilateral talks would've gone through without any difficulty, President Clinton ended up having to fight very hard for NAFTA, which survived by a very narrow majority. In order to win NAFTA, he had to give in on things like labor standards and so on. That's when all these social things became part of trade deals. From there, it never looked back.

So in retrospect, I would say, because of the concessions they had to make, Clinton started us down a road which really has been counterproductive.

There is another thing to worry about. When you look at a trade agreement like NAFTA, it's about that thick (*holds his hands about two feet apart*). When I debate people like Lori Wallach of Public Citizen, she arrives with a lot of books, and among them is this NAFTA treaty she carries for effect. I hope she gets a hernia from doing this often enough, because it looks pretty heavy to me. I wouldn't be carrying it around. Anyway, she shows this book and asks, "Is this free trade?" And mad as

she is, she's right to raise that issue. You should be able to say maybe in 10 pages that in these sectors we are going to liberalize and so on. But nine-tenths of what's in these agreements are things which have nothing to do with trade. Labor standards, environmental standards, intellectual property rights. If I were Jane Fonda, in order to sell more workout tapes, I could put into the agreement a clause that the president of Mexico has to do his exercise to my tapes. And it would go in, because ours is a lobbying culture and nobody really would know that it's there. Because who opens these things except the lobbyists?

So many developing countries are now waking up to the fact that they're being sold a bill of goods in the form of trade agreements.

reason: Do you think a global externality problem like global warming poses a fundamental threat to free trade?

Bhagwati: I think it depends on the way you do it. First, you've got to decide whether there is a problem of an externality. I have doubts about these scientists who claim to have a consensus on global warming because, you know, Freeman Dyson, a great scientific figure, says these guys are really low-level scientists and I'm told by many that they, in fact, are. And if they reach a consensus, I don't care. I mean, that's the consensus of incompetents.

But so long as only the scientists were talking about global warming, nobody paid the slightest attention. Remember, not a single senator voted for the Kyoto resolution back in the '90s. Even Al Gore and Clinton had to walk away from Kyoto. But then the polar bears were threatened, the glaciers began to melt, and then that great French film about the penguins, which touched all our hearts came out. So these were three whammies. Even if you live in Peoria you will understand, wrongly maybe, that global warming is a problem. I tell all my students: If they think of something like that for free trade, please let me know.

What countries like India and China are saying is that if the CO_2 was accumulating and it's going to create a disaster, then that took a lot of time to establish. So they want the West to bear primary responsibility for the damage it has caused in the past. If America applies some kind of a carbon tax and it says that if India and China don't impose a similar tax, it's going to use what is called border tax adjustment, then that is protectionism. And there's no reason why Indians and Chinese have to accept this. Just as America was not willing to accept it when it didn't sign onto Kyoto and Europe started threatening a countervailing duty on American exports. But everybody reacted to that talk and said this is a cockeyed thing to do. Peter Mandelson, who was the EU Commissioner, said it was very unwise because the United States will retaliate.

It's ironic that we are now using exactly that kind of threat on India and China. But America's fuel tax is so much lower than that of most other countries, except the Middle East. So India and China are going to hit us because we had a low gas tax for a long time. And all hell would break loose. India and China are big guys. They can get legal [World Trade Organization] retaliation against the U.S. Or India could take away contracts from Boeing and give them to Air France. It can have nuclear reactors go to France rather than to G.E. Caterpillar would be shut out.

So I suggest a different way. If in our own U.S. system you're going to get your companies to clean up under the Superfund Act, that's a tort principle which we accept. Then we ought to be willing to pay in some form to other poor countries for the past damages. The West has completely ignored this suggestion so far. It has provided maybe a few million dollars in assistance to Third World countries for this purpose. But if the West seriously starts contributing to this fund, Third World countries could get anywhere from $150 million to $1 billion to mitigate global warming.

reason: This is a political non-starter, you know.

Bhagwati: Yes. But the president actually has made some remarks about border tax adjustments not being such a good idea. He's got to do more than that. He's got to say this is a crazy thing to do. He's still very cool—he needs to lose his temper once in a while. Because it's too important. The U.S. is one of the biggest trading nations in the world. We want the rule of law. We don't want retaliation, which would be massive. India and China are not Zaire or Zimbabwe. They're not little countries you can push around. We don't want to unleash that kind of trade war, because it would be very hard to control, I'm afraid.

UNIT 2

International Finance

Unit Selections

Key Points to Consider

- How do you think the global financial crisis affected world trade? Do you think the debt that is being accumulated by the developing world will affect its ability to come out of the recession? Do you think this debt will affect its ability to grow?

- What were some of the causes of the financial crisis? How do you think they could have been prevented? Do you think those steps are being taken? Why or why not?

- What are some of the things that international financial and other global organizations, like the World Trade Organization, might be able to do to help prevent the kind of melt-down in the financial markets that occurred in 2008?

- Do you think that harmonizing the accounting reports on a global basis is a good idea?

Student Website

www.mhhe.com/cls

Internet References

Foreign Direct Investment is on the Rise Around the World
www.neweconomyindex.org

India Finance and Investment Guide
financeindiamart.com/

Institute of International Bankers (IIB)
www.iib.org

International Monetary Fund
www.imf.org/

Lex Mercatoria: International Trade Law Monitor
Lexmercatoria.net

North American Free Trade Association (NAFTA)
www.nafta-sec-alena.org

Resources for Economists on the Internet
www.rfe.org

World Bank
www.worldbank.org

World Trade Organization
www.wto.org

Further information regarding these websites may be found in the book's preface or online.

In October of 2008, the international financial markets came crashing down and all the aspects of global business changed for the foreseeable future. It was not only Wall Street in the United States that experienced the crisis, but the financial markets of London, Japan and the rest of the world that spun out of control. Financial institutions that were thought to be solid and secure were suddenly found to be insolvent; corporations whose stock resided in the most conservative portfolios suddenly revealed themselves to be mere shadows of their corporate images; and the financial system began to collapse like a house of cards before the autumn winds.

Governments, corporations, central bankers, financial institutions, and global organizations scrambled first to stop the slide into what everyone feared would be the coming of the next Great Depression and then to find a way out of what has become what some have called the Great Recession. "The World Economy: The Global Financial Crisis and the Collapse in World Trade," and what will happen in the next several years is what is on everyone's mind, and what everyone is attempting to find an answer to. What will be the GDP in places like China, India, Indonesia, and the United States?—the four largest countries in the world in terms of population. How much and how will Europe and Japan grow in this crisis? It is going to take time for the financial markets to recover from the shocks that occurred in 2008 and it is going to take longer for other sectors of the economy to rebound from the shocks that shook the global markets in the fall of 2008. However, evidence suggests that the developing world is recovering faster than the developed world where the people had more to loose, and lost it, while in the developing world, people had less to loose, so when they lost it, it did not matter as much. As a result, people in the developing world have less to make-up than people in the developed world because they were not as exposed to the risks that the financial markets had created through their irresponsible behavior and are now growing while the developed world remains bogged-down in a deep, prolonged recession.

For the global economy to successfully recover from the current recession, as one article puts it, "Everyone Needs to Rethink Everything: Reflections from the IMF's Former Chief Economist." What no one could anticipate was the actions that governments would take and the way that would cause global confidence to disintegrate. The system of world trade, including the financial system of world trade and the way the government regulatory agencies interact with the marketplace needs to be evaluated. There are agencies, such as the International Monetary Fund (IMF) and the World Bank that are designed to address some of these issues. "Potential Future Functions of the World Trade Organization," and those of the IMF and the World Bank as well as regional trade associations such as the European Union (EU) and the North American Free Trade Association (NAFTA), also need to be addressed. But, these are complicated problems that are not easily solved. The financial markets have been at the heart of the economic problem that has gripped international business. "The Wicked Problem of Good Financial Markets," will not lend itself to a single magic solution. It is far too complicated. The conditions that brought on

Idealink Photography / Alamy Images RF

the financial crisis and global economic recession will require more than just a single solution. The solutions will also require political will on the part of the global community that might not yet be present as the current crisis may not be dire enough. It may take a truly terrible economic collapse to provide the political will to institute the necessary reforms to prevent a global economic melt-down from happening. The success that institutions have currently experienced in avoiding that kind of disaster is unlikely to lead to the necessary changes to the reform of the global economic system.

Despite the upheavals of the global marketplace and the problems of the international financial markets, global business and global trade continues to move on. While, perhaps not at the rate that it did prior to the autumn 2008 crash, investments are still made, goods are still transported and sold, and people continue to invest in the future.

China represents an alluring market for investment by large and small firms. One of the first economies to come out of the recession, China represents a unique opportunity for direct foreign investment. Most of the very large companies are already there, but opportunities remain for small organizations to participate in the largest market in the world. "Engaging China: Strategies for the Small Internationalizing Firm," offers some interesting approaches for the small multinational corporation to enter the Chinese market through direct foreign investment. While these companies may have lost the "first mover" advantage to their larger cousins, they have the advantage of learning from the mistakes the big multinationals made in going into the Chinese market earlier on.

Changes are also afoot in the way that financial results are going to be reported. The Securities and Exchange Commission (SEC) is going to be requiring American firms doing business outside the country to start reporting their results using the International Financial Reporting Standards (IFRS) instead of FASB in 2011. This is certain to result in some very different reporting from what would have been previously reported under the old standards. It is true that reporting under IFRS standards will put the U.S. firms more in line with the rest of the international community in reporting their financial results, but in the short-term, this is bound to lead to some confusion on the part of investors, especially during a time of economic uncertainty.

The financial markets continue to be a focus of uncertainty for many involved in international trade. The worldwide interconnection of the financial markets was made more than evident during the crisis and has been reaffirmed by the continuing inability of the developed countries to bring themselves out of the morass. Until the financial crisis is resolved, whether that starts in the United States, Europe or Japan, world trade will continue to lag and this will affect the growth of the economies of the world.

The Global Debt Bomb

Spending our way out of Worldwide Recession will Take Years to Pay Back—and Create a Lot of Pain.

DANIEL FISHER

K yle bass has bet the house against Japan—his own house, that is. The Dallas hedge fund manager (no relation to the famous Bass family of Fort Worth) is so convinced the Japanese government's profligate spending will drive the nation to the brink of default that he financed his home with a five-year loan denominated in yen, which he hopes will be cheaper to pay back than dollars. Through his hedge fund, Hayman Advisors, Bass has also bought $6 million worth of securities that will jump in value if interest rates on ten-year Japanese government bonds, currently a minuscule 1.3%, rise to something more like ten-year Treasuries in the U.S. (a recent 3.4%). A former Bear Stearns trader, Bass turned $110 million into $700 million by betting against subprime debt in 2006. "Japan is the most asymmetric opportunity I have ever seen," he says, "way better than subprime."

Bass could be wrong on Japan. The island nation (and the world's second-largest economy) has defied skeptics for so long that experienced traders call betting against it "the widowmaker." But he may be right on the bigger picture. If 2008 was the year of the subprime meltdown, 2010, he thinks, will be the year entire nations start going broke.

The world has issued so much debt in the past two years fighting the Great Recession that paying it all back is going to be hell—for Americans, along with everybody else. Taxes will have to rise around the globe, hobbling job growth and economic recovery. Traders like Bass could make a lot of money betting against sovereign debt the way they shorted subprime loans at the peak of the housing bubble.

National governments will issue an estimated $4.5 trillion in debt this year, almost triple the average for mature economies over the preceding five years. The U.S. has allowed the total federal debt (including debt held by

government agencies, like the Social Security fund) to balloon by 50% since 2006 to $12.3 trillion. The pain of repayment is not yet being felt, because interest rates are so low—close to 0% on short-term Treasury bills. Someday those rates are going to rise. Then the taxpayer will have the devil to pay.

Whether or not you believe the spending spree was morally justified, you have to be concerned about the prospect of a dismal, debt-burdened fiscal future. More debt weighs heavily on GDP, says Carmen Reinhart, a University of Maryland economist. The coauthor, with Harvard professor Kenneth Rogoff, of *This Time It's Different: Eight Centuries of Financial Folly* (Princeton, 2009), Reinhart has found that a 90% ratio of government debt to GDP is a tipping point in economic growth. Beyond that, developed economies have growth rates two percentage points lower, on average, than economies that have not yet crossed the line. (The danger point is lower in emerging markets.) "It's not a linear process," she says. "You increase it over and beyond a high threshold, and boom!" The U.S. government-debt-to-GDP ratio is 84%.

We've been through this scenario before. It's especially ugly because we get hit by inflation, too. In the years immediately after World War II inflation surged past 6%, while economic growth flagged and the government-debt-to-GDP level exceeded 90%, note Reinhart and Rogoff. The country worked that ratio down over the next half-century. Now the ratio is shooting up again.

America is a nation of spendthrifts, addicted to easy credit and dependent on the kindness of savers overseas to keep us comfortable. Our retail industry hangs on credit cards and our real estate on 95% financing and the tax rewards for mortgage interest. The personal savings rate has climbed from negative 0.4% in 2006 to a positive 4.5% rate now, but that is still a pathetic figure for a

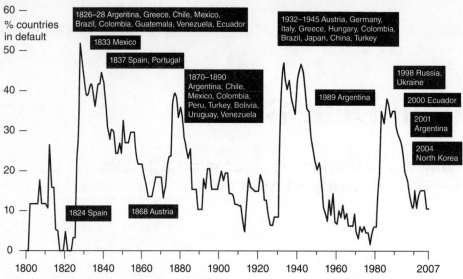

The Stumble Cycle Sovereign defaults—when a country stops paying its bills—go in waves, often following global financial crises, wars or the boom-bust cycles of commodities. Some countries, like Spain and Austria, mend their ways; others, like Argentina, are repeat offenders.

Sources: Standard & Poor's; Kenneth Rogoff, Harvard; Carmen Reinhart, U. Maryland.

Graph: David Lada for Forbes Magazine

nation whose government is un-saving all that and more with its deficit budget. Politicians on this continent are good at compassion, whether trying to help people stay in their overpriced homes or offering health care to millions of those without it. They are not so adept at nurturing growth.

If the GDP doesn't expand at "normal" rates of 3% to 5% coming out of this recession, wrestling down the debt will be very tough, indeed—perhaps impossible without drastic cuts in spending and higher tax rates on many fronts. The Congressional Budget Office currently projects the fiscal deficit will decline from 10% of GDP next year to around 4.4% from 2013 to 2015. But that assumes economic expansion of at least 4%, not the 2% predicted in the study by Reinhart and Rogoff. You see the vicious cycle here: Debt depresses growth, and then low growth makes paying down the debt an impossible task.

U.S. corporate income tax receipts were down 55% in the year ended Sept. 30, 2009 to $138 billion. It may be a long while before these tax collections get back to where they were. As corporate profits recover, factory utilization will be up and inflation will be close behind. At that point the 0% yield on Treasury bills will be history. Rolling over the national debt will become a lot more expensive. Higher rates on Treasuries will work their way through the debt market, driving up the cost of money for homeowners, businesses and already struggling state and local governments.

"The economy over the last six months has been on a sugar high," says Benn Steil, senior fellow at the Council on Foreign Relations and author of *Money, Markets and Sovereignty* (Yale, 2009), a survey of the relationship between money and the state. If Congress and the Obama Administration don't trim deficits, he says, "we will get to the point where credit is much more expensive in the U.S. than it ever has been in the past."

Most states are already having trouble paying their bills and, of course, don't have printing presses with which to finance their debts. They are turning to Washington for help and may succeed in putting some of their liabilities on the federal balance sheet. With growing off-balance-sheet obligations, notably unfunded pension liabilities, the states will be competing for years with the federal government for scarce taxpayer dollars.

"U.S. states are like emerging markets," says Reinhart. "They spend a lot during the boom years and then are forced to retrench during the down years." Cutting expenses sounds good theoretically, but look at California: Students (and faculty) are up in arms over proposed tuition increases and cutbacks at the state's once prestigious university system; state employees are mounting a fierce legal battle against furloughs and other wage concessions.

Mainstream credit analysts are worried. The U.S. has been able to sell vast amounts of debt because the Treasury market, with $500 billion a day in turnover, is

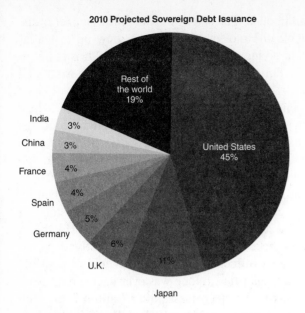

2010 Projected Sovereign Debt Issuance

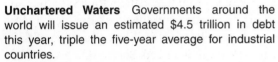

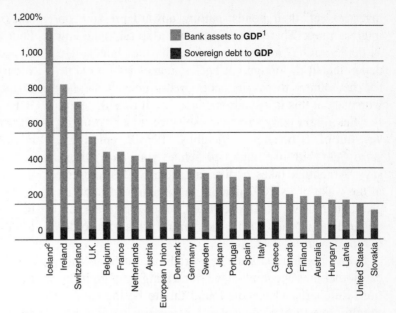

Unchartered Waters Governments around the world will issue an estimated $4.5 trillion in debt this year, triple the five-year average for industrial countries.

Sources: IMF World Economic Outlook and other various public sources, including news media and respective government data; Hayman Advisors estimates.

It's the Total Debt, Stupid Private banking assets tend to become public problems in a crisis. By that measure European countries are far worse off than the U.S.

[1]Assets for five largest banks. [2]Iceland data represent pre-financial-crisis conditions.
Source: Hayman Advisors.

Graph: David Lada for Forbes Magazine

considered safe and dwarfs all other debt markets. But Brian Coulton, head of global economics at Fitch Ratings in London, warns that once rock-solid economies like the U.S. and the U.K. could join shakier nations like Japan and Ireland in losing their AAA ratings if they don't get their bad habits under control. "While AAAs can borrow in the short term, very high and rising government debt-to-GDP ratios are ultimately not consistent with AAA status," Coulton says.

A FORBES survey of sovereign credit, taking into account trends in spending and revenue, economic freedom and the price of the debt insurance, a.k.a. credit default swaps, ranks the U.S. number 35 in a class of 85, below Germany, the Netherlands and China. The CDS market is priced to imply a 3.1% chance of default over five years on Treasury debt. Other countries are likely to hit the debt wall sooner, and with greater impact. The U.K., for example, is 38 on the list, two notches above Slovenia. One culprit is much higher levels of private banking debt that could land on the British government balance sheet à la Fannie Mae and Freddie Mac in the U.S. The sovereign debt of the U.K., plus the assets of its five largest banks, exceeds 500% of GDP, compared with 200% in the U.S. Even closer to the edge is Ireland. Sovereign debt is at 41% of GDP. But total banking-system assets are another 800% of GDP *(see graph)*. If those assets sour, the government will almost certainly step in

to protect the banking system, as Iceland was forced to do in 2008. Iceland's currency and stock market collapsed soon thereafter, and its president recently blocked a law to repay $5 billion-plus to British and Dutch investors. That move puts at risk a pending bailout package for Iceland from the International Monetary Fund and its application to join the European Union.

Most investors seem to believe, as the late Citibank chairman Walter Wriston put it, that "countries don't go bust." The opposite is true. "There was a massive default wave in 1980s and 1990s," says Reinhart. Investors may not have paid much attention since the defaults were mostly in emerging market countries like Guatemala and Romania. But the deadbeats included current investor favorites like Brazil, which defaulted in 1983, went through a bout of hyperinflation in 1990 and effectively defaulted again, for the same reason, in 2000. Reinhart and Rogoff show that, on average, nations add 86% to their debt loads within three years of a credit crisis. At the same time, government revenue falls an average of 2% in the second year after the onset of the troubles.

The combination can be fatal for investors holding bonds issued by financially shaky countries like Argentina or Greece, which sell a lot of their debt outside their own borders (as does the U.S.—45% of all publicly held debt). As a nation's finances deteriorate, foreign investors sell their bonds, putting upward pressure on interest rates. That usually sets off a spiral including a deteriorating currency, which, if the bonds are denominated in foreign currencies, makes it impossible for the country to pay its debt. Greece doesn't have to worry about this last syndrome, because it uses the euro. But that might make things worse since it can't print its way out of its financial difficulties. "It's like entering a prize fight with one hand tied behind your back," Bass says. Argentina takes a different tack. Still struggling in the wake of its 2002 default on foreign-held debt, its president recently tried, and failed, to seize central-bank dollar deposits (and cashier her central banker) in order to repay overseas debt.

Even if countries don't stiff creditors outright, they can sometimes accomplish the same thing through inflation. Reinhart and Rogoff found this to be the case in roughly one-third of the countries they tracked that had currency depreciation rates above 15% a year, following the 1980–81 recession. Of course, this works only for debt denominated in the home currency and only if investors are taken by surprise. If they see inflation and devaluation coming, they price it into the interest they collect.

Making money on sovereign defaults isn't as easy as picking off subprime mortgages. Credit default swaps on potential basket cases like Dubai, Greece and Ukraine have doubled and tripled in price over the past 12 months as their debt loads grew. To buy insurance against a default in Greece over the next five years costs 3.4% a year.

How about Switzerland—once considered an impregnable money center? Credit default swaps on Swiss debt cost 46 basis points (0.46% a year), compared with 33 for the U.S. The Swiss government is not itself deeply in hock, but it may have to bail out its private banks in the manner of Iceland or Uncle Sam. Swiss private-bank debt is seven times GDP. The U.S. isn't a disinterested bystander: The Swiss central bank borrowed $40 billion from the Federal Reserve under a little-known swaps program last year to remove bad assets denominated in dollars from private banks. The Fed considers the transaction low risk because the Swiss promise to repay in dollars. But it signals how losses on private loans—in this case, U.S. subprime mortgages—can cycle back into a problem for the Swiss government. As hedge fund operator Bass notes, a 10% hit on Swiss banking assets would represent 80% of its 2008 GDP of $488 billion and 400% of annual government revenue. "You can invest a very small portion of capital, so if you're wrong it costs very little," says Bass. "If you're right it can pay hundreds of percent."

Shorting countries comes naturally to Bass, 40, who has spent most of his career investigating overvalued

stocks and bonds. The son of the onetime manager of the Fountainbleau Hotel in Miami, Bass grew up in Dallas and won a diving scholarship from Texas Christian University in Fort Worth, where he studied real estate and finance.

He spent most of the 1990s at Bear Stearns in Dallas, attracting a group of well-heeled clients who took his advice on shorting stocks like Delgratia Mining Corp. of Vancouver, B.C., which plunged after a highly touted gold find in Nevada turned out to be a hoax.

Around that time Bass learned the danger of betting too much on his own research. He shorted the stock of RadiSys, a telecom technology maker in Hillsboro, Ore., after he called the company's recently departed chief financial officer at home and was told of possible financial irregularities. (None was ever uncovered.) Bass was forced to take steep losses after Carlton Lutz, then an influential stock promoter, called RadiSys "the son of Intel" in his newsletter and the stock doubled. (More recently the company lost $58 million on revenue of $320 million in the 12 months ended Sept. 30.) "Even when you do great investigative work and you understand the accounting, it doesn't matter if you know everything," Bass says. "You can still lose a fortune."

Last spring Bass lost $110 million buying credit default swaps on Portugal, Ireland, Italy and Greece. He may have been right but too early. He is holding on.

His biggest potential score is in Japan. Government debt has soared to 190% of GDP from 50% in the mid-1990s, hitting an estimated $10 trillion in 2009. But because interest rates are so low, the government paid only 2.6% of GDP to service its debt in 2008, less than the U.S. at 2.9%.

Yet low rates mask a growing problem for Japan. The government took in $500 billion in taxes last year, plus another $100 billion in other revenue that included money borrowed by a government investment program. But the Tokyo feds spent $980 billion, including $100 billion-plus on interest and $190 billion or so it transferred to regional and municipal governments. That left a $360 billion hole it could plug only by writing more IOUs, on top of the debt it must roll over each year as bonds mature.

Today Japan can borrow all it wants from its own citizens. Over the decades they have dutifully (if mechanically) piled up a $7.7 trillion cache of savings they keep mostly in low-yielding bank deposits. Those savings equal two-thirds of the total household wealth of Germany, France and the U.K. combined, says John Richards, North American head of strategy at RBS, who spent the early 1990s in Japan trying to build a channel for selling Japanese government bonds overseas (the country still sells but 6% of its debt to foreigners). "You

Debt Weight Scorecard

Free-spending America isn't quite a banana republic yet. But in a FORBES ranking of sovereign debt the U.S. comes out number 35, one rung below Estonia, on a global list of 85.

How do the 50 U.S. states stack up against one another? Have a look at the best and worst below. We considered a dozen or so factors, including unfunded pension liabilities, changes in tax revenue, debt as a percentage of GDP, debt per capita, growth expectations for employment and the state economy, net migrations and a moocher ratio that compares government employees, pension burdens and Medicaid enrollees to private-sector employment. Utah finished first overall thanks to AAA ratings from both Moody's and S&P, as well as a debt per capita of only $447. Bringing up the rear is Illinois, which lagged several high-tax, debt-burdened states in the Northeast. More people left the Prairie State than took up residence over the past five years, and its unfunded pension obligations are fifth highest in the country.

—Kurt Badenhausen

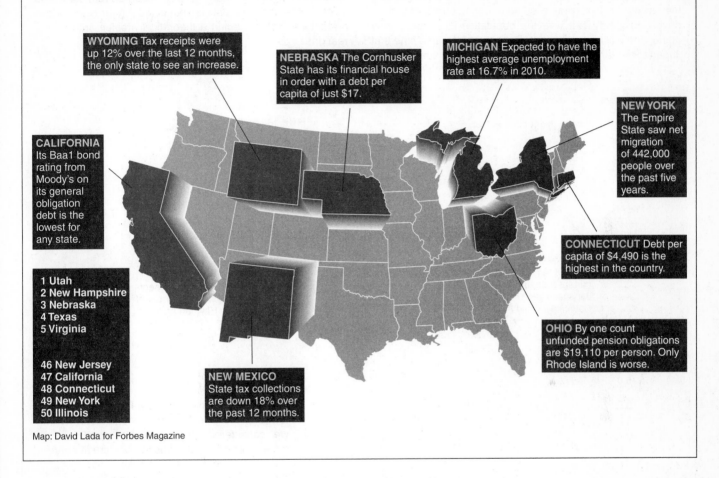

WYOMING Tax receipts were up 12% over the last 12 months, the only state to see an increase.

NEBRASKA The Cornhusker State has its financial house in order with a debt per capita of just $17.

MICHIGAN Expected to have the highest average unemployment rate at 16.7% in 2010.

NEW YORK The Empire State saw net migration of 442,000 people over the past five years.

CALIFORNIA Its Baa1 bond rating from Moody's on its general obligation debt is the lowest for any state.

CONNECTICUT Debt per capita of $4,490 is the highest in the country.

OHIO By one count unfunded pension obligations are $19,110 per person. Only Rhode Island is worse.

NEW MEXICO State tax collections are down 18% over the past 12 months.

1 Utah
2 New Hampshire
3 Nebraska
4 Texas
5 Virginia

46 New Jersey
47 California
48 Connecticut
49 New York
50 Illinois

Map: David Lada for Forbes Magazine

ask how would Japan turn into a sovereign debt crisis and you can't find the trigger," Richards says. "Shorting the yen because you think there's going to be a rollover crisis makes no sense at all."

The trigger could be demographics. Japan's population is aging quickly. Today 22% of Japanese are 65 or older; in 20 years it will rise to 30% or so (compared with a current 13% of Americans and 20% in 2030). At the same time Japan's total population peaked at 128 million in 2004 and has settled into long-term decline.

The combination means Japan's government pension fund has become a net seller of government bonds, while the nation's savings rate has plunged from 18.4% in 1982 to 3.3% today. When that drops to zero, Japan will be forced to look overseas for financing—and risks exposing itself to international rates.

JPMorgan Chase analyst Masaaki Kanno in Tokyo says that Japanese bonds are in a bubble that could pop in the next three to five years, as savings rates drop. Even if the government can somehow keep borrowing at a 1.4% interest rate, he says, interest expense will rise to roughly $200 billion by 2019, or 45% of government revenue, unless it pushes through a big increase in the national value-added tax.

But those rates are unlikely to hold. For years the government has been able to replace bonds paying as much as 7% interest with steadily lower-rate debt. The favorable rollovers ended in 2007, leaving the government much more vulnerable if it has to sell debt overseas,

Setting Sun
With an Aging Population and Ballooning Debt, Japan Soon May Have Trouble Financing Itself

It's a measure of Japan's mounting fiscal problems that its finance minister, Hirohisa Fujii, resigned in early January because of exhaustion. Nobody can come up with an elegant way out of Japan's dilemma.

The island nation has historically financed itself, tapping the savings of its citizens piled up during decades of export-driven prosperity. But now the population is shrinking and aging, and savings rates have plunged at the same time that Japan's left-leaning Hatoyama administration is spending like

never before. The chart below shows what's likely to happen next: Debt per working citizen will surge as growing fiscal deficits are spread across a shrinking population.

The crunch may come soon after Japan's current account balance—net export income, plus income from overseas investment—slips to a deficit. That could trigger rising prices and interest rates, turning a theoretical problem into a very real one.

—*D.F.*

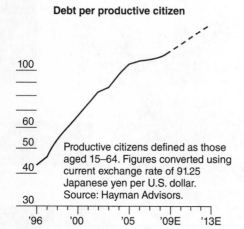

Debt per productive citizen

Productive citizens defined as those aged 15–64. Figures converted using current exchange rate of 91.25 Japanese yen per U.S. dollar. Source: Hayman Advisors.

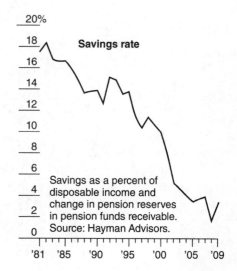

Savings rate

Savings as a percent of disposable income and change in pension reserves in pension funds receivable. Source: Hayman Advisors.

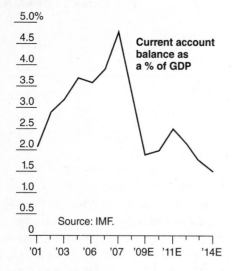

Current account balance as a % of GDP

Source: IMF.

Credit Crunch

To compile a ranking of soveregin debt for 85 of the world's largest economies, we considered, among other factors, default probabilities based on credit default spreads, trade balances, credit agency ratings and debt as apercentage of GDP.

Best
1 Qatar
2 Hong Kong
3 China
4 Luxembourg
5 Singapore

Worst
81 Serbia
82 Argentina
83 Venezuela
84 Pakistan
85 Ukraine

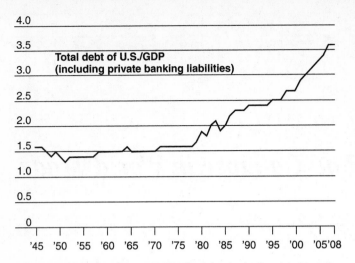

Total debt of U.S./GDP (including private banking liabilities)

The Leverage Factor Total U.S. debt, including banking liabilities, has soared relative to economic growth over the past 20 years.

Source: Federal Reserve.

where ten-year rates are two to three percentage points higher than Japan's. If rates rise past 3%—the scenario Bass is betting on—interest expense will exceed total government revenue by 2019.

The process will accelerate if the yen falls and interest rates rise, prompting Japanese savers to pull their money from low-yielding bank accounts, which, in turn, are invested in government bonds. "That will be the beginning of a vicious cycle," Kanno says, when "consumers will realize what is happening" and shift their money to more attractive investments overseas. Bass thinks the crisis will come sooner. For $6 million he has secured options on $12 billion in ten-year government bonds that will pay $125 million if Japanese rates rise to 4%.

"The good news is the wolf's at the door in Japan and that we in the U.S. have front row seats to see what's going to happen," he says. "I hope we learn something from it."

The World Economy
The Global Financial Crisis and Collapse in World Trade

DAWN HOLLAND ET AL.

The global financial crisis has been compounded by an exceptionally sharp drop in world trade, and we are now facing the most widespread global recession in over sixty years. World GDP is expected to record an annual decline this year for the first time since 1946.[1] As the economic crisis has developed, policymakers have stepped in across the globe to help stabilise the world economy. In the absence of fiscal and monetary easing initiated since 2008, world output would have been expected to decline by 1.7 per cent this year, compared to our current forecast decline of 0.5 per cent. However, while policy actions in the banking sector were sufficient to stabilise what appeared to be the imminent collapse of the global financial system last October, there is little concrete evidence that policy initiatives have successfully started to ease lending conditions. The key risks to our forecast hinge on the speed with which financing conditions normalise, the speed with which world trade reverts to equilibrium and the path of inventories.

Recovery from the recession is expected to be gradual. The far-reaching nature of this global recession means that recovery must be primarily driven by renewed strength in domestic demand in some of the larger economies, as the world currently lacks a leader for an export-driven revival. Figure 1 illustrates our quarterly profile for GDP growth in the world, US, Euro Area and Japan. Following the onset of the subprime crisis in the US in August 2007, bank lending conditions tightened, and a large number of economies had already dipped into a mild recession by mid-2008. Financial markets erupted in crisis in September 2008, as major bankruptcies and interventions raised perceptions of risk to levels last seen in the 1930s and, as a consequence, about 55 per cent of OECD economies fell into recession (OECD, 2009). A few economies, such as Greece, Slovakia and several major oil exporters, including Russia and Norway, recorded positive growth in the final quarter of 2008, but exceptionally sharp quarter-on-quarter output declines of more than 3 per cent were recorded in Japan, South Korea, Taiwan, Brazil, Ireland, Slovenia and the Baltic states. Most of these countries recorded exceptionally steep contractions in domestic demand, and on top of this external demand contracted sharply. Global trade in goods and services declined by 6.7 per cent in the final quarter of 2008, the most severe contraction since at least 1965, when quarterly statistics become

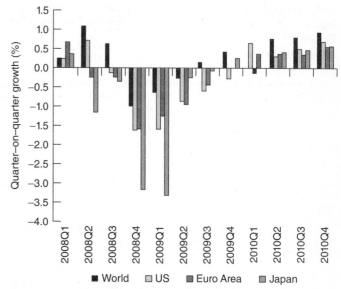

Figure 1   Quarterly profile of GDP growth

Note: This chart incorporates the advance estimate of US GDP released on 29 April, after our forecast figures were finalised. The outturn was approximately 0.7 percentage points weaker than anticipated.

available. Only a few economies for which data are available recorded an increase in export volumes in the final quarter of 2008, notably India and Norway.

The available information points to quarterly declines in GDP of a similar magnitude in the first quarter of 2009, as illustrated in the figure. While the sharpest declines are believed to be behind us, we expect to see further declines in output for at least another two quarters. Japan's export markets should benefit from an anticipated recovery in the level of world trade, so growth may come sooner there than elsewhere. Our central forecast sees six or seven consecutive quarters of output decline in the US, Japan, the Euro Area and the UK. In Figure 2 we illustrate the probability of the recession extending to up to nine consecutive quarters, based on a series of stochastic simulations around our current forecast. While our central forecast sees growth returning to Japan earlier than in the other economies, Japan also faces the greatest risk of a more prolonged recession lasting up to nine consecutive quarters.

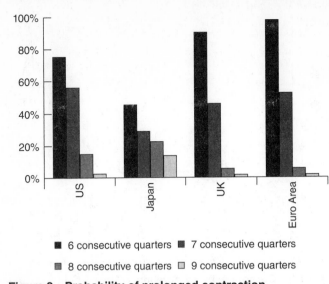

Figure 2 Probability of prolonged contraction

Note: These figures are based on stochastic simulation results using NiGEM and illustrate the probability of output declining for 6, 7, 8 and 9 consecutive quarters, starting between 2008q1 and 2009q1.

Our forecasts for GDP growth and inflation in the major economies are reported in Table 1. The sharpest annual declines in the major economies are anticipated in Japan and Germany this year. Both are sensitive to the car market, which

has collapsed, while Japan is also hampered externally by its strong exchange rate. Although the yen has receded from peaks reached in the first quarter of the year, it remains about 15 per cent above its average level in the first three quarters of 2008 in effective terms. Japanese exports are highly price sensitive, so the appreciation can be expected to have a significant effect on Japanese exports. While China is expected to record positive growth this year, growth will ease to 6.4 per cent, well below the Government's target of 8 per cent, in order to maintain a stable employment rate.

Growth is expected to return to most economies by the end of next year, and we forecast global growth of 2.1 per cent in 2010. However, we expect GDP growth to remain below recent trend rates in most of the major economies in 2011 and in some cases in 2012. From 2013, growth should rise above trend rates to pull the economies back towards a new, lower, equilibrium. The financial crisis will leave permanent scarring in most major economies, as lenders are expected to retain higher risk premia than before the crisis, so that the level of potential output will be permanently lower than forecast before the crisis. The magnitude of scarring will vary across countries, depending on the extent to which lenders underestimated risk prior to the crisis.

The roots of the financial crisis lie in a sharp drop in the value of bank assets, leaving banks with insufficient capital to maintain their crucial role of providing loans on both a short and

Table 1   Forecast Summary   *Percentage Change*

Real GDP[a]

	World	China	OECD	EU-27	Euro Area	USA	Japan	Germany	France	Italy	UK	Canada	World Trade[b]
2005	4.5	10.4	2.7	2.1	1.8	2.9	1.9	0.9	1.9	0.8	2.1	2.9	8.1
2006	5.1	11.6	3.1	3.2	3.0	2.8	2.1	3.2	2.4	2.1	2.8	3.1	9.4
2007	5.0	11.9	2.7	2.9	2.7	2.0	2.4	2.6	2.1	1.5	3.0	2.7	6.9
2008	3.2	9.0	1.0	0.8	0.7	1.1	−0.7	1.0	0.7	−1.0	0.7	0.5	1.8
2009	−0.5	6.4	−3.3	−3.5	−3.5	−2.8	−6.2	−5.1	−2.9	−3.3	−4.3	−1.9	−8.2
2010	2.1	7.4	0.5	0.7	0.4	−0.2	0.7	0.9	0.7	−1.2	0.9	1.1	7.7
1999–2004	3.6	8.9	2.5	2.3	2.1	2.8	1.2	1.2	2.2	1.5	2.9	3.4	7.1
2011–2015	3.9	8.1	2.4	2.2	2.0	2.5	1.6	1.7	1.8	1.8	2.6	2.6	5.4

Private Consumption Deflator | | | | | | | | | | World Prices | |

	OECD	EU-15	Euro Area	USA	Japan	Germany	France	Italy	UK	Canada	Exports ($)[c]	Oil($ per Barrel)[d]
2005	2.2	2.1	2.0	2.9	−0.8	1.5	1.4	2.3	2.5	1.7	3.6	51.8
2006	2.2	2.1	2.1	2.8	−0.2	1.2	1.7	2.7	2.3	1.5	3.2	63.4
2007	2.2	2.1	2.1	2.6	−0.4	1.7	1.3	2.2	2.5	1.6	7.4	70.5
2008	3.0	2.7	2.8	3.3	0.5	2.2	2.2	3.2	2.4	1.7	8.0	95.7
2009	0.3	0.5	0.4	−0.6	−1.5	−0.4	0.4	0.7	1.1	1.2	−9.2	51.6
2010	0.4	0.8	0.7	−0.4	0.0	0.1	0.4	0.9	1.3	1.0	0.1	60.6
1999–2004	1.9	1.9	2.1	2.0	−1.0	1.2	1.3	2.7	1.6	1.8	1.6	26.0
2011–2015	2.0	1.7	1.7	2.2	1.7	1.4	1.6	1.6	1.7	1.4	1.7	79.1

Notes: (a) GDP growth at market prices. Regional aggregates are based on PPP shares. (b) Trade in goods and services. (c) Non-commodity export prices. (d) Average of Dubai and Brent spot prices.

long-term basis to allow the smooth functioning of the economy. As economic conditions have worsened, credit losses have continued to accumulate, especially where house price declines and share price falls have been steepest. While a wide number of measures to stabilise banks have been introduced around the world, there remains a high level of uncertainty related to the value of troubled assets, and these measures have so far proved insufficient to restart bank lending. Since October, policymakers have been urged to act quickly and decisively to ensure banks have adequate capital to operate. Any delay will only increase the expected costs to taxpayers, which we know will be large. In our last *Review,* we estimated that delay to taking decisive action between October 2008 and January 2009 had cost the global economy $550 billion, or 0.8 per cent of GDP.

The authorities initially focussed on shoring up the liabilities side of bank balance sheets, with capital injections that could be implemented quickly in order to stave off a complete collapse of the banking system. Policymakers are now turning to the asset side of the balance sheet, and it is crucial that the magnitude of losses on the asset side are recognised in order to relieve the uncertainty regarding the underlying value of financial institutions and regain confidence in the banking system. The IMF's Global Financial Stability Report estimates that total write-downs related to the crisis could reach $4 trillion over the next two years, approximately two-thirds of which may be taken by banks, and the remainder by insurance companies, pension funds, hedge funds and other intermediaries. So far, banks have recognised less than one-third of estimated losses. Measures to separate toxic assets from healthy assets have recently been introduced in the US, Germany, UK, Canada, Italy, Spain, Ireland, Switzerland and South Korea and it is likely that similar measures will be required in other countries as well.

Actions taken thus far appear to have stabilised financial markets, although there is limited evidence that lending conditions have improved. One of the key indicators that we monitor is the corporate bond spread, measured as the yield on Baa corporate bonds (bonds that are considered investment grade, but bear some degree of risk) against 10-year government bond yields (as illustrated in Figure 3). In October 2008, corporate spreads in the US, UK and Euro Area widened to their highest level since the 1930s. Corporate bond spreads give an indication of the cost and accessibility of credit to firms, which can in normal times raise money either through bank borrowing, bond issue or share issue. Corporate spreads in the US have fluctuated between 5¼ and 6½ percentage points since October, with no clear inclination to rise or fall. Spreads in Europe, on the other hand, continued to rise until March, but now appear to be on a downward path.

Bank lending to the private sector across Europe and America has slowed since late 2008, as asset losses have left banks undercapitalised and unable to issue loans. Senior loan officer surveys from the major central banks point to continued tightening of loan conditions in the first half of 2009, but the rate of tightening has eased, especially for businesses, with only about 20 per cent of banks expecting to tighten further this quarter in the Euro Area and the UK, while 60–80 per cent of banks in North America and Europe tightened lending to businesses in the final quarter of 2008.

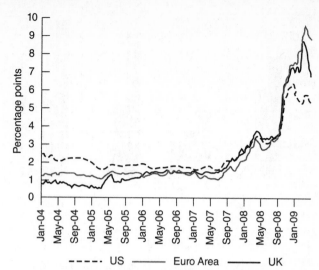

Figure 3 Corporate bond spreads *Spread between Baa corporate and government bond yields*
Source: Derived from Datastream series.

Our forecast assumptions for investment risk premia and corporate borrowing constraints are largely based on our assessment of corporate bond spreads, and take into account the views expressed in surveys of credit conditions. We continue to believe that risk premia peaked in the first quarter of 2009, and expect premia to recede gradually over the forecast horizon. However, we expect risk premia to remain high for the rest of 2009, and return to long-term levels only in 2012, while maintaining a margin of 1 point on average above precrisis levels. These assumptions are essentially unchanged since January. Our assumptions regarding credit rationing to consumers are also essentially unchanged since January, except where actual data outturns have indicated an over- or under-assessment. Credit conditions for consumers are expected to remain tight until 2012. The lack of access to credit is exacerbated by asset price developments and a collapse in household wealth. House prices are declining across most of the OECD economies, with sharp drops in the US, UK, Canada, Denmark, Ireland, Norway and New Zealand. Share prices reached a trough in early March, and have recovered some ground, but remain well below the levels of last September when the crisis hit. We are forecasting declines in consumer spending of about 1–2 per cent this year in most of the major economies, although consumer spending in Germany is expected to out-perform the other G7 economies, supported by fiscal incentives for car purchases.

The recession has taken an expectedly severe toll on the global car market. Spending on cars always contracts in a recession, as both households and firms delay spending on expensive items when budgets are constrained. A lack of access to finance for car purchases by potential car buyers has greatly exacerbated the decline in demand for cars. On top of this, exporters suffered a freeze in advance financing for shipment of goods, and this has affected not just the car market but merchandise trade in general. In addition to cars, global trade in capital goods has contracted severely, due to the sharp drop in investment across the world.

Box A
The Impact of Policy Reactions to the Financial Crisis

In the last *Review,* we included a note that analysed the impact of the global policy response to the financial crisis (Barrell, Fic and Holland, 2009). This Box builds on our earlier analysis to incorporate additional measures of monetary and fiscal easing that have been introduced since January 2009. By January 2009, interest rates had been cut essentially to zero in the US and Japan, and stood at 1 per cent in Canada and 1½ per cent in the UK and the Euro Area. While a further half point cut was anticipated in the UK, financial markets at that time had not priced in any further changes to intervention rates. Yields on longer-term bonds suggested that rates were expected to rise gradually, starting in the second or third quarters of 2010. Since January, intervention rates in the UK and Canada have been cut to ½ per cent, while Euro Area rates have been cut to 1 per cent. In addition, the major central banks have also engaged in quantitative easing. While specific policies differ across countries, the ultimate aim is the same, which is to flatten the yield curve by convincing financial markets that policy rates will be maintained at current low levels for an extended period.

Table 2 reports the interest rate assumptions underlying our current forecast. We now expect interest rates to remain at current levels until the end of 2010, as quantitative easing measures have successfully pushed down yields on 1, 2 and 3-year bonds. In addition to the monetary easing measures, we have updated the fiscal package for the US, which remained under

debate in January, to reflect more accurately the budget plans approved in February 2009. The US stimulus is worth 2 per cent of GDP in 2009, with an additional stimulus worth 0.8 per cent of GDP in 2010. The revised figures increase US policy initiatives by about $150 billion in 2009 and 2010 compared with our January estimate. In addition to the US package, we have included a fiscal stimulus in China of approximately 3.5 per cent of GDP in 2009 and 2010. This can be thought of as the lower bound of the actual Chinese stimulus that is likely to be introduced, and is consistent with the data observed in the first quarter of 2009.

We use NIESR's model NiGEM to strip the policy actions off in a sequence that allows us to quantify the effects of policy to date. Figure A1 illustrates the impact that policy changes since January 2009 are expected to have on GDP growth in the major economies, while Figure A2 illustrates the impact of all policy initiative since the beginning of 2008. Changes to the US fiscal package primarily affect the outlook for 2009, and are expected to offset about 0.1 percentage points in the decline in US output this year. Monetary easing measures have been more significant in the Euro Area, Canada and the UK since January, but also give a small stimulus to Japan in 2009 and 2010. Policy initiatives since the beginning of 2008 offset about 1–1¾ percentage points in the potential declines in the major economies this year, except in Italy, where fiscal expansion has been minimal.

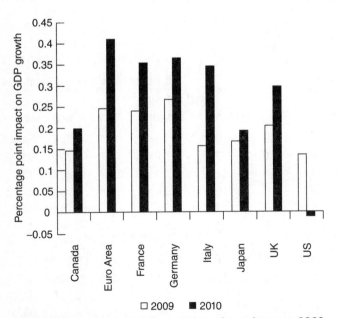

Figure A1 Impact of policy easing since January 2009 on GDP growth

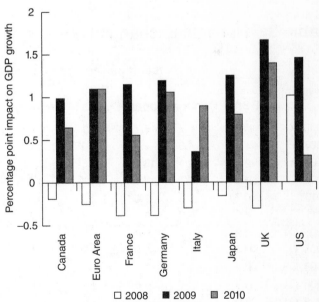

Figure A2 Cumulative impact of policy easing since 2008 on GDP growth

Compounding demand and financing factors, very sharp exchange rate realignments have caused temporary disruption to global supply networks, as importers in countries with

depreciated currencies suddenly find it too costly to import goods at previously agreed prices. Global capital flows have contracted sharply in response to the crisis, and the 'flight to

Table 2 Interest Rates

Percent Per Annum

| | Central bank intervention rates | | | | | Long-Term Interest Rates | | | | |
	USA	Canada	Japan	Euro Area	UK	USA	Canada	Japan	Euro Area	UK
2006	5.0	4.0	0.2	2.8	4.6	4.8	4.2	1.7	3.8	4.5
2007	5.1	4.4	0.5	3.8	5.5	4.6	4.3	1.7	4.3	5.0
2008	2.1	3.0	0.5	3.9	4.7	3.6	3.6	1.5	4.2	4.5
2009	0.3	0.6	0.1	1.2	0.6	3.1	3.2	1.3	3.9	3.6
2010	0.3	0.5	0.1	1.0	0.5	3.9	4.0	1.3	4.3	4.2
2011	1.4	1.6	0.5	2.3	1.8	4.4	4.4	1.5	4.7	4.6
2012	2.6	2.6	0.7	3.6	3.4	4.7	4.7	1.7	4.9	4.8
2013	3.6	3.6	0.9	4.6	4.4	4.9	4.9	1.9	5.0	5.0
2014–2017	4.9	4.9	1.4	5.0	5.0	5.0	5.0	2.4	5.0	5.0
2008 Q1	3.2	3.9	0.5	4.0	5.4	3.6	3.7	1.4	4.1	4.5
2008 Q2	2.1	3.1	0.5	4.0	5.0	3.9	3.7	1.6	4.4	4.8
2008 Q3	2.0	3.0	0.5	4.2	5.0	3.8	3.6	1.5	4.5	4.7
2008 Q4	1.1	2.1	0.3	3.4	3.3	3.2	3.4	1.4	3.9	4.0
2009 Q1	0.3	0.9	0.1	2.0	1.1	2.7	2.8	1.3	3.7	3.5
2009 Q2	0.3	0.5	0.1	1.0	0.5	2.8	2.8	1.5	3.8	3.2
2009 Q3	0.3	0.5	0.1	1.0	0.5	3.5	3.5	1.1	3.9	3.7
2009 Q4	0.3	0.5	0.1	1.0	0.5	3.6	3.7	1.1	4.0	3.9
2010 Q1	0.3	0.5	0.1	1.0	0.5	3.7	3.8	1.2	4.1	4.0
2010 Q2	0.3	0.5	0.1	1.0	0.5	3.9	3.9	1.3	4.2	4.1
2010 Q3	0.3	0.5	0.1	1.0	0.5	4.0	4.0	1.3	4.3	4.2
2010 Q4	0.3	0.5	0.1	1.0	0.5	4.1	4.1	1.4	4.4	4.3

Table 3 Nominal Exchange Rates

| | Percentage Change in Effective Rate | | | | | | | | Bilateral Rate per US Dollar | | | |
	USA	Canada	Japan	Euro Area	Germany	France	Italy	UK	Canadian Dollar	Yen	Euro	Sterling
2006	−1.5	6.7	−6.7	0.1	0.0	0.1	0.0	0.7	1.13	116.3	0.797	0.543
2007	−4.4	4.8	−4.5	4.0	1.8	2.0	2.0	2.3	1.07	117.8	0.731	0.500
2008	−2.2	0.1	13.1	5.8	2.2	2.9	2.8	−11.8	1.07	103.4	0.683	0.545
2009	11.8	−12.1	12.1	1.7	1.3	0.7	1.1	−13.3	1.24	98.5	0.755	0.683
2010	0.7	0.3	−2.6	1.3	0.5	0.6	0.7	1.0	1.24	101.5	0.754	0.680
2011	1.6	0.2	−0.4	1.7	0.7	0.7	0.9	1.2	1.24	103.3	0.760	0.681
2008 Q1	−1.2	−2.7	6.4	2.3	0.9	1.2	1.2	−5.4	1.00	105.2	0.667	0.505
2008 Q2	−1.4	−1.0	−0.3	2.9	1.2	1.4	1.4	−3.0	1.01	104.6	0.640	0.507
2008 Q3	2.3	−2.5	−1.3	−2.1	−1.1	−0.9	−1.2	−1.3	1.04	107.6	0.666	0.529
2008 Q4	11.9	−12.1	20.6	−2.4	−0.9	−1.2	−0.9	−8.1	1.21	96.1	0.757	0.637
2009 Q1	3.0	−2.0	4.3	3.2	2.0	1.3	1.8	−7.0	1.24	93.7	0.766	0.696
2009 Q2	−1.2	0.7	−7.4	1.0	0.3	0.5	0.4	1.1	1.23	100.1	0.751	0.679
2009 Q3	0.0	0.0	0.0	0.0	0.0	0.0	0.0	0.0	1.23	100.1	0.751	0.679
2009 Q4	0.0	0.0	0.0	0.0	0.0	0.0	0.0	0.0	1.23	100.1	0.751	0.679
2010 Q1	0.4	0.0	−0.3	0.4	0.2	0.2	0.2	0.3	1.23	100.7	0.752	0.679
2010 Q2	0.4	0.0	−0.3	0.4	0.2	0.2	0.2	0.3	1.23	101.3	0.754	0.680
2010 Q3	0.4	0.0	−0.2	0.4	0.2	0.2	0.2	0.3	1.24	101.8	0.755	0.680
2010 Q4	0.4	0.0	−0.2	0.4	0.2	0.2	0.2	0.3	1.24	102.3	0.756	0.681

safety' has strengthened the US dollar, the euro and the yen since September 2008, while a number of emerging market economies have suffered steep depreciations. Effective exchange rates in Brazil, Hungary, Mexico, Poland, Russia and South Korea have all depreciated by more than 15 per cent since September 2008. These countries together account for about 8 per cent of world trade, so the disruption to trade in these countries can have a significant impact at the global level.

Even after taking account of all these negative influences on world trade, most statistical models significantly overpredicted the actual outturn for global trade in the final quarter of 2008. The available trade data for the first quarter of 2009 point to a global decline in trade of a similar magnitude to that observed in the final quarter of 2008. This is based on available information on export volumes in the US, which declined by 8.5 per cent relative to the previous quarter; merchandise export volumes in Japan and the UK, which declined by 39.2 per cent and 9 per cent respectively in the first two months of the year relative to the first two months of the previous quarter, and extra-EU export volumes, which declined by 21.4 per cent in January relative to October 2008, while inter-EU export volumes declined by 13.7 per cent over the same period. Available information on bilateral trade suggests that decline in export demand was widespread across the world, with only some of the major oil exporting economies maintaining import demand. There was a clear bias against trade in cars, and vehicle exports from the US declined by 45 per cent in the first two months of the year relative to the first two months of the previous quarter, while Japanese exports of cars declined by over 60 per cent in the first quarter relative to a year earlier and UK exports of cars dropped by 30 per cent in the three months to February relative to the previous three months.

Figure 4 illustrates the ratio of car exports to GDP in a number of countries, to help identify where the collapse in global vehicle trade is expected to have the biggest impacts. The Slovak Republic stands out as being one of the most sensitive economies to global car sales, while car exports also account for more than 5 per cent of GDP in Austria, Belgium, Canada, the Czech Republic, Germany, Hungary, Poland, South Korea, Slovenia, Spain and Sweden. These economies can be expected to be particularly affected by the slump in the global car industry. However, evidence suggests that countries such as the Slovak Republic and Poland have recently gained market share in the global or at least European car market, as purchases have switched to less expensive, fuel-efficient cars.

In order to model the contraction in world trade accurately in our forecast, we need to reduce import volumes in most countries in the first quarter of the year over and above what our model equation predicts. As the car market is clearly over-represented in the contraction of world trade, we have designed the forecasting shock to imports by considering the share of cars in total imports in each economy, as well as available information on car sales in each country in the first quarter of 2009. As can be seen in Figure 5, cars account for a large share of total imports in Canada, Spain and Russia, particularly, while Asian economies such as China, India and Japan have relatively low import shares.

Figure 6 illustrates the ratio of world trade to world GDP. This ratio has clearly been on a steady upward trend, rising from 10 per cent in 1970 to 35 per cent in 2007, reflecting increasing globalisation and rising import penetration ratios in all countries. Our view is that import penetration ratios are unlikely to shift so dramatically on a permanent or medium-term basis. We have, therefore, assumed a recovery in world trade starts in the second half of 2009, allowing the ratio of world trade to GDP to revert to previous trend levels by about 2012. If world trade recovers more gradually than anticipated,

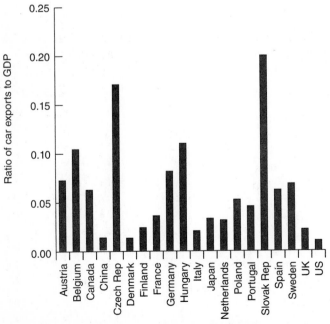

Figure 4   Car exports as a share of GDP (2006)

Source: Derived from UN Comtrade data and NiGEM database.

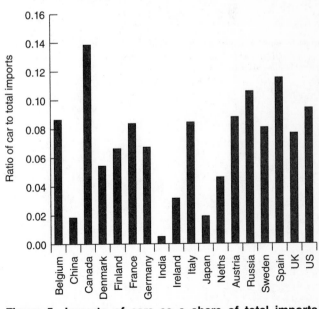

Figure 5   Imports of cars as a share of total imports (2006)

Source: Derived from UN Comtrade data, adjusted for services share of imports from IMF International Financial Statistics.

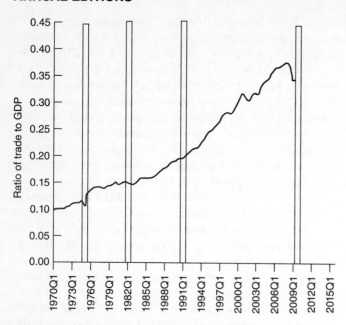

Figure 6   Ratio of world trade to world GDP

Note: Forecast in grey. Areas in boxes indicate periods of global recession as identified in IMF (2009).

this would imply weaker growth in many trade sensitive economies in 2010 than currently forecast.

The unexpectedly steep drop in world demand has led to a sharp rise in inventory levels since September 2008 in the US, Japan and the Euro Area, as firms have found themselves with excess stock that they are unable to sell. There is less evidence of excessive stock build-up in Canada. We expect to see a significant degree of destocking in all the major economies this year, in order to adjust inventories to normal levels in relation to expected sales. This destocking alone is expected to reduce GDP growth by 0.4 percentage points this year in the US,

by 1 percentage point in the Euro Area and by 0.8 percentage points in Japan. The path of inventories is difficult to predict accurately. Evidence points to significant destocking across the world at the turn of the year, and this is thought to be an important factor behind the collapse in world trade. It is possible that businesses have made a one-off adjustment to their stock levels, and stockbuilding may resume earlier than currently forecast. On the other hand, we may have underestimated the required levels of destocking needed in some countries, which would deepen the recessions forecast for this year.

The oil price has risen by about $15 per barrel since the lows reached in January 2009, but remains moderate relative to prices last year. This will continue to restrain inflation and act as a mitigating impact on recessions in oil importing economies. The decline in the oil price from an average of $95 per barrel in 2008 to an average of just over $50 per barrel in 2009 can be expected to reduce inflation in the OECD economies by about 1.8 percentage points this year. On top of the disinflationary impacts of widening output gaps and rising unemployment, this will push inflation rates close to zero in many countries, with a significant possibility of deflation. Prices have already declined on a year-on-year basis in Japan, China, Taiwan, Hong Kong, Spain, Portugal, Ireland, Luxembourg and Switzerland. In addition, they have declined on a quarter-on-quarter basis in the US, Canada, Germany, France, the UK, Italy, Belgium, Greece, Sweden, Slovenia, Estonia and in several economies in East Asia. We project an annual decline in prices in the US, Japan and Germany this year, as well as Taiwan, Ireland and Portugal. However, we do not expect deflation to become entrenched, and forecast price inflation in all economies by 2011. Low rates of deflation for a short period do not pose a threat to these economies, although if deflation becomes entrenched it can push up real interest rates and increase debt burdens on households and business, raising the risk of default and putting bank solvency in jeopardy.

International Special Report

A *Financial Crisis to the West—a Fundamental Crisis to the East*

IAN TRAYNOR

The large inflatable columns toppled one after the other in Berlin on Monday night in a play on democracy's chain reaction in 1989. Twenty years on in Budapest, Daniel Bebesy has a gloomier domino theory.

"Western banks and business have made huge profits in this region for years. Now there's a reluctance to support us," said the economic analyst and fund manager at a large foreign bank in Hungary. "If one of our countries defaults, it will be contagious. There will be a domino effect."

The Hungarians are the Cassandras of central Europe. Bebesy's pessimistic vision of spiralling debt, tumbling economies, and political mayhem may be overwrought.

But for the newish democracies and market economies of the region, 2009 has been a rude awakening, the biggest shock since they switched from Soviet communism to western capitalism 20 years ago. "There is no doubt the region is in deep crisis," said the European Bank for Reconstruction and Development last week. "The worst output collapse since the great recession that followed the end of communism."

The financial and economic crisis was made in the west, but has hit hardest in the east. After years of growth far outstripping rates in the west, governments in Hungary, Latvia, and Romania have fallen, economies have slumped, and leaders have had to call in the salvage squads from the International Monetary Fund, whose tens of billions in bail-out funds are conditioned on swingeing budget cuts.

The US and western Europe this year saw the comeback of the state, nationalising banks and car companies, taxpayers shelling out squillions to buy bad debt, toxic assets, and high street fixtures. But in eastern Europe states are weak and small, the banks are western-owned. The resources for coping with the crisis are thin.

The west does fiscal stimulus. The east cannot afford to.

"The crisis signals the inevitable end of the political and economic cycle that central Europe has come through since 1989," Jacques Rupnik, a Czech political scientist in Paris, wrote recently in an obituary for neoliberal economics in the region.

Pal Tamas, a Hungarian sociologist, said that the problems went much deeper. "This is not a financial crisis, as in western Europe. Here it is a fundamental crisis, a paradigm shift. The 20-year transition since the end of communism has come to an end. The model that we saw being implemented in the 1990s and 2000s is finished."

In Latvia, whose economy is expected to shrink by more than a quarter before the upturn begins, scores of schools and hospitals are being closed as budgets are slashed. Public sector wages have been cut by up to 40%, pensions reduced, and under the 2010 budget agreed last week there will be further steep public spending cuts.

Since overthrowing communism two decades ago the new democracies of eastern and central Europe have eagerly embraced the western free market model lock, stock, and barrel.

Not only did they join the European Union and Nato, but they handed their banks to the big western players, closed down their communist-era industries, privatised what was left and sold them to western multinationals, opened their economies entirely to the forces of globalisation, and fuelled their race to prosperity through a huge western-supplied cheap credit boom that has come to an abrupt halt.

In Latvia, for example, the Swedish banks dominate the market. They helped to create one of the world's biggest property bubbles through profligate lending in euros. The bubble burst. Property prices collapsed. The new middle class finds itself in negative equity.

This is a new phenomenon for these capitalist neophytes. Only 15 years ago there was barely any household debt.

"We had unlimited belief in the capacity of the markets to regulate themselves. Most believed that property prices cannot fall, that it was a law of physics," said a Latvian economist working at one of the big Scandinavian banks in Riga.

In Budapest, Bebesy used to restore old buildings before losing his job to a leg injury. He fell for the slick advertising and the western offers of easy loans to feed, as with many Hungarians, a consumption binge. The 36-year-old took out two mortgages on two flats, one in Swiss francs, the other in euros. Then the Hungarian forint slumped against the euro, meaning his monthly repayments soared by 50%.

"It's a catastrophe. Everything is under a frog's arse," he complained, using a salty Hungarian expression meaning things could not get worse.

Veronika Mildenberger is also at her wit's end, fearing her retirement nest-egg will be devoured by the crisis. After 40 years' work in Budapest as a typist, the 76-year-old has 7m forints in the Italian-owned bank.

That is euros 25,000 (pounds 22,460). A year ago it was euros 30,000. Although the Austrian and Italian banks which dominate the Hungarian market have promised not to abandon the country, her confidence is slight. "I'm very afraid that the Italian bank will close down and move back to Italy. If that happens I'll lose everything. It's sad, but that's what we wake up to every morning."

In Riga and Budapest there is a sense that governments failed to exploit the boom years to secure future economic prospects, and anger with the western banks and a conviction that they should share the blame and the costs for the mess.

"The banks were too willing to lend," said Valdis Dombrovskis, the Latvian prime minister. "We've had some issues with the Swedish banks. The debt levels were mainly driven by them. And when the crisis came, it stopped abruptly. The banks stopped lending and made the recession worse."

In Budapest, Gyoergy Czirmes, a Hungarian lawyer, is campaigning to force the foreign banks to limit repayments by struggling customers. "I'm trying to raise awareness that the banks should not be allowed simply to raise the monthly instalments. If the currency is devalued [as in Hungary], the client and the bank should share the costs."

But the crisis is more systemic, not confined to the mess in the housing market. Eastern Europe has been kept afloat by cheap international credit for more than a decade, with western banks lending more than a trillion euros to households and companies across the region.

That era looks to be over, complicating the outlook for any quick recovery. Gordon Brown said earlier this year that global international capital flows collapsed by 80% last year. Private capital flows to eastern Europe are drying up, expected to drop to $30bn (pounds 18bn) this year from $254bn last year, according to the Institute of International Finance.

This spells a big shock to a system which, unlike in the west, is young, fragile, and has shallow roots.

The revolutions of 1989 threw up winners and losers. The losers were the elderly, the poor and ill-educated, the small towns and rural populations, the eastern parts of countries. The winners were the well-educated, metropolitan, flexible younger generation for whom a new life of opportunity beckoned—owning an apartment, buying a new (western) car, winter skiing in Austria, summer holidays in Croatia. For young Hungarians, Poles or Slovaks, life just kept getting better.

It is this new middle class, the bedrock of the new democracies, that is being hit hardest for the first time since communism collapsed.

According to Tamas, the director of Hungary's Institute of Sociology: "International liberalism in its Atlantic form, we've only had it for two decades, and it's dead. In financial terms, the middle-class dream is over here."

Bebesy, the 30-year-old fund manager, was one of the winners. "This is all we talk about in the cafes in the evening. Who's kept his job, who's losing his job. You can't borrow money any more. There are nominal wage cuts, short-time working, firms closing down, people getting fired. We couldn't imagine this happening. It's a big shock, the first crisis since the changeover [post-1989]."

There is no palpable nostalgia across central Europe for the bad old days on the wrong side of the iron curtain. But there is growing grievance.

The structure of the economies in "new Europe"—more open, more global and less experienced than those of "old Europe"—means they are at the mercy of Germany and western Europe.

When they opened up to the west, countries like Hungary or Slovakia willingly turned themselves into cheap assembly plants, inside the European single market, for western giants manufacturing cars, car parts, mobile phone handsets, computer components or plasma TV screens.

"What you have in central Europe is cheap labour production for the big west European companies with the output going back to western Europe to be consumed," said Zsoltan Pogatsa, who teaches the economics of European integration at the University of Western Hungary.

This was the tacit bargain struck in the 1990s, an arrangement that would gradually haul the east toward parity with the west, embedded in Europe's prosperous single currency zone.

At the very least, the crisis has delayed that process of convergence.

But given where they are coming from, the resilience of the east Europeans suggests they are well placed to cope with the hard times.

"Many political systems could have collapsed under this kind of stress," said the Latvian bank economist. "Life got too easy after we joined the EU. But I remember the Soviet lifestyle. Things are still a lot better now. We've probably been set back five years, but there's no need for a new paradigm."

Nils Muiznieks, a Latvian political scientist and former government minister, is also sanguine.

"The 20-30-year-olds are hard hit. They borrowed lots of money for cars and apartments and the market cannot sustain their expectations. Many of them will emigrate," he said. "But we had hyperinflation in the early 90s. People have weathered crises before and they will do again. There's a lot of stoicism."

Tomorrow: The history wars: Europe is divided over the past but the east is insisting its version is heard.

"Everyone Needs to Rethink Everything"
Reflections from the IMF's Former Chief Economist

SIMON JOHNSON

Multinational Monitor: *In a nutshell, what's the reason for the current financial crisis?*
Simon Johnson: The severity of the crisis, which I think is the interesting point in question, is because confidence in credit markets and financial institutions collapsed in the middle of September due to the actions the government took with regard to first Lehman and then AIG.

They decided to let Lehman fail, which was a pretty big judgment call, and then they decided to save AIG two days later, but they saved it in a way that took a lot of value away from the creditors. The creditors were very shocked by this. Creditors, and the credit market, interpreted this as meaning that while companies were too big to fail, no one was big enough to protect its creditors. That generated a wave of panic around the world that cascaded. And [Treasury Secretary Henry] Paulson's response was slow. By the time Mr. Paulson acted [in October, when he announced the Treasury Department would buy shares in banks, not just buy their troubled assets], it seemed it was too late.

MM: *Is it correct to say that your interpretation of events is that the financial crisis is driving the bigger-scale economic problems?*
Johnson: Yes. A little more than a month ago [in early September], I would have told you that we were heading toward a mild recession because of the problems that had emerged out of the housing sector and the difficulties the financial sector was having. I think that was the more or less correct view at the time, or at least a sensible baseline view to have.

What no one could anticipate was the actions that the government would take and the way that would cause global confidence to disintegrate. We've never seen anything like that in our lives. That has already triggered lots of adverse economic consequences, and there may be a lot more coming.

> **What no one could anticipate was the actions that the government would take and the way that would cause global confidence to disintegrate. We've never seen anything like that in our lives.**

MM: *In terms of the recent actions from the Europeans and the revised actions by the Treasury and the Fed and FDIC, do you believe they are now going down the right path?*
Johnson: Yes. We talked about this privately for quite a long time and went public with a document on September 29 on our website. We laid out what we thought was going on, and made a case for more radical policy actions, including a kind of bank recapitalization. If they had adopted our measures on September 29, I can't tell you that that would have definitely saved the day. What I can tell you is they waited two weeks and it doesn't seemed to have saved the day.

MM: *Now, a few weeks later, is it too late to deal with the confidence problem, to undo the loss of confidence?*
Johnson: Well, you certainly can't put the genie back in the bottle. Any last hope that that might be possible disintegrated after the G-7 [the group of seven leading industrial nations] and their close friends did the right thing with bank recapitalization and put a lot of public funds on the line. It seemed as if the markets looked at this and decided that there was a severe recession coming anyway. That triggers a lot of adjustment in asset prices that then has consequences for emerging markets and for developing countries, and then comes back and feeds further downward movement in the U.S. and in Europe.

Confidence will return, obviously. It's not the end of the world or the end of the world economy. Nothing ends with a financial crisis. But it is going to be a pretty long way down and a pretty painful climb back up.

MM: *Are the lenders being rational in being so reluctant to extend credit?*
Johnson: Yes, of course. Everyone is being pretty rational. With the information they have and all the uncertainties around them, they want to hold on to their cash—that's why they don't lend.

I think the measures put in place in the U.S. and probably in Europe will make you feel confident that the core banks will be solvent. With that will come more lending between banks. But that, at this point, is more of a symptom rather than anything deeper.

Underlying the issue is, will the banks lend to non-bank institutions or organizations? There, the story is very clear. They're already cutting back quite drastically on loans to all kinds of categories. We see it in auto loans, we see it in student loans and small business loans, and I imagine we'll see it in credit cards fairly soon. We'll probably see it in mortgage application approvals.

The banks are overleveraged. They have a small amount of capital on a very large balance sheet. And what they'd like to do right now is unwind on the loans side and make themselves smaller. Smaller is less vulnerable in this kind of situation. That will take some time and is going to be quite painful.

MM: *Is there something wrong with the way the financial system is set up that a difference of two weeks of when the government takes what is, by any recent standard, a very bold action has this massive impact? Is the world on too much of a hair-trigger system?*

Johnson: Yes, absolutely. We didn't know it was a hair-trigger. The government, to give it some credit, didn't know it was some big tripwire that they would set off, otherwise they wouldn't have done it. They didn't do it intentionally.

By our calculations, all the things the Fed and Treasury are doing amount to close to 70 percent of GDP [gross domestic product]. A few months ago, if I told you they'd do this for 5 percent of GDP, it would have been shocking. In fact, in September when they asked 5 percent of GDP [$700 billion] it was shocking. Now they're doing 70 percent. That's not going to be the total final increase in debt burden, but that's the amount of stuff the Fed is now guaranteeing one way or another, or promising to buy if necessary.

A few months ago, that would have been revolutionary, and I could have been expelled from the American Economic Association for suggesting it.

If this was a novel on the beach that you were reading, this summer, you'd have put it down in disgust and said, "This is a really bad novel. I'm going to go read something less sensational."

MM: *If the financial system has these kinds of hair triggers, is there something that should be done to make it less hypersensitive? What are those things?*

Johnson: First of all, it's a bit late. The horse has bolted; the horse has left the stable. We should go back and spend a lot of time studying stable doors and understanding why this one sprang open as it did. But to try and prevent it from happening again is not a top priority now, to be honest. A top priority is to try and push into the recession and try to get a recovery underway sooner rather than later. And that's a heck of a lot of work.

Down the road, we definitely have to look at what went wrong and how to avoid it. Presumably, the key thing is you can't let people take hard-to-understand risks, on any kind of scale relative to the national economy. It could also be that, perhaps, you shouldn't let your banks get too big relative to the national economy. You have in the U.K. a situation where bank assets and liabilities are about six times GDP. If those banks go into trouble, and the government is guaranteeing their liabilities, that's a lot of debt the government has to take on. That's

not an attractive way to run an economy. I don't care if it gives you 10 years of good growth, or 20 years of good growth, at the end of the day there's going to be a reckoning and you're going to be quite miserable for five years, in a good scenario.

> **Presumably, the key thing is you can't let people take hard-to-understand risks, on any kind of scale relative to the national economy. It could also be that, perhaps, you shouldn't let your banks get too big relative to the national economy.**

MM: *The governments have made a lot of commitments, but there are clearly going to be a lot more problems in the banking sector. How would you recommend managing it? Do you see a need to start closing down banks?*

Johnson: Potentially not. I think you need to go further down the road they started with the bank recapitalizations. They have the TARP money—the Troubled Asset Release Program—which is $700 billion. And they say they're going to put $250 billion into bank recapitalization and use the rest to buy troubled assets. We published a piece in the Washington Post saying that that split doesn't make sense. The auctions to buy troubled assets are completely irrelevant right now, and at worse, a signal that the government doesn't understand what's really going on. What you should do is put the remaining $450 billion in a war chest in the president's office with a big label on the top that says, "open in case of severe recession," because then you will need more capital for the banks. That, first and foremost, should be done.

> **What you should do is put the remaining $450 billion in a war chest in the president's office with a big label on the top that says, "open in case of severe recession," because then you will need more capital for the banks.**

In addition, the Fed is doing a lot of things to support the financial system, including buying commercial paper, providing various kinds of guarantees for money market funds and the like. They have a lot of pieces in place, but they need to stay focused on providing capital.

MM: *What are the similarities and differences in the problems facing the European financial institutions? Is it the same set of problems?*

Johnson: Yes, but worse, because their banks are more highly leveraged. Their asset-to-capital ratio is more like 30- or 50-to-one, compared to the United States, which is somewhere between 10- and 20-to-one. They have more potential deleveraging. And their banks are also bigger relative to the size of their economy.

MM: *If the financial panic was the thing that's taken the recession from mild to severe, and the panic is being quieted, why can't a severe recession be avoided?*

Johnson: This is the idea that you can't put the genie back in the bottle. If you could suddenly, miraculously, make everyone confident enough to lend, then yes, you could avoid recession. But that's not going to happen. Once these organizations turn and the markets turn, then it takes years to get back.

I was recently on a panel at the Council for Foreign Relations, and some prominent people told me that I'm far too optimistic about the prospects for recovery in the United States. These people are not just interesting, smart people. They actually move a lot of money around the world. I am just an academic and a former official. These guys are actually the decision makers. They say, "The psychology is ruined. It won't come back for a long time." And if they believe that, of course, it's self-fulfilling.

I'm not saying that they are causing the problem. They are reading the market situation correctly.

MM: *How do you expect that the financial crisis and the recession will affect developing countries?*

Johnson: It's going to be very bad. They're going to be hit in a two-fold way. First, commodity prices are going to go down a lot. That's part of the adjustment we're already seeing both in commodity prices and the prices of mineral-producing companies. Second, they will not get as much aid as they have become accustomed to, because everyone will cut their aid budgets.

> **Developing countries are going to be hit in a two-fold way. First, commodity prices are going to go down a lot. Second, they will not get as much aid as they have become accustomed to, because everyone will cut their aid budgets.**

Developing countries are in for a very tough half decade, at least.

MM: *You've also written that developing countries will have problems as capital flows dry up.*

Johnson: Most of them don't have that many reserves. China has a lot of reserves, as do a few others, but most developing countries do not. And of the ones which do have reserves, many let their private sectors borrow quite heavily. In the case of Russia, the government has a lot of reserves and very little debt. The private sector has a lot of debt in foreign currency. So when things start to fall apart and the currency comes under pressure, the government either has to let the private sector fail, or it has to step in and take over that debt. Then the question is, who do they choose to let survive? They are picking winners as we speak.

MM: *Are those countries helpless victims in this or are there things that they might have done to position themselves differently?*

Johnson: They probably could have been more conservative. But what we're looking at here is a once in a hundred years storm, and nobody runs their economy—aside from one or two countries—anticipating the once in a hundred years storm.

We built a system that was much more dangerous than anyone thought, than anyone realized.

A few people, no doubt, did criticize the system, and it turns out they were right. And even those people didn't fully understand what was going to happen.

MM: *The standard storyline now is that deregulation really helped drive this problem. Is that one you agree with?*

Johnson: Yes, certainly deregulation played a role. There's something for everyone in this crisis. It's hard to find any entity or person who was involved in major macro regulatory decision making that can't have some piece of the blame.

There's a nice piece that recently appeared in the *Washington Post* that traced some of the deregulation back to the Democrats under Clinton. But there are lots of other people, including Republicans in Congress and in the Bush administration, who fully supported deregulation.

Deregulation has worked well in some industries. But deregulation turns out to have had rather unfortunate unintended consequences in the financial sector.

MM: *Looking back on your old job as chief economist at the IMF, do you think that the IMF needs to rethink support for financial liberalization?*

Johnson: I think everyone needs to rethink everything, to be honest. Not just financial liberalization, but financial development.

One of the mantras of the last 15 or 20 years has been that more financial development is good. Allowing your banks to grow and doing away with what's called financial repression—where you keep interest rates artificially low—was considered to be a good thing. Now I think we have to question that.

> **One of the mantras of the last 15 or 20 years has been that more financial development is good. Allowing your banks to grow was considered to be a good thing. Now I think we have to question that.**

I don't think you want to go back to the repressed financial systems of the 1950s and 1960s, but maybe you have to think about the kinds of constraints you put on financial activities and you have to keep finance more plain vanilla. One constraint might be that no bank should do anything that it can't explain in an 800 word op-ed, or that its CEO does not understand.

MM: *What do you think governments in the United States and elsewhere ought to be doing to lessen the severity of the recession?*

Johnson: There's a lot. There's a bit more that you could do with monetary policy in the U.S., though it won't have that much effect at this stage. You could do a pretty big fiscal expansion.

Getting money into the hands of state and local governments strikes me as being pretty important because they're starting to cut back already. Putting money into education would also strike me as being a very smart short-term move, because we know that classroom sizes are going up as people move out of fee-paying schools to public schools. Some sort of income transfer scheme could be worth consideration. People will tend to save the extra money you give them, not spend it in this context, so you have to take that into consideration. In the U.S. context, I would want to link that very closely with spending public money on mortgage restructuring programs. You've got to find ways to break this death spiral of declining house prices, foreclosures, forced sales and further house price declines.

In Europe, I think there's big room for monetary policy easing. It's remarkable they haven't cut interest rates so far this week [October 13]—it tells you that they don't really get the situation. There is also some room for fiscal expansion. The problem is their government balance sheets aren't that good to start with, and they've taken on these massive banks, so that is really going to constrain them. Obviously, if you go way overboard with fiscal, you're going to undermine confidence. It's a very fickle beast, confidence.

So, priorities are: U.S., fiscal; Europe, monetary and fiscal; mortgage restructuring in the U.S. and in some European countries, particularly in the U.K., Ireland and Spain. A number of Asian countries could do fiscal expansions also. They're scope is limited; they're not that big; and the amount of fiscal expansion China could actually put on the table in the next 12 months, just as a practical matter, is pretty small.

MM: *Why is Europe so reluctant to loosen up on the monetary side?*
Johnson: They're still obsessed with inflation. They are reliving the 1970s in their own minds. That was a formative experience for many of them and for their institutions. In the 1970s, you had recession and you had inflation for a particular circumstance related to the oil price shocks and wage-price dynamics. They think that's going to happen again, so they think they must guard against inflation while trying to be somewhat more helpful now on the real economy.

I think it's a mistake. I think we're heading into a deflationary spiral. I think inflation is the last thing to worry about at this stage.

MM: *Do the middle-income countries and the poor countries have any policy flexibility at this point?*
Johnson: They have a bit. They have to decide when to use their reserves, that's an important decision. Do you hold the exchange rate at where it is, or do you let it go to some degree? Letting it go often means people are going to fail, and then you have to decide who to save and how to organize workouts and so on.

The classic mistake would be to try and hold exchange rates at what is now an overvalued level, or a level you can't defend. Then people attack the exchange rate, you lose your reserves, you have a big depreciation anyway, and you no longer have the reserves—making it much harder to bring stability back into the picture.

So there are lots of tough choices ahead for them, and those choices do actually make a difference.

SIMON JOHNSON is former chief economist of the International Monetary Fund. He is a professor at the Massachusetts Institute of Technology Sloan School of Management and a senior fellow at the Peterson Institute for International Economics. He is a co-founder of The Baseline Scenario, a website dedicated to providing a "baseline" view of the current economic crisis. <http://baselinescenario.com>

The Balance of Payments
Office for National Statistics

GRAEME CHAMBERLIN

The Balance of Payments records one nation's transactions with the rest of the world. This not only includes the conventional flows of goods and services that make up international trade, but also cross-border payments associated with the international ownership of financial assets and current transfers, including remittances by workers from one country to another. In fact, remittances have become increasingly important in recent decades as capital and labour becomes increasingly mobile and financial markets in different countries more strongly integrated. Therefore the means of production are becoming just as likely to move across borders as the actual goods and services produced.

The purpose of this article is to outline the main structure of the UK Balance of Payments so the reader can understand how international trade in goods, services and financial assets and cross-border income flows are recorded in the National Accounts[1]. In doing this the changing patterns over time are presented, along with a more recent analysis of how the current global economic downturn is being reflected in key parts of the Balance of Payments.

The Balance of Payments can effectively be broken down into two parts. The Current Account records international trade in goods and services, international income flows and current transfers. The Capital Account and Financial Account form the counter part to this, recording the changing pattern in the international ownership of assets. While the Financial Account records changes in the cross-border flows of assets, the International Investment Position measures the total stocks of foreign assets and liabilities held by a nation. Some features of this, in particular its relation to investment income, are also analysed in this article.

Current Account

The Current Account consists of four parts:

- Trade in goods
- Trade in services
- Net income flows
- Current transfers

Table 1 presents the UK Current Account for 2007. Although data for 2008 are available these have been significantly affected by the turmoil in the global financial markets and the world recession so are not the best to use for demonstration purposes.

The trade in goods balance is the difference between the value of goods exported and the value of goods imported. Hence, in 2007 a £220.9 billion credit to the Current Account resulted from goods exports and a £310.6 billion debit from imports giving an overall deficit of £89.8 billion. The trade in services is recorded in the same way, with credits to the Current Account reflecting services exports and debits services imports. In 2007, the UK ran an overall surplus of £44.8 billion on the balance of trade in services.

An often cited measure is the trade balance which is the overall balance in the trade in goods and services. In 2007 this would have been negative to the tune of £45.0 billion, as the deficit in goods trades outweighs the surplus in services trade. The trade balance though is not to be confused with the overall Current Account which consists of two further, but less well-known, items.

Table 1 UK Current Account in 2007

	£ billions		
	Credit	**Debit**	**Balance**
Goods trade	220.9	310.6	−89.8
Services trade	150.6	105.8	44.8
Net income flows	291.3	270.5	20.8
Current transfers	14.0	27.6	−13.5
Current Account (total)	676.8	714.6	−37.7

Source: ONS Balance of Payments.

Net income flows reflect international payments associated with the ownership of the factors of production (land, labour and capital).

Two types of income transactions are distinguished; compensation of employees which is paid to non-resident workers involved in the production process and investment income which is the return for providing financial assets and rent for natural resources.

In 2007, net compensation of employees debits (outflows) exceeded credits (inflows) by £734 million. However, this clearly accounts for only a small proportion of the total given UK net income was £20.8 billion in surplus in 2007.

The remainder of net income relates to investment income—these are the payments associated with the international ownership of financial assets such as interest payments and dividends. For example, if a UK citizen owned shares in a foreign company, then any dividends earned from this would be counted as a credit. Alternatively, if a UK company borrowed money from a foreign bank then any interest payments accrued would be recorded as a debit.

As financial markets around the world become increasingly integrated it is likely that residents (households, firms, financial institutions such as banks and pension funds, nonprofit institutions and the public sector) in one country will seek to diversify their portfolios of financial assets to take advantage of higher returns overseas and reduce exposures to individual country risks. Therefore the ownership of foreign assets and foreigner's ownership of UK assets have grown rapidly and investment income flows are becoming a major determinant of the Current Account.

Current transfers are the final component of the Current Account. This records a miscellaneous set of net payments including workers remittances, social security, foreign aid and contributions to international organisations such as the European Union (EU). As Table 1 shows, these flows are small compared to other parts of the Current Account and in 2007 were in overall deficit of £13.5 billion.

Current Account—Some History

In sum the UK Current Account deficit was £37.7 billion or 2.7 per cent of Gross Domestic Product (GDP) in 2007. The longer-term history of the UK Current Account and its main components are presented in Table 2, and here it can be clearly seen that the overall UK Current Account has been predominately in deficit over the last 40 years.

The main factor behind the UK's persistent Current Account deficit has been the deficit on the balance of trade in goods. In fact, since 1946 this has been in deficit every year bar five. An average surplus was recorded between 1980–84 when UK goods trade was aided by

Table 2 The UK Current Account and Its Main Components

Year	Percentage of GDP (five year averages except later years)				
	Goods Trade	Services Trade	Net Income	Current Transfers	Current Account
1955–59	−0.4	0.4	0.8	0.0	0.9
1960–64	−0.9	0.1	0.9	−0.1	0.0
1965–69	−0.9	0.4	0.8	−0.2	0.0
1970–74	−2.1	1.2	0.9	−0.3	−0.3
1975–79	−2.0	2.2	−0.1	−0.6	−0.5
1980–84	0.1	1.8	−0.6	−0.5	0.7
1985–89	−3.1	1.8	−0.4	−0.7	−2.4
1990–94	−2.1	1.1	−0.4	−0.7	−2.1
1995–99	−2.1	1.7	0.2	−0.8	−1.0
2000–04	−4.2	1.9	1.2	−0.8	−2.0
2005	−5.5	2.1	1.7	−0.9	−2.6
2006	−5.8	2.6	0.7	−0.9	−3.3
2007	−6.4	3.2	1.5	−1.0	−2.7
2008	−6.4	3.8	1.9	−0.9	−1.7

Source: ONS Balance of Payments.

North Sea oil production and high oil prices, but since then the deficit has consistently grown as a proportion of GDP to 6.4 per cent in both 2007 and 2008.

As manufacturing goods make up the largest proportion of goods trade then the relative decline in UK manufacturing output might suggest why this deficit has grown over the last two decades. The emergence of low cost producers in emerging markets have meant that the bulk of UK manufacturing including automobiles, clothing and footwear, consumer electronics and materials processing have seen its global market share fall. However, the UK has managed to increase its export share in smaller higher technology manufactures such as medical and pharmaceuticals, communications equipment, office machinery and computers.

On the other hand exports of services have exceeded imports every year since 1951 except two, and surpluses as a proportion of GDP have grown continuously since EU membership in 1973. This is consistent with the changing composition of UK output, with the largest surpluses in financial and business services—and is evidence that structural change in the UK economy has followed its comparative advantage in international trade[2].

Net income has been more erratic over the years reflecting the inherent volatility in financial markets. It was last negative as recently as 1999 due to the impact of the Asian financial crisis, but during the last decade has generally made a positive contribution to the Current Account.

In comparison current transfers have made a negative contribution to the Current Account but the deficit has been fairly stable as a proportion of GDP over the last 30 years. The typical deficit reflects net contributions to the EU and the cost of foreign aid.

Capital and Financial Accounts

So what does it mean if the UK ran a Current Account deficit of £37.7 billion in 2007? Basically it states that foreigners are adding to their stock of UK assets by a sum of £37.7 billion more than UK residents are adding to their stock of foreign assets—or that the UK is essentially increasing its net liabilities to the rest of the world by this amount.

The Capital and Financial Accounts records the counterparts to the Current Account, which are the offsetting changes in the ownership of financial assets as implied by the Current Account surplus or deficit. In fact, Table 3 shows that in 2007 both UK residents have added to their stock of foreign assets and foreign residents have added to their stock of UK assets by over £1,000 billion (£1 trillion)—but the key is that foreigners have added to their stock of assets by somewhat (£37.7 billion) more.

In Table 3, the credit column refers to money spent by foreign residents on UK assets and the debit column to money spent by UK residents on foreign assets.

The Capital Account consists of several miscellaneous items such as land purchases and sales associated with

Table 3   UK Capital and Financial Accounts in 2007

| | £ billions | | |
	Credit	Debit	Balance
Capital Account	4.6	2.0	2.6
Financial Account			
Direct investment	98.2	136.1	−38.0
Portfolio investment	203.3	92.0	111.3
Other investment	725.9	767.5	−41.6
Total	1027.4	995.7	31.7
Balancing item			3.4
Grand total			37.7

Source: ONS Balance of Payments.

embassies, the transfers of migrants, EU regional development fund payments and so on. It is small relative to the Financial Account, and in 2007 credits exceeded debits by £2.6 billion.

The Financial Account has been broken down according to the main types of assets.

Direct investments refer to the purchase by the residents of one country of a significant part of an enterprise in another country. This not only consists of factories or production units but larger shareholdings (in excess of 10 per cent of total equity) which is considered to give the owner influence over the management of the enterprise and the set level of dividends.

The purchase of British Airports Association (BAA) by the Spanish company Ferrovial and British Energy Group by Electricite de France (EDF) are examples of direct investment credits in the Financial Account. Likewise, the purchase of the German telecoms firm Mannesmann by Vodafone and Atlantic Richfield by BP Amoco would be examples of significant direct investment debits. Major (in excess of £5 billion) direct investment acquisitions of foreign companies by UK companies and vice-versa during the last ten years are recorded in Table 4.

Portfolio investments relate to the smaller purchases of equity (less than 10 per cent of the total) and also debt securities.

Other investments in the main refer to financial intermediation services. For example, a deposit made by a UK local authority in an Icelandic bank would have been scored as a debit. Alternatively a loan from a foreign bank to a UK household would be classified as a credit.

The sums recorded in both the debit and credit columns in the other investment category are huge, representing around 70 per cent of UK Gross Domestic Product. This is because the UK financial system is highly integrated with the rest of the world's financial markets and plays a large intermediary role between them.

For example, a UK bank may receive £1 billion in deposits from a German pension fund that it then lends to US firms. In this case both the credit and debit columns of the other investment category will increase by £1 billion. Alternatively, the UK bank may decide to lend the £1 billion to a UK firm that purchases a majority shareholding in a foreign company. In this case the debit column in the other investment category and the credit column in the direct investment category will both increase by £1 billion. Because these types of intermediary transactions are so commonplace it is easy to understand how the size of credits and debits in the Financial Account may be a large proportion of GDP but the difference between them is relatively small. This is demonstrated in Figure 1, where both foreign assets and liabilities (holdings of

Table 4 Major Direct Investment Acquisitions by/of UK Companies in the Last Decade by Value

Outwards Acquisitions of Foreign Companies

£113.0 billion: Mannesmann AG by Vodafone (2000 Q1)

£37.5 billion: Airtouch by Vodafone (1999 Q2)

£32.6 billion: Amoco Corp by British Petroleum (BP) (1998 Q4)

£21.0 billion: Zeneca PLC by Astra AB (1999 Q2)

£18.5 billion: Alcan Inc by Rio Tinto (2007 Q4)

£18.0 billion: Atlantic Richfield by BP Amoco (2000 Q2)

£9.3 billion: Altadis SA by Imperial Tobacco Group (2008 Q1)

£9.1 billion: Household International by HSBC (2003 Q1)

£7.7 billion: MedImmune Inc by AstraZeneca (2007 Q3)

£6.6 billion: Credit Commerciale de France by HSBC (2000 Q3)

£5.8 billion: Charter 1 by Royal Bank of Scotland (RBS) (2004 Q3)

£5.5 billion: Hutchison Essar by Vodafone Group (2007 Q2)

£5.0 billion: Innovene Inc by Ineos Group (2005 Q4)

Inward acquisitions of UK companies

£23.5 billion: Orange PLC by France Telecom (2000 Q3)

£19.5 billion: Orange PLC by Mannesmann AG (1999 Q4)

£17.7 billion: O2 by Telefonica (2006 Q1)

£12.5 billion: British Energy by Electricite de France (EDF) (2009 Q1)

£11.0 billion: Alliance Boots PLC by AB Acquisitions Ltd

£10.1 billion: British Airports Association (BAA) by Ferrovial (2006 Q2)

£9.0 billion: Abbey National by Banco Santander (2004 Q4)

£8.5 billion: Reuters Group by Thomson Corporation (2008 Q2)

£8.3 billion: Hanson PLC by Heidellberg Cement AG (2007 Q3)

£8.2 billion: BOC Group PLC by Linde AC (2006 Q3)

£8.1 billion: Imperial Chemical Industries by AKZO Nobel (2008 Q1)

£7.5 billion: Scottish & Newcastle by Sunrise Acquisitions Ltd (2008 Q2)

£6.7 billion: ASDA by Wal-Mart (1999 Q3)

£5.3 billion: Amersham PLC by General Electric Group (2004 Q2)

£5.2 billion: Powergen by E. on (2002 Q3)

Source: ONS Balance of Payments.

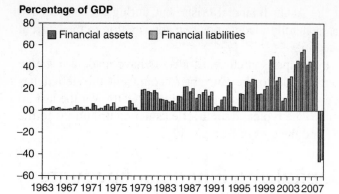

Figure 1 Net acquisitions of financial assets and liabilities

Source: ONS Balance of Payments.

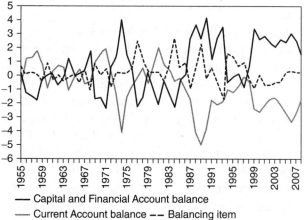

Figure 2 Balancing the Balance of Payments

Source: ONS Balance of Payments.

Figure 2 shows the long-term history of the UK Current Account balance, the Capital and Financial Accounts balances, and the balancing item as a percentage of GDP. Clearly there is an offsetting relationship between the two main parts of the Balance of Payments, so the data behaves as expected. The balancing item exhibits some volatility but in recent years has been relatively minor.

International Investment Position

While the Financial Account records international flows in the acquisition and disposals of financial assets, the stock positions are presented in the International Investment Position (IIP). This is the difference in the value of foreign assets held by UK residents (UK's foreign assets) and UK assets held by foreign residents (UK's foreign liabilities). Therefore it is also referred to as the net-asset position.

Like Financial Account flows in Figure 1, the UK's stocks of foreign assets and liabilities have grown rapidly

UK assets by foreigners) have grown significantly as a proportion of GDP yet in each year differ by a relatively small amount.

The final element, which does not officially form part of the Capital or Financial Accounts is the balancing item. Although in theory the Capital and Financial Accounts should offset the Current Account, in practise it rarely does due to errors and omissions. The purpose of the balancing item is therefore reconcile the two sides of the Balance of Payments.

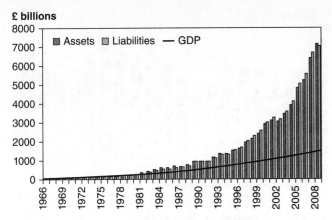

Figure 3   International Investment Position

Source: ONS Balance of Payments.

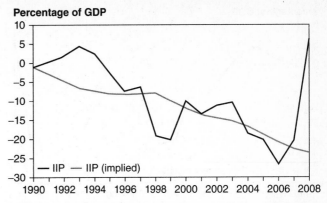

Figure 4   International Investment Position and the Current Account

Source: ONS Balance of Payments.

and now far outstrip GDP. As Figure 3 shows, stocks of foreign assets and liabilities are near £7,000 billion (£7 trillion) or about 4 and half times GDP. This ratio is much higher than in most developed countries (for the US stocks of foreign assets and liabilities were around 100 per cent of GDP in 2005) and is a strong indication of the relative openness of the UK economy, and in particular its financial sector, to the rest of the world.

And like the balance on the Financial Account, in any one year the IIP or net asset position is relatively small given the size of the asset stocks, further indication of the intermediary role played by UK financial institutions in the global economy.

As the IIP and Financial Account are linked by a stock-flow relationship, in theory, there should also be a relationship between the IIP and the Current Account. The UK's persistent Current Account deficit over the last thirty years implies that the nation has been living beyond its means for a considerable period of time requiring offsetting surpluses on the Financial Account. Therefore, as this feeds through into asset stocks it would be expected that a long run decline in the IIP would result.

Figure 4 plots the actual UK IIP since 1990, and the IIP implied by the accumulation of Current Account deficits. Up until 2007 the IIP has generally behaved as expected, deteriorating in line with Current Account deficits. However, in 2008, the IIP jumped sharply into positive territory for the first time since 1994.

This can be explained by looking at what determines the actual dynamics of the IIP between time period (t) and (t-1):

$$IIP(t) = IIP(t-1) + Current\ Account(t) + asset\ revaluations(t)$$

where asset revaluations = price changes + exchange rate changes + other adjustments

That is changes in the net asset position do not just reflect Financial (Current) Account flows but also revaluations of those assets. Furthermore, revaluations of assets do not just reflect the volatility in equity and bond markets but also in exchange rates. Almost the entire jump in the UK IIP during 2008 can be accounted for by the depreciation of sterling.

As foreign assets are expressed in foreign currency, depreciation of sterling against that foreign currency means that the valuation of that asset in sterling terms increases. If UK liabilities (UK assets held by foreigners) are valued in sterling then there is no change following depreciation. But were they also valued in foreign currency then the sterling value of liabilities would also rise following depreciation. However this is generally not the case. The majority of UK foreign assets will be valued in foreign currency and the majority of UK assets held by foreigners will be valued in sterling so sterling depreciation improves the IIP and sterling appreciation deteriorates the IIP.

Given that the trade-weighted effective sterling exchange rate fell by about 25 per cent during 2008 and the stock of foreign assets held by UK residents amounts to 4 and a half times GDP then it is quite plausible to explain how such a large jump in the IIP was possible. The jump in the value of foreign assets can be seen in Figure 3 as well as in the IIP in Figure 4.

International Investment Position and Net Investment Income

Until last year (2008) the declining UK IIP was a curiosity in that net international investment income continued to be positive (see Figure 5)—suggesting that an increasingly negative net asset position was managing to create robust positive net investment income[3]. An explanation for the divergence in IIP and net investment income requires the

Percentage of GDP

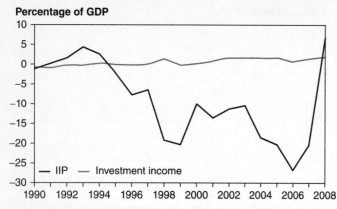

Figure 5   International Investment Position and net investment income

Source: ONS Balance of Payments.

Percentage of GDP

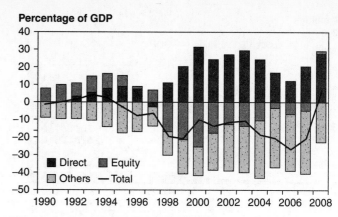

Figure 7   IIP breakdown by asset type

Source: ONS Balance of Payments.

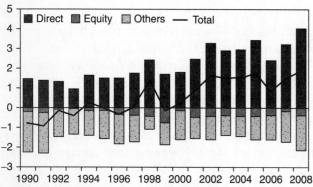
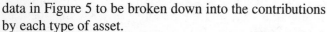

Figure 6   Breakdown of investment income by asset type

Source: ONS Balance of Payments.

Percent

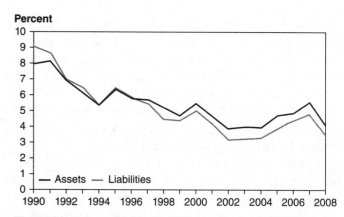

Figure 8   Rates of return on UK assets and liabilities

Source: ONS Balance of Payments.

data in Figure 5 to be broken down into the contributions by each type of asset.

Starting with net investment income, Figure 6 presents a breakdown by three main asset classes: direct investments, equity investments and other investments which are predominately interest bearing financial assets including debt securities. Surpluses on the investment income balance have clearly been driven from direct investment, while the other two asset classes make negative contributions.

Figure 7 presents the composition of the UK IIP according to the same asset categories. Although the aggregate IIP is generally in deficit, primarily due to the contribution of other investments, the UK has managed to sustain a robust surplus in direct investment assets.

For a negative IIP to generate a surplus in net investment income it must be the case that the UK's stock of foreign assets are generating higher returns than the stock of UK assets held by foreigners. This is confirmed in Figure 8. Rates of return[4] on the UK's foreign assets and liabilities have generally fallen since the early 1990s in line with

global interest rates, but since the mid 1990s the UK has enjoyed a distinct rate of return advantage. It is this that accounts for the positive investment income despite the overall negative position on the IIP.

Figure 9, by presenting rates of return for each asset class, ties together the trends in Figures 6, 7 and 8. There are a number of observations that can be made:

• Rates of return in direct investment can be volatile, reflecting the global economic cycle, but on the whole exceed those of other asset classes. This differential has grown in the last decade as the fall in global interest rates pushes down on income from other investments including debt securities which are predominately interest bearing.

• Direct investments, which include equity holdings of over 10 per cent of an enterprise, offer far higher rates of return than smaller equity investments (minority shareholdings). This implies that exercising some degree of control over

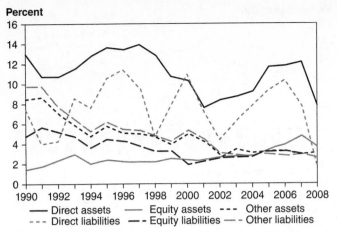

Figure 9   Rates of return by types of asset and liability
Source: ONS Balance of Payments.

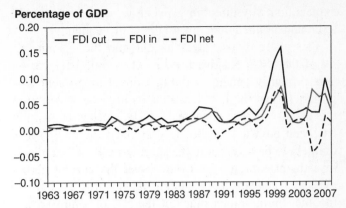

Figure 10   UK Foreign Direct Investment
Source: ONS Balance of Payments.

the enterprise including the power to influence dividend payments yields a superior return.

• Returns on UK held foreign direct investments have generally exceeded those of foreign direct investments into the UK, while there is little rate of return difference in equity and other assets.

Therefore the UK's rate of return advantage is down to two factors.

First, it has a strong net-asset position in higher yielding direct investments. In this respect, Nickell (2006) describes the UK IIP as similar to a successful venture capitalist by borrowing cheap interest bearing funds through its negative IIP in other investment assets and maintaining a surplus in its IIP of more lucrative direct investment assets.

Second, even within the direct investment category the UK has a rate of return advantage. In addition to the successful venture capitalist argument that the UK is just relatively good at picking profitable FDI opportunities three other explanations for this advantage have been suggested.

The US also enjoys a rate of return advantage in FDI, which Hausmann and Sturzenegger (2006) put down to exports of 'dark matter[5]'. These are the unseen intangibles (or knowledge capital) such as managerial expertise, organisational structure, brand names, IT systems, design and technical (R&D) capabilities that usually accompany direct investments and make it more successful. The same reasoning may also apply to the UK–that its direct investments abroad are supported by significant transfers of quality intangibles. This reasoning may also account for the rate of return advantage of direct investments over smaller equity investments.

Another explanation is that, for one reason or another, foreigners may be prepared to accept a relatively lower

rate of return on their direct investments in the UK. It might be considered as a price for accessing the large EU market allowing firms to benefit from economies of scale in production. The UK is also considered to be a less risky environment in which to do business than other economies, mainly due to the superior development of its legal and financial institutions. As a result, the risk premium and yields on inward FDI to the UK would be correspondingly lower.

It might also be the case that firms deliberately report lower profits on their UK operations to reduce tax liabilities of the UK. As the production process becomes more vertically integrated across borders it gives firms scope to move profits through transfer pricing (also known as toll processing). For example, if the UK was considered a relatively high tax country then companies would face an incentive to reduce their reported earnings in the UK. This could be achieved by raising the internal prices of the output produced downstream, or reducing the prices charged upstream, as either would squeeze the margins on UK operations relative to the parts of the production process undertaken in other countries.

Finally, the rate of return on UK direct investments abroad may be exaggerated by underestimating the value of these direct investments and hence the overall IIP. Most financial assets such as equity and debt securities are frequently traded so that they can be valued using established market prices. Direct investments though are large, unique and illiquid assets for which market prices do not exist and the actual value can differ significantly from book or historic values—making life difficult for statisticians. As a result an undervaluation of the value of direct investment abroad would lead to an overstatement of the rate of return. But it should also be acknowledged that the same argument could be applied to inward foreign direct investment, so this reasoning would require an explanation why direct investment abroad is more likely to be undervalued than inward direct investment.

This analysis also gives insight into the sustainability of the UK's positive investment income balance. As it is primarily generated through direct investment it is important that the UK maintains its net asset position in this asset type. And given that the UK's net asset position has been built up over many years (see Figure 10) it is unlikely to be reversed in the short term. However, direct investment earnings are cyclical and the current global recession appears to be putting downward pressure on income. Furthermore, much of the rate of return advantage enjoyed by the UK has resulted from falling global interest rates making it easier to fund its large negative IIP in other (predominately interest bearing) assets. So should global interest rates start to push upwards it would put downward pressure on UK net investment income.

Recent Trends in the UK Balance of Payments

In this final section more recent trends in the UK Balance of Payments are analysed. These are of special interest given the global nature of the current recession and financial crisis.

Figure 11 shows, as a percentage of GDP and on a quarterly basis, the main component parts of the UK Current Account. Most striking is that since the beginning of 2008 the UK Current Account deficit has grown, despite the balance of trade (goods and services) improving. Transfers have been very stable, so the deterioration over the last year has been primarily driven by falling net investment income.

In Figure 12 the exports and imports of goods are presented. As most of the balance on goods trade is determined by manufactures (semi and finished goods) then both exports and imports have fallen quickly as a result

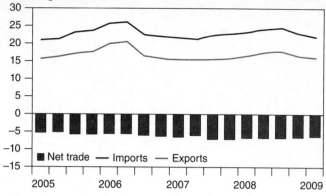

Percentage of GDP

Figure 12   Trade in goods
Source: ONS Balance of Payments.

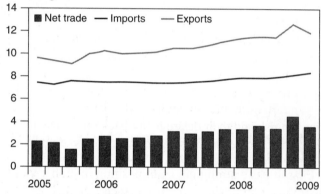

Percentage of GDP

Figure 13   Trade in services
Source: ONS Balance of Payments.

of the global economic downturn being concentrated in the manufacturing sector. However, because UK imports have fallen faster than exports the overall goods deficit has narrowed in recent quarters.

Services trade though has been relatively robust through the recession. In fact, as Figure 13 shows, there has been no notable downturn as a proportion of GDP and the overall UK balance has improved. One area that appears to have been doing well is the financial sector, ironically as a result of the global financial crisis.

Financial sector output consists of two main parts. First there are activities for which fee and commission income is earned, and as expected, this has fallen in line with business activity in the global recession. These are direct outputs, known as Financial Intermediation Services Directly Measured (FISDM). However, much of the output of the financial services sector is not charged for directly, such as current account services. Here incomes are usually made by a spread between deposit (savings) and credit (lending) rates—this output is known as Financial Intermediation Services Indirectly Measured

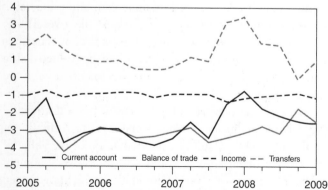

Percentage of GDP

Figure 11   Current Account
Source: ONS Balance of payments.

Percentage of GDP

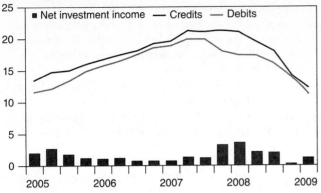

Figure 14   Net investment income

Source: ONS Balance of Payments.

Percentage of GDP

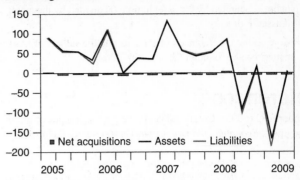

Figure 15   Financial Account transactions

Source: ONS Balance of Payments.

(FISIM). One of the consequences of the financial crisis is that these spreads have widened. Central banks around the world have been aggressive in cutting interest rates which have been passed on quickly into deposit rates. But lending rates have come down less quickly, and for many consumer loans they have actually not come down at all or gone up—a reflection of the banking sectors updated view on risk and their desire to cut back on some lending. Given that the deposit base hasn't changed that much this has led to a large jump in calculated FISIM output in the last year. And because the UK financial services sector is large and operates on a global scale it is likely that FISIM exports will have increased as well.

Net investment income though, despite continuing to make a positive contribution to the Current Account, has fallen sharply in recent quarters. Although it must also be acknowledged that net income had been particularly strong in 2007, so much of the reversal may just be trend correcting. Strong investment income was the main factor closing the Current Account in early 2008, and has been the main factor in the widening deficit thereafter.

Given the UK's strong net asset position in direct investment, most of the deterioration can be traced to this asset class. Earnings on direct investment abroad, and on foreign earnings on direct investments in the UK have fallen, mostly likely as a consequence of the global recession and credit crunch on company profits. Particularly affected are the earnings of financial corporations. As direct investment in the UK from overseas are highly concentrated in the banking sector it explains why income flows out of the UK have fallen faster than flows to the UK in recent years.

As explained already, Capital and Financial Account transactions are the mirror of Current Account transactions. Hence the deterioration in the Current Account would be associated with a growing surplus on the Capital

and Financial Accounts as the UK reduces its net-asset position vis-á-vis the rest of the world.

However, it is still worth looking at because while the balance may actually be quite small, there have been very large recent movements in the flows of financial assets. This is shown quite clearly in Figure 1, where the UK's cross-border accumulation of financial assets and liabilities was massively negative in 2008.

The quarterly figures underline the recent volatility in financial markets (see Figure 15). The striking feature which is also picked up in Figure 1 are the periods of large disinvestment–where UK residents cut back on their stocks of foreign assets and foreign residents on their stocks of UK assets. This could be to reduce more 'risky' holdings of foreign assets or simply to repatriate assets to cover domestic losses and shore up balance sheets. For example, securities have been one of the financial asset classes most affected by the fallout from the US sub-prime mortgage market and the credit crunch and much of the volatility in the UK Financial Account has resulted from disinvestments in these assets. In the past, net disinvestment in equities has frequently coincided with financial shocks—for example the UK's exit from the Exchange Rate Mechanism in 1992, the Asian financial crisis in 1997 and the collapse in equity markets in 2002. The most recent crisis though is more unique in that disinvestment has happened across a broad range of asset classes, not just the more volatile ones.

Notes

1. Much of this article follows and updates the analysis in Nickell (2006).

2. Chamberlin (2008) provides further evidence on the shifting composition of UK output and trade including its implications for the terms of trade.

3. Similar analysis and background on the UK International Investment Position can be found in Nickell (2006) and Whitaker (2006).

4. The rate of return on an asset in time (t) is calculated as the income generated by the asset in time (t) divided by the stock of asset in time (t-1).

5. More on the US Balance of Payments and the subject of 'dark matter' can be found in Chamberlin (2009).

References

Chamberlin G (2008) 'Command GDP: the purchasing power of UK output', *Economic and Labour Market Review* (September).

Chamberlin G (2009) 'Dark matter. Does it matter?' in Linda Yueh (ed) 'The law and economics of globalisation', Edward Elgar.

Hausmann R and Sturzenegger F (2006) 'Global imbalances or bad accounting? The missing dark matter in the wealth of nations', Centre for International Development, Harvard University, *Working Paper* no. 124, January.

Nickell S (2006) 'The current account and all that', *Bank of England Quarterly Bulletin* Summer.

Whitaker S (2006) 'The UK international investment position', *Bank of England Quarterly Bulletin* 2006 Q3.

From *Economic and Labour Market Review,* vol. 3, no. 9, published by Palgrave Macmillan, September 2009, pp. 44–51. Source: Office for National Statistics. Crown Copyright material is reproduced with the permission of the Office of Public Sector Information (OPSI). www.palgrave-journals.com

Potential Future Functions of the World Trade Organization

Patrick Low

In thinking about the World Trade Organization's role in the future governance of the global trade system, there are at least six issues worthy of consideration:

1. Agenda formation in the WTO.
2. Relationships with other international organizations.
3. The relationship between the trade liberalization and rule-making functions of the WTO.
4. A "missing middle" in the functions of the WTO?
5. Systemic threats to the system (regionalism).
6. Variable geometry and possibilities for critical mass approaches to WTO obligations.

At first blush, these issues may appear to be discrete, yet they are interrelated. Part of what determines the functions of the WTO is obviously the reach of its mandate in terms of policy area coverage. That, in turn, will influence relationships with other intergovernmental agencies for international cooperation. Both agenda formation and the nature of interagency relationships are relevant to the balance of emphasis in the WTO between liberalization, rule making and nonlitigious deliberation (the missing middle). The notion that the explosion of regionalism poses a systemic threat to the multilateral trading system is core to a consideration of the future functions of the WTO, particularly in relation to the balance between liberalization and rule making. Finally, the status of the consensus rule in the WTO will influence processes and outcomes in relation both to agenda formation and the balance of emphasis in defining the WTO's priorities and core functions.[1]

Agenda Formation

This issue can be seen as a question about the boundaries of the WTO. We do not have a theory or a conceptual framework that would permit us to determine *ex ante* whether a particular issue or subject area should be negotiated in the WTO. Perhaps it would be useful to try (as some authors have) to define such a framework. In the meantime, it may help to think about why governments might seek to expand the WTO agenda. Here are some possible reasons:

- To protect *acquis*—the accumulated rules and law of the General Agreement on Tariffs and Trade (GATT) and

the WTO. What we are thinking about here is essentially the elaboration of existing provisions.[2] Two things about these types of negotiations are noteworthy. First, we have no way of determining which existing provisions in GATT or the WTO should be elaborated. Second, when such elaboration or clarification of existing provisions occurs, this may also entail an extension of provisions, thus introducing new disciplines. So in practice, the desire to protect acquis may also involve an extended trade agenda, blurring the distinction between this and negotiations that would change the conditions of competition, as discussed below.

- To change the conditions of competition. This is about introducing new areas of regulation where a primary, but not necessarily exclusive, concern is with gaining a competitive advantage. This could account, for example, for the desire to introduce rules on government procurement. A problem here, of course, is that other motivations may be adduced in arguing for the inclusion of a new issue. Those wishing to bring labor rights into the WTO are likely, for example, to argue in terms of social values rather than economic advantage. This example sounds a cautionary note on the utility of a taxonomy that relies on the attribution of motive.

- To enhance efficiency. The easiest example here is of international disciplines relating to environmental protection in order to manage spillovers, but there are doubtless others, including prisoners' dilemma situations. Aspects of regulatory harmonization through international agreement can also be presented in efficiency terms. Any situation where international cooperation is key to reducing trade costs or transactions costs would fit under this rubric.

- To find trade-offs through a broader agenda. If a government wants something in one area, it may introduce or entertain agenda expansion in order to secure a negotiating trade-off. Some have attributed this motive as a partial explanation for the European Union (EU) proposals on the Singapore issues.

- To secure domestic tie-in or influence the domestic politics of policymaking. Here, the idea is that, if one internationalizes rights and obligations in a given area, a policy stance may be reinforced, rendered more easily attainable, or more consistent. These ideas are quite well developed theoretically, and we have examples like that of China where internationalizing the domestic policy regime was a vital plank in the reform process. But concrete examples of where such considerations might have driven agenda formation or debates about agenda formation in the WTO are elusive.

- To enhance enforceability. Consideration of this motivation for bringing issues to the WTO provides a convenient bridge to thinking about the relationship between the WTO and other international institutions. The classic example given of where this motivation was prominent is in the desire of some governments to bring the Agreement on Trade Related Aspects of Intellectual Property Rights (TRIPs) into the WTO. This has much to do with the ability to resort to a functioning dispute settlement system where, for a variety of reasons, the likelihood of compliance is high and the threat of trade retaliation may well influence the seriousness with which governments take their international commitments. This is about choosing among international agencies, as opposed to bringing something new onto the international agenda.

This taxonomy is not complete. Nor does it establish mutually exclusive motivational categories for positions taken by governments on agenda formation. Thus, it does not provide definitive guidance on principles for setting the agenda. But perhaps it does help us to think about what questions to ask, and even maybe how to begin to set priorities. And this way of thinking about the issue certainly assists in discarding such notions as "trade-relatedness" as a guiding principle for agenda formation. We need more thought and analysis on this question. The approach thus far makes it hard to avoid the conclusion that time- and place-specific politics, along with power relationships, loom large in agenda formation. The quest for a principle-based, consensual prior agreement on what is legitimate and what is not in terms of the scope of the WTO agenda may be a fool's errand.

Relationships with Other Organizations

The architecture and functions of the existing network of intergovernmental institutions designed to manage global governance result largely from independent decisions taken through time. Many factors have influenced the shape of the present landscape, including power relationships, competing interests among different branches of government at the domestic level, and the influence of some of the international bureaucracies staffing the institutions. Institutions are highly path dependent and absent crises, so thoroughgoing reform of the structures, functions, and functioning of international institutions is extraordinarily difficult. Therefore, any consideration of how the WTO interacts with other agencies in the context of its own (evolving) agenda can only raise issues at the margin.

In considering this question, the following points seem pertinent:

- Most government and nongovernment stakeholders seem to favor interagency cooperation where this is feasible. Article V of the Marrakesh agreement, which established the WTO, instructs the General Council to make appropriate arrangements for effective cooperation with other agencies whose mandates are relevant to the WTO. Under current WTO leadership, greater emphasis has been placed on joint work, which on the research front has resulted in joint published work and ongoing projects with the International Labour Organization, joint published work with the United Nations Environment Programme, a joint project with the Organisation for Economic Co-operation and Development, and discussions of similar activities with other agencies.

- Interagency initiatives relating to technical cooperation and capacity building have grown in prominence (e.g., the Integrated Framework for Trade-Related Technical Assistance to Least Developed Countries, Aid for Trade, and joint agency work on food standards).

- The coherence mandate on global economic policymaking (Article III:5 of the Marrakesh agreement) calls for appropriate cooperation with the International Monetary Fund (IMF) and World Bank. It has not always been obvious what the nature of this cooperation should be, but presumably the core of it should focus on links between trade, finance, and development. Interactions have intensified in recent years, particularly with the World Bank. This is perhaps an issue for further reflection.

The above relationships, even if not always easy, are important because they help to avoid incoherence and duplication and they sharpen appreciation of the interrelatedness of issues outside the narrower mandates of individual institutions. They are likely to contribute to better international governance.

But all this is tangential to the question of how the WTO's relationship with other agencies is affected by its own agenda and changes in that agenda. Clearly, there are ways in which changes in the WTO's agenda could generate conflict with other agencies that feel their territory is being invaded.

An interesting issue in the event of such an occurrence is whether WTO rules replace or build on existing international obligations. The spectrum of choice in this regard is well illustrated by the TRIPs agreement on the one hand, which in some key substantive respects redefined the intellectual property regime, and the Sanitary and Phytosanitary (SPS) agreement, which did not seek to redefine the substantive standards of other international regimes—the Codex (Alimentarius) Commission, the International Office of Epizotics, and the International Plant Protection Convention.

By way of conclusion, however, it probably should be said that, if time- and place-specific politics, along with power relationships, loom large in agenda formation (as concluded in the Agenda Formation section above), there is no reason to suppose that the situation will be different when it comes to managing the fallout from agenda formation decisions on interagency relationships.

The Relationship between the Trade Liberalization and Rule-Making Functions of the WTO

When we look at GATT and the WTO historically, the only major trade liberalization achievement has been the reduction of (most) industrial tariffs in industrial countries over five decades. In addition, the WTO scored some success eleven years ago in telecoms and financial services. Countries acceding to the WTO have had to liberalize considerably as part of the entry price. But in agriculture and services, the record is modest, and developing countries in general have liberalized very little on the altar of the WTO.

Trade liberalization is not something that the WTO uniquely supplies. Countries move on this front unilaterally, bilaterally, and regionally. The quantum of liberalization achieved through preferential trade agreements (PTAs) over the past two decades exceeds anything attained so far by GATT and the WTO in the same period.

By contrast, the WTO is the unique supplier of the global public good of universal rules. This includes rules about market access in the form of tariff bindings and all the other rules that entail precommitment in policy behavior, generating greater certainty and a richer information environment. The rules also reduce power asymmetry between strong and weak or large and small players.

Perhaps we have not done enough to emphasize the WTO's rule-making role. The image of an institution hell-bent on prizing open markets has been dominant, weakening the WTO's legitimacy in the minds of many critics. This is not an argument against liberalization—far from it—but rather a comment on the balance of the message, the WTO's public image, and therefore the effectiveness of the institution.

A Missing Middle in the Functions of the WTO?

In his Foreword to the WTO's *World Trade Report 2007,* WTO director-general Pascal Lamy wrote: "As an institution we legislate and litigate, and I believe we do this reasonably well. But is there something of a 'missing middle' where we should be engaged more in fostering dialogue that can bolster cooperation?"[3] The intellectual underpinning for this idea may be found in constructivist theories that maintain this kind of interaction can change the dynamic and improve the quality of international cooperation. In other words, the WTO would be able to function better, including in terms of setting its agenda and determining its scope of competence, if more nonlitigious dialogue occurred among governments outside a negotiating framework.

A danger, of course, is that the WTO could begin to look more like a "talk shop" than a place to conduct substantive trade policy business. This is a matter of balance, and it would be important to ensure that dialogue did not replace a negotiating agenda nor blunt commitment to effective dispute settlement. The benefits that enhanced dialogue could bring are essentially twofold. First, it would improve the knowledge base for informed decisions and discussions on trade policy.

Information and data are simply lacking in a wide range of areas, and improving this situation in the context of an engagement in dialogue could make a contribution to enhanced cooperation and increased welfare. And, second, dialogue promotes understanding and sensitizes parties to the needs, priorities, and perspectives of their counterparts. To the extent that this occurs, it will help to shape the contours of cooperation and increase the likelihood of mutually beneficial outcomes. This idea is not entirely novel in GATT and the WTO. Perhaps it would be worth evaluating the Trade Policy Review Mechanism and the recently established Transparency Mechanism for regional trade agreements (RTAs) to evaluate both how far these exercises are making a positive contribution and what more might be done to foster dialogue of this kind.

Systemic Threats to the System—Regionalism

The number of RTAs has exploded in the past couple of decades. They come in many forms, often serving a variety of objectives that go beyond trade policy as narrowly defined. They are more or less far-reaching, depending on their underlying objectives. The only thing that all RTAs have in common is that they have not been judged on conformity grounds under the WTO. Lawyers might argue that, in the absence of formal challenge under the WTO, the default is approval.

Whether or not this legal point is correct, the fact is we do not have a clear idea of how far RTAs are undermining the tenets of WTO discipline. We might take some comfort in the notion that few RTAs could be characterized as determinedly discriminatory and exclusive in terms of their primary objectives. But this does not guarantee against distortionary effects or the generation of additional trade costs and lost trading opportunities for some. Neither does it mean the integrity of multilateralism is safe.

So although it is pointless to rail against the growth of regionalism from a multilateral perspective, and rather meaningless to continue to insist on the inviolability of GATT/WTO rules in a vacuum, it seems that any consideration of the future functions of the WTO cannot disregard the systemic challenge posed by regionalism. Presumably, the decision by members to fast-track the application of the transparency decision in the Doha Round reflects this thinking.

The present challenge is to think about how WTO members might respond positively to the challenge of building mutually reinforcing synergies between the specificities of regional agreements and the universalist aspirations of the multilateral trading system. Possible elements for political consideration and further research include the following:

- If governments have already shown willingness through the fledgling Transparency Mechanism to share information and dialogue in relation to their RTAs, surely this exercise should be strengthened and used as a vehicle for thinking more about the underlying issue of discrimination in trade policy.
- Work might be done on further liberalizing and geographically extending rules of origin affecting goods

trade, as was done under the pan-European system of cumulation. This should be feasible if the underlying motivation of these rules is not protectionist.

- Other aspects of multilateralizing regionalism should be examined more closely to see where obstacles lie to the extension on nondiscriminatory access to a wider set of countries. Preliminary evidence suggests that obstacles to such action may not be as far-reaching as may have been feared with respect to nontariff and regulatory policy aspects of preferential arrangements.

- More analysis might be undertaken of a new role for the WTO in developing best policy practices in RTAs with a view to informing and reinforcing commitment to a new look at the role the WTO should play in the future, including in terms of substantive legal obligations that would apply to all RTAs among WTO members.

Variable Geometry and Possibilities for Critical Mass Approaches to WTO Obligations

Some argue that the consensus rule in WTO rule making frustrates work, makes it harder to ensure that the WTO agenda can keep up with the times, and favors an excessively status quo and lowest-common-denominator approach to decisions in the WTO, especially but not only in relation to questions of agenda formation. Others argue that the linkage between consensus and the Uruguay Round-style "single undertaking" resulted in overcommitment among many WTO members, engendering resistance to any further extension of the WTO agenda. According to this view, the single undertaking experience poisoned the atmosphere in the debate over the Singapore issues, and led to their rejection (except trade facilitation) on grounds that were independent of any serious consideration of their merit.

The removal of veto power through a relaxation of consensus via critical mass decisionmaking and acceptance of an additional degree of variable geometry under WTO rules are not strictly the same thing. Consensus decisionmaking could still be required while less than the full membership accepted new obligations. Alternatively, critical mass agreements could be legitimized by decisions among those parties accepting new obligations, with no veto rights on the part of those who are not accepting new obligations. In the latter case, critical mass applies both to defining the obligations in a new policy area for a subset of the membership as well as to decisions about the outcome and its adoption.

For any consideration of this more varied approach to defining the functions of the multilateral trading system, the point at which veto rights disappear is vital. For those with an interest in developing the WTO agenda, the argument might well be that those taking on new obligations should also be allowed to decide what is in the WTO and what is out, provided the interests of all WTO parties are protected.[4]

For those who eschew agenda expansion, or value their veto for reasons other than the particular issue at hand, the argument may well be that agreements adding obligations for some and rights for all could in principle go ahead, but that any decision even to start negotiating, or about the adoption of results, would still have to be taken on a consensus basis.

This is the nub of the issue when it comes to designing new ways of ensuring the WTO's relevance while protecting the rights of all members. This is a core issue for the future functioning of the WTO.

Notes

Patrick Low is chief economist at the World Trade Organization, and has served previously as chief of staff for the WTO director-general (1999–2001), at the World Bank's International Trade Division (1990–1994), and in the GATT Secretariat (1980–1987).

1. This essay is written in the author's personal capacity and does not represent the views of the members of the WTO or the WTO secretariat.

2. For example, some of the nontariff negotiations that took place in the Tokyo Round (agreements on antidumping, subsidies and countervailing measures, customs valuation, standards, and import licensing), in the Uruguay Round (further elaboration of some of the Tokyo Round agreements plus additional elements such as the agreements on SPS Measures, trade-related investment measures, safeguards, and the dispute settlement mechanism), and in the Doha Round (trade facilitation—GATT Articles V, VIII, and X).

3. World Trade Organization, *World Trade Report 2007* (Geneva: WTO, 2007).

4. The kind of critical mass scenarios discussed here would protect the interests of those who commit to new obligations because they form part of the critical mass. The interests of the rest of the membership would also be protected because they would not be excluded in debate nor be prevented from joining critical mass agreements later on, and they would not lose any WTO rights (including most-favored-nation status). These types of safeguards could be added to and spelled out in more detail if ideas such as critical mass as a mode of operation in agenda formation were to go forward.

The Wicked Problem of Good Financial Markets

Michael Mainelli

The Problem of Wicked Finance

There is a huge problem in the world. It's responsible for the upheaval of the entire global economy, the displacement of populations, the loss of significant assets and the likely impoverishment of future generations. No, not climate change—I refer to the global financial system. In today's world we are supposed to reflect on the big global risks, of which there are a tremendous number. In past pieces I've discussed the Copenhagen Consensus issues, among them malaria, AIDS/HIV, corruption, armed conflict, governance, pandemics and climate change. We have many scarcity issues—water, cropland, living space or fish. We have many quality of life issues, such as obesity, longevity, genetic modification, access to medicine or employment opportunities.

Given that financial markets are more and more frequently the mechanism by which global risks and rewards are transmitted, e.g. micro-finance, internalisation of carbon emissions, or motivations for drug companies to research tropical diseases, the robustness and resilience of financial markets themselves is a global risk. The 2007 Credit Crunch has led more and more people to believe that financial markets are a problem needing a solution. The "wicked" nature of financial markets needs to be controlled. There are numerous proposals for action. But can we predict the outline of the likely outcome and what it might mean for financial firms?

Global risks are events or circumstances that are beyond any particular party's capacity to control, that may adversely impact multiple parties across geographic borders, industries, and/or sectors. However abstract they may be, global risks affect enterprises, even those not apparently involved, in different ways—disruption to a distribution channel, impairment of facilities, network interruption, reputation harm, higher commodity costs, and more—that are concrete enough to manage but still beyond any particular enterprise's capacity to control. Some risks have their origins in business activity, such as accounting misconduct, but entail a broader threat to society.

Commercial enterprises strive to create value for shareholders and other stakeholders, and have mechanisms that allow them to respond both to their existing environment and to anticipate change. Enterprises specifically work to reduce risk, i.e. they attempt to reduce the likelihood of adverse events or the impact on the enterprise if the risk materialises. Enterprise risk management systems focus on competitive advantage for the individual enterprise. Global risks are characteristically low probability and high impact, rendering them too complex and uncertain for any single entity, working in isolation, to manage. Kunreuther and Heal [2002] point to the threat of systematic underinvestment in risk management where "the incentive to invest in protection approaches zero as the number of unprotected agents increases."

Because organisations have a bias toward assigning greatest importance to those risks that are within the enterprise's control and their risk systems classify global risks as "beyond our control", they give insufficient attention to global risks. In the case of Wicked Finance, it's not just the threat to the world from finance, but the threat to Finance from global society. Are risk managers thinking about how societal reaction to the Credit Crunch is likely to affect their firms' reputations, freedom to manoeuvre, likely odds in court cases, repayment rates or insurability, just to name a few immediate risks to financial firms.

What We Have Here Is a Failure to Allocate

But what can we actually do about these risks? Are not they all too complex? Is not the globalization of finance increasing linkages among these risks? Evans and Steven (2008) point out that the international system's increasing complexity is due to a "growing number of actors confronted by fluid and interlinked threats". They believe that:

> Two drivers of change stand out: *scarcity,* limits to the sustainable consumption of highly strategic commodities such as energy, land, water, food and "atmospheric space" for emissions; and *instability,* the tendency for complex systems to experience unpredictable and unsettling shifts.

Arguably, population growth is at the root of many of our scarcity problems. Huge populations combined with rapid communications give us a number of feed-forward/ positive feedback problems that increase the instability Evans and Steven (2007) fear.

Doyne Farmer of the Santa Fe Institute observes that:

> One of the most fundamental principles in financial economics is called market efficiency. This principle takes many forms: A market is informationally efficient if prices reflect all available information; it is arbitrage efficient if it is impossible for investors to make "excess profits", and it is allocationally efficient if prices are set so that they in some sense maximize everyone's welfare. [Farmer *et al.,* 2005, p. 3).

Markets are self-organising information processing systems that direct societies. Markets can and do help to set goals through prices. These three types of efficiency imply certain goals. Information efficiency should mean that prices are not predictable but that prices help to communicate values through society and therefore direct commercial efforts. You need no further proof than to look at various manias and panics such as tulip bulbs or credit crunches. The goals may be odd, but markets set them. Good markets should provide information that permits improved decision-making. Arbitrage efficiency should mean that it is impossible to make money without taking risks. Good markets encourage people to take risks that other people are prepared to reward. One can argue that a market is incomplete if all relevant risks can't be hedged. Finally, allocation efficiency should mean that it's impossible to make somebody better off without making someone else worse off. Markets satisfy the goal of helping to allocate risks and rewards through society. Markets should maximise social welfare.

A few paradoxes arise. If information efficiency is strong, then innovation should be kept secret. If one firm is successful but grows too large, secrecy is lost. If arbitrage efficiency is high, then there are few ways to make large amounts of money and interest in work and innovation might collapse. Finally, highly efficient allocation may not be equitable and may lead to reallocation outside the market, e.g. by force or taxation. While nodding towards Rawls and Nozick, I would like to quote from an online conversation I've had with Doug Sunshine.

> [I]n any "immaculately conceived" initial distribution of resources, normal activity will take place until there is some exogenous change that will inevitably benefit some and hurt others. All political evidence, however, points to the fact that the "losers" of said change prefer to be compensated by the "winners" than to bear their loss silently. If their numbers are great enough, they will agitate for political action to be compensated—you are now exiting Nozick's Utopia. (Doug Sunshine, 7 April 2008).

Anticipation 1: enviable losses. Societal discomfort with financial services compensation and pay (allocative efficiency) will continue to intensify. Society is also likely to continue to seek to reduce arbitrage opportunities, as has already happened on short selling. This leaves financial services firms needing to make the most out of information efficiencies. Unfortunately, this rational action firm-by-firm could be seen by society as an industry becoming more secretive, at just the time it needs to be perceived as a societal enhancer.

Wicked Problems

My colleague, Alexander Knapp, directed me to the concept of "Wicked Problems". The term was originally proposed by Horst Rittel (a pioneering theorist of design and planning at the University of California, Berkeley) and Melvin Webber in a treatise for planning. Rittel explored ill-defined design and planning problems which he termed "wicked", i.e. messy, circular and aggressive. These problems are not the comparatively tame problems most decision theorists study, for example chess, game theory or puzzle solving. The real world is messy, circular and aggressive. According to Laurence J Peter of The Peter Principle fame, "Some problems are so complex that you have to be highly intelligent and well informed just to be undecided about them." Jeff Conklin summarises Horst Rittel's problems with wicked problems:

- "You don't understand the problem until you have developed a solution". Indeed, there is no definitive statement of "The Problem." The problem is ill-structured, an evolving set of interlocking issues and constraints.

- Wicked problems have no stopping rule. Since there is no definitive "The Problem", there is also no definitive "The Solution." The problem solving process ends when you run out of resources.

- Solutions to wicked problems are not right or wrong, simply "better," "worse," "good enough," or "not good enough."

- Every wicked problem is essentially unique and novel. There are so many factors and conditions, all embedded in a dynamic social context, that no two wicked problems are alike, and the solutions to them will always be custom designed and fitted.
- Every solution to a wicked problem is a "one-shot operation," every attempt has consequences. As Rittel says, "One cannot build a freeway to see how it works." This is the "Catch 22" about wicked problems: you can't learn about the problem without trying solutions, but every solution you try is expensive and has lasting unintended consequences which are likely to spawn new wicked problems.
- Wicked problems have no given alternative solutions. There may be no solutions, or there may be a host of potential solutions that are devised, and another host that are never even thought of. (http://cognexus.org/wpf/wickedproblems.pdf).

Wicked problems are not just about global risks. Building a new power station or credit risk system can be a wicked problem. Wherever the problem affects the solution and vice versa, where solutions are enmeshed in society and everyone cares, you probably have a wicked problem. Certainly most global risks, with long timescales, distant countries and, when it grabs their attention, everyone wanting to do something immediately, qualify as wicked problems. People want solutions that don't damage economic growth at home, but if it didn't cost anything it would be happening now. The rare few who state "if we want it so much let's pay for it" are considered either scuppering realists or unrealistic idealists.

One of the big problems with wicked problems is determining how much it matters to act now. When people talk about risks, I often contend that something isn't a risk if no one is prepared to pay to avoid it or its effects. Take a frivolous example, the risk that the sky might turn from blue to purple. Assume that if the sky turns purple there are no other physical dangers, just a colour change. Assume too that people can make a payment to reduce the chance of the sky turning purple. If no one wants to pay, then I call the sky colour change an event, not a risk. On the other hand, perhaps people are prepared to pay to avoid having to adjust to new colour schemes or to keep cultural continuity with old masters' paintings, then the sky colour change is a risk. You may find it frivolous that people will spend money to avoid something that has no negative effects, but if they pay to avoid it, it's a risk.

Wicked problems are plagued with a tension between the room for action versus uncertainty. As uncertainty decreases over time, the room for action diminishes.

But as the room for action diminishes, people are more certain about what to do. This tension is why things are frequently left so late. It can be difficult to distinguish "waiting for enough information to act responsibly" from "acting because our backs are against the wall". If you wait, you may find new ways of solving problems, but the problem also grows in scale.

Anticipation 2: plus ça change. It is unlikely that all of the proposals and discussions about how to reform the world of finance are going to bring about radical change. There is little willingness to pay for large-scale changes directly. There are already "hidden" charges mitigating awareness, e.g. taxpayers bearing risks without compensation on Freddie Mac and Fannie Mae and Northern Rock, yet not understanding the scale. There are also "hidden" ways of making financial services firms pay for change such as regulatory costs or transaction taxes or punitive, compulsory insurance schemes.

Resilient or Robust Solutions?

Actions are of two types, resilient actions or robust actions. Resilient actions get by—resilient systems perform within the range of historic volatility. Robust actions try to solve the problem or handle a previously unreasonable scale—robust systems handle step changes in volatility. A lot of the difficulty with global problems is people getting used to them. A resilient approach to famine is to establish a reasonable disaster relief programme. Let us just get by for now. A robust approach to famine is to overhaul everything from agriculture to transportation to markets to governance to try and prevent famine from happening. Let us solve it once and for all. In some cases, robust approaches aren't attempted because of lack of confidence. In other cases, robust approaches are overdone, e.g. seeking a silver bullet technology such as nuclear fusion these many years. In some cases, robust approaches have achieved wonders, such as the eradication of smallpox. But solving wicked problems via robust approaches involves a lot of different activities, acting in some degree of concert.

A few single approaches to solving global risk problems can be ruled out. We can start with government on its own. For many wicked problems dinner party answers start with the phrase "somebody ought to . . ." Of course we really mean some omniscient, omnipotent being who will come down and make everyone else act properly, pay to fix things and avoid all future problems. In the financial markets right now, everyone awaits the coming of new super-regulators who won't make the credit crunch mistakes of those who came before them. Sadly, neither that government nor that regulator exist, nor to the dismay of Pastafarians, does the Flying Spaghetti Monster exist. Less flippantly, Muhammad Yunus, founder of Grameen Bank and winner of the 2006 Nobel Peace Prize, says:

> Governments can do much to address social problems. They are large and powerful, with access to almost every corner of society, and through taxes they can mobilize vast resources [. . .] So it is tempting to simply dump our world's social problems into the lap of government and say, "Here, fix this". But if this approach were effective, the problems would have been solved long ago . . . governments can be inefficient, slow, prone to corruption, bureaucratic and self-perpetuating. These are all side effects of the advantages governments possess: Their vast size, power, and reach almost inevitably make them unwieldy as well as attractive to those who want to use them to amass power and wealth for themselves. (Yunus 2007, p. 8).

Another truism is that solutions to wicked problems are not "top-down" imposed solutions. Jeremy Hunt, the UK Conservative's Shadow Secretary of State for Culture, Media and Sport remarked at a City event in March on philanthropy—"If you want to solve the big social problems of the day you can't just do it through money and targets".

Likewise we must brake a slide towards the idea that wicked solutions are just about Commerce; that today's problems are all caused by poor government and we can just sit back and wait for the free market to save the day. The invisible hand will arrive and all will be cured. Rischard of the World Bank makes an extremely pointed warning. He talks of four stresses in the "new world economy", 1—"adapting to the new rules of the game" (speed, boundary-free, knowledge intensive, hypercompetitive), 2—"growing disparities", 3—"turbulence and fragility" ". . . [F]ourth stress associated with the new world economy is subtler. It has to do with excessive trust in the market, and the complacency that results from it." (Rischard 2002, p. 34).

Wicked problems involve many policy issues, many political issues, many commercial issues, many project management issues and many implementation issues. We have to recognise "everything, everywhere at all times"—ownership, enforcement, multiple players, multiple player interactions. Complex global risks imply messy diverse solutions, no silver bullet. I group mechanisms into four general methods:

- *Knowledge:* the degree to which risk management is enhanced by sharing information and knowledge or conducting research with other entities about severity, likelihood and effectiveness of responses;
- *Markets:* the degree to which market mechanisms price risk and reward improvement, a richness of supporting financial methods and, in many cases, direct financial support;
- *Standards:* the degree to which standards and the audit of standards can help to set goals, share knowledge, improve the effectiveness of market forces and provide signals from consumers to producers;
- *Policies:* how well intelligent guidelines, legislation, regulation and enforcement underpin public and private sector responses.

Anticipation 3: messy interventions. Solutions to wicked problems are likely to be wickedly complex—give markets a chance, but alongside everything else, sharing knowledge, developing standards and setting policies.

Credit Crunch 2007 is, so far, a "diffuse" crisis—no single baddy, no single incident, no single owner. Without a clear problem, a wicked problem such as financial services reform elicits a series of messy answers. It is likely that some smaller, more pointed reforms may get through, but then there is the danger that piecemeal reforms often don't work because the environment hasn't changed enough. "My Reform X would have worked, but I was counting on reforms Y and Z as well."

One may start with economics and rationality, but at the end of all social science is contingency theory. Credit Crunch 2007 is not likely to lead to major reforms, just a muddle through. The financial services industry is neither wicked nor good and, despite the designs some of us may have on radical reform, it isn't an abject failure. As Deng Xiaoping pointed out: "It doesn't matter if a cat is black or white, so long as it catches mice." The financial services industry has had a series of major failings and needs major reforms at some point, but Credit Crunch 2007 was not crisis enough to jolt radical reform, yet.

References

Evans, A. and Steven, D. (2007), "Climate change: the state of the debate", The London Accord, City of London Corporation, December, available at: www.london-accord.co.uk/final_report/reports/b1.htm.

Evans, A. and Steven, D. (2008), "Shooting the rapids: multilateralism and global risks", paper presented to heads of state at the Progressive Governance Summit, 5 April, available at: http://globaldashboard.org/wp-content/uploads/2008/04/Shooting_the_rapids.pdf.

Farmer, J. D.,Shubik, M. and Smith, E. (2005), "Economics: the next physical science?", Cowles Foundation Discussion Paper Number 1520, June, available at: http://cowles.econ.yale.edu/P/cd/d15a/d1520.pdf.

Kunreuther, H. and Heal, G. (2002), "Interdependent security", *Journal of Risk and Uncertainty*, Vol. 26 Nos 2/3, pp. 231–49, available at: http://opim.wharton.upenn.edu/risk/downloads/02-06-HK.pdf (accessed March 2003).

Rischard, J. F. (2002), *High Noon: Twenty Global Problems, Twenty Years To Solve Them*, Basic Books, New York, NY.

Rittel, H. and Webber, M. (1973), "Dilemmas in a general theory of planning", *Policy Sciences,* Vol. 4, Elsevier Scientific Publishing Company, Amsterdam, pp. 155–69 (reprinted in N. Cross (Ed.) (1984), *Developments in Design Methodology*, Wiley, Chichester, pp. 135–144).

Yunus, M. (2007), *Creating a World Without Poverty: Social Business and the Future of Capitalism*, PublicAffairs, New York, NY.

Further Reading

Sandia National Laboratories (2007), Sandia National Laboratory's views on Wicked Problems, available at: www.sandia.gov/news/resources/releases/2007/wickedproblems.html.

Waverman, L., Meschi, M. and Fuss, M. (2005), "The impact of telecoms on economic growth in developing countries", The Vodafone Policy Paper Series 2, available at: www.london.edu/assets/documents/PDF/L_Waverman_Telecoms_Growth_in_Dev_Countries.pdf.

Engaging China: Strategies for the Small Internationalizing Firm

Rolf D. Cremer and Bala Ramasamy

Foreign Investments in China: Large or Small?

Despite concerns of an over-heating economy, increasing operational costs, dominance in important world markets, and widening income gaps within China, the Chinese economy continues to grow relentlessly. In 2007, China's real gross domestic product (GDP) grew by more than 10 percent—again. The continuing expansion is due in large part also to its international economic relations. China's foreign trade volume surpassed US$1.1 trillion in 2004, replacing Japan as the third largest trading nation after the USA and Germany. In 2003, China overtook the USA as the most popular destination for foreign direct investment (FDI), with inflows of $53 billion. In 2006, FDI inflow increased further to US$70 billion. There are more than half a million foreign enterprises active in China. The US-China Business Council (n.d.) reports indicate that since 1990 foreign multinationals like P&G, YUM!, AIG, Alcatel, Carrefour, Motorola, Nestle, Siemens, and Volkswagen are generating higher profits from their China ventures.

It is not surprising then that companies from around the globe—big and small—are considering China ventures seriously. However, the chances of making mistakes and failing in China are daunting. Cases of messy joint ventures, negotiations that have gone bad, fierce price competition, intellectual property rights (IPR) problems and betrayals, or market promises that never existed are also part of the business reality in China.

Nevertheless, after 30 years of reforms, the Chinese economy is fast approaching normalcy. Membership in the WTO, the presence and influence of many multinationals, as well as many important reforms and adjustments in the legal system, have made China much more predictable today than in the past. Mechem in 2004 claimed that predictability, more than anything else, has made it possible for even smaller firms to consider their China dream (Mechem, 2004).

While literature on the internationalization of small firms has proliferated, most research on how to do business in China tends to be biased towards larger multinationals. This is perhaps due to the attention that these multinationals receive in the media or simply because 400 of the *Fortune* 500 companies are already in China. The result of this is a lack of attention in the literature regarding the specific situation of smaller firms. Consider the data in Table I. The average value of projects contracted in 2003 is a mere US$1.3 million. The average size of investment is not much different between a joint venture and a wholly owned enterprise. With more than 40,000 relatively small projects, one could imagine that most projects involve relatively small firms.

This suggests that there is a problem: Most of the firms and/or investments entering the Chinese market are, in fact, small. On the other hand, many proposed strategies for doing business in China are derived from studying multinationals. For instance, Wong and Maher's (1997) study that appeared in the *Business Horizons* in 1997 was based on two major US multinationals. Reports on doing business in China by consultancy firms like McKinsey (see for example, Woetzel (2004) and Chen and Penhirin (2004)) are based on fast-moving consumer goods giants like Procter and Gamble. Although many of these strategies may be workable for companies whatever their size, smaller firms are different in terms of availability of resources, capabilities and core competencies, as well as how they are perceived by the Chinese market and authorities.

In this paper, we focus on those smaller firms planning to expand their operations to China, either for trade or for investment purposes. The definition of small and medium-sized companies (SMEs) varies across countries. In the European Union (EU), SMEs are those firms with fewer than 250 employees, but in the USA these include firms with fewer than 500 employees. On the other hand, Waste Management New Zealand—a company listed among the top 200 New Zealand firms—employs only

Table I FDI in China, By Type, 2003

	No. of projects	Contracted value (billion US$)	Used value (billion US$)	Average contracted value (million US$)	Average used value (million US$)
Total FDI	41,081	115.1	53.5	2.8	1.3
Joint ventures	12,521	25.5	15.4	2.0	1.2
Wholly owned	26,943	81.6	33.4	3.0	1.2

Source: National Bureau of Statistics of China (2004)

870 employees and contractors. Given these variations, for the current study, we define small firms as those that do not have strong core competencies embedded in technology, marketing networks or brand names; and those firms that have limited accessibility to resources, be they financial or managerial. In this study, we identify some core strategies and mindsets that are required by such firms for successful engagements in China.

The Study
The Small Internationalizing Firm

Figure 1 provides a visual of our research focus and its ensuing strategies. The size-time matrix distinguishes four main fields. The two fields on the left refer to firms that entered China in the early stages of the reform era. They comprise large multinationals like Volkswagen and Philips, who obtained early mover advantages in the 1980s and 1990s.

There were also smaller enterprises that entered the Chinese market when it opened up to the outside world. We call these firms explorers. A large number of companies from greater China (particularly Hong Kong and Macau) belong in this bottom left field.

After 15 to 20 years of reform, however, China, and especially the coastal regions, no longer offer any early mover advantages. Firms that have ventured into China more recently fall in the fields on the right of Figure 1.

Large multinationals are still making their moves into China. For instance, Ford and several Japanese and Korean multinationals could fall into this category. But they are latecomers. This does not necessarily imply an earlier mistake, as the example of Daimler-Chrysler shows a long tradition of targeting maturing markets for their luxury brand. Our research, however, focuses on the firms in the bottom right field, representing small and medium-sized late movers. This field comprises three types of players that we group together and call small internationalizing firms (SIFs).

1. The first category of SIFs comprises small multinationals. While these are multinationals in that they operate in more than one country, they typically do not possess the kind of resources or intangible assets (e.g., brand names) of their larger counterparts. These firms exist everywhere, obviously, but in some countries like New Zealand, Australia, Canada, and for newly industrializing economies like Korea and Singapore, they are the dominant class of internationalizing firms.

2. The second category of SIFs comprises professional service providers and includes, for example, legal, advertising, public relations, design, accounting and consultancy firms. As with other internationalizing service firms (Li and Guisinger, 1992), their primary reason for setting up operations in China is usually to extend support services to their clients who have moved to China, and only secondly to expand their market to other foreign subsidiaries as well as to domestic enterprises.

3. The final category of SIFs comprises single entrepreneurs. They are no different from the explorers in the early stage of China's reform era. One could argue that they are not really international firms, but rather a form of business migrant venturing into China with an idea and a great deal of confidence that they will be able to carve out a small piece of the action.

For the purpose of this research, we have chosen New Zealand companies as our population. New Zealand was the first nation to reach an agreement on China's accession to the WTO as well as the first developed country to start negotiations for a free trade agreement (FTA) with China. In 2003, China became New Zealand's fourth largest trading partner, overtaking the UK, historically the most important trading partner. Between 1990 and 2006, bilateral trade between the two countries grew at an average annual rate of 98.5 percent, compared to 9.1 and 5.1 percent for Australia and the USA respectively.

By global standards, New Zealand's foreign direct investment into China is small. Up to the end of December 2003, the stock of New Zealand's contractual investment in China amounted to US$812 million in 819 projects,

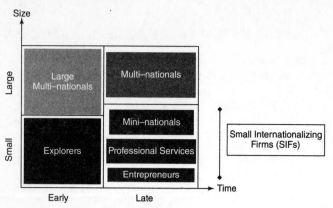

Figure 1 The size-time matrix.

with actual investment of US$405 million. One of New Zealand's largest investments in China was Lion Nathan's US$280 million investment in a brewery in Suzhou and a purchase of another brewery in Wuxi. Apart from the Lion Nathan investment, the size of investment projects is typically small, in terms of visibility, relative size and extent of resource commitment to the China business. Hence, New Zealand's firms are suitable for the purposes of this study.

Research Methods: Questionnaire and Focus Group Discussion

We followed a two-pronged methodology. The first stage involved mailing a questionnaire to the 200 largest companies in New Zealand as listed in the *New Zealand Management* magazine. Comprising 29 questions in five sections, the questionnaire solicited information on the current state of business activities in China, the strategies employed, obstacles faced in China and expected assistance from the authorities. The purpose of the questionnaire was to gauge the views regarding the China engagement from an overseas located headquarter perspective. Questionnaires were sent out to 191 of the 200 companies. In nine cases, the postal and email addresses were incorrect or unavailable. A total of 50 companies responded (26 percent); 40 of the returned questionnaires were relevant. Responses from ten companies were excluded as they had no past, present or planned engagement with China. The responses of the survey participants were analyzed and relevant issues were drawn out for the second stage of the research process.

The second part of the study was designed to seek indepth views of the opportunities and challenges faced by New Zealand businesses at "ground zero". The primary purpose of this part was to identify experience-based key success factors for SIFs, proven in the day-to-day struggle for survival and success. A secondary purpose was to draw out a comparison on China, on the Chinese and on doing

business in China between decision makers based at overseas headquarters and managers actually based in China. A questionnaire-based study among New Zealand businesses in China was not statistically feasible as the number of known companies was too small to produce meaningful quantitative results. As an alternative, a focus group approach was used. The advantage of a focus group discussion is that it can capture perceptions on a specific area of interest in a permissive, non-threatening environment.

Four focus group discussions were organized—two each in Beijing and Shanghai. The members were drawn from an incomplete list of NZ companies complied by NZ Consulates General in China. The discussions involved 14 companies in total, with representatives from all three categories of SIFs explained above—small multinationals, professional services providers and single entrepreneurs. They also represented various industries including agriculture (forestry), manufacturing and services. There was an average of six participants per discussion, allowing for in-depth discussion. The discussions revolved around five issues: core competencies of New Zealand businesses in China, mode of entry, challenges faced by New Zealand firms in China, the Chinese consumer market and role of government assistance.

Strategies for Success in China
Manager Characteristics and Vision

In a 1990 seminal article in the *Harvard Business Review,* Prahalad and Hamel (1990) wrote that "only if the company is conceived of as a hierarchy of core competencies, core products, and market-focused business units will it be fit to fight". For many large multinationals, the core competency might lie in their technology know-how and IPR, in the range of their distribution networks, or in their brand names. Still, even multinationals state time and again that their key concern in China, with its dominance of relationship-based business practices as opposed to the transaction-based business practices of the West, is talent management, i.e. the recruitment, development and retention of key personnel.

Our findings suggest that SIFs do not normally possess the advantages typical of multinationals. This in turn means that the remaining factor—the skills of their leading people—becomes even more critical; in particular, the individual traits of the manager and the personal relationships they have with business people in China. When asked what core competencies New Zealand firms have in China, our respondents in both Shanghai and Beijing were unanimous and had this to say:

> New Zealand people are quite a likeable people and the Chinese tend to respond to the New Zealanders' personality a little better than to an American or European.

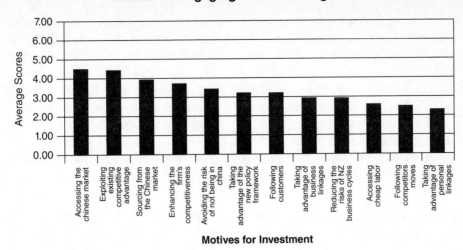

Figure 2   Investment motives in China.

We're not so steeped into tradition and formal ways [. . .] we are willing to give anything a try, we can be innovative. We're often very adaptable, we just get on and get the job done. Others may be more inhibitive.

When you say you're a New Zealander [. . .] the reaction is very visual, very noticeable.

It is important to note that these interpersonal relational skills are of little impact, unless they are brought actively into play. The selection of the right people to open markets in China thus is critical for small multinationals. Virtues like sincerity, caring, open-mindedness and adaptability may be more forthcoming among executives who come from smaller and lesser-known countries like New Zealand. Further, the perception that the Chinese have of such countries is a bonus. For instance, the perception that New Zealand is clean, agriculture-based and neutral in its international relations helps build initial relationships with the Chinese.

It must be emphasized that inter-personal relational skills are necessary, but not a sufficient condition for success in China. Indeed, a core competency based on individual traits alone has limitations if not combined with a visionary mindset. Relying on a pool of likeable but small-minded people might not take a company far in China. Consider, for instance, the following comment from a discussant from Beijing:

[In my Timaru coffee shop] I had ten people there, or three, or sometimes 20. In Zhenjiang, I have 3,500 customers every lunch.

Kedia and Mukherji (1999), in the *Journal of World Business*, state that managers need to have a growth mindset from the outset, even before leaving their local shores. This global mindset is aptly described by Rhinesmith (1993) as "a way of being rather than a set of skills. It is

an orientation of the world that allows one to see certain things that others do not". SIFs that originate from market bases that are small, like New Zealand or Singapore, need to visualize the enormous magnitude of the China market and have the confidence that this is within their capabilities, although the size of their operation may be several times the size they are used to at home.

Business Focus

At an estimated 0.87 percent growth annually, China's population grows by about 11.2 million people a year. It is not surprising that rapid economic growth and penetration into the China market have been listed as important motivations for investing in China by surveys done by consulting firms like PriceWaterhouseCoopers (2004). Market-related factors are also seen to be the more important reasons in our survey of New Zealand businesses (see Figure 2). However, the size of the market may prove to be elusive for small multinationals. Studwell (2003), in *The China Dream,* for instance, describes the limited success experienced by firms attracted to China's billion customers. Zeng and Williamson (2003) explain that the number of local enterprises competing in markets ranging from beer to computers has increased competition to unprofitable levels. Still, China has in recent years become the hotbed for fast-moving consumer goods companies, attracting world-renowned brand names.

[. . .] the number of local enterprises competing in markets ranging from beer to computers has increased competition to unprofitable levels. Still, China has in recent years become the hotbed for fast-moving consumer goods companies, attracting world-renowned brand names.

How then does an SIF avoid the cutthroat competition of the mass-product markets yet still take advantage of the size of China? Our findings suggest that to survive and profit in China, small multinationals must steer clear from large mass markets and focus on small niche markets.

Sheth and Sisodia (2002) discovered that in mature markets, three big companies dominate, with the remaining players concentrated in niche markets. Niche markets may be small but the scope of being small in China is obviously relative. One focus group discussant in the carpet industry stated:

[. . .] in New Zealand, 1000 square meters is a big order, but in China this might involve 2 million square meters per order for a new hotel [. . .] In 2002, we sold nearly 700,000 square meters.

Targeting niche markets has been recommended when markets are globalized or when competition becomes excessive. In a Business Sector Round Table discussion organized by the International Trade Council in Brussels in May 2001, successful exporters from least-developed countries were those who were able to find:

[. . .] niche products for niche markets, moving up the value chain through processing and design, responding to the ever rising demand from consumers for higher quality standards; entering brand new markets like services' or shortening the distribution chain to capture a greater share of the value.

Dalgic and Leeuw (1994) characterize niche markets as those that have:

- sufficient size and are potentially profitable;
- no real competitors or have been overlooked by other players;
- growth potential;
- the necessary purchasing ability;
- a need for special treatment;
- customer goodwill; and
- opportunities for a company to exercise its superior competence.

Craig and Douglas (1997) advise smaller multinationals to identify niches that are not large enough to attract other Western firms or those which require customization of product or services. They highlight the ability of a firm to leverage its core competency within the niche market through a positive association with the country of origin. Our focus group discussants in the wool carpet and fitness industries confirm that niche markets can be secured using the country of origin as an advantage (in our case, New Zealand). Niche markets also exist in the manufacturing sector. A focus group discussant in Shanghai represented Scott Technology, a Dunedin-based firm that specializes exclusively in the design and manufacture of large-scale automation systems for the major domestic appliance industries of the world. Scott Technologies is one of four firms producing such systems worldwide.

SIFs should therefore identify their specific position in the relevant emerging international, multi-firm supply chain and concentrate their resources in developing a niche for themselves in this position. A related question is, how does an SIF develop a niche in a consumer market which is overzealous on brand names and international recognition? The China market is a demanding one where brand names of international repute not only compete with their global competitors, but also with local brand names and counterfeiters. Our findings on the niche market strategy suggest focusing on the industrial/commercial buyer who may provide small multinationals with the answer to the question posed above. A business to business (B2B) focus also provides the following advantages:

- A smaller number of potential buyers who buy in bulk. This could reduce the amount of resources required for marketing purposes, such as advertising.
- Less price competition as industrial buyers may be willing to pay for quality. Industrial buyers are professionals who are paid to make the right buying decision. Hence, quality and after-sales service would be considered more seriously than the impulse buying behavior of consumers.
- Smaller quantity purchase, but an emphasis on custom-made product/service. Note, however, that small is relative, but could be within the capabilities of smaller multinationals.
- Personal relationship is critical and small multinationals may excel in their relationship compared to their larger counterparts.

The fourth advantage listed above requires further elaboration as it relates to other dimensions described in this study. Bell and Zacharilla (2003) state that B2B buying decisions are influenced by three factors: reputation, referrals and references. Faced with scarce resources allocated by the head office, small multinationals need to work on their relationships with Chinese businesses and through them acquire greater contacts, i.e. develop *guanxi* with a few businesses and expand the network base over time.

A discussant in the Beijing focus group explained how B2B relationships work for the SIF:

[. . .] There are two ways of doing business in China. First, if you are selling goods like toothpaste or toothbrushes or products that everyone uses—especially if you are one of those large American

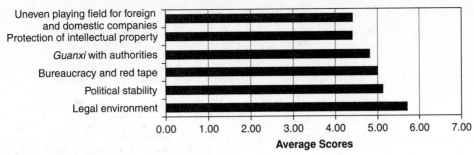

Figure 3   Legal and political challenges in China.

companies—you give it free for about two years and then you use large billboards and spend a lot on advertisements. This is the American way, the big guys in the business can do this. But for small companies, the best way is to join the relevant associations. For example, we are a member of the tourism and hotels association, the American Chamber of Commerce in China, the Australian Chamber of Commerce (but they were too small) and you know people and they know the product that you deal with [. . .] and they will contact you if they need anything. I have had business with seven embassies in Beijing.

Developing Guanxi (Networks)

An important factor that contributes to the success of business in China is *guanxi* or connections. Fan (2002) describes *guanxi* as a potential solution to the obstacles faced when entering and operating in China, where individuals can be more powerful than the legal system. It is considered the lifeblood of the Chinese community, without which nothing gets done. In a survey carried out by PriceWaterhouseCoopers, building *guanxi* with local and provincial governments was ranked as the second greatest legal challenge faced by multinationals operating in China. Similarly, in our survey of New Zealand businesses, *guanxi* also appeared to be an important challenge (see Figure 3).

"[. . .] building *guanxi* with local and provincial governments was ranked as the second greatest legal challenge faced by multinationals operating in China."

Even after a quarter century of reforms, the role, authority and influence of government and government officials continue to play an important role in China. Gordon and Li (1991) state that as a result of economic reforms, the decentralization of decision-making has moved to the

level of the local or provincial government. Their role is not expected to diminish either as most developing countries that have long adhered to market economy principles continue to place senior government officials on a pedestal. Media reports of ministers and mayors opening business premises, cutting ribbons, digging the first dirt and other photo opportunities are common in many developing Asian economies. In a study on Singaporean investments in China, Yeung (2000) states that it is imperative for foreign firms to collaborate with local officials and party cadres to facilitate business operations.

Thus, SIFs in China, in particular, need to take heed of the governmental relationships in business. A company like GM or Toyota might have a direct route into the mayor's office of a Chinese city, but this may not be the case for small multinationals. *Guanxi* is helpful, but for new multinationals the right *guanxi* may not be forthcoming. It is in this context that the assistance of home governments is useful.

What type of assistance are New Zealand businesses expecting from their home government? Our headquarters survey reveals that respondents are primarily looking for information assistance regarding the workings of business in China. Among the list of options provided, they ranked advice on legal matters and information on local business partners at the top of their priority list. Within the context of our study, the role of the New Zealand government in providing such information becomes imperative if it seeks to strengthen the economic relationship with China. Similarly, informal discussion with experienced people in China-related affairs is also considered important. The list of assistance, as shown in Figure 4, clearly shows the need for general information. More specific information like accounting and M&A advice seems less important.

Discussants in our focus groups were more pragmatic. They wanted physical government presence in China. For example, a discussant in Shanghai explained:

[. . .] for small businesses in China, if the government officials could assist you to meet the Vice Mayor or other officials, it helps. In my case, our

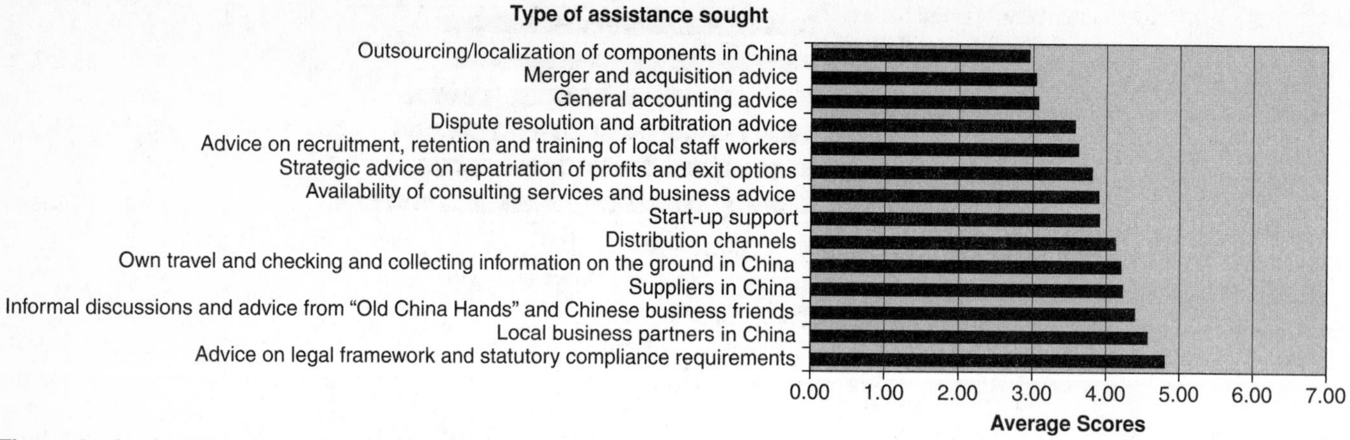

Type of assistance sought

Figure 4   Assistance sought by New Zealand businesses.

single biggest problem is getting natural gas connected to the houses we're building. I really need to get this done [. . .] If someone like the Trade Commissioner invites me for lunch and I get to sit next to the head of the Gas Bureau, well [. . .]

In home countries, access to senior government officials like ministers, ambassadors or trade officials can be easier in smaller countries like New Zealand. In China, the level of protocol and bureaucracy may hinder the contact between the SIF and government officials. However, apart from size, the position of government officials of home countries is equivalent to those of the host country. For instance, the mayor of Ashburton (population: 15,800) might have a better chance of meeting the mayor of Xiamen (population: 1.24 million) than a senior executive based in China. Thus senior officials of embassies in Beijing, Shanghai and Guangzhou have a critical role to play as facilitators of business in China. It is well worth the investment for governments to allocate more resources to these embassies if they wish to see more businesses engaging China.

Inter-governmental *guanxi* is important, but relying on this alone may be unwise. SIFs need to build their own *guanxi* for sustainable success in China. These firms might have overlooked an important resource in their own home country to develop *guanxi*—the thousands of Chinese tourists and students who visit every year. As overseas education and travel is still a luxury good, those who can afford such travels are likely to be "someone" in China, or know someone in China's business or political hierarchy. In New Zealand, for example, 56.8 percent of foreign students for the academic year 2003/2004 were from China. There were also more than 84,000 tourists from China who visited New Zealand in the year ending March 2005.

Chinese students, in particular are excellent resources as they can help businesses by sharing the *guanxi* that

they and their family might have. Additionally, these foreign-trained students can also make up the managerial talent that China lacks.

As explained earlier, the image of the country serves as a comparative advantage for small multinationals and it is beneficial for policy makers to provide the right impression to Chinese tourists who visit. While the physical environment of New Zealand speaks for itself, the human touch exemplified through good manners, due diligence, patience and goodwill—virtues important in the Chinese culture—can be instrumental in building the foundations needed to support the complex web of relationships required to be successful in China.

SIFs from smaller economies can also enhance their political and economic clout by promoting relationships with selected cities in China. We find, for example, that "well-managed sister-city relationships can play an important role in international trade and investment, which in turn can provide the development of cultural and social ties with a lasting economically viable foundation".

Finally, another approach for developing *guanxi* is to promote what we refer to as the "reverse Colombo Plan". The well-known Colombo Plan was initiated by the developed countries of the British Commonwealth in 1950 with a view to highlight the needs and requirement of the poorer members of the organization. The primary purpose of the plan was to develop human resources in the region. The plan's most successful activity was the aid given to bright young scholars of developing countries to pursue their studies in institutions of higher learning in the more developed nations like the UK, Australia and New Zealand. The reverse Colombo Plan refers to the idea of sending open-minded young executives to China with the intention of studying in some of the good universities there. China boasts several universities with international reputations, including Beijing University and Fudan University. These universities have joint programs with top business schools from the USA and Europe. Living in China for a period of one-to-two years, learning in China with equally bright Chinese scholars, familiarizing themselves with the culture and language all contribute to both the understanding and appreciating the Chinese culture as well as developing *guanxi* among future business leaders of China. While this may be a long-term strategy, such is the nature of *guanxi* and the learning of culture. Given the opportunities in China, such long-term investments may provide the SIFs with the competitive edge to succeed in China.

Conclusion

China's economic growth continues to mesmerize international firms the world over. Unabated GDP growth has surpassed 9 percent for nine consecutive quarters since the end of 2003. In the first three quarters of 2005, exports grew 31.3 percent despite a revaluation of the *renminbi*. No doubt, an increasingly affluent market and a perceived abundance of natural and human resources continue to attract firms into China. Today, no firm can truly claim to be international if it does not have some form of Chinese connection. We do not aver that China is a bed of roses. Even after 27 years of economic reforms, a weak rule of law and corruption continue to be major issues, as attested by Ahlstrom *et al.* (2002). Perhaps it is due to, rather than despite of, poor governance in China that direct investment is more popular than other forms of investment, e.g. portfolio investment. Li in 2005, explained that direct engagement with China is necessary although it seems more "time consuming, complicated and illiquid, thus exposing investors to greater risks" (Li, 2005).

Unabated GDP growth has surpassed 9 percent for nine consecutive quarters since the end of 2003.

The purpose of this paper is to equip managers with several strategic mindsets that would strengthen their respective core competency. Our main focus is on SIFs, multinationals that are small by global standards with limited access to resources and core competencies, particularly those originating from small countries. We believe that these firms need to have strategies that may be different from their larger counterparts, due to their size, capabilities and core competencies.

Our findings, based on both the questionnaires and the focus group discussions, reveal three inter-related dimensions that characterize successful SIFs. These dimensions are visualized in Figure 5. At the heart of success—and

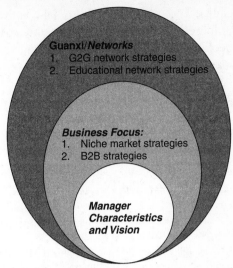

Figure 5   Key dimensions of success.

also of failure—of SIFs in China lies a human factor embedded in the respective business leader, regardless of whether this leader is on the ground in China or primarily located overseas. More specifically, the core competency of the management of an SIF lies with the interpersonal relational skills, the personality and the vision of the leader(s). The second dimension for success relates to the operational strategies of the business in terms of its market focus. Faced with such a large and complicated market, the chances of an SIF being engulfed by the market are high. This is particularly true if an SIF undertakes marketing strategies akin to those of larger multinationals. We find that focusing on niche markets through a B2B approach increases the rate of success. Finally, the third dimension refers to the environment in which the SIF, or for that matter all business in China, operates. Particularly for a small firm, the web of connections or *guanxi*, determines its survival in China. Our findings highlight two approaches towards building *guanxi*, namely by capitalizing on home government networks as well as through Chinese students studying abroad. The latter approach can be considered a specific factor that creates the equivalent of an overseas-Chinese network.

We find that focusing on niche markets through a B2B approach increases the rate of success.

China will continue to attract foreign firms both large and small and it is unlikely that the opening of markets will be scaled back. The mindsets and strategic moves proposed in our study are relevant for any company entering China. The point we wish to make is that these strategic mindsets are particularly crucial for SIFs as they can decrease the risks in the China engagement and increase success rates.

References

Ahlstrom, D., Young, M. N. and Nair, A. (2002), "Deceptive managerial practices in China: strategies for foreign firms", *Business Horizons*, November-December, pp. 49–59.

Bell, R. and Zacharilla, L. (2003), *B2B without the BS: The Business to Business Sales and Marketing Manual*, Alan Anthony, New York, NY.

Chen, Y. and Penhirin, J. (2004), "Marketing to China's consumers", *McKinsey Quarterly*, April 11, special issue.

Craig, C. S. and Douglas, C. P. (1997), "Managing the transnational value chain—strategies for firms from emerging markets", *Journal of International Marketing*, Vol. 5 No. 3, pp. 71–84.

Dalgic, T. and Leeuw, M. (1994), "Niche marketing revisited: concept, applications and some European cases", *European Journal of Marketing*, Vol. 28 No. 4, pp. 39–55.

Fan, Y. (2002), "Questioning *guanxi:* definition, classification and implications", *International Business Review*, Vol. 11 No. 5, pp. 543–61.

Gordon, R. H. and Li, W. (1991), "Chinese enterprise behavior under the reform", *American Economic Review*, Vol. 81 No. 2, pp. 202–6.

Kedia, B. L. and Mukherji, A. (1999), "Global managers: developing a mindset for global competitiveness", *Journal of World Business*, Vol. 34 No. 3, pp. 230–51.

Li, J. and Guisinger, S. (1992), "The globalisation of service multinationals in the triad regions: Japan, Western Europe, and North America", *Journal of International Business Studies*, Vol. 23 No. 4, pp. 675–96.

Li, S. (2005), "Why a poor governance environment does not deter foreign direct investment: the case of China and its implications for investment protection", *Business Horizons*, Vol. 48 No. 4, pp. 297–302.

Mechem, R. M. (2004), "Strategies for investing in China", *The China Business Review*, September-October.

National Bureau of Statistics of China (2004), *China Statistical Yearbook, 2004*, China Statistics Press, Beijing.

Prahalad, C. K. and Hamel, G. (1990), "The core competence of the corporation",*Harvard Business Review*, May-June, pp. 79–91.

PriceWaterhouseCoopers (2004), *Doing Business in China*, PriceWaterhouseCoopers, Hong Kong.

Rhinesmith, S. H. (1993), *A Manager's Guide to Globalization: Six Keys to Success in a Changing World*, Irwin, New York, NY.

Sheth, J. and Sisodia, R. (2002), *The Rule of Three: Surviving and Thriving in Competitive Markets*, Free Press, New York, NY.

Studwell, J. (2003),*The China Dream: The Quest for the Last Great Untapped Market on Earth*, Grove Press, New York, NY.

US-China Business Council (n.d.), "Foreign direct investment in China", available at: www.uschina.org/statistics/fdi_cumulative.html

Woetzel, J. R. (2004), "A guide to doing business in China", *McKinsey Quarterly*, April 11, special issue.

Wong, Y. Y. and Maher, T. E. (1997), "New key success factors for China's growing market", *Business Horizons*, Vol. 40 No. 3, pp. 43–52.

Yeung, H. W. (2000), "Local politics and foreign ventures in China's transitional economy: the political economy of Singaporean investment in China", *Political Geography*, Vol. 19, pp. 808–40.

Zeng, M. and Williamson, P. J. (2003), "The hidden dragons", *Harvard Business Review*, Vol. 81 No. 10, pp. 104–12.

Further Reading

International Trade Forum (2001), "A new generation of LDC exporters emerges", No. 1, Brussels.

Ramasamy, B. and Cremer, R. D. (1998), "Cities, commerce and culture: the economic role of international sister city relationships", *Journal of the Asia Pacific Economy*, Vol. 3 No. 3, pp. 446–61.

Rolf D. Cremer is Dean of the China Europe International Business School and Professor of Economics. He works and lives in China. His research focuses on foreign direct investment, international trade and international business strategies involving China.

Bala Ramasamy is Professor of Economics at the China Europe International Business School. His research focuses on foreign direct investment, international trade and international business strategies involving China. Bala Ramasamy is the corresponding author and can be contacted at: bramasamy@ceibs.edu

ROLF D. CREMER is Dean and Professor of Economics and **BALA RAMASAMY** is Professor of Economics, both at the China Europe International Business School, Shanghai, China.

From *Journal of Business Strategy*, vol. 30, no. 6, 2009, pp. 15–26. Copyright © 2009 by Emerald Group Publishing Ltd. All rights reserved. Reprinted by permission via Rightslink.

Planning Ahead for IFRS 1
Initial Adoption of IFRS by U.S. Companies

Joseph M. Langmead and Jalal Soroosh

On November 14, 2008, the SEC issued its proposed road map addressing when and under what circumstances U.S. public companies might be permitted or required to adopt International Financial Reporting Standards (IFRS) when preparing their financial statements with the SEC. The road map does not include a fixed IFRS adoption date as such. Rather, it states that adoption of IFRS will be considered in 2011 in light of stated conditions at that time. It also provides an option for early adoption by a defined set of companies. While the adoption of IFRS by U.S. public companies likely will, if it comes to pass, occur over several years, the opportunity for some public companies may arrive soon. For all others, the time for planning such a transition is now.

The differences and similarities between IFRS and U.S. GAAP have been covered extensively. (For example, see "International Financial Reporting Standards: The Road Ahead," by Joseph M. Langmead and Jalal Soroosh, *The CPA Journal,* March 2009; "Dual Reporting Under U.S. GAAP and IFRS," by Francesco Bellandi, *The CPA Journal,* December 2007; and "Shaking Up Financial Statement Presentation," by Guy McClain and Andrew J. McLelland, *Journal of Accountancy,* November 2008.) The discussion below will instead explore several of the important technical and practical considerations for a U.S. public company adopting IFRS for the first time. The focus is on the issues deriving from applicable accounting standards regarding initial adoption.

Emergence of IFRS for U.S. Companies

IFRS is a comprehensive set of accounting standards promulgated by the International Accounting Standards Board (IASB). In December 2007, in a step which surprised many, the SEC eliminated the requirement for many foreign company filers using IFRS to provide supplemental information on a U.S. GAAP basis. One important reason behind the SEC's proposed road map is that IFRS has become the de facto international accounting language, used (or scheduled to be used) in more than 100 countries. Because comparability between companies is highly valued by both investors and the SEC, and because

U.S. GAAP has not achieved similar acceptance around the world, the SEC sees IFRS as the logical next step. The momentum in this direction has been assisted by the convergence efforts undertaken by the FASB and the IASB over the past several years. The two standards setters have been working from a common agenda to eliminate as many differences as possible between them over time. The SEC, however, appears to consider the matter more urgent than the gradual convergence process would allow. The many current differences between the two sets of standards are a significant consideration when a U.S. company adopts IFRS initially.

Much progress has been made to reduce the differences between U.S. GAAP and IFRS, and several major remaining ones are on track for convergence in the near term. Nevertheless, a reasonably large company approaching the switch to IFRS might identify 10 or more such differences which are material and which may require important changes to its information systems as well as to compensation arrangements, debt covenants, income tax decisions, and a variety of other aspects of its business. All of these dimensions are important and require substantial lead time in a transition to IFRS, usually within an overall project management framework.

The technical and practical accounting considerations associated with the initial adoption of IFRS can, by themselves, influence the timing and timetable of a conversion, especially in a period where adoption is optional and the timing is flexible, as may be the case for a number of public companies (the SEC estimates 110) as soon as the road map is adopted. Even in the later phase of implementation, where the timing will depend upon the size of the company (2014 for the largest public companies; 2016 for the smallest), these adoption-related accounting considerations can influence how early one should start making important measurements. In some cases, analysis may indicate that some action should be taken as early as this year.

Accounting and Reporting Framework for Initial Adoption

IFRS 1, *First-time Adoption of International Financial Reporting Standards,* was issued by the IASB in 2003 and has since been amended (most recently on July 23, 2009). It establishes

Exhibit 1
Identifying Operative Dates

Example A:

Company A is a calendar-year U.S. company and is required by the SEC to adopt IFRS in 2014.

First reporting date: December 31, 2014
Transition date: January 1, 2012

Required financial statements: As of and for each of the years in the three-year period ending December 31, 2014, plus balance sheet at January 1, 2012

Basis of accounting: IFRS as in effect at December 31, 2014, applied as though in effect consistently for all periods, including before 2012 (subject to exceptions discussed).

Example B:

Company B is a U.S. company with a June 30 year-end and is permitted by the SEC to adopt IFRS as early as 2010 and elects to do so beginning July 1, 2010.

First reporting date: June 30, 2011
Transition date: July 1, 2008

Required financial statements: As of and for each of the years in the three-year period ending June 30, 2011, plus balance sheet at July 1, 2008

Basis of accounting: IFRS as in effect at June 30, 2011, applied as though in effect consistently for all periods, including before July 2008 (subject to exceptions).

the provisions that govern companies when adopting IFRS. The standard provides a number of practical provisions to ease the burden of such a transition and contains exceptions to what might otherwise be the full retroactive application of IFRS.

There are two related considerations in any adoption of a new accounting model:

- Identifying the operative effective date of the change, and
- Implementing any retroactive ("retrospective" in IFRS 1) features required by the change (including how many prior periods are to be presented).

IFRS 1 provides that a first reporting date be established at the end of the period in which IFRS is adopted. It then defines a transition date as the beginning of the earliest period whose financial statement information is required for comparative purposes in the year of adoption. It prescribes that opening balance sheet measurements under IFRS be made at the transition date and that IFRS be consistently applied from then to the first reporting date based on IFRS standards in effect at the first reporting date, even though standards may have changed between those dates. The period between those dates is generally two years under IFRS 1, and the SEC accepted this two-year standard when many European companies first adopted IFRS in 2005. But for U.S. companies, based on the proposed road map, the SEC will likely require three years and further clarify that adoption must take place only as of the end of a fiscal year.

Thus "period" in IFRS 1 means "year" and the transition date is the beginning of the three-year period ending with the first reporting date (which is the year-end date as of which IFRS is first adopted). This three-year period must reflect a consistent application of IFRS, as if the standards in effect at the end of the current fiscal year were in effect throughout the period.

Similarly, subject to defined exceptions discussed below, the three-year period begins its measurements with an opening balance sheet (statement of financial position) composed of assets and liabilities measured in conformity with IFRS in effect at the end of the three-year period. This consistency provision applies for new adopters, even though individual IFRS standards may

have become effective between the transition date and the first reporting date, and even though some IFRS standards include special transitional guidance which might depart from full retroactivity. A further element of this framework is that the financial statement form and classification requirements of IFRS be in full effect for all periods on the basis of IFRS requirements at the first reporting date. *Exhibit 1* provides examples capturing these key provisions.

Given this framework, a host of implementation issues arise. The opening balance sheet requirement in particular reinforces the basic challenge that differences between IFRS and U.S. GAAP that remain unconverged at the end of the year of adoption must be measured and adjusted consistently not only for all three years presented but for all transactions and events in earlier years which have residual effects on the opening balance sheet. Such a challenge can be formidable for many companies, and IFRS 1 contains two strategies for reducing the magnitude of the challenge. The first is noted above: IFRS 1 removes the problem that IFRS itself has been changing over time by identifying a single date (the first reporting date) as of which IFRS standards are identified and applied to all earlier transactions and events. Note that this does not alter the fact that U.S. GAAP has also been changing over time.

The second strategy IFRS 1 employs is to make exceptions to full retroactivity for more complex categories of transactions. These exceptions, particularly the optional ones, are integrated into IFRS 1 in recognition that any conversion or adoption to a new basis of accounting presents practical challenges when applying new standards retroactively. By reviewing these exceptions from the standpoint of a U.S. company, one can address the more significant accounting challenges inherent in first-time adoption.

Exceptions to Full Retroactivity

Implicit in the three-year retroactive requirement is that all transactions preceding this period must also be remeasured using those standards, at least to the extent of the residual effects of those earlier transactions on the transition date

Exhibit 2
Business Combination Examples

Example A:

Company A is a calendar-year U.S. company and is required by the SEC to adopt IFRS in 2014. It consummated a major business combination on May 15, 2005 and plans to restate its accounting for that combination consistent with IFRS.

First reporting date: December 31, 2014

Transition date: January 1, 2012

Required financial statements: As of and for each of the years in the three-year period ending December 31, 2014, plus the balance sheet at January 1, 2012.

Basis of accounting: IFRS as in effect at December 31, 2014, applied as though in effect consistently for all periods, including before 2012 (subject to exceptions discussed)

Accounting for business combinations: All business combinations consummated after May 14, 2005, must be restated using IFRS in effect at December 31, 2014 (with the effects of the restatements reflected in the January 1, 2012, balance sheet for combinations consummated between May 15, 2005, and December 31, 2011).

Example B:

Company B is a U.S. company with a June 30 year-end and is permitted by the SEC to adopt IFRS as early as 2010 and elects to do so beginning July 1, 2010. It has consummated a number of business combinations over the years but does not wish to restate any more of them than are required.

First reporting date: June 30, 2011

Transition date: July 1, 2008

Required financial statements: As of and for each of the years in the three-year period ending June 30, 2011 plus balance sheet at July 1, 2008

Basis of accounting: IFRS as in effect at June 30, 2011, applied as though in effect consistently for all periods, including pre-July 2008 (subject to exceptions discussed).

Accounting for business combinations: All business combinations consummated after June 30, 2008, must be restated using IFRS in effect at June 30, 2011.

---

balance sheet. The challenge of having many current differences between U.S. GAAP and IFRS is increased when considering that U.S. GAAP and IFRS were even less converged in earlier years than at present. In an effort to make the transition to IFRS less onerous, the IASB included additional provisions in IFRS 1 to reduce the practical burdens of retroactive application. These include both optional and mandatory exceptions to the general principle that the opening transition date balance sheet should reflect all standards in effect at the first reporting date. Each of these exceptions represents a potentially important element in a U.S. company's strategy regarding when and how to adopt IFRS initially.

Optional Exceptions

In the interests of practicality, IFRS 1 specifies 15 available, but not required, exceptions (exemptions) from the general principle that the transition date opening balance sheet should reflect the same accounting principles as those employed throughout the initial three-year period ending with the first reporting date. Some are less relevant to U.S. companies than others and are discussed and summarized below. Users should read IFRS 1 completely for further details and possible exceptions.

Business Combinations

Business combinations are potentially the most onerous and complex accounting category involved in any retroactive application. IFRS 1 provides no exception to the requirement that all periods presented (probably three years for U.S. companies) should reflect consistent application of IFRS in effect at the end of the period. That requirement thus includes all business combinations consummated within that three-year period. IFRS provides

an exception, however, for business combinations consummated before that period despite the further requirement that the transition date (opening) balance sheet be similarly prepared on the basis of IFRS applied during the three-year period through the first reporting date. To put the basis for this exception in fuller perspective, note that, while both U.S. GAAP and IFRS now require the use of purchase accounting, both systems allowed for pooling-of-interests accounting (uniting of interests in IFRS) in (differing) defined circumstances in earlier periods, and, in any case, the application of purchase accounting was different in the two systems. Even now, this area is not fully converged.

IFRS 1 permits the initial adoption of IFRS without revising or restating business combinations which occurred prior to the transition date, even if some or all were accounted for using the pooling-of-interests method. It also permits the revision or restatement of some or all earlier combinations, but once any such earlier combination is identified for revision to conform to current IFRS standards, all combinations after that date must be similarly revised.

Exhibit 2 expands upon the previous examples and addresses the business combinations exemption. In considering this option, the focus is on the effects on assets and liabilities in the transition date balance sheet. Thus, accounting differences from earlier business combinations whose effects on that balance sheet are no longer significant are not relevant. Another implication of the focus on the transition date balance sheet is the IFRS 1 requirement that, even after an election not to revise the accounting for earlier business combinations, the transition date balance sheet must generally reflect all assets and liabilities that are recognizable under current IFRS and exclude those that are not. The effect of this requirement is to reopen some aspects of earlier business combinations that the company

ANNUAL EDITIONS

would otherwise choose not to restate. For example, an earlier urestated business combination may have given rise to an asset or liability under U.S. GAAP (all or some of which remains at the transition date) that cannot be recognized under IFRS.

While this should become increasingly rare as convergence efforts progress, the recognition criteria for certain contingent and intangible assets and contingent liabilities differ under SFAS 141 and the corresponding IFRS standards (IFRS 3 and IAS 37). To the extent this situation arises, the opening transition balance sheet must reflect removal of the ineligible asset or liability with possible corresponding effects on the remaining goodwill related to the earlier acquisition. This is a rare case where goodwill might be affected in adjusting other assets or liabilities to their IFRS basis on the opening balance sheet. The more usual case is that opening balance sheet adjustments to conform to IFRS requirements are offset through retained earnings. Similarly, liabilities recognizable under IFRS must generally be reflected in the transition date balance sheet—even those liabilities which arose in earlier business combinations not reflected by the accounting at the time. These latter effects would also generally be reflected as cumulative adjustments to retained earnings as of the date of the transition balance sheet.

Goodwill arising from an earlier combination which is not otherwise revised or restated needs to be evaluated for impairment at the transition date pursuant to the IFRS standards (impairment testing and measurement continues to be different under IFRS) in effect at the first reporting date, and an impairment write-down may need to be reflected in the related transition balance sheet along with corresponding effects on retained earnings. A special provision of IFRS 1 requires that any earlier goodwill that has been written down or written off prior to the transition date under U.S. GAAP may not be reinstated as part of the transition to IFRS, regardless of the conditions at the date of the transition.

Related to business combinations is the issue of where a new basis of accounting was warranted under U.S. GAAP (changes in control and similar uses of push-down accounting before the transition date). These and other narrow applications are beyond the scope of this article; a thorough reading of IFRS standards is warranted in any actual conversion situation.

Besides earlier business combinations, a number of other specialized areas enjoy optional special treatment in IFRS 1 to mitigate the burden of full retroactive restatement as of the transition date balance sheet. The more relevant issues are discussed below.

Property, Plant, and Equipment and Certain Other Noncurrent Assets

The second exemption identified in IFRS 1 can sometimes be the next most useful. IFRS (irrespective of new adopters) has long provided the option for an entity to revalue its property, plant, and equipment and certain other noncurrent assets, including certain intangibles, at fair value and then calculate future depreciation based on that new basis. Periodic subsequent valuations are required to maintain such assets at approximate fair value. Alternatively, IFRS permits the historical cost basis and a variety of depreciation methods similar to the requirements of U.S. GAAP. An important difference in the historical cost alternative is that IFRS places more emphasis on unbundling components

of an asset (e.g., a building) that have substantially differing useful lives (e.g., the heating system or the roof) for the calculation of depreciation. IFRS 1 allows companies adopting IFRS for the first time to elect to use fair value amounts for these assets based on fair values as of the opening balance sheet date or an earlier date if a similar valuation exercise had been performed earlier for other purposes. If an earlier date is chosen, related accumulated depreciation through the transition date should also be reflected in the transition balance sheet in accordance with IFRS (including adequate consideration of the componentization requirement). The effects of restating these asset amounts should also be reflected in retained earnings at the transition date, even if some of the assets were acquired in an earlier un-restated business combination. Thus, a U.S. company may wish to exercise the fair value option for these assets both because of its effect on the balance sheet and because it supersedes the need to retroactively align historical cost depreciation to the more demanding IFRS requirements regarding componentization.

Defined Benefit Pension Plans

Defined benefit pension plans are generally accounted for similarly under U.S. GAAP and IFRS, but the detailed actuarial options and calculations can be different in several cases. A potentially significant example concerns actuarial gains and losses not recognized immediately. The deferral and amortization approach to actuarial gains and losses (pursuant to a so-called corridor approach) can result in different amortized and unamortized amounts under IFRS. Retroactive restatement to include the cumulative effects of such differences on the transition opening balance sheet (and subsequent periods) can be onerous and expensive. IFRS 1 permits initial adopters of IFRS the option of considering all unamortized actuarial gains and losses as having been realized as of the transition date as long as this option is applied to all such plans. A company and its actuaries can then apply a deferral and amortization strategy for new actuarial gains and losses in line with IFRS methodology.

Foreign Currency Translation Adjustment

The cumulative foreign currency translation adjustment related to foreign operations and activities (a separate component of equity) may be eliminated at the transition date as long as it is eliminated for all such operations and activities (reset to zero). All subsequent translation adjustments are measured and accounted for in line with IFRS thereafter, including each of the years in the three-year period immediately prior to the first reporting date. This is a useful option when other cumulative IFRS adjustments made at the transition date have effects on foreign assets and liabilities that are difficult to measure or where the detailed application of IFRS to foreign currency translation before the transition date would have differed from U.S. GAAP.

Compound Financial Instruments

IFRS (IAS 32) requires that financial instruments that have both debt and equity features (e.g., convertible debt) be accounted for in two separate parts, with the amount allocated to equity persisting even if the instrument is not converted and the debt is fully paid off. IFRS 1 allows this provision to be ignored for all such cases where the debt has been fully paid off as of the transition date. Thereafter, the IFRS bifurcation requirement applies, including during the three-year period immediately prior to the first reporting date.

Certain Affiliates

The effects of adopting IFRS at the transition date can be different if a subsidiary or other specified affiliate has adopted IFRS earlier. Similarly, if a U.S. company adopting IFRS is a subsidiary or specified affiliate of a parent who has already adopted IFRS, certain other options apply.

Certain Financial Assets and Liabilities

U.S. GAAP and IFRS require that certain defined financial assets be classified as available for sale (subject to mark-to-market accounting through other comprehensive income, a separate component of shareholders' equity) or trading (subject to mark-to-market accounting through the income statement). Certain financial liabilities can similarly be designated as subject to mark-to-market accounting through the income statement. IFRS 1 allows a one-time opportunity, as of the transition date, to redesignate assets as available for sale and assets and liabilities as subject to mark-to-market accounting through the income statement, irrespective of their earlier designations under U.S. GAAP, subject to specific conditions. Because these IFRS classifications are virtually identical to those under U.S. GAAP, it would likely be difficult to justify the use of this option except for items not previously marked-to-market under U.S. GAAP.

Certain Share-Based Compensation

SFAS 123(R), *Share-based Payments,* requires a fair value accounting approach for share-based compensation awards that is generally similar to IFRS 2. One would thus expect IFRS to require restatement for any awards prior to the 2005 effective date of SFAS 123(R), but IFRS 1 provides an optional exception to the restatement requirement for any awards that have been fully vested prior to the transition date.

In all these cases, and for other optional exceptions not discussed here (due to their limited relevance and in light of recent convergence efforts), a thorough reading of IFRS standards is warranted in any actual conversion situation. Electing any one of these optional elections does not require electing any of the others.

Mandatory Exceptions

IFRS 1 recognizes that certain kinds of retroactive or retrospective changes made along with a change from one accounting model to another can have negative effects and rob such a transition of important credibility and objectivity. IFRS 1 thus specifies a set of core accounting judgments that should not be revisited as part of an initial retroactive adoption of IFRS. In broad terms, these include the more typical instances where estimates and judgments are required by management, such

as credit loss allowances, warranty obligations, and other contingent liability exposures. In these cases, a company adopting IFRS is prohibited from employing any information which became available subsequent to the original estimates as long as management employed all of the relevant information available at the time of the original estimate. Recordable amounts for contingent liabilities can sometimes be different under IFRS due to different methodologies and thresholds. Such differences must still be applied retroactively but only by employing information available at the time of the original estimates.

In a similar vein, both IFRS and U.S. GAAP contain documentation and designation requirements to support various forms of hedge accounting. These are generally applicable at the initiation of a hedge, making the use of hindsight problematic. Thus, IFRS 1 generally prohibits any retroactive designations. Only designations documented as having been made on a timely basis at the initiation of a transaction can be employed in the retroactive application of IFRS. Since U.S. GAAP has reasonably stringent requirements regarding timely designation, the effect of this prohibition simply precludes the use of hindsight to achieve hedge accounting where it was not already applicable under U.S. GAAP.

Prospective Changes in IFRS at the First Reporting Date

As a result of convergence efforts, both U.S. GAAP and IFRS now provide that changes in accounting principle, particularly those required by a new accounting standard, be implemented retroactively for all periods presented. Formerly, U.S. GAAP usually required a one-time cumulative catch-up adjustment in the year of change without restatement of earlier periods. Like U.S. GAAP, when a new IFRS standard is finalized, its effective date may be in the future but an option for earlier adoption is often available and encouraged. Companies adopting IFRS should consider early adoption if it is advantageous. The attractions may include not only the actual accounting effects of the new standards, but also the avoidance of future restatements. IFRS 1 allows for such early adoption of newer standards in connection with initial adoption as long as the newer standards are applied consistently across all periods presented, as well as in the transition date balance sheet. If more than one newer standard is available for early adoption at the first reporting date, a decision to adopt one early does not trigger the early adoption of others. These considerations alone can influence the selection of a first reporting date for companies where IFRS adoption is optional.

Required Disclosures in Initial Adoption

As noted above, IFRS 1 requires the measurement of a transition date opening balance sheet (opening IFRS statement of financial position) to capture the full cumulative retroactive effects of the application of IFRS up to the beginning (transition date) of the comparative periods (three years) required to be presented in (the year of adoption (the end of which is the first reporting date). The plain language of IFRS 1 seems to require the actual presentation of this opening balance sheet in the year of adoption. Even if this awkward requirement were to be waived by the SEC for U.S. companies, such a balance sheet, at least in summarized form, may be useful in the notes to meet the disclosure requirements of IFRS 1 regarding the various financial statement effects of the conversion to IFRS and a related required reconciliation of total shareholders' equity at the transition date. IFRS 1 also requires reconciliation of key financial statement amounts (shareholders' equity and comprehensive income) from the preceding year's U.S. GAAP statements to the corresponding IFRS amounts.

The SEC's road map requires more elaborate U.S. GAAP disclosures, particularly for those companies that, under the proposal, may adopt IFRS earlier than 2014. A prudent approach would be to assume that U.S. GAAP information will need to be compiled alongside IFRS information through 2014.

Regarding disclosures in general, IFRS has its own set of required disclosures which can be more extensive in some areas than U.S. GAAP. A U.S. company considering its IFRS conversion strategy and timing should include this within its planning.

Preparing for Change

The discussion above has focused on the particular accounting and reporting implications at the time of the first adoption of IFRS and thus excludes discussion of the many other dimensions of such a significant change in a company's basis of accounting. Other relevant subjects include the remaining not-yet-converged differences between IFRS and U.S. GAAP and the substantial organizational impact, including the education and training implications, the importance of knowledgeable commitments from the board of directors and senior management, the changes to information systems and business processes, and the need for an effective overall project management structure. Perhaps just as important is the degree to which management will be challenged to use more judgment in applying accounting standards, because IFRS remains generally less rules-based and more principles-based than U.S. GAAP, an attribute that is lauded by some and criticized by others.

Most importantly, every U.S. public company should carefully consider the technical accounting implications of the initial adoption of IFRS, including the particular options available in IFRS 1, and, for those companies that may be eligible to adopt IFRS early, the considerations for selecting the year in which to adopt.

JOSEPH M. LANGMEAD, STD, MBA, CPA, is an executive in residence at the Sellinger School of Business and Management, Loyola University Maryland, Baltimore. **JALAL SOROOSH, PhD, CMA,** is a professor of accounting at the Sellinger School of Business and Management, Loyola University Maryland, Baltimore.

From *The CPA Journal* by Joseph M. Longmead and Jalal Soroosh, October 2009, pp. 24–29. Copyright © 2009 by The CPA Journal. Reprinted by permission of the New York State Society of Certified Public Accountants.

The Global Financial Crisis: What Went Wrong?

Management accountants are often asked what caused the crisis, but the complexity of the financial system makes the key reasons hard to pinpoint.

RICHARD MALLETT AND VICTOR SMART

The crisis began to surface in the spring of 2007 with rumblings about sub-prime loans, but the true starting point is seen as August 9, 2007, when investment bank BNP Paribas told investors that they would not be able to withdraw money from two of its funds. The reason: a "complete evaporation of liquidity" from the market.

The next milestone was the run on Northern Rock on September 14, 2007. Then, a year and a day later, came the spectacular collapse of Lehman Brothers after a weekend of desperate negotiations in September 2008.

This was the tipping point. The financial system went into meltdown as confidence and trust in the markets and among banks vanished. As Mervyn King, governor of the Bank of England, recently declared: "It is difficult to exaggerate the severity and importance of those events. Not since the beginning of World War I has our banking system been so close to collapse."

The real economy had already been damaged. Now, vast swathes of industry began to struggle and countries that had thought that they were immune learned that they were facing a savage downturn. The crisis had gone global. No one could accuse central banks and governments of failing to see the gravity of the situation. Their attempts to salvage the banking system and reduce the severity of the recession included measures that were unorthodox and that, only a few weeks earlier, would have been criticised as downright reckless.

> **"Failure stemmed from a chain of events, no one of which appeared to threaten stability, but which taken together led to the worst financial crisis that any of us can recall"**
>
> —Mervyn King, governor of the Bank of England

Few commentators predicted the crisis or how it would unfold. It resulted from the explosive interaction of many complex factors—which are summarised on the following two pages—and was exacerbated by the length of the preceding boom. As King explained, the "failure stemmed from a chain of events, no one of which alone appeared to threaten stability, but which taken together led to the worst financial crisis that any of us can recall".

The Major Causes
A More Complex, but Less Differentiated, Configuration of Players

- Distinctions among different types of players were blurred and the connections between them became more opaque.
- Opportunities were created for increasing leverage and shifting risk in opaque ways that were harder for markets and regulators to assess.
- There was significant growth in leverage among financial institutions. From the early nineties to 2007, total debt in the UK relative to GDP almost doubled. About two-thirds of this increase was accounted for by lending within the financial sector. Debt also expanded in the US and the eurozone.
- Maturity transformation (lending long but funding short) increased and took place through a wider range of institutions, often relying on liquidity through marketability (counting long-term assets as available to sell in a day). These were often structured investment vehicles and conduits that were not banks and so fell outside the banking rules.

Pro-Cyclical Capital Requirements and Accounting

- Risk can be pro-cyclical in both up-swings and down-swings. This is significant in terms of regulatory capital, but also possibly for remuneration and its influence on motivation (irrational exuberance).

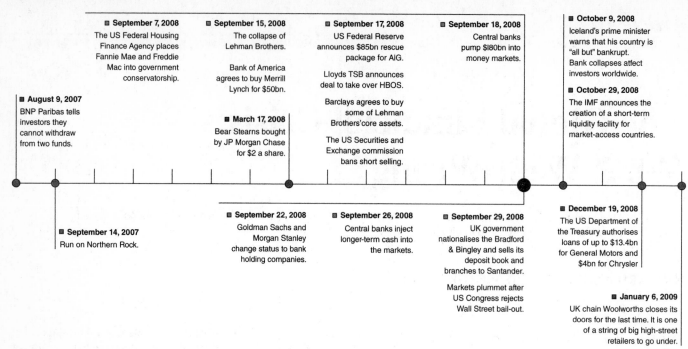

September 7, 2008
The US Federal Housing
Finance Agency places
Fannie Mae and Freddie
Mac into government
conservatorship.

September 15, 2008
The collapse of
Lehman Brothers.

Bank of America
agrees to buy Merrill
Lynch for $50bn.

September 17, 2008
US Federal Reserve
announces $85bn rescue
package for AIG.

Lloyds TSB announces
deal to take over HBOS.

Barclays agrees to buy
some of Lehman
Brothers'core assets.

The US Securities and
Exchange commission
bans short selling.

September 18, 2008
Central banks
pump $180bn into
money markets.

October 9, 2008
Iceland's prime minister
warns that his country is
"all but" bankrupt.
Bank collapses affect
investors worldwide.

October 29, 2008
The IMF announces the
creation of a short-term
liquidity facility for
market-access countries.

August 9, 2007
BNP Paribas tells
investors they
cannot withdraw
from two funds.

March 17, 2008
Bear Stearns bought
by JP Morgan Chase
for $2 a share.

September 14, 2007
Run on Northern Rock.

September 22, 2008
Goldman Sachs and
Morgan Stanley
change status to bank
holding companies.

September 26, 2008
Central banks inject
longer-term cash into
the markets.

September 29, 2008
UK government
nationalises the Bradford
& Bingley and sells its
deposit book and
branches to Santander.

Markets plummet after
US Congress rejects
Wall Street bail-out.

December 19, 2008
The US Department of
the Treasury authorises
loans of up to $13.4bn
for General Motors and
$4bn for Chrysler

January 6, 2009
UK chain Woolworths closes its
doors for the last time. It is one
of a string of big high-street
retailers to go under.

Credit crunch countdown: a chronology of key events

A General Failure to Price Risk Or "Stress Test" Adequately

- "Disaster myopia"—that is, the tendency to underestimate the probability of adverse outcomes—became more widespread.

- Data was biased towards the "golden" decade up to 2007, when outcomes were less variable than they had been historically.

- Externally, this increased problems and uncertainties with networks. For example, fewer people knew their counterparty's counterparties and there were assumptions about correlations, which at times of stress inevitably tend towards one.

- Incentives were misaligned and principal-agent issues arose. Risk managers and risk takers in financial institutions were influenced by the need to keep up with competitors, as well as a tendency to follow the herd.

- Problems arose between financial institutions and regulators when the former were implicitly guaranteed by governments as too important to fail.

Global Imbalances and Housing Bubbles

- Global macroeconomic imbalances arose. For example, while China, Japan and many oil-exporting countries built massive economic surpluses, the US, UK, Ireland and Spain ran large deficits. This resulted in artificially low real interest rates, which helped to drive rapid growth and fuelled asset price bubbles.

- Low and stable rates of inflation meant that nominal interest rates fell to historically low levels.

- Money was lent on easy terms—for example, "covlite" (weak covenant) loan agreements—to individuals and companies.

- Low interest rates led investors to search harder for returns, so increasing their appetite for risk.

- Government measures to encourage people to buy homes—for example, tax subsidies on interest payments and/or capital gains, the US Community Reinvestment Act and the establishment and growth of Freddie Mac and Fannie Mae—contributed to a housing bubble.

Excessive Market-Based, Backward-Looking Risk Management Methods Predicated on Historical Data

- Due diligence and the analysis of fundamentals were neglected.

- Market participants used similar models, which exacerbated systemic risk—that is, the likelihood that not only one organisation but an entire system or market could collapse.

- The fact that regulatory ratios were being met may have made directors less diligent.

Destabilising Incentives

- Shareholders and employees in financial institutions had incentives to increase returns by taking excessive long-term tail risks (the probability of an extreme event).

- Information asymmetries (where one participant knew more than another) were exploited to shift risks to the future or to less informed players in the market.

- The explosion of credit and credit derivatives was supported by, and drove, big increases in financial institutions' leverage.

A Disregard for Systemic Risk

- This disregard was shared by bankers, regulators, central banks, ministers and academics. Regulators focused on institutions while central banks focused on inflation targets.
- Financial institutions and managers had incentives to follow the herd to retain market share and achieve compensation based on relative performance. Many expected that losses from systemic risks would be "socialised" by the taxpayer and saw their organisations as being too big to fail.
- The Basel II system relied on an arbitrary risk-weighted approach to assets that led to regulatory arbitrage by banks to limit capital requirements.

Innovation and Structural Change

- The originate-to-distribute model (where a lender sells mortgages and other asset-based securities to a third party) increased the complexity and the use of wholesale funding.
- The level of aggregate risk-taking increased.
- Uncertainty increased about the distribution of risks among market participants.
- Increasingly complex financial products combined with a dramatic rise in the volume of credit derivatives enabled hedging and created synthetic credit exposure (where investment in products merely mimics the price movements of underlying financial products).

- The banks' use of special purpose vehicles (SPVs) relied on wholesale markets and so incurred maturity mismatches without an adequate consideration of the risk that wholesale funding—that is, funding directly from the market rather than from banks—could evaporate.
- Originating and arranging organisations lacked appropriate credit screening and monitoring incentives, while investors failed to question this sufficiently.
- Retail borrowers deceived themselves and others that they could service huge loans and were sometimes mis-sold products. Ethics and integrity declined along most of the origination-and-distribute supply chain.
- Credit ratings agencies had conflicts of interest and used limited historical data, flawed models and inadequate due diligence. Financial institutions then outsourced too much risk management to these agencies.
- Financial institutions disclosed too little of their on- and off-balance sheet risk exposures, particularly for structured products such as collateralised debt obligations.
- A lot of securitised credit ended up on the balance sheets (directly or through SPVs) of highly geared banks and bank-like institutions, rather than on those of end investors—that is, the banks performed both "acquire and arbitrage".
- Players believed that slicing and dicing risk made the overall financial system "more resilient" (International Monetary Fund, April 2006). With hindsight, we know that risk was becoming systemic.

RICHARD MALLETT, CIMA's technical director, and **VICTOR SMART,** head of corporate communications, offer their summary of the main factors.

UNIT 3

International Organizations and Operations

Unit Selections

Key Points to Consider

- What do you think the opportunities are for companies in the global environment? Do you think that they are only available for large multinationals or do you think that small companies can be involved also?

- Do multinational firms only come from the developed world or do they also come from the developing world?

- When most people think about marketing in international business, they tend to think about marketing in the developed world. What about opportunities in the developing world? Can companies from the developing world produce world-class products for the luxury market?

- Human resources becomes very complicated in a global environment. How would you handle training for cultural differences that might involve what could be considered illegal activities in the United States or another country?

- Off-shoring is becoming more common as jobs leave the developed world for more cost-effective venues. How would you respond to this problem of jobs going off-shore?

- Investment in the United States by off-shore corporations is becoming more common. The purchase of American companies by non-U.S. firms means that the U.S. operations are now under the control of non-U.S. executives who may not be familiar with domestic laws and customs. How would you get them from becoming the "Ugly Foreigner?"

- Global operations management is the way that companies become more efficient and more competitive in the marketplace. What ways can you think of to improve efficiency? How do you think you could increase profits? What are some strategies?

Student Website
www.mhhe.com/cls

International organizations come in all shapes and sizes from the large multinational corporation to the import/exporter who is doing business on a shoestring. While most people tend to focus on the larger companies, the small firm should not be overlooked. Well over half of the exports from the United States come from small businesses, not from multinational corporations. There are opportunities for these small companies in international trade and the U.S. government is willing to help as seen in "The Work Left Undone: Perspectives on Small Business Opportunities in International Trade."

When people think of large organizations, they tend to think of firms that are rooted in the developed countries. But, while that may have been the case 40 or 50 years ago, that is no longer the case today. Large companies can also be found with their roots in the developing world. Many of them are multinational in scope while some of them are in markets that are so large that their international ventures have been very limited.

Global corporate strategy is a key to the success of global organizations, especially in an era of extreme economic uncertainty. Each company must develop a strategic plan that is unique to its particular strengths, weaknesses, opportunities and the threats that their market and industry present. This applies to consumer goods, industrial goods, services, indeed, to all of the types of businesses in the global marketplace. Multinational companies from developing countries can aspire to being the leading company in a particular business as Vale is doing as "Brazil's Iron Giant Reaches for the Top." Tata Industries of India has pursued a strategy of growth that involves the purchase of divisions of other corporations that seem to be troubled and turning them around. While most organizations that use this approach to grow their business often engage in a kind of "slash and burn" strategy for the newly acquired division, Tata leaves most of the management and workers intact and tries to develop the newly acquired business into a profitable unit using people who know the business best. Tata has become known as the "Master of the Gentle Approach." Companies from developed countries can also have a global strategy, even if they are small and essentially entrepreneurial in nature. In "NanoTech Firm Takes Passage to India," there is an excellent example of an essentially entrepreneurial, high-tech organization taking its manufacturing, testing, and marketing to the developing world before taking it to the developed world; going global before going domestic. An interesting and possibly growing trend.

An axiom of international business is to "think global, but act local," But now, that is being challenged. There are really few global brands that this can be applied to. Thinking global may be an ideal situation, but the fact is that most markets are local. For a brand to be successful, it must be a part of the local culture and few brands have been successful in achieving that status on a world-wide basis. Opportunities for achieving global brand status may lie at the base of the economic pyramid. There are four billion people who live on US$ 2.00 a day or less. This represents about half or so of the world's population. These people have needs for consumer goods just like everyone else and they live in countries where the price purchase parity makes that US$ 2.00 a day go much further than in the developed world.

© Manchan/Getty Images RF

For example, a potato in the United States may cost twenty-five cents, but in a place where the average daily income is US$2.00 a day that same potato may only cost five cents. "Expanding Opportunity at the Base of the Pyramid," may be a way for companies to truly think local and establish themselves as global brands.

Chinese companies face a particular problem when trying to market their goods outside the Middle Kingdom. Chinese products often have the reputation of being of lesser quality than goods produced elsewhere. This is because they generally cost less to produce and there have been some unfortunate incidents involving the safety and quality of goods manufactured in China. However, this does not apply to all of the goods produced in China. Hailun Piano is producing quality pianos at an affordable price for the export market for a number of years. Because of the tax laws in China, Hailun, a privately held firm, was forced to produce products for the export market early on in its history, but is now selling in the domestic market in China because the Chinese recognize its superior quality over other pianos available in the Chinese market. But the people at Hailun are not satisfied with just being a contender in the world market for pianos, or the domestic market in China. What Hailun Piano wants is recognition as among the best pianos in the world.

Human resources offer another aspect of organization and operations of global business that is far more complicated than domestic operations. Dealing with corrupt foreign practices that may be common in other societies, but completely illegal in the United States can present problems for American executives and the companies they represent. The Corrupt Foreign Practices Act makes illegal practices that in some countries are simply a part of doing business and American firms and their executives are sometimes caught doing them and have to pay a price.

Off-shoring has become very controversial. It is certain that companies will continue to do what is best for their stockholders, especially in a world of ruthless competition. That is going to mean cutting costs wherever possible and that is often going to mean off-shoring jobs. How governments and societies respond to this is going to determine how developed countries are going to prosper in the coming decades. There is really no way to stop this from happening, but societies can prepare themselves to deal with it so as to minimize the damage and to take advantage of the opportunities that will be available.

The question of off-shoring leads to a larger question of international operations and the cost of doing business. Right now, the global economy is in recession so the price of nearly everything is down, but when the global economy recovers and demand starts to climb, it is a virtual certainty that the price of nearly everything will start to climb as discussed in "A Material World." The cost of everything, everywhere will increase and businesses will be further challenged to keep their costs down as much as possible. Businesses will be looking for lower cost venues with more enthusiasm than they do today and governments, faced with the same increases in costs, will be looking for additional revenue sources. The situation leads to a conundrum outlined in "Whose income is it? How Business Is Caught in the Global Competition and Controversy for Tax Revenues." Businesses need to make money and governments need tax revenue. The question is how to maximize both for each. Businesses do not like to pay taxes, but governments need to collect taxes so that they can provide the necessary services for businesses to be able to do business so that they can make a profit. The two are not mutually exclusive, but are dependant upon each other. But when do taxes become too burdensome for industry? When do other tax authorities offer more attractive tax codes for industry so as to attract industry to their location? What taxing authority has the right to tax profits, assets, and other aspects of the business, for how much and when? These are all questions that are going to become more important in the future as taxing authorities become more aggressive in their quest for additional funds to run their operations.

Internet References

CIA Homepage
http://cia.gov

European Union
http://europa.eu

Harvard Business School
www.hbs.edu

International Business Resources on the www
www.globaledge.msu.edu/ibid/ibrd.asap.

International Labor Organization
www.ilo.org

Outsourcing Center
www.outsourcingcenter.com

Sales and Marketing Executives International (SME)
www.smei.org

United States Trade Representative
www.ustr.gov

Further information regarding these websites may be found in this book's preface or online.

The Work Left Undone

Perspectives on Small Business Opportunities in International Trade

Matthew Carr

There's an old adage that "art imitates life." In the musical *Annie*, the red-haired orphan escapes from the diabolical Miss Hannigan in search of the parents that had left her on the doorstep of the Municipal Girls Orphanage years earlier, promising to return. While on the run and exploring the streets of New York City during the Great Depression, Annie not only finds her famous sidekick Sandy, but she also shares a meal (and a song) with a Hoovervile of individuals made homeless by the recent economic collapse. In classic musical logic, while hovering around the communal cauldron, the shanty town breaks into song, singing:

We'd like to thank you, Herbert Hoover/For really showing us the way/You dirty rat, you Bureaucrat, you/Made us what we are today. . .

Now, there's plenty of evidence to demonstrate that placing the blame for the stock market crash and the resulting depression solely on the shoulders of former President Herbert Hoover is short-sighted. During the Great Depression, just like in our modern crisis, greed, questionable corporate ethics and insufficient regulation were the ultimate villains. Nonetheless, the psychological need to single out a lone individual as the guilty party always trumps reality.

There are many parallels between *Annie*'s story and what is currently happening in the United States today. Unemployment has surged into double-digit territory and Americans from coast-to-coast are losing their homes. Animosity is brewing because President Barack Obama hasn't already delivered salvation, and bleak and weak economic indicators provide a steady chain of ammunition. And maybe some of that hostility is understandable as it would've been as difficult for Hoover to explain to the unemployed and homeless in *Annie*'s Hooverville that it wasn't his fault as it would for Obama or former President George W. Bush to do so today.

The world has just experienced one of the greatest eras of economic turmoil ever, maybe second only to the Great Depression. Not surprisingly, it has earned the moniker the "Great Recession," as global markets were held hostage for more than 20 months, more than twice as long as the average duration of a normal recession. And the world still isn't out of the woods yet.

Global trade, the one reliable ally through the sinking bog of the economic downturn, became shaky and has slowly returned over the last several months, ebbing and flowing as nations emerge and then recede back into uncertainty. The United States was buoyed from sinking into a depression by a surge in export activity, spurred on by the weakening dollar. Germany's first unsteady steps from the fog of recession in the second quarter have since been strengthened by export stimulus, while the rest of Europe continues to trail behind. Canada is now confident that recovery is imminent, despite its strong reliance on the United States, while emerging Asian markets continue to bud and blossom.

Many experts had predicted that a rebound would be in full swing at this point and that the third quarter for most of the world would be one of flourishing revived economies. In part, that is true. The United States continues to plod forward, regaining ground at a modest pace, but has slipped along the way due to a still-elusive consumer confidence. Germany and France have long since been free of recession and the rest of Western Europe is making progress. In all likelihood, the light at the end of the tunnel is drawing near, but the upticks in recovery have been nowhere near as steep as anticipated.

Many experts had predicted that a rebound would be in full swing at this point and that the third quarter for most of the world would be one of flourishing revived economies.

Unfortunately, recovery is not uniform and in business the meek aren't clearly destined to inherit anything.

Cut Down to Size

To strengthen the country's foundation and help speed recovery, the United States has made small businesses and small business exporting its top priority. The Obama Administration has worked with legislators and the Office of the United States Trade Representative (USTR) to clear any obstacles from the path of businesses looking to make the leap from Main Street to International Drive. The Small Business Administration (SBA) has partnered in the initiative and has revamped its size limitations on loans, while the U.S. Export-Import Bank (Ex-Im Bank) has been on a campaign to make sure every interested enterprise knows that it's there.

"As an economy, we have to really figure out how to get better tools for small businesses so that they can get the cash flow moving through their business and into other small businesses and throughout the entire ecosystem that's out there," said Jim Swift, CEO and president, Cortera, Inc. Swift is skeptical that the federal moves will have much impact, particularly those from the SBA. "It's helpful and maybe it gives that business the predictable cash to go and hire that person that they've been waiting to hire because they were unsure about things, but what it doesn't ensure is that that company is going to pay its suppliers who also need the money," he said.

There are obviously significant differences between small and larger companies. Larger enterprises are typically better suited to survive economic uncertainties because they have a broader pool of resources to lean on to steady their footing. That has been the onus behind trying to make more capital available to smaller businesses as the financial downturn lags on, exponentially increasing the impacts from a lack of credit and consumer confidence, and slow payments from debtors. Cortera tracks payment trends throughout the supply chain with its Supply Chain Index (SCI). Right now, commercial accounts receivable (A/R) debt more than 30 days past due is 50% higher than what was seen in September 2007 just prior to the official start of the recession. Overall, payments are also arriving 40% later than in September 2007, demonstrating the lingering effects of the crisis. "Everyone kind of hoarded cash for a while," said Swift.

Now, all eyes are on the returns from the holiday shopping season as a barometer for the economic climate. During the months leading up to the big winter retail rush, manufacturers, retailers and suppliers typically take on additional trade credit debt as they prepare for this season. This is usually represented in the SCI as an annual spike in late A/R from November to the end of the year, but in 2009, the spike in accounts days beyond terms (DBT) arrived in September, two months earlier than normal.

Swift thinks that the early arrival of the DBT uptick in October may be because U.S. companies are stretching out payments on that seasonal debt. Every fall and winter, companies dramatically slow down payments to suppliers as they try to manage their capital for the holidays. Under normal conditions, this slowdown happens in November or December and then quickly recedes after the New Year when companies—sitting on a cache of cash—begin paying off debts again. He said that it could also be that overall confidence in the economy's recovery has taken a severe blow.

The biggest problem continues to be the disparity between how large companies and small companies are paying. Late payments from larger companies have dwindled, but the situation seems to be exacerbated for smaller firms. "I'm kind of surprised we don't see a rebound in how fast small businesses are paying," said Swift. "It's still 28% or so higher than it was

at this point two years ago and they're not showing any signs that they're speeding up payments." He added, "It looks like it's taking longer for those companies to feel the effects of the economic rebound shake down to their business."

The return to normalcy also appears to be much more measured for smaller domestic firms as evidenced by the National Federation of Independent Business' (NFIB) Index of Small Business Optimism that found outlook inched upward only slightly in October. Since the second lowest reading ever in the index's history in March 2009, there has been a steady upward trend to a reading of 89.1. That's a significant benchmark because, during the recession from 1980–82, the NFIB's optimism index fell below 90 only once. Throughout this prolonged downturn, the index has been below 90 six times, reflecting the pure severity of the decline.

"Just because a business gets a loan, that business still has to be confident in the other parts of its operation and whether its customers will continue to pay and flow cash through. That's the key," said Swift. "The government, I don't think, can really do anything about it and shouldn't necessarily pretend that they can get businesses to get that cash flow moving. It's really up to the businesses themselves."

In the United States, the debate will continue about the effectiveness of the current strategies to nurture recovery. Nonetheless, there may finally be some success in pushing more American companies to diversify by getting them involved in international trade.

"I haven't seen any game-changing initiatives," said Iosh Green, CEO and president, Panjiva, Inc. of the current federal moves. "I think the economic forces are the key drivers here. Perhaps one of the legacies of this downturn could be a rise in entrepreneurship. People are out of jobs. They can't find somebody to give them a job, so they create a job for themselves. And that wouldn't surprise me at all if some of those jobs related to importing."

Profits of Doom

As the U.S. government urges more and more businesses to get involved in international trade, the World Trade Organization (WTO) warned all last year that global trade will be on the decline in 2010. Despite the fact that the weak dollar made U.S. goods and commodities like crude and gold more affordable on the international level, the mood has become more subdued in the global marketplace, particularly compared to brimming enthusiasm witnessed even just a handful of months ago. This makes it even more harrowing for small businesses either importing or exporting that are already at a disadvantage by having fewer resources than their large counterparts, let alone lacking the resources on the ground in emerging markets.

"I really encourage people to consider the multitude of risks," said Green. "People are very accustomed to thinking about financial risk: the risk that the company they are doing business with will go out of business. The reality is there are more than just financial risks that you need to worry about, particularly if you are doing business internationally."

Anybody involved in international trade already understands that it isn't a plug-and-go/turn-key endeavor. There are the many activities an overseas partner company can be engaged in to put a company's brand at risk, including capacity risk, pricing risk, currency risk, and political risk. "I think it's important that as people do business internationally, they do it with eyes wide open about the variety of risks and the ways to manage those risks," Green said.

According to Panjiva, Inc., from August to September 2009, the number of global manufacturers shipping to the United States slipped as international trade buckled. Then, in October, global trade regained steam and there was a slight uptick. Specifically, there was a 3% increase in the number of global manufacturers shipping to the U.S. market. At the same time, there was a 2% increase in the number of U.S. companies receiving waterborne shipments.

Of course, even during a global recession, any sort of panic in a major consuming economy like the United States can have significant impacts for distributors around the world. The great thing about international trade is that it's a two-way street. On one side, there was a sense of disappointment when the Department of Commerce announced that the U.S. trade deficit increased dramatically in September to $36.5 billion from August's $30.8 billion. On the other, those numbers included the effects of the media love affair with H1N1 and the predicted impending crisis the "swine flu" virus would create. "We had a hunch that given the swine flu scare, hand sanitizer shipments would be up significantly," said Green. "We looked into the data and, sure enough, there was a massive spike in shipments to the United States."

Spike is a relative term. During the three months ending in September, Panjiva discovered that shipments of waterborne hand sanitizer to the United States had increased 129% year-over-year. In the third quarter of 2009, there were 128 shipments destined for the U.S., compared to 56 such shipments in the third quarter of 2008. The cargo loads also represented a threefold increase when analyzed on a weight basis.

What these numbers also reveal is the wide range of opportunities that exist in the global market that make it attractive for small enterprises.

The Road Ahead

Since global trade hit bottom in February 2009, it has been recovering at a modest pace, in fits and starts. Import activity in the U.S. has recovered, although the absolute level of activity is still well below pre-recession numbers. Unfortunately, rebound is anticipated to be slow and there are few people who expect a great improvement any time soon.

"Some people were hoping to see one with the holiday season, but that didn't materialize," said Green. "My best guess at this point is that we'll continue to see a slow recovery. Obviously, any further macroeconomic shocks could change that dynamic."

Despite all the talk over the last year about trade shifting from China and more toward Central and South America, the change hasn't been enormous. Coface expects 2009 growth for China and India to come in at 8.5% and 6% respectively. For 2010, Coface reports that growth for China will remain strong, increasing to 10%, while India's growth will trend upward to 8%.

"People need to go beyond just thinking about countries," said Green. "Having a country orientation when you're thinking about where to buy products and where risks lie is really inappropriate. You need to think about the company level. You really need to dig in and understand what's going on with the companies you are interacting with and are considering interacting with because that's where the bulk of the risks lie."

In the business world, companies are constantly relying on the cash inflows from their customers to go out the back door.

Companies like Panjiva offer an array of informational services on international distributors and Green said his company feels that information is critical. "The way I look at it, it's not about any one business; it's about the interaction between the businesses," said Swift. "If you think of the economy as a whole, the more confident we are about things, the more money we spend. Knowing that we're going to get paid, we're going to get jobs, we're going to spend more and those people are then going to spend more and you really can't put your finger on it, but in a thriving economy everyone has confidence and the money flows freely. In the business world, companies are constantly relying on the cash inflows from their customers to go out the back door. The confidence is a huge factor in all of this."

From *Business Credit*, January 2010, pp. 40–43. Copyright © 2010 by Business Credit Magazine, the official publication of the National Association of Credit Management (NACM). Reprinted by permission.

Brazil's Iron Giant Reaches for the Top

Vale Has a Shot at Becoming the World's No. 1 Mining Company, If It Can Outfox Rivals—Including China.

Joshua Schneyer

Steelmakers might not see Vale as a natural ally. The Rio de Janeiro company is, after all, the world's leading supplier of iron ore, and on Feb. 18 and 19 it forced steel producers in Japan, Korea, and Germany to eat a 65% price hike. Worse, the increase comes as Vale is considering a bid for Switzerland's Xstrata, the world's No. 6 mining company. Such a combination would give the Brazilians even greater pricing power vis-à-vis steelmakers.

But Roger Agnelli, Vale's chief executive, would say his merger plans are in the best interests of players across the industry, providing a counterweight to China's growing clout in global markets for iron ore and steel. Western industrialists should "wake up" to China's strength, Agnelli said at the American Chamber of Commerce in Rio in October.

The way he sees it, everyone in the consolidating mining industry is either predator or prey. The 48-year-old Agnelli expects Vale, formerly Companhia Vale do Rio Doce, to be one of the winners and aims to make it the world's top mining company. He's now within striking range. Since Agnelli took over in 2001, Vale has bought more than a dozen mining and metals companies in Brazil and abroad, and now spans six continents. Under Agnelli, shareholders have seen Amazonian returns of 64% a year.

Key to Agnelli's ambitions is owning Xstrata. The Swiss company is a major player in copper, nickel, and coal, with operations in 18 countries, including Brazil and the U.S. Vale won't discuss the bid publicly, but industry sources say the company is close to lining up some $50 billion in loans to help cover the cash portion of its offer, which could total more than $90 billion.

Tug-of-War

The Chinese, though, appear to have other plans. China has already shown it will write big checks to gain control of resources. On Feb. 1, state-run Aluminum Corp. of China (Chalco) teamed up with Pittsburgh-based Alcoa to buy 9% of London-based Rio Tinto, the world's No. 3 mining company, for $14 billion. Rio Tinto, meanwhile, is the target of a

$147 billion hostile takeover bid from Australia's BHP Billiton. Though Chalco hasn't disclosed its motives for the purchase, China would be a clear loser if BHP succeeds (the combined company would have far greater pricing power), so many expect the Chinese to use their new inside position to try to scuttle that deal. Some analysts speculate China may go after a chunk of Xstrata to keep it out of Vale's hands, for similar reasons.

Of course, both partners in this strange tango need each other. Since 2002, Vale has quintupled its ore shipments to China, to 100 million metric tons in 2007. This year, Chinese steelmakers will likely consume almost half the world's iron-ore output, including 40% of Vale's exports. After Japanese and Korean producers agreed to the price hike—the sixth straight year of increases from Vale—the Chinese will likely have to follow suit.

The heart of Vale's mining operations is a vast complex in the central Amazon known as Carajás. The company has three mines in the area, where workers sometimes catch glimpses of big jungle cats and the eerie groan of howler monkeys is seldom far off. Day and night, a fleet of more than 100 trucks as big as houses climb in and out of pits carved 1,500 feet deep into the rain forest. They move a million tons of rusty earth every day, unloading huge chunks into "jaw-crushers," which process the rock into iron ore.

Vale believes its biggest customer—China, more than 13,000 miles away—is too distant. Rising freight costs for the 45-day journey around Africa's southern tip are becoming a bigger disadvantage for the Brazilians than for rivals in Australia. So Agnelli is seeking to sell more ore to the U.S., just a one-week sail, or Europe, two weeks away. "China is our main market, but it's not our natural market," says Tito Martins, a top deputy to Agnelli.

Better yet, Vale wants big clients to set up shop in Brazil. Some heavyweights have already signed on to do so. Luxembourg-based ArcelorMittal, Germany's ThyssenKrupp, and Korea's Dongkuk are all planning steelworks in Brazil and expect to buy Vale's ore. Even Shanghai-based Baosteel can't resist the pull of Brazil's plentiful resources. The company, China's biggest steelmaker, is building a $5 billion plant in the southeastern Brazilian city of Vitória. All told, Brazil expects to nearly double its 34 million-ton steel output by 2013.

Despite Vale's growing global profile, some Brazilians worry that its international push will weaken the management of its domestic operations. "Vale should tend its own backyard, which is Brazil," says Novarck de Oliveira, a Vale union leader. Vale's Martins counters that the best way to ensure the company's future—and its leading role in Brazil—is to keep growing any way it can. To prosper, says Martins, "we need old resources, new resources, acquisitions, and organic growth."

NanoTech Firm Takes Passage to India

PETER GWYNNE

A small high-tech company in New England is going global in an ambitious way. The firm, Nanobiosym, has started a collaboration with the governments of India and two Indian states on a public-private partnership that will give it and other Western companies a local presence on the subcontinent from which they can carry out R&D—as well as manufacturing and marketing their technologies.

The project is in its early phases. Nanobiosym does not want to reveal details of its discussions with potential corporate collaborators, although it is still prepared to welcome business partners from North America and Europe to the venture. However, the company's experience so far provides valuable insights into ways in which technology companies can gain a foothold in a country with a potentially large middle-class market that has begun to overturn a longstanding tradition of protectionism.

Physicist-physician Anita Goel, M.D., founded Nanobiosym, Inc. in Medford, Massachusetts in 2004, with the goal, she says, "of creating an environment in which physics, biology, and nanotechnology could be combined as a nexus." The company initially worked in R&D, earning contracts from the United States Department of Energy and other government agencies.

Genetic Fingerprints

One project developed proprietary nanochip technology capable of detecting the genetic fingerprints of any biological organism fast and accurately. The technology, called Gene-RADAR, has potential use in homeland security, by detecting pathogens in food, water and the air, for example.

Dr. Goel, who is Nanobiosym's chairman and CEO, created a subsidiary firm, Nanobiosym Diagnostics, to commercialize that and other advances. She realized that portable devices based on the Gene-RADAR technology had medical value in third-world nations. The devices could diagnose infections and other illnesses within a few minutes of receiving a drop of blood or saliva. "The technology takes the ability to diagnose disease outside the pathology lab and into handheld devices," she explains. "That would be a paradigm shift."

Equally important, Dr. Goel saw the need to continue research and development on the technology, as well as manufacturing and marketing the devices, in the developing world. She quickly identified India as the initial target. Why India? "It's an emerging market," Dr. Goel explains. "We have a technology platform. My vision is to bring it to emerging markets. India represented a place that would be a foothold to help drive down the costs of our products, especially as we scale up our technology to bring it into new markets in the developing world." Dr. Goel's heritage helped steer her toward India. Her parents had emigrated from there to the U.S. before she was born.

A Worldwide Stage

From the beginning, Dr. Goel wanted more than a conventional agreement in which a Western company sets up overseas manufacturing sites. For a start, she determined to work on a worldwide stage. "Our vision is more global," she says, "with India being a piece of that." Just as important, she aimed to use Nanobiosym's opportunity as the gateway for taking a burst of Western technology into India and other developing countries. "Initially, the Indian government said: 'Why don't you manufacture your products over here and create jobs over here?'" she recalls. "We have the vision of something bigger—a test bed ecosystem where cutting edge technologies can be introduced into emerging markets. There's a different science and art in bringing products into these markets than into the more developed markets of the West, for example."

The initial result of her negotiations is land for a 500-acre science park in Himachal Pradesh state, about two hours north of the Indian capital of New Delhi, along with the corporate-government institutional structure that will enable the project. The park, Dr. Goel says, "will harness the resources of the local environment and also bring in global players to create a bridge to the global economy. We have a broad vision of creating an ecosystem where companies from around the world can come together to bring emerging technologies into emerging markets. Many companies are approaching us to explore innovative partnership models, as well as ideas of how best to create a win-win symbiotic relationship with the local communities." India's western-most state of Gujarat has signed up to work on a similar project with Nanobiosym.

Global Showcase

The projects are in the early stages and remain open to participation. "We're looking for special kinds of partners—best-of-breed people who share our sense of global mission, Dr. Goel says. We're very open to companies, enterprises, and organizations that feel they have a niche in this ecosystem we're building. We're building a global consortium of all kinds of partners—manufacturing, R&D, education, and even entertainment. It's the idea of a global showcase in which we all learn from each other."

The agreements have come at an appropriate time. India's long-skeptical attitude toward overseas corporations has begun to mellow in recent years. Both the ruling Congress Party and the main opposition Bharatiya Janata Party have indicated that they welcome the presence of overseas corporations as well as the goods and services they produce. And at the beginning of 2005, the Indian Patent Office brought the country's patent act in line with the requirements of the World Trade Organization's Agreement on Trade Related Aspects of Intellectual Property. That change permitted the first local filings of product patents on compounds for use as drugs and other medications. "Traditionally they focused on outsourcing," Dr. Goel notes. "They seem now to be wanting to take a step toward innovation."

But change does not take root overnight. In a recent case, an Indian court upheld the patent office's decision to reject a patent application by Swiss pharmaceutical firm Novartis for its chronic myeloid leukemia drug Gleevec. Its contention: The drug represented only a small improvement to an existing drug. In addition, Indian bureaucracy has not entirely shed its reputation of being difficult and time-consuming to navigate.

Two Indias

In her negotiations, Dr. Goel has seen evidence of both changing attitudes and the old style of doing business. "There are two Indias," she says. "One seems to be very progressive, moving to the future, and high-tech friendly. The other is still living in the past and living up to its reputation. At every step—in government, corporations, and other institutions—you are dealing with both Indias."

How does Dr. Goel deal with the two? "There's no magic bullet," she says. "It's a process—not as deliberate as it may look. We had these products we wanted to bring into an emerging market. Our company is focused on innovation where physics, medicine, and nanotechnology meet to develop new ways of attacking global problems. A series of events luckily happened that brought this unique opportunity about."

Some of those events came about by design. Last fall, for example, Dr. Goel brought Ratan Tata, chairman of India's giant Tata Group and perhaps India's best-known technology executive, to Nanobiosym's global advisory board. "I am inspired by his example, which provides us with a practical road map for bringing cutting-edge technologies into emerging global economies and extending our reach to broad markets at the bottom of the pyramid," Dr. Goel said. The appointment helped to seal the relationship with India. In addition, she worked with such organizations as the USA-India Chamber of Commerce. As to her Indian heritage: "It sometimes helps and sometimes hurts, depending perhaps on which India you are dealing with" she says.

Words of Advice

What advice does Dr. Goel have for technology-based corporations whose executives want to create a presence in India in particular and the developing world in general? "I would encourage companies, whether they are small, medium or large, to join us," she says. "We're building partnerships in a very collaborative way, including R&D, manufacturing, innovation, education, and even entertainment in an ecosystem that plays into the local economy. We are eco-friendly, green and fitting into the local markets. We're thinking in a global context. I'm sure that many companies interested in going global and bringing their technologies into those markets are thinking that way. In my opinion, they should be evolving beyond the idea of being perceived as Western companies exploiting local labor, into global enterprises seeking to address the needs of the local economies."

From *Research-Technology Management*, May–June 2009, pp. 7–8. Copyright © 2009 by Industrial Research Institute, Inc. Reprinted by permission.

Tata: Master of the Gentle Approach

The Indian giant has found a way to acquire companies across the globe—and still tread lightly.

MANJEET KRIPALANI

R avi Kant was shocked. As head of commercial vehicles at India's Tata Motors, Kant had traveled to the Korean port city of Gunsan to examine the failing Daewoo conglomerate's truck division, which was being auctioned. When Kant asked a midlevel Daewoo manager which bidder he preferred, the Korean replied that a European suitor would best secure his company's future. "I realized we had to change our entire strategy," Kant recalls, "and tell the Koreans what Tata was about."

Kant quickly put together a massive public-relations effort: Tata executives were enrolled in Korean language classes, company brochures were translated into Korean, and Tata began making presentations to employees, the local auto association chief, the mayor of Gunsan, officials in Seoul, even Korea's Prime Minister. If Tata were chosen, Kant's team explained, it would preserve jobs, build Daewoo into a major exporter, and blend the outfit seamlessly with the parent company. "Tata had done its homework in everything needed to do business here," says Chae Kwang Ok, chief executive of Tata Daewoo. The Indians won the auction, paying $102 million.

Americans often associate takeovers with layoffs and factory closings. Tata, India's premier industrial group, with an expected $50 billion in sales this year, has a different way to merge—more strategic partner than vulture capitalist. It has applied this approach to $18 billion in overseas deals since 2000, when it acquired Tetley Tea for $400 million. After buying British and Italian engineering and design houses, tony American hotels, Asian and European steelmakers, and software companies around the globe, Tata now has 333,000 employees worldwide, 26% of them outside India. In the latest move, Tata Chemicals on Jan. 31 bought Wyoming's General Chemical Industrial Products, a leading producer of soda ash. And Tata is the front-runner in the bidding to buy Ford Motor's Jaguar-Rover operations for an estimated $1 billion.

In all its deals, Tata has been careful to signal its respect for workers. While it chooses its targets carefully and doesn't do a lot of bottom-fishing, Tata is nonetheless unusual in that it hasn't laid off any workers or shuttered any facilities following its overseas acquisitions (though it has had layoffs at home in the past decade). "Tata buys companies overseas not to reduce costs but to improve [its own] capabilities," says Arun Maira, Boston Consulting Group's chairman in India. And Tata's Indian background has given it plenty of experience in managing a diverse workforce. Its employees in India come from various castes, religions, and ethnic origins and speak any of dozens of languages or dialects.

With its overseas acquisitions, Tata typically leaves executives in place. Instead of dispatching legions of Indians to the new company, Tata sets up a joint management board, which decides on issues ranging from growth targets to the development of new talent. Working groups find common goals, and managers of the acquired company are asked to help smooth out any cultural differences. This approach takes time, says Philippe Varin, chief executive of Corus, which Tata Steel bought for $12 billion last year. But it allows Tata to stay focused on bigger strategic issues "without sweating the small stuff," Varin says.

At Daewoo, Tata knew not to act like an occupation force. The company formed a joint board of directors, and Daewoo CEO Chae was given the freedom to keep running the business his way. Kant wanted two Tata executives to act as advisers. Chae welcomed them but insisted on incorporating them into his management team, with one caveat for the Indians: They had to shave their mustaches, as Koreans preferred a "clean" look.

The Indians helped devise a strategy to expand Daewoo's product line and boost exports. "It's turned out to be a win-win situation," says Choi Jai Choon, a union leader there. While the company had been largely focused on its domestic market, the new Tata Daewoo accounts for two-thirds of Korea's heavy truck exports, up from 20% three years ago. Sales are expected to hit $670 million for the year ending in March—more than double their level before the takeover. That success, says Kim Ki Chan, an auto industry specialist at the Catholic University of Korea, can be attributed to Tata's capital injection of $176 million, as well as its hands-off approach to the company. "It would have been difficult to find a better suitor than Tata," says Kim.

Tata's unique shareholder structure makes it easier for the group to tread lightly. Since its founding in 1868, Tata has been controlled by charitable trusts. Today, they own 66% of parent Tata Sons' shares and aren't as focused on short-term gains as most investors. The trusts, says R.K. Krishna Kumar, a director with Tata Sons, have long insulated employees "from the greed that is sweeping the corporate world." As the company gets more deeply enmeshed in the global economy, that gentility will be put to the test. Says Harvard Business School professor Tarun Khanna: "There's a different kind of rough-and-tumble to competitive pressures outside of India."

Rethinking Globalization
Does "Think Global, Act Local" Still Apply?

Nigel Hollis

It is received wisdom that, in order to be successful, a global brand should seek to become part of the local culture, adapting to the unique needs, values and desires of the population. But what evidence do we have that this is really still true? At the beginning of 2008, a global survey, sponsored by Millward Brown, was designed to understand the importance of the local touch. We wanted to answer these questions:

- What role do factors like culture and local production play in people's likelihood to buy a brand?
- Is there a difference between global and local brands in terms of what motivates people to buy them?

Although the overall conclusion, that getting close to local culture does still matter, has been reported elsewhere, this article delves deeper into the research and summarizes new findings and implications for marketers. The Global Brand survey was conducted in eight countries: (from west to east) the United States, Mexico, Brazil, the United Kingdom, Germany, Russia, India and China.

In each country, we compared two global brands to two local brands in each of five categories: cars, beer, fast food, shampoo/conditioners and soft drinks. In total, we interviewed 3,307 people about 91 different brands. About 400 people were interviewed in each country. A single respondent could answer for up to three categories for which they qualified. (The qualification was that they were likely to buy or use a brand in the category.) The fact that the surveys were conducted online limited the sample to people with at least moderate levels of income and education, and quotas were applied to achieve a balance across age groups.

In reality there are relatively few truly global brands and fewer still that manage to create a really strong connection with consumers in many countries. And so, even though the global brands we selected for study were well-known players (McDonald's, KFC, Budweiser, Heineken, Toyota, Ford, Pantene Pro-V, Dove, Coca-Cola and Pepsi), in some countries we had to make substitutions for one or more of these brands. For example, in Russia, we replaced Budweiser with Miller. It is not that Budweiser is not present in Russia, but simply that its presence there is too low for it to serve as a meaningful example of a global brand.

Local brands were selected on a similar basis in each country. They had to be well-known enough for the majority of people to have an opinion of them. Again, we had to make some adjustments for certain countries and categories. For example, because there are no major car brands that are truly "local" to Brazil, we had to select two foreign-owned brands (Volkswagen and Fiat) that are regarded as local because they have been manufactured in Brazil for many years. In one or two cases we deliberately selected a brand in order to enable cross-country comparisons (e.g., Buick in the United States and China; Corona in the United States and Mexico).

Strong Global Brands Are Rare

Before delving into the results of our survey, we need to put the findings in context. This survey was designed to contrast a consistent set of global brands with their local competitors. This design forced us to choose from the very limited set of brands that have already created strong relationships with consumers in multiple countries. As a result, our set of global brands is an unusually strong one. Because the strength of this set of brands might appear to overstate the advantages of global brands, it is important to interpret the results in the light of the following facts.

First, Millward Brown's BrandZ equity database holds data on more than 10,000 brands across almost 100 countries,

Executive Summary

By now all marketers should know they need to "think global and act local" when trying to extend a brand to new countries and cultures. Global media companies and the Internet ensure that popular culture and news is generally available to all. When people have so much in common, is it still necessary to make that local connection with them? Using results of an extensive Millward Brown survey, this article examines that question.

Table 1 Average Percent Mentioning a Brand

	Average Percent Mentioning Any Global Or Local Brand		Significant in Relation to Purchase	
	Global %	Local %	Global %	Local %
First choice or seriously considered for purchase	53	40		
Are very easy to recognize	63	56	*	
Have very distinctive identities	52	43	*	
Are very high-quality brands	48	39	*	*
Have a strong heritage	42	31	*	*
Are brands that are setting the trends	42	27	*	*
Are made in (country)	25	56		*
Are part of our (nationality) culture	21	42	*	*

Note: An * indicates that regression analysis (conducted separately for global and local brands) has identified a statistically significant relationship between the image statement and the probability of people purchasing a brand at the 95% level of confidence.

but only 3 percent of those brands were measured in seven or more countries. The overwhelming majority of brands—84 percent—were measured in only one. (It should be noted that BrandZ typically measures the brands that account for 80 percent of category volume in a market. If a brand is only measured in one country, it implies it does not have a significant share elsewhere.)

Second, on average, the brands measured by BrandZ in just one country created a stronger attitudinal bond with their consumers than those measured in seven or more countries.

Third, an analysis designed to identify brands that created strong attitudinal bonds with consumers across countries and cultures found very few brands that did so. Of the 3 percent of brands measured in seven or more countries, only one in four were classified as being strong in at least half of the countries in which they were studied.

This is really not surprising. Most global brands started out as local brands. As they extended their reach, they had to build relationships from scratch in each new market. Local brands enjoy the advantage of being familiar with local tastes and customs and therefore have a better chance of getting firmly entrenched in the local culture.

In considering the results of The Global Brand survey, readers must remember that the global brands in this study are truly la crème de la crème.

Global vs. Local

The aggregate results of the survey are summarized in Table 1. The first two columns show the average percentage of people mentioning any global or local brand across the five product categories and eight countries studied. In the two rightmost columns, an asterick denotes that regression analysis (conducted separately for global and local brands) identified a statistically significant relationship between the image statement and the probability of people purchasing a brand.

It is apparent from the data that the global brands included in our survey are stronger than the local ones. They are more often considered for purchase and receive higher scores on all statements, except those related to where they were made or whether they were part of the local national culture.

In part, this stronger performance derives from the strong, scalable business models these brands have developed over time. Advantages of scale also accrue to global brands in terms of centralized R&D, redeploying marketing practices and assets that have proved successful elsewhere and so on.

Advantages like these have allowed these global brands to enter new markets successfully by disrupting the status quo in a category. Innovation and perceptions of higher quality help them establish a competitive advantage over the competition. In our research, this is reflected by a far stronger perception that they are "setting the trends." The global brands in our survey also lead local brands in being mentioned as "very easy to recognize" and having "very distinctive identities."

Being Part of the National Culture Drives Purchase Probability for Both Global and Local Brands

Not everything is stacked in favor of the global brands, however. Local brands typically score far higher than global ones on being seen as part of the national culture, an attribute which, at the aggregate level, is a driver of purchase intent for all brands, both global and local.

This finding confirms that brands that are identified with local culture will perform better than others (all other things being equal). While it has less impact on purchase probability than perceptions that a brand is high quality or setting trends, association with local culture is definitely a benefit. With notable exceptions, our analysis suggests that global brands owe their strength to their reliance on the basics of brand-building. By contrast, local brands, which may lack the business acumen and deep pockets of the MNC brands, draw strength from the home-field advantage (provided that they qualify as strong brands in their own right).

Table 2 Percent Agreeing with Each Statement

	Russia	Germany	U.K.	Brazil	U.S.	India	Mexico	China
I always try to buy brands produced in my own country	23%	30%	31%	47%	49%	50%	54%	62%
More concerned with getting a specific brand rather than the best price	81%	65%	64%	69%	65%	79%	74%	75%

Finally, the analysis also finds that being produced locally is a significant driver for local brands but not global ones. In practice, this advantage is often negated by MNCs establishing local production facilities (e.g., Toyota building cars in the United States or Motorola making mobile phones in China). However, the survey results suggest it is still a potential benefit to some local brands in some countries.

Not Every Country Thinks Local Is Better

As with all research conducted across countries and categories, the preceding "global" results hide several differences and exceptions. Most notable for brand marketers are the differences by country.

Regression analysis conducted across the five product categories within individual countries found that two countries deviate from our general finding: Russia and the United Kingdom. The reasons behind these differences point to the innate complexity of marketing brands across countries and cultures.

In Russia, for a brand to be seen as part of the national culture actually appears to undermine purchase intent. The relationship between both national culture and local production is significant but negative. As shown in Table 2, Russians are the most likely of the eight nationalities to think choosing the right brand is important (as opposed to getting the right price), but the least likely to agree they always try to buy locally produced brands.

Memories of poor quality goods from the communist era still influence Russian's beliefs today; therefore foreign brands are held in much higher regard. The belief that foreign brands are typically higher quality or that their consumption helps indicate a person's status is by no means limited to Russia, but only there do we find such a strong, negative view of local brands.

In the U.K., the relationship between local culture, local production and purchase intent is statistically insignificant, a finding that supports government concern that the British no longer value their cultural origins. But then, the British have long been exposed to influences from many different cultures and countries, including foreign brands, and they are much more likely to travel abroad on a regular basis than their peers in other countries (except Germany). Analysis of Global Target Group Index (TGI) data confirms that, in most countries, regular international travelers are more likely to buy foreign brands than their stay-at-home peers.

Like people in other Western countries with developed economies, the British are more likely to believe that most brands are good quality and, lacking any other means to differentiate between them, buy on price (as reported in Table 2). This selection process often favors brands produced abroad.

Are Other Countries Destined to Share the West's Outlook on Brands?

As I talked to many marketers in the United States and Europe, I encounter an implicit assumption that, as disposable income levels rise around the world, consumers' needs, wants and desires will become more homogeneous. But is this assumption true? The findings reported here suggest there are still significant differences in attitudes toward brands across countries, but will these differences fade with time?

Our survey can only shed light on the current situation. However, other indicators help anticipate whether the world will become more homogenized or not. Analysis of TGI data reveals that the rich and poor within a country have largely similar values, but big differences still exist between people with relatively high standards of living across countries. This is consistent with analysis by Marieke de Mooij, who concluded that "Countries may be converging with respect to income levels but they are not converging with respect to values of national culture." (See her September 1997 ESOMAR paper, "Mapping Cultural Values for Global Marketing and Advertising.")

If history is to be our guide, the developing economies of Asia and South America are likely to follow the examples of Japan and Korea and retain a strong degree of cultural identity. Since its rise as a global powerhouse, Japan has shown little sign of losing its unique culture. Developing brands and marketing communication that will succeed there still presents a significant challenge to global marketers.

Whatever the future brings, it seems unlikely that people's needs, wants and desires will become irrevocably homogenized any time soon. If anything, rising income levels may allow people to celebrate their own cultural identity rather than blindly adopting that of the West. Global brands will still need to win at the local level in order to become successful on a global scale.

Table 3 Brands That Blend in

	U.S.	Brazil	U.K.	Germany	India	China	Mexico	Russia
McDonald's	81%	44%	29%	22%	15%	7%	6%	6%
Coca-Cola	80%	64%	30%	26%	18%	9%	47%	8%

Strategies for Adaptation

How much a brand needs to blend into local culture is dictated by the nature of the product category, the country and the competitive context. Information technology brands are often selling to a relatively upscale group of consumers around the world, particularly in business-to-business categories. Even in the consumer domain, IT products serve mostly as interfaces to content and therefore are less susceptible to the influences of culture. The music and videos I have on my MP3 player will probably be very different from what you have on yours; likewise I may view very different content online from my laptop. The technology, however, is the same for both of us. By comparison with IT brands, however, food and drink brands are much more susceptible to the demands of local tastes and thus require a greater degree of adaptation.

Two brands that stood out in our survey as having succeeded on the world stage through effective adaptation were Coca-Cola and McDonald's. Both brands achieved high purchase intent scores across our eight countries. Not surprisingly, both brands scored very highly on being seen as part of the national culture in the United States. They are identified as American brands by most people interviewed. In spite of this strong American heritage, however, a significant proportion of people in some countries outside of the United States admitted to feeling that these brands were part of their own national culture, as evidenced by the data in Table 3.

This is no mean feat for such iconic American brands. While aspiration for the American lifestyle has no doubt played a strong part in the success of these brands, two other factors are also at work: local adaptation and time in market.

Combining Global Positioning with Local Adaptation

McDonald's is the world's largest chain of fast food restaurants, currently serving in more than 100 countries in the world. While the brand's presence outside of the United States used to reflect its American heritage, that is no longer true. Menu items, store design and marketing communication are all adapted to meet local needs and values.

The company's launch into India reflects its willingness to adapt to meet local needs. In respect to Hindu and Muslim beliefs, no beef or pork is offered on the menu. The signature Big Mac is replaced by the Chicken Maharaja Mac. While the brand's positioning—good food served fast and at a reasonable price—remains the same, its marketing communication reflects local needs.

Initially, advertising was designed to establish the brand's positioning and create an emotional connection between Indian families and the brand. The latest campaign features father-son duos from the Bollywood film industry. Various strategies help ensure that the brand is accessible and relevant. The Happy Price Menu extends its appeal to younger consumers as well as those in socio-economic group B, which consists of higher income, well-educated, urban consumers. A one-minute service guarantee, kitchen tours and home delivery all help to encourage trial and repeat use. Today, 30 percent of Indians interviewed in our survey agreed McDonald's is their first choice for fast food.

Coca-Cola has been similarly successful in building up a strong relationship with consumers across countries and cultures. Unknown to many of its consumers, the Coca-Cola product varies around the world. One only has to travel from the brand's homeland, the United States, to Mexico to find a formulation that uses cane sugar instead of corn syrup. Many Mexican immigrants living in the United States regard this as the "real thing" and will transport cases of the signature glass bottles across the border from Mexico.

Coke is extremely strong in Mexico, and, in spite of the fact that people know it is an American brand, nearly one in two Mexicans agree that it is part of their national culture. Strong distribution and visibility combined with the use of locally produced ads that complement global campaigns contribute to the brand's strength. However, there is one other factor that many marketers would do well to remember: Relationships take time to develop. Just as it takes time to build a strong relationship with another person, it takes time to build a strong relationship between people and a brand. The authorization to bottle Coca-Cola in Mexico was granted in 1926, and therefore most Mexicans have grown up with the brand.

For both McDonald's and Coca-Cola, time in market helps explain the degree to which the brand is seen to be part of the local culture. Looking across the countries studied (excluding the U.S.), the correlation between number of years in market (or from re-entry, in the case of Coca-Cola in India and China) and the proportion perceiving the brand to be part of local culture is 0.66 for Coca-Cola and 0.61 for McDonald's.

Combining Global Strengths with a Local Face

The aim of successful global brands is to strike the balance between business scale and brand strength that allows them to connect with consumers around the world. With this in mind, branding expert Martin Lindstrom proposes that a global brand needs to maintain a consistent name, logo and color scheme in order to combine marketing efficiencies with the flexibility to localize positioning and communications. (See AdAge video, http://adage.com/article?article_id=115637.)

On face value, this seems to be an appealing proposition, but there are many examples of global brands that flout these guidelines. For example, history has left Unilever with several brands that share the same positioning but have different names in different parts of the world. By retaining local names but sharing a common product formulation, packaging and positioning, Unilever can keep the local connection while leveraging the advantages of scale.

One such brand is the shampoo brand that is known as Sedal in Mexico, Seda in Brazil and Sunsilk in India, the United States and elsewhere. In Brazil, Seda combines the strengths of a multinational brand with those of a local one. Time in market has given it a high profile and it maintains a distinctive positioning. Many people think that Seda, like its sibling brand, Dove, is setting the trends for the category (44 percent vs. 57 percent, respectively). Like its Brazilian-owned competitor, Natura, Seda is also seen to be part of the Brazilian national culture (56 percent agree this is true of both brands). The combination has helped Seda retain brand leadership in the Brazilian hair care category.

Does Foreign Ownership Really Matter?

In days gone by, automotive manufacturers used to be a source of significant national pride. Today well-known British brands like Jaguar and Land Rover have been bought and sold by Indian and American companies, and local producers like Seat and Skoda are owned by the German Volkswagen Audi Group. One would think that today no one really cares who owns what. Indeed, substantial confusion often exists over whether a brand is actually owned by a foreign company or not. Even so, our data points to the subtle influence of the local connection in people's attitudes to automotive brands.

In the U.K., 65 percent of people believe the new MINI is part of their country's national culture. Only a minority realizes that it is actually designed and manufactured by the German company BMW. When apprised of this fact, most people greeted the news with indifference, suggesting it would make no difference in the way they viewed the brand. Germany, after all, has a well-established reputation for manufacturing quality automobiles.

By comparison, 68 percent of Germans believe that GM's Opel is a German car brand, and 48 percent think it is part of their national culture. When informed that Opel is owned by an American company (General Motors), 16 percent said it made them feel less favorable about the brand. Only 5 percent felt more favorable. This negative reaction was most notable among the younger respondents, with 31 percent of 16-to-29-year-olds suggesting their opinion of the brand had been lowered. Younger Germans probably do not see the U.S., and particularly the U.S. auto industry, as positively as their older compatriots.

But foreign ownership may not be a bad thing, provided the brand is locally produced. Volkswagen has been produced in Mexico for many years, and the Beetle taxicab, affectionately known as "Vocho," is an icon of the Mexico City streets. In fact, the beloved "Vocho" was so popular that its discontinuation in 2003 was marked with grief. Five years later, 59 percent of Mexicans think that Volkswagen is a part of their national culture in spite of the fact that the majority know of its German origins.

A similar story plays itself out in China with the American brand Buick. In the United States, Buick is not a brand that elicits desire. Along with other U.S. automotive brands, it has suffered from an undue reliance on "cash on the hood" to get people to buy. But, in China, Buick is an aspirational brand. In our global survey, Chinese perceptions of Buick's quality match those of Toyota. The Chinese also gave Buick a slight edge over Toyota on setting the trends in the category. Like many successful global brands in China, Buick markets its sub-brands to separate audiences. Regal targets the winners, the ones with "conquering spirit" who have made it to the top. Excelle, on the other hand, goes after those who are on the move, applauding those who actively play the game. Our data confirms the vast difference in perception between the two countries.

However, in the year since our survey was taken, the situation for GM in China has gotten tougher. While the new Buick Regal, released in China last fall, was greeted with enthusiastic reviews, competition from Honda and Toyota has increased, and affluent Chinese consumers who want a luxury car are increasingly able to afford European makes like Audi and BMW. A combination of American heritage and locally inspired design has powered Buick's success so far, but in the face of increased competition and the news of GM's financial difficulties at home, Buick cannot afford to rest on its laurels.

Being Seen as Part of Local Culture Is Not a Necessity

Our regression analysis confirms that, on an overall basis, being seen as part of the national culture is a driver of purchase intent for global brands. But unlike perceptions of high quality or a distinctive positioning, being part of the local culture is not a necessity. Three globally successful brands in our study achieved universally low scores on this measure (across the eight countries studied) but still achieved relatively high purchase intent. These brands were Heineken, Toyota and Pantene Pro-V.

To find a beer brand that has achieved success in multiple countries outside its homeland is very unusual. Heineken has achieved strong (if not dominant) consideration scores in most of our eight countries, even though the brand is not seen as part of local culture in any of them. That said, few people can accurately identify what Heineken's nationality really is. Rather than deriving distinction from association with a particular place, Heineken has achieved its current lofty status through innovation, strong marketing and a long history.

Founded in The Netherlands in 1863, Heineken used an innovative brewing process that produced a shelf-stable beer that was well-suited to export. The company became the first serious exporter of beer when it extended distribution to England, Belgium and Northern France. The beer and its distinctive packaging remain consistent around the world and, while the brand's marketing communication varies according to local needs and culture, it remains true to the brand's global "feeling."

Like Heineken, Toyota achieves relatively high purchase consideration scores across the countries in our survey, but is not typically seen to be part of the national culture. Toyota differs from Heineken in that the majority of people in each country know that the brand originates in Japan.

The origins of Procter & Gamble's Pantene Pro-V are less clearly identifiable than those of Toyota. A slightly higher proportion of people suggest the brand is American than state they are not sure of the brand's nationality. Like Heineken, however, Pantene Pro-V shares the characteristics of a successful global brand: high quality, distinctive identity, trend-setting and easy to recognize.

Overall, our research suggests that the "think global act local" mantra does in fact still apply. As with any assessment of the global scene, however, there are exceptions. We cannot assume that the principle will apply in all cultures or that every category or brand will be viewed the same way within a country. The real conclusion from our analysis is that no hard and fast rules apply. The strategy that will produce the best return on investment will vary depending on brand, competition, context and culture. When seeking to develop a strong brand on the global stage, each new opportunity must be judged on its own merits, and the brand offer adapted accordingly. Insightful market research must be a critical element of that process. •

Additional Reading

Hollis, Nigel (2008), *The Global Brand*. London: Palgrave Macmillan.

NIGEL HOLLIS, Millward Brown's Chief Global Analyst. A 28-year research veteran, Nigel draws on his experience and understanding of how marketing communications can build brands in addressing the issues facing marketers in today's fast changing world.

After a four-year stint with Cadbury Schweppes in the UK, Nigel joined Millward Brown, where he has worked with clients in many different industries and countries, and has been instrumental in developing some of Millward Brown's most successful research solutions.

Nigel is a four-time winner of WPP's Atticus Award for original thinking in marketing services. His latest thoughts on the world of marketing and market research can be found at www.mb-blog.com.

From *Marketing Research*, Spring 2009, pp. 12–14, 16–18. Copyright © 2009 by American Marketing Association. Reprinted by permission.

Expanding Opportunity at the Base of the Pyramid

In the last decade, C. K. Prahalad and others have argued that the 4 billion people living on less than $2 a day—a group in society that wields trillions of dollars in economic power—is a major, untapped market (Prahalad, 2006). Indeed, there is mounting evidence that the world's poorest people are not only viable producers for a host of products and services, but they also are eager consumers of the basic necessities of the developed world—from mobile phones to soap to banking and insurance products.

DAVID G. ALTMAN, LYNDON REGO, AND PEG ROSS

Recognizing this opportunity, a number of multinational companies launched initiatives to explore the untapped market potential at the base of the economic pyramid (BoP). These multinationals, however, are not focused solely on developing new markets. They are becoming aware, through the efforts of some government organizations, NGOs and philanthropic organizations, that an effective way to eliminate poverty is to provide the poor with access to markets and credit, meaningful goods and services, and opportunities to enhance their skills and business practices. By exploring BoP opportunities, these companies also can have a positive impact on the lives of the poor.

Given the global financial crisis and the ever-expanding gap between the rich and the poor, we may be at the nexus of a major societal shift. A shared view is developing across diverse constituencies that the poorest of the world are a source of abundant resources rather than a societal burden. This is an ideal time to bring diverse players together to experiment with innovative approaches to pressing challenges.

This is an ideal time to bring diverse players together to experiment with innovative approaches to pressing challenges.

By joining forces, the commercial and nonprofit sectors can work together "to enable the poor, especially the poorest, to create a world without poverty" (Grameen Foundation, 2008). From this vantage we explore five lessons learned from organizations that actively are engaged in work at the base of the pyramid and the implications for human resource leaders working in these companies.

Lesson 1: The BoP Has Consumers *and* Producers

The first shift in thinking that needs to be made is how we define people at the BoP. The consumer's goal in this space is to secure affordable food, housing, health care, economic livelihood, education and other essential products and services. In pursuit of these goals, the BoP customer has a few key concerns:

1. easy access to known, needed goods at affordable prices;
2. solutions to daily life challenges; and
3. the opportunity to participate in economically productive activities.

Organizations serving the BoP market strive to accomplish these tasks:

1. generate revenue from existing products;
2. develop new products to meet new market needs; and
3. be good global citizens by using their products and expertise to help solve fundamental social problems.

To meet the needs of the BoP market, companies will need to pursue relationships with local delivery providers, social development players, entrepreneurs, government officials and potential customers.

Beyond an enormous untapped consumer market, those at the lowest levels of the global economy can be effective and viable producers, contributing real economic value to themselves and their business partners. A stunning example is the Indian dairy cooperative, Gujarat Cooperative Milk Marketing Federation (GCMMF), which operates under the brand name Amul (GCMMF, 2009). Poor rural farmers sell the daily output of their few buffaloes to the cooperative of which they are part owners. The cooperative takes care of everything else, from picking up of milk in the village to manufacturing and marketing the end products.

The scale of the business is impressive: 2.7 million producers are responsible for a daily output of more than 10 million liters of milk that accounted for more than $1.3 billion in sales in 2008. Individually, these poor producers would not have access to efficient markets, but when their production capacity is combined they are powerful—GCMMF is India's largest food products marketing organization.

It is difficult to see a group needier or more removed from our traditional notions of producers or consumers than beggars in Bangladesh. Yet micro-lender Grameen Bank saw things differently. In his Nobel Prize acceptance speech, Grameen Bank founder, Muhammad Yunus, recounts:

"Three years ago we started an exclusive programme focusing on the beggars. Loans are interest-free; they can pay whatever amount they wish, whenever they wish. We gave them the idea to carry small merchandise, such as snacks, toys or household items, when they went from house to house for begging. The idea worked. There are now 85,000 beggars in the program. About 5,000 of them have already stopped begging completely. The typical loan to a beggar is $12." (Yunus, 2006)

Lesson No. 1 teaches us that the poor of the world should not be viewed only through the lens of charity.

Lesson 2: Public/Private Partnerships Create Opportunities at the BoP

Inspired by the work of Yunus and Grameen Bank, Grameen Foundation (GF), a U.S.-based nonprofit that has supported the global microfinance industry since the mid 1990s, provides products and services that enable microfinance institutions to use both microfinance and technology to grow and reach ever greater numbers of the world's poorest.

Sometimes called "banking for the poor," microfinance gives very poor people around the world access to credit and other financial services to empower them to pull themselves out of poverty. Relying on their traditional skills, entrepreneurial instincts and hard work, microfinance clients, mostly women, use small loans (usually less than US$200) and other financial services to run small businesses. GF has developed deep business partnerships with BoP customers and organizations serving the BoP. The foundation intends to change mindsets and challenge conventional wisdom by demonstrating to the private and public sectors that these alliances can benefit all parties involved by creating meaningful self-employment opportunities that improve lives.

Wireless Reach

One example is how Qualcomm, the large telecommunications company, works in partnership with Grameen to provide phones to poor people. The initiative started in 2006 with an initial grant from Qualcomm's Wireless Reach initiative that enabled Grameen Foundation's Technology Center to test the feasibility of expanding its successful Village Phone program to Indonesia. Based on the pioneering work of the Grameen Village Phone in Bangladesh, Village Phone and Village Phone Direct extend the benefits of affordable telecommunications access in a sustainable, profitable and empowering way.

Designed to create profitable micro-franchise telecommunications businesses owned and run by poor entrepreneurs, these Village Phone Operators (VPOs) operate their businesses in rural villages where no telecommunications services previously existed. They rent the use of the phone to their community on a per-call basis. The VPOs provide affordable rates to their patrons while earning enough to repay their loans and earn profits that allow them to make investments in their children's health, nutrition and education, and in other business ventures.

In July 2008, GF, Qualcomm's Wireless Reach initiative, a local telecommunications operator and microfinance partners launched Indonesia's first Village Phone program. This program has created more than 137 new businesses in West Java and Banten, all owned and operated by women. Going forward, the partnership will focus on developing the capacity of wireless telecommunications and microfinance institutions by expanding the program to at least 1,000 new Village Phone businesses, reaching up to 500,000 poor Indonesians who currently do not have access to telecommunications services.

This collaboration has evolved into a successful public/private alliance where Qualcomm and GF have been able to combine expertise and experience to spur innovative business solutions for the poor. It also is enabling both organizations to meet their missions.

For Qualcomm, this alliance is a good fit with its Wireless Reach initiative, which supports programs and solutions that bring the benefits of 3G connectivity to developing communities globally. For GF, the relationship with Qualcomm provides a multiplier effect for the limited resources it has to invest.

Grameen-Jameel

In 2003, GF formed a unique partnership with Abdul Latif Jameel Group, a Saudi conglomerate, to support the growth and impact of microfinance across the Arab world. Poverty is an endemic problem in the region, where an estimated 75 million people live on less than $2 a day. This alliance was consolidated in 2007 to form Grameen-Jameel Pan-Arab Microfinance Limited (Grameen-Jameel), a for-profit company headquartered in Dubai, UAE. Jointly owned by GF and Bab Rizq Jameel Limited, a subsidiary of Abdul Latif Jameel Group, Grameen-Jameel is modeled after the social business enterprise concept promoted by Yunus. It reinvests all of its profits into the business rather than distributing dividends. Grameen-Jameel's vision is to reach 1 million new active microfinance clients in the Arab world by 2011 by forming strategic partnerships with microfinance institutions (MFIs) that share its values.

The partners receive a wide range of support, including financing through its $50 million guarantee fund, technical assistance, training and access to best practices resources that have been translated into Arabic. Grameen-Jameel already has reached more than 300,000 new microfinance clients through its partners in Egypt, Jordan, Lebanon, Morocco, Tunisia and Yemen. It is the first social business in the Arab world and an example of how two very different organizations, a Western nonprofit and a for-profit, privately held Saudi company, can come together for a common social good.

As these and other examples illustrate, the challenge of the customer-organization interface at the BoP is to manage relationships between the for-profit players and local organizations that will be involved in implementing the market solutions. There are many questions at the heart of these relationships:

- What profit is enough (and too much) for the for-profit partner?
- How can the impact on alleviating poverty be measured?
- How can tradeoffs between doing well (financially) and doing good (improving the lives of those at the BoP) be managed effectively when competing interests exist?
- What unintended effects, both positive and negative, occur to organizations and BoP customers when innovations are introduced?

Lesson No. 2 teaches us that, despite these questions, non-traditional partners can come together to create new opportunities for those at the BoP.

Lesson 3: The BoP Can Drive Innovation

Some organizations have begun to recognize that the BoP can be a driver of innovation. Cosmos Ignite Innovations developed a product designed to meet the need of the poor for access to lighting. The product also addresses the health and environmental problems associated with using polluting kerosene lamps. The company started by studying the problem at the grassroots. Cosmos Ignite wanted to understand the social need and what barriers existed that its solution would have to overcome.

The company's Mighty Light product uses the latest LED technology combined with solar energy and it is waterproof and shock proof. It has multiple functions, as a room light, reading light or flashlight. The light is strong enough to illuminate an entire room, holds an hour charge and is designed to last 100,000 hours, the equivalent of 30 years of daily use.

It is not difficult to imagine how lighting will change the lives of the more than 1.6 billion people without regular lighting—children can complete their school work after agricultural chores are completed, handwork can be done into the evening providing additional sources of income and families' health is improved with the elimination of kerosene lamps. Mighty Light is used effectively in India, Afghanistan, Pakistan, Cambodia, Nigeria, Kenya, Rwanda, Panama, Guyana and Colombia (Kapur, 2007).

Consider the work of Dr. Devi Shetty, a cardiac surgeon based in Bangalore, India. Shetty has pioneered a series of innovative solutions that have placed health care within the reach of many millions of people in India, regardless of their ability to pay.

One of the vexing challenges Shetty tackled was figuring out how to get quality health care to the large populations living in remote areas of the country. India, like many developing nations, has a population that lives largely in remote, rural villages. While 70 percent of the country's population resides in villages, 70 percent of the nation's doctors live in cities. As Shetty pondered this problem, he found that solutions existed in his own backyard.

Shetty tapped Bangalore's world-class information technology prowess and enlisted India's space agency, also headquartered in the city, to establish a telemedicine network, connected by satellite, between urban hospitals and villages. Patients in rural areas of India can be "seen" by specialists, aided by local paramedical staff who operate the rural clinics. Doctors prescribe treatment administered by the local representative, or request that serious cases be brought to urban centers for treatment.

The system improves access to health care for the rural poor, creates jobs in villages for the paramedical staff that runs the clinics, and maximizes urban doctors' efficiency and reach (Rego & Bhandary, 2006).

Lesson 3 reinforces the importance of viewing the BoP as a seedbed of innovation, grounded in overcoming need and necessity. Nurturing these seeds can unleash innovation in all sectors of society.

Lesson 4: Respond to Market Needs at the BoP with Design Thinking

In the past few years, the Center for Creative Leadership (CCL) has been experimenting with a number of models to make leadership development more affordable and accessible to people around the world (**http://leadbeyond.org/**). The goal of this work is to democratize and scale leadership development. As we embarked on this work, we first began by reading and analyzing the literature, writing reports and preparing scenario documents.

While our analysis was solid, our progress was quite incremental. We hired two of the top design and innovation firms in the world (IDEO and Continuum) to help us shift gears using "design thinking." Design thinking includes ethnographic data collection, brainstorming and rapid prototyping to uncover unmet customer needs and to create innovative solutions to meet these needs.

Continuum and IDEO encouraged us to immerse ourselves in the developing countries in which we wanted to work. The immersions and subsequent product experiments spanned developing and developed countries; corporate, nonprofit and government organizations; and different approaches to product design and delivery. These immersions brought to life the needs and aspirations of underserved populations and took us in directions we could not have envisioned via analysis of the detailed data alone. The deep insights we gained gave form to a spectrum of solutions that CCL is implementing to make leadership development more affordable and accessible for social-sector organizations, youth and young professionals in developed and developing countries.

The design-driven way of working has been mastered by a number of corporations and social enterprises that see emerging markets and low-income populations as prime growth markets. Nokia is an example of a multinational that has been exceptionally successful in BoP markets. It has three R&D facilities in India that have produced innovations such as a phone that operates for more than two weeks on a single charge and comes with a flashlight for those who live without access to dependable electricity. The phone also allows families and friends to share a device by maintaining as many as five separate phone books and providing controls for how much an individual user can talk or spend (Ewing, 2007).

The design-driven way of working has been mastered by a number of corporations and social enterprises that see emerging markets and low-income populations as prime growth markets.

Similarly, companies such as P&G, which generates $20 billion from developing markets, find that localizing capacity is essential to keeping costs down and leveraging local knowledge and relationships. For example, P&G products often wound up hidden under the cashier's counter in crowded retail stores, to be sold on request. By hiring local sales agents, P&G was able to build ties to store owners and better negotiate display space (Byron, 2007).

In some cases, the solutions are inspired by bringing together disparate concepts that span developing and developed worlds. For example, Dr. Govindappa Venkataswamy (or Dr. V as he is commonly known) of Aravind Eye Care in Madurai, India, was inspired by McDonald's Hamburger University. Through studying the hamburger chain's operations, he saw that low-cost, high-quality and volume could be attained through carefully managed operations. The model he created has enabled eye doctors to conduct 2,600 surgeries each year, compared to the current prevailing average of 400 operations (Miller, 2006).

BoP solutions often set improbably lofty goals that are brought to life through iterative experimentation. The One Laptop per Child Project had a three-year gestation period through which a network of hardware and software designers experimented with a variety of features and options to address key BoP limitations. The initial product specs called for a laptop that was intuitive to children, heat-proof, dust-proof, drop-proof, spill-proof, designed to work with limited power and Internet access, and priced at a fifth the price of the cheapest laptop available. The product that made it to market, named the XO, was priced closer to $200 but has accomplished many of its seemingly unrealistic objectives (Pogue, 2007).

As these examples illustrate, success in BoP markets requires the kind of empathetic and imaginative approaches that design thinking incorporates as a best practice. It also requires leveraging local talent to acquire insights, maintain relationships and trim costs. Fortunately there is no deficit of talent at the BoP, only the need to see the abundant opportunity and unlock the vast human potential that exists within it.

Lesson 5: The BoP is a Source of Employees

For most multinational corporations, success in emerging markets necessitates identifying, hiring, developing and utilizing local talent. Pantaloon, a large Indian retail giant, has had commercial success hiring employees at the BoP. They recruit and train youth from India's slums to become clerks and baristas, some of whom go on to become managers and entrepreneurs. The head of training at Pantaloon, K.C. Kurien, reports that he built the company's leadership-training program on an insight he had at a traffic intersection in Mumbai. Watching beggars work the line of cars, he noticed that those with greater social skills were more successful. If self-confidence and social skills work for beggars, he asked himself, what could they do for motivated people from the slums? Pantaloon's program has been highly successful in driving employee engagement, customer service, innovation and growth.

Along similar lines, Mobile Metrix is an on-the-ground marketing organization that works in developing countries to help public- and private-sector organizations collect grassroots data that inform product and service development for the BoP market. To obtain these data, they hire local young people (ages 16–24), provide them with training on how to use handheld computers and then send them into their communities to collect data on community needs. After products are developed, these young people also have the opportunity to be employed in marketing and distribution, benefiting both them and the organizations that now have access to hard-to-reach communities and consumers.

Another innovative organization that is bringing essential products, jobs and empowerment to disadvantaged populations is VisionSpring (formerly Scojo Foundation). VisionSpring is working to provide reading glasses to the poor; 700 million of the world's poorest suffer from presbyopia (blurry up-close vision), which undermines their ability to do many work tasks such as sewing or sorting grain. The organization's business model is to train and engage local women as "vision entrepreneurs," which in many cases leads to a doubling of their income. The company operates in more than a dozen countries, and as of 2008 had sold nearly 90,000 pairs of reading glasses and trained more than 1,000 Vision Entrepreneurs (MacMillan, 2008).

If Grameen Bank can turn beggars into successful entrepreneurs, if Pantaloon can turn slum dwellers into confident store clerks and managers, if Mobile Metrix can successfully employ youth in hard-to-reach communities to help drive product development and sales, and if VisionSpring can employ poor women to help improve the eyesight of others, consider the societal impact if thousands of organizations were to include the BoP as a source of employees.

Relevance to HR Leaders

The vast untapped market at the BoP represents a potential opportunity for organizations that find their traditional markets are becoming saturated and their profit margins are shrinking. The IMF notes that India and China—countries made up largely of poor people—are the main engines of world growth (Callen, 2007). The World Bank reports that developing countries are responsible for 40 percent of the world's economy (World Bank, 2007).

Success at the BoP requires a new orientation however. Working at the BoP requires a rejection of the notion that the poor are passive recipients of charity, incapable of being consumers or producers. It also requires innovation to create or adapt product, services and business models. This, in turn, requires new capabilities within organizations and their people.

For senior HR leaders, these new business opportunities will require developing people (and teams) who can work successfully in BoP environments and with non-profit partners. What corporations can learn from non-profits is how to work with scarce resources, create broad alliances and build movements and tap passion and unlock potential. The head of a corporation in Chile explained that young people who join the corporate sector after completing a service learning program in rural Chile are much in demand and are deemed able to think more holistically and be more persevering and resilient.

From another lens, engaging with BoP markets provides a lever for organizational transformation, increased employee engagement and stronger community relations. Employees can gain opportunities to develop their strengths and apply them in service of social as well as business goals, enhancing organizations' effectiveness as well as corporate brands. In an era of growing demands for triple-bottom-line approaches, a company that serves the BoP can be more attractive to customers and employees.

The greatest barrier to traverse is that of mindset. Mohammed Yunus likens the untapped potential of the poor, limited by the lack of opportunity, to a seed of a tree that is planted in a tiny pot. The same seed planted in the fertile ground can grow to be a great tree (Knowledge@Wharton, 2005). The potential for companies with the BoP is much the same. If planted in a small pot of opportunity they will yield little. Nurtured in a supportive corporate culture, however, the BoP represents significant growth potential for organizations and their shareholders, employees and customers. HR leaders can lead the way by helping create cultures that enable this transformation.

References

Byron, E. (2007, July 16). P&G's global target: Shelves of tiny stores. *The Wall Street Journal*, p. A1.

Callen, T. (2007, October 17). Emerging markets main engine of growth. *IMF Survey Magazine*, p. 195.

Ewing, J. (2007, May 4). First mover in mobile. *BusinessWeek*, p. 60.

Grameen Foundation. (2008). *Mission statement*. Washington, DC: Author.

Gujarat Cooperative Milk Marketing Federation (GCMMF). (2009). Retrieved March 6, 2009, from www.amul.com

Kapur, S. (2007, August 14). Innovating for the bottom of the pyramid. *Business Standard*. Retrieved March 6, 2009, from www.business-standard.com/india/storypage.php?autono=294343

Knowledge@Wharton. (2005). *Muhammad Yunus, banker to the world's poorest citizens, makes his case*. Retrieved April 5, 2009, from http://knowledge.wharton.upenn.edu/article.cfm?articleid=1147

MacMillan, G. (2008). *45 social entrepreneurs who are changing the world*. Retrieved March 13, 2009, from www.fastcompany.com/social/2008/profiles/scojo-foundation.html

Miller, S. (2006, August 5). McSurgery: A man who saved 2.4 million eyes. *The Wall Street Journal*, p. A6.

Pogue, D. (2007, October 4). Laptop with a mission widens its audience. *The New York Times*. Retrieved from www.nytimes.com/2007/10/04/technology/circuits/04pogue.html

Prahalad, C. K. (2006). *The fortune at the bottom of the pyramid: Eradicating poverty through profits*. Upper Saddle River, NJ: Pearson.

Rego, L., & Bhandary, A. (2006). New model: A social entrepreneur changes the landscape. *Leadership in Action*, 26(1), 8-11.

Yunus, M. (2006). Nobel Lecture, Oslo, December 10, 2006. Retrieved February 14, 2009, from http://nobelprize.org/nobel_prizes/peace/laureates/2006/yunus-lecture-en.html

DAVID G. ALTMAN, PHD., is executive vice president, Research, Innovation and Product Development at the Center for Creative Leadership (CCL), a global non-profit organization. Prior to joining CCL, he spent 20 years as a public health researcher, advocate and professor.

LYNDON REGO, MBA, is director, Innovation Incubator at the Center for Creative Leadership, where he helps steer a broad initiative to extend leadership development to underserved populations across the world.

PEG ROSS is director of the Human Capital Center at Grameen Foundation, where she helps microfinance institutions strengthen their people practices and align them with business strategy. She has held corporate HR leadership positions in a variety of industries and obtained her master's degree in Organization Development from Loyola University of Chicago.

From *HRPS People & Strategy*, vol. 32, issue 2, June 2009, pp. 47–51. Copyright © 2009 by Human Resource Planning Society. All rights reserved. Reprinted by permission. www.hrps.org

Hailun Piano and the Quest for Quality

Hindered in the domestic Chinese market by peculiar tax laws, Hailun was forced to build a better product or perish. This tough lesson has served the company well as it expands its global presence.

On the Saturday before the opening of the Music China Fair in Shanghai, a multinational team of piano designers is crowded around a hand-carved piano at the Hailun Piano factory in Ningbo, 175 miles to the south. The special edition concert grand with its images of Chinese landscapes carved in rosewood will be the centerpiece of Hailun's exhibit at the show. Voicing specialist Sibin Zlatkovic is making his final adjustments to its exposed strings while the rest of the team looks on. "We did this kind of work at Bösendorfer," says Basilios Strmec, an Austrian who is now president of Hailun USA. "This is gorgeous, all hand-carved. It took 19 months to build."

The show piece piano represents a first step into the luxury market for Hailun, whose mid-priced pianos have taken hold throughout North America and Europe as well in as in the domestic Chinese market. Last year the brand received worldwide exposure in the form of a red lacquered grand piano built for ceremonies in the run-up to the Beijing Olympic Games.

Behind the scenes, Hailun's team of artistic and technical experts is as international as its aspirations. In China for the upcoming trade show, along with Strmec, are American Frank Emerson, who designed pianos for Baldwin and later for Mason & Hamlin, is a recipient of the Friendship Medal, the highest honor presented by the Chinese government to foreigners who have made outstanding contributions to China's economic and social progress. Veletzky, the owner of Austrian piano maker Wendl & Lung, is Hailun's senior technical advisor and directs the distribution of Hailun in the European market. Zlatkovic, also of Wendl & Lung, is Hailun's director of voicing and tuning and instructor to the company's team of voicers at the factory in Ningbo.

In about two days the whole team will make the road trip to Music China over the newly constructed Hangzhou Bay Bridge, which has reduced the travel time between Ningbo and Shanghai from a circuitous four hours to a straight shot of two-and-a-half. It's just one example of a rapid modernization that touches everything from China's infrastructure to its economy and the lifestyle of its people.

Middle aged Chinese people can remember being taught as children about the evils of capitalism, Western culture, and all of its trappings, including classical music. Today, knowledge and appreciation of classical music is regarded as a mark of sophistication. As in Western countries, ownership of a high-caliber piano—even among those who don't play—is considered a status symbol. "Twenty or 25 years ago, there probably wasn't a piano in the city of Ningbo," says Emerson. "And now we're building them by the hundreds."

The explosion of China's middle class, usually estimated between 200 and 300 million, has made China the fastest-growing market for Hailun, whose domestic sales have risen 40% in two years. Moreover, market research shows that Chinese people, particularly the younger generation, aren't just able to buy more things—they have higher expectations for the products they purchase than ever before. "There's a different turn in Chinese perceptions and values," says Strmec. "They have awakened to the idea of quality."

The history of the Hailun Piano Company will illustrate how circumstances pushed the company to market its pianos on quality rather than price. Founder Hailun Chen, who came from a background in tool manufacturing, started the company in 1987 as a parts manufacturer for other piano makers. When Hailun shifted into piano production in 2002, it built its first pianos for export only to avoid the tax penalty imposed by the Chinese government on private businesses competing with government-owned companies in the Chinese domestic market. Later the company did introduce its pianos to the domestic market, but the embedded cost of the tax would make it impossible to compete with other Chinese-made pianos on price alone. "Hailun had to build a higher-quality piano to justify the higher price," says Emerson. "This gave them even more incentive to produce the best product they could."

Once established as a piano maker, Hailun dedicated a $44 million capital outlay capital outlay toward equipping its 430,000-square-foot factory with custom-designed CNC machinery. A rigorous apprenticeship program was established, recruiting 40 engineering students per year from the Ningbo Institute of Technology. Only the top three are offered permanent jobs. All Hailun workers are trained for at least one year—four years for those involved in tuning and voicing—before being allowed to work on pianos headed for the market. They are paid 25% more than the average Chinese factory worker. "We want to ensure that what we send out is a product of integrity, that there's quality behind it," says Strmec.

Four years ago, Strmec was vice president for U.S. marketing and sales for Bösendorfer, whose exclusive reputation is built on its annual production of 400 and retail prices of $120,000 and more. Hailun, with its annual production of 8,000 and typical price points between $10,000 and $20,000, demands a different mindset, but some of the principles still apply.

"Bösendorfer continues to survive and command prices of $120,000 and $130,000 because they do not cut corners," says Strmec. "We can't compromise on little things to make our pianos two dollars cheaper. If you're trained in the mentality that people value quality, you'll have the courage to go out on the market and say, 'This is quality—try it and see for yourself,' instead of apologizing for the price."

> We can't compromise on little things to make our pianos two dollars cheaper. People value quality. You need the courage to say, 'This is quality—try it and see for yourself.' instead of apologizing for the price.

Indicating a soundboard in production on the factory floor, he says, "Do you see the grain of the wood, how the rings are close together? A good soundboard has very close-together rings—that means the wood has grown very slowly and has greater resonance." Later, in a room of finished pianos due for transport to the Music China Fair, he points out the characteristic texture of the genuine ebony keys on one of Hailun's higher-end grands. "It's a little bit rougher; it gives the pianist a better grip," he says.

On this trip to the factory in Ningbo, Hailun's design team is refining its newest high-end feature, the inclusion of a sostenuto pedal on two upright models, the HU 6 and HU 7, due to be presented at the winter NAMM show. By incorporating the sostenuto, considered a feature for the professional market, the designers aim to match the range of expression found in a fine European instrument. "It's the mark of a high-end piano," says Emerson. "If you want to be counted among that class of piano, you have to have it."

As a Chinese manufacturer, Hailun faces the preconceptions of consumers in the West, where Chinese products sometimes carry associations with product recalls and quality-control snafus. Even within the music products industry, Hailun fights the perception that the lower cost of Chinese-made products indicates shoddy workmanship more than the lower cost of doing business in China. Zlatkovic counters, "If I were to build the same piano in Boston or Vienna, it would have to cost three to four times more because of the cost of the electricity, the real estate, the insurance, etc. Everything would be more expensive. By building it in China, I can sell it as a less expensive piano, but that doesn't make it a lower-quality piano."

Strmec says, "It's a shame that the word 'Chinese' should be associated with poor quality. We want to change that perception to reflect the tremendous history of this country and the integrity behind our product."

Considering, incidentally, the range of multinational influences behind Hailun pianos, it's fair to pose the question of whether they should be considered Chinese instruments at all.

"What is the word President Obama used to describe himself during the election?" says Strmec. "Our pianos are mutts. On the Chinese side they reflect considerable ingenuity and investment in both machinery and people. But the genius behind them is also American, is Austrian, is French—it's the best ideas coming together."

> Our pianos are mutts. On the Chinese side they reflect considerable investment in machinery and people. But the genius behind them is also American, Austrian, French—it's the best ideas come together.

A Family Business

Hailun personnel say the company is very much a family business. Several members of the upper level management are related to Hailun Chen, including his cousin May Wang, who is vice president of sales to the U.S. market and also serves as primary translator among the Chinese personnel and visiting experts from the Europe and the U.S. But those who have worked there for any length of time say the sense of family extends to the entire team—even foreigners—to a degree that's unusual for China, where close friendships and casual socializing among colleagues is less common than in the U.S. For lunch at the factory, Hailun executives and visiting designers eat family style at a round table, where at least three languages are often spoken at once but communication proceeds with surprising fluency. After a round of cards with a group of Hailun factory employees, Strmec says, "At what other company would a guy who works in the factory be allowed to win money from the president of the U.S. branch of the company? Other companies try to create that camaraderie, but they keep it at arm's length. There's none of that here. There is a unique skill that Mr. Chen brings to this company that has nothing to do with building pianos and everything to do with building positive international relationships."

The Voice of the Piano

Because there's no global consensus on what a piano ought to sound like, Hailun builds and voices its various models according to the tastes of the markets they're destined for. Zlatkovic can deliver a scholarly synopsis of voicing preferences around the world, from the delicate tone favored by the Europeans to the bolder tastes of the Americans. Time, too, has altered overall norms in voicing. Zlatkovic will tell you that trends in piano voicing, which ran to the warm and mellow during the 1920s and '30s and shifted to favor a harsher, stronger sound through the latter part of the 20th century, have come full circle in the early part of the 21st century. "If you transported a pianist from 30 years ago and had him play on one of the mellower-sounding pianos we're voicing today, he wouldn't like it because he wouldn't think it sounded aggressive enough," says Zlatkovic.

More an art than a science, voicing is said to be one of the most difficult concepts to impart to students of the trade. Compounding the challenge for Zlatkovic and his trainees is the lost knowledge that comes from China's long prohibition on Western music and culture. "What I can't give my voicing students is my experience of all the other instruments I have in my mental library," says Zlatkovic. "They have the talent, but they don't have the same cultural reference point as we have in the West. That's why they welcome the expertise we can bring them from the U.S. and Europe, where the piano tradition has existed for so long."

The European Strategy

With a 300-year legacy in piano building, the European markets present special challenges for a new, foreign-made piano. Hailun's European strategy relies heavily on its association with Wendl & Lung, the century-old Viennese piano manufacturer now owned by Peter Veletzky. Veletzky, who at the age of 22 became Austria's youngest master piano builder, represents the fourth generation of his family to head the company. Since forming a partnership with Hailun in 2003, Veletzky has overseen the distribution of Hailun pianos in Europe, where they are sold under the Wendl & Lung name. "Peter's participation has created a lot of credibility for us, both in Europe and in other parts of the world," says Strmec.

In Europe, as in North America, the repercussions of the economic crisis have created an opening for a mid-priced piano modeled after the European tradition in fine piano making.

"With our products that offer a lot of value at a very modest price, we are better positioned in this economic climate than many European manufacturers," says Veletzky. "I say that with both a smile and a tear: a smile, because we've done well in Europe, very well, and a tear for the European piano industry, which in large part is suffering."

The Future of Hailun Piano

After the Music China Fair, Hailun's hand-carved concert grand, called Dreams of the East, sold to a Chinese businessman for approximately $347,000. Following the blockbuster sale, Hailun plans tentatively to craft a similar piano for the 2011 winter NAMM show, and eventually to build up to 50 such instruments each year for the luxury market. But within its primary mid-priced niche, Hailun maintains its focus on building what many say is the missing piece for some of China's most promising companies: a brand that commands recognition and respect in the West. A sleek new Hailun Piano website, tailored to the U.S. market, was scheduled to launch around the first of the year. On other fronts, Hailun is pursuing artist endorsements to match faces and sounds with the Hailun name. "Ultimately, Hailun wants to serve the stages of concert halls and recording studios with instruments worthy of musicians and music connoisseurs of every musical persuasion," says Strmec. "My conviction is that a brand constitutes a promise that is consistently fulfilled to its customers. For Hailun to develop into a brand that follows through on that promise would be my greatest source of pride."

Distant Dilemmas

Before sending executives on assignments in countries with questionable business practices, HR professionals must help prepare them for the ethical predicaments that may await them there.

MARK McGRAW

No one is naïve enough to think that bribery, kickbacks and other corrupt business practices don't exist here in the United States. But it's also understood that such practices are, at best, unethical and, at worst, illegal—not to mention potentially costly for companies caught engaging in them.

But in some countries, bribes, illegal payments and other underhanded activities are simply an accepted part of doing business. And if recent statistics are any indication, the current recession is only compounding the problem.

According to a recent Ernst & Young survey, half of the 2,246 respondents in major countries across Europe said they felt that one or more types of unethical business behaviors was acceptable, including 25 percent who thought it fine to give a cash bribe to win work. By country, that figure rose as high as 38 percent in Spain, 43 percent in the Czech Republic and 53 percent in Turkey.

In the same survey by the New York-based business and financial advisory firm, more than half of respondents said they expected corporate fraud to increase over the next few years, with 54 percent of participants from Western Europe and 55 percent from Central and Eastern Europe expressing the same sentiment.

While questionable business practices may become more accepted by workers in some places, governments in revenue-starved countries are focusing more closely than ever on violations of international anti-corruption laws and the accompanying fines that can be doled out.

Expatriates can easily, even unwittingly, violate such laws, especially when they are relocated to a country awash in corruption. Corporate counsel may be aware of this growing concern, but experts say HR must take on an equally large role in preparing expatriates for the vastly different business environments they may find themselves in overseas.

Hard Lessons

Some companies have discovered the hard way that the cost of an expatriate's unethical behavior can be steep. Consider Lucent Technologies, for example, the former telecommunications giant that merged with Alcatel to become Alcatel-Lucent, based in Murray Hill, N.J., in 2006.

In 2004, the company fired four China-based executives for alleged violations of the Foreign Corrupt Practices Act. No arrests were made, but, as part of an intercession agreement reached with the United States Department of Justice in December 2007 the company agreed to pay $2.5 million in civil penalties and fines to settle the allegations—which included making payments to Chinese government officials to travel to the United States and elsewhere for sightseeing and entertainment between 2000 and 2003.

According to a suit filed in the United States District Court for the District of Columbia, the Securities and Exchange Commission alleged that Lucent spent upwards of $10 million in travel and entertainment expenses for about 1,000 employees of state-owned or state-controlled telecommunications businesses in China that were prospective or existing Lucent customers. The suit alleged that the foreign officials spent little or no time actually visiting Lucent facilities, and that the company improperly recorded the expenses in its corporate books.

In December of last year, Siemens paid $1.6 billion—the largest fine for bribery in modern corporate history, according to the *New York Times*—in a settlement with the Justice Department and the Securities and Exchange Commission. As part of the settlement, Siemens also pleaded guilty to violating accounting provisions of the FCPA. The agreement came two years after midlevel executive Reinhard Siekaczek was arrested for his role in overseeing "an annual bribery budget of about $40 million to $50 million" to make payments to well-placed officials in countries such as Vietnam, Venezuela, Italy and Israel, according to the *Times*.

The payments, Siekaczek told the paper, were "vital to maintaining the competitiveness of Siemens overseas.

"It was about keeping the business unit alive," he said, "and not jeopardizing thousands of jobs overnight."

Granted, Siekaczek's intentions, at least in his mind, may have simply been to keep the business afloat in trying times, by whatever means necessary. Regardless, say experts consulted for this story, it should be clear to expatriates that bribery and other corrupt practices are unacceptable, regardless of the setting or circumstances.

HR must play a key role in hammering that message home, says Stewart Black, associate dean of executive development programs at INSEAD, an international graduate business school with North American offices in New York.

"If you make the situation difficult enough, even 'ethical people' will make bad choices."

—STEWART BLACK, INSEAD

"If you make the situation difficult enough, even 'ethical people' will make bad choices," says Black, who is also an affiliate professor of organization behavior at INSEAD, and the executive director of the INSEAD Center for Human Resources in Singapore. "Part of HR's role is to highlight the human, social [and] relational side of a situation. The more demanding the situation, the more careful the selection [of the employee to handle it] and the more intensive the training needs to be."

The best companies decrease the likelihood of potential expats making "bad choices" in foreign countries by looking beyond their technical skills when evaluating them for overseas assignments, says William Sheridan, vice president of international human resource services at the New York office of the National Foreign Trade Council.

"Smarter companies," he says, "don't rely solely on an employee's performance record in [his or her] home country—or the employee's manager's recommendation alone—but are aware that working in a foreign setting is different, and that social skills are as important as accumulated business skills, perhaps even more important.

"Adaptability to new situations is critical," Sheridan says. "Often, the more adaptable employee will outperform a colleague who had higher job-performance ratings in the home country."

Training, Training, Training

Selecting an executive with a consistent moral compass and an ability to adjust is a good start to ensuring ethical behavior overseas.

Pinpointing such employees requires some legwork on HR's part, says William Devaney, co-chair of the Foreign Corrupt Practices Act and Anti-Corruption Group at Washington-based business law firm Venable.

"Look at their reviews, speak to their supervisors and speak to the employees themselves," Devaney says. "You want to try to identify the employee who will not take the expedient route over the ethical when faced with the challenge of dealing with corrupt bureaucracies."

But, moreover, HR should be heavily involved in extensive training for these employees about to go abroad, experts say.

First and foremost, HR must work closely with corporate counsel to ensure that expatriates understand the implications of the Foreign Corrupt Practices Act and other anti-corruption measures, Devaney says.

The U.S. employee needs to understand that the FCPA, which addresses accounting-transparency requirements under the Securities Exchange Act and contains anti-bribery provisions, applies to individuals specifically, even when working abroad and/or working for a non-U.S. company or a non-U.S. affiliate, he adds.

Such training should be conducted in person at least once a year, and should be overseen "by in-house counsel well-versed in the FCPA or outside counsel [with expertise on] the FCPA," Devaney says. "That way, the employees can discuss real-life [events] and walk through various situations that might present themselves [in other countries]. If live training is not possible, there are Internet training programs available that can be bolstered by training programs that management conducts."

Executives overseas should be made aware they have a responsibility beyond themselves, too.

"The [executive] also needs to understand that he, as well as the company, is responsible for the company's agents in the foreign country," Devaney says. "The employee must ensure that the local agents or contractors he is dealing with are not making corrupt payments."

"This can be difficult in areas of the world where such payments are the norm," he says. "But turning a blind eye to the issue can cost the company untold millions in fines and expose the employee to criminal prosecution."

HR, along with the general counsel's office, must also ensure "there is worldwide training, so that anti-corruption is a worldwide initiative and not something viewed internally as stopping at the U.S. border," he says.

Most companies have a code of conduct that employees must be in compliance with wherever they do business, says Achim Mossmann, managing director of global mobility advisory services in KPMG International Executive Services practice, based in New York.

However, some countries' practices may pose a dilemma to expatriates, he says.

"For example, in some countries, gift-giving is seen as an acceptable way to 'move a transaction along.' Training can help employees understand what specific business practices to expect in certain countries and what behavior is acceptable in certain situations," he says.

"Role playing, training scenarios and case studies can help employees understand acceptable gift-giving—a $30 bottle of wine, perhaps—versus what could be characterized as bribery or corruption—a $1,000 cash payment."

HR should play a sizable role in orchestrating local and global training for expatriates, Mossman says. Setting up a companywide program is typically done with help from outside vendors, he says, "to assist with the development and implementation of this type of training."

When searching for a vendor to lead expat training, HR should develop a general outline explaining the type of training they would like to provide, issue a request for proposal and select a vendor capable of developing the necessary content and materials, he adds.

The actual training can happen in two ways, Mossman says. The vendor can conduct in-person training or develop a

Web-based training module. Or, after developing the program, the vendor "trains the trainer," in many cases an HR professional, who then delivers the training.

"Many organizations like this model, because it allows them to hire someone from the outside with the expertise to develop the training content and materials, and then have an in-house HR professional who knows the organization conduct the training, which helps from a credibility standpoint."

Thoroughly documenting that expatriates have received such training will help distance the company from the unscrupulous actions of a rogue employee, says Mossman, who advises HR executives on managing international-assignment programs.

"In these scenarios, there are always two potential culprits—the employee and the employer," he says. "The employer will need to show an investigating authority that it provided the employee with sufficient information and training, as a first line of defense. Appropriate documentation can demonstrate that the employer has made sufficient efforts to ensure that the employee has received adequate training and information."

Monitoring the Situation

There are clearly questions to answer and scenarios to consider before sending an executive on assignment to a country with corrupt business practices. But the company's—and the HR executive's—job isn't over once the expatriate gets on the plane.

HR executives should stay in frequent contact with the recently transferred executive, Devaney says, and establish a support system that offers expatriates guidance in the event that ethical quandaries arise.

"The company should have a hotline, where any anti-corruption questions or issues can be openly and, if necessary, anonymously discussed," he says. "If the HR executive sees any problems in the anti-corruption area, he or she should notify the general counsel's office immediately."

"Without a sounding board," Black adds, "the expat is on his or her own. HR needs to be close enough to the employee that he or she feels comfortable enough to discuss questionable situations," he says, "without the immediate pressures of business results that are often implicitly or explicitly there in discussions of the same issue with line executives."

The careful selection and appropriate training of expatriates is lacking at many companies, but even when both are done well, HR must still help keep a close eye on operations in countries with questionable business ethics, says Black.

"To not have HR as a sounding board in a knowingly corrupt country is like deciding not to buy flood insurance when you are in an established flood plain," he says.

Ultimately, he says, that decision could cost an organization millions of dollars, not to mention destroy the good will it has worked hard to create among its customers and public.

"Trust me," Black says, "the *International Herald Tribune* does not care that the situation was almost impossible. They only care that an ethical lapse makes for a great story."

"It takes decades to build up public trust and credibility, and it can take only minutes for it to go up in a toxic cloud," he adds.

From *Human Resource Executive,* January 2010. Copyright © 2010 by Human Resource Executive. Reprinted by permission of LRP Publications.

Jobs on Another Shore

Outsourcing of service jobs to other countries could affect industrial countries' economies and attitudes toward globalization.

David T. Coe

China and, more recently, India are emerging as major trading countries at the same time that a new form of international commerce is taking shape—technologically assisted offshoring of jobs, especially of jobs once thought immune to international competition.

China's burgeoning share of world exports and the increase in India's share (see Chart 1) have been recognized as a major development in international economics with a significant impact on employment, wages, and production in developed countries. Now it is becoming clear that offshoring—the outsourcing to other countries of jobs or tasks that produce intermediate inputs, including services—could have potentially long-lived effects on employment, relative wages, and the job security of workers in advanced economies.

In the long run, most economists and policymakers agree, this recent acceleration of globalization will have beneficial economic effects, in both advanced economies and their emerging market trading partners. But in the short run, particularly in countries with less flexible labor markets, there could be large disruptions. Moreover, the sizable number of potentially offshorable jobs has exposed new groups of workers to international competition, and these workers may increasingly be a receptive audience for special-interest protectionists.

The recent phenomenon of the offshoring of business services has stimulated a debate in many advanced economies. The two sides of the academic debate in the United States are probably best exemplified by the attitudes of Harvard economist Gregory Mankiw and Princeton economist Alan Blinder.

In 2004, when he was chairman of the U.S. Council of Economic Advisers (CEA), Mankiw called offshoring a long-run plus for the economy, with effects that are not qualitatively different from those of conventional trade in goods. Blinder—a member of President Bill Clinton's CEA and former vice chair of the Federal Reserve Board—has said the debate is not about basic economic gains, which he acknowledges, but about whether offshoring and the entrance of China and India into the world economy are a "big deal" or simply "business as usual." Blinder (2007) says the developments *are* a big deal because they will force major changes in industrial structure and types

of jobs, as well as in wages, job security, labor turnover, and—at least in the short run—employment and unemployment.

Whether offshoring is a big deal or business as usual depends on a number of factors: how many jobs have already been "lost," how many jobs might be lost, how rapidly new jobs are created, the potential impact on incomes and job security for different types of workers, and how long or smooth the transition is likely to be.

The Offshoring Threat

Hard data are scarce on how many jobs in advanced economies have actually been lost because of offshoring, but estimates suggest the effects have been limited to about 0.3–0.7 percent of total employment in the United States and those European countries for which estimates are available (Baldwin, 2006). There is also evidence, however, that service offshoring has been steadily increasing in recent years.

The potential number of service sector jobs that could be affected by offshoring is much larger. Van Welsum and Vickery (2005) estimate that in 2003 close to 20 percent of total

(percent of total world exports of goods and services)

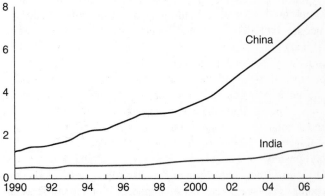

Chart 1 Growing presence Since 1990, China's share of world exports has grown dramatically, while India's has also increased.

Source: IMF, World Economic Outlook database.

113

employment in the European Union countries, Australia, Canada, and the United States could potentially have been affected by offshoring of services enabled by information and communications technology. Blinder has higher estimates for the United States: 22–29 percent. Other studies also produce large estimates.

The distinction between estimates of the *potential* number of service sector jobs that could be exposed to international competition and the *actual* number of job losses is often missed in the public debate. That debate often implicitly assumes that industrial countries will have no comparative advantage in *any* of the service sector jobs newly exposed to international competition. That is, industrial countries will only *offshore,* not attract, or *onshore,* jobs. Yet the United States, the United Kingdom, and a number of other advanced economies are net exporters of services, and in many cases this net surplus has been increasing in recent years. It is possible that advanced economies will onshore more services than they offshore. In addition, productivity increases in offshoring enterprises may lead them to increase hiring, potentially resulting in a net increase in jobs. In the United Kingdom, for example, firms that import services have faster employment growth than those that do not (Hijzen and others, 2007).

Incomes and Job Security

A key issue is whether offshoring will affect the relative wages of workers differently than did earlier episodes of globalization. It is more likely that offshoring will be a big deal in advanced economies if offshoring reduces incomes of medium- and high-skilled workers, many of whom were not previously exposed to international competition, rather than mainly restraining wages of low-skilled workers, as skill-biased technical change and globalization have tended to do in the past. The possibility of downward pressure on wages of skilled workers is suggested by ample anecdotal evidence: workers in India reading X-rays of patients in advanced economies, developing software for firms in advanced economies, and preparing tax forms for citizens of advanced economies. Moreover, some low-skill tasks, such as those performed by gardeners, garbage collectors, and caregivers, are, with current technology, not able to be done abroad, suggesting that wages for these types of jobs are unlikely to be affected by offshoring.

Whether, on balance, highly skilled service tasks are offshored or onshored in a specific country, with concomitant pressures on incomes, will depend on that country's comparative advantage. Although offshoring of some skilled services has grown rapidly in Indian cities such as Bangalore, it seems likely that the comparative advantage of emerging market countries, such as China and India, will remain in low- or medium-skill tasks for some time, given the challenges of increasing the quality of education and average levels of education of their vast populations.

In general, offshoring does not appear to be having a disproportionately large effect on skilled tasks in advanced economies. Of course, this could change if high-skilled jobs in industrial countries that are potentially offshorable get offshored. Thus far, however, the effects of offshoring appear to be consistent with findings in the broader literature indicating that skill-biased technical change tends to reduce the wages of low-skilled workers.

Offshoring may also have important effects on workers' actual or perceived job security and on labor's bargaining power. Evidence

of this is found in the United States, for example, where workers in industries and occupations involved in tradable goods express higher levels of economic insecurity than other workers. Needless to say, insecurity will increase if the impact of offshoring on workers is sudden and unpredictable, as has generally been the case.

How Bumpy the Transition?

Whether increased offshoring occurs smoothly or in a massive and disruptive transition will depend on a variety of macroeconomic and structural factors. Important factors are the macroeconomic, trade, and exchange rate policies in China and India and in their industrial country trading partners that will determine the overall size and configuration of world current account balances. Structural policies are also important because countries with flexible labor and product markets, good education institutions and training systems, and effective employment and innovation policies will more easily and rapidly adapt to the challenges and opportunities from increased trade and offshoring.

The actual number of tasks that become tradable and how rapidly they start to be traded will also depend on the capacity in China, India, and other developing countries to take on new types of tasks from advanced economies. As noted, it seems likely that it will take some time before China and India develop a broad-based comparative advantage in more technologically advanced services. Capacity to onshore new types of tasks will also require improvements in infrastructure in India; in China, it will depend on strengthened English-language skills, property rights, intellectual property rights enforcement, and rule of law. These structural issues suggest a drawn-out transition.

The transition will also depend on wage developments for the limited number of suitably skilled workers in China and India. There are already tentative signs of rising real wages and anecdotal evidence of labor shortages in the coastal regions of China and in Bangalore. Other things being equal, rising real wages in key regions in China and India will erode these countries' comparative advantages and limit the number of tasks they take on from developed economies.

A final question is how many other developing and transition countries will join the party as offshoring destinations— and how rapidly. So far, the participation of many countries in sub-Saharan Africa, the Middle East, Central Asia, and South America appears nonexistent. For a number of reasons related to geographic proximity, cultural and linguistic similarities, and the unique roles of the Chinese and Indian diasporas, other countries may find it difficult to emulate China's and India's recent successes as offshoring destinations (Coe, 2007).

The longer the transition takes, the less likely it is to be disruptive. But regardless of how long the transition is, it is clear that the ongoing integration of China and India into the world economy is likely to have lasting effects on the distribution of income and on job security in advanced economies.

Globalization and Inequality

The recent intensification of globalization has occurred while many workers in industrial countries perceive an ongoing and sustained rise in economic inequality. The causes of the rise in income

Gini index (percent)

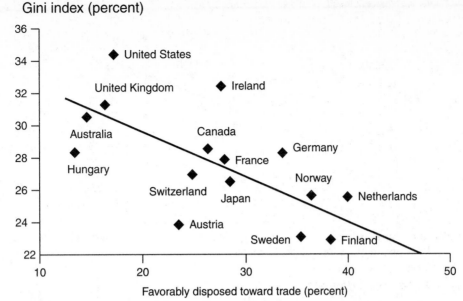

Chart 2 Inequality and trade views In industrial countries, the higher the level of income inequality, the less positive are the attitudes toward trade.

Sources: Förster and Pearson (2002); and International Social Survey Programme (2007).

Note: The Gini Index is a measure of income inequality. At 0, there is perfect equality (everyone has the same income); at 100, there is total inequality (one person has all the income). The Gini index here is from the mid-1990s. The attitudes toward trade are from a 2003 survey.

inequality are not fully understood, but the balance of empirical research indicates that skill-biased technical change has been a more powerful driver of increased wage dispersion than globalization, itself a reflection of technological advance (IMF, 2007).

Although the increase in inequality has been fairly general, it has been particularly large in countries such as the United States, the United Kingdom, and Australia. It has often been especially pronounced when comparing the very top of the income distribution with the rest of the population. In the United States, for example, on some measures, income inequality is greater today than at any time since the 1920s. And it is not only the low-skilled who are affected: workers with relatively high levels of education are also experiencing declining real wages (Aldonas, Lawrence, and Slaughter, 2007).

That the acceleration of globalization has coincided with rises in income inequality in some countries has important implications for public support for globalization. Voters whose incomes remain stagnant while globalization is boosting the incomes of a few may see themselves as outsiders not benefiting from globalization and may increasingly identify with the losers from globalization. This may even be the case if voters—correctly—view technology as the driving force behind income developments, because increased trade may be the most evident manifestation of technological change. Moreover, voters have the political power to influence policies that can slow, halt, or even reverse the process of globalization, whereas they are largely unable to influence the pace of technological advance.

Public opinion surveys in many countries indicate that an individual's relative economic status has a very strong positive association with pro-trade attitudes (see Chart 2). Aldonas, Lawrence, and Slaughter (2007) argue, for example, that the U.S. public is becoming more protectionist because of stagnant

or falling incomes, not because of a failure to understand the benefits of globalization. This suggests that the public appreciates that the gains to the winners from trade liberalization exceed the losses of the losers. But they also understand that liberalization is an improvement for the nation as a whole only if the losers are *actually* compensated, which they seldom are.

The most important policy implication of the emergence of China and India and of the increase in offshoring may stem from their coincidence with the perception of widespread increases in economic inequality in many advanced economies. The large number of *potentially* offshorable jobs exposes new groups of white-collar workers, many of whom may be politically active, to international competition. If large numbers of workers believe their jobs are potentially at risk of being offshored and the benefits from globalization are not being shared fairly, they are likely to be increasingly receptive to special-interest protectionists.

Creating a Consensus

Policymakers need to ensure that the gains from trade are broadly shared and that social policies are in place to facilitate adjustment of those workers adversely affected by globalization and technological change. One way to do this is to improve education and training, which is crucial to adapt successfully to globalization. But this is likely to have only limited effects in the short run. Education reforms are often difficult to implement and have an impact only as new generations of students complete their education.

In the time frame relevant for political decisions, redistribution policies to compensate losers or outsiders may be key to obtaining political support for continued participation in—or to prevent a retreat from—globalization. This appears to be the case in the European Union: countries that do relatively more

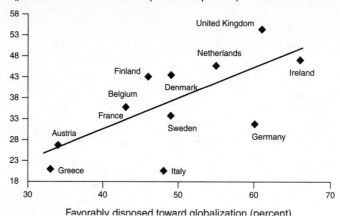

(percent transfer of income to poorest 30 percent)

Favorably disposed toward globalization (percent)

Chart 3   Income transfer and globalization   In the euro area, the more income that is redistributed to the poorest 30 percent of the population, the more positive are attitudes toward globalization.

Sources: Förster and Pearson (2002): and European Commission (2003).

Note: Income transfer data are from the mid-1990s; attitudes toward globalization from a 2003 survey.

redistribution, proxied by the percent of total benefit payments that are paid to the lowest 30 percent of the working-age population, are those in which the population is most in favor of globalization (see Chart 3).

Although the need to compensate the losers from globalization has been widely appreciated, the question of how best to do so has not received much attention. The changing nature of globalization in recent years, however, suggests that this issue may become increasingly important in some countries because larger groups of workers may now consider themselves losers. To maintain political support for globalization, therefore, compensation may need to be broadened beyond the narrowly defined group of workers who lose their jobs as a result of trade liberalization to include employed workers at the low end of the income distribution.

Redistribution, however, will have adverse incentive effects, reducing the economic gains from globalization. This highlights the importance of designing efficient redistribution schemes to maximize the net gains from globalization. Redistribution schemes that do a relatively good job of preserving the incentive to work allow a country to derive relatively large net benefits from globalization (Snower and Coe, 2008).

Fortunately, there are examples of relatively efficient redistribution schemes: the Earned Income Tax Credit in the United States and the Working Families Tax Credit in the United Kingdom, among others (OECD, 2006). But this is only one aspect of the issue. There is also the question of whether the amount of redistribution being done is sufficient to create and maintain a consensus for globalization.

References

Aldonas, Grant, Robert Lawrence, and Matthew Slaughter, 2007, "Succeeding in the Global Economy: A New Policy Agenda for the American Worker," Financial Services Forum Policy Research Paper, June.

Baldwin, Richard, 2006, "Globalization: the great unbundling(s)," paper for the Finnish Prime Minister's Office, Economic Council of Finland, as part of EU Presidency, September.

Blinder, Alan, 2007, "Offshoring: Big Deal, or Business as Usual?" CEPS Working Paper No. 149 (Princeton, NJ: Princeton University).

Coe, David, 2007, *"Globalisation and Labour Markets: Policy Issues Arising from the Emergence of China and India," OECD Social, Employment and Migration Working Papers No. 63 (Paris: Organization for Economic Cooperation and Development).*

European Commission, 2003, "Globalization," Flash Eurobarometer No. 151b.

Förster, Michael, and Mark Pearson, 2002, "Income Distribution and Poverty in the OECD Area: Trends and Driving Forces," OECD Economic Studies, No. 34, pp. 7–39 (Paris).

Hijzen, Alexander, Mauro Pisu, Richard Upward, and Peter Wright, 2007, "Employment, Job Turnover and Trade in Producer Services: Firm-Level Evidence," University of Nottingham GEP Working Paper 2007/37, August.

IMF, 2007, *World Economic Outlook.* October (Washington).

International Social Survey Programme, 2007, "National Identity."

OECD, 2006, *Boosting Jobs and Incomes: Policy Lessons from Reassessing the OECD Jobs Strategy* (Paris).

Snower, Dennis, and David Coe, 2008, "Globalization Through Redistribution," Kiel Institute for the World Economy Working Paper (forthcoming).

van Welsum, Desirée, and Graham Vickery, 2005, "Potential Offshoring of ICT-Intensive Using Occupations," DSTI Information Economy Working Paper DSTI/ICCP/IE(2004)19/FINAL/ (Paris: Organization for Economic Cooperation and Development).

For references to additional papers, see Coe (2007).

DAVID COE is a Senior Advisor in the IMF's Asia and Pacific Department.

From *Finance & Development*, March 2008, pp. 48–51. Copyright © 2008 by The International Monetary Fund and the World Bank. Reprinted by permission of The International Monetary Fund and the World Bank via the Copyright Clearance Center.

Offshored Headquarters

Global human resources becomes a top priority—fast— when foreign companies buy U.S. operations.

ALLEN SMITH

It's not every day that companies such as General Motors (GM)—once the largest private employer in the world—go bankrupt. Sichuan Tengzhong Heavy Industrial Machinery Co.'s purchase of the Hummer brand as part of GM's bankruptch plan, announced June 2, may not be just the end of an era for GM. It may signal the purchase of other U.S. businesses by companies based abroad, a trend that shouldn't be too surprising in light of the global economy.

Of the four most populous countries—China, India, the United States and Indonesia—only the United States was predicted to have a shrinking gross domestic product (GDP) in 2009. Last June, the Organisation for Economic Co-operation and Development, based in Paris, projected that the GDP in China would grow by 7.7 percent in 2009, India's would rise 5.9 percent and Indonesia's 3.5 percent.

Would you be ready if your corporate headquarters suddenly went offshore? Any merger can be challenging for HR professionals, but that's especially true when the C-suite suddenly flies across the globe.

Fortunately, HR leaders can learn lessons from those who have been through this. When Doosan, based in Seoul, South Korea, bought the Bobcat unit from Ingersoll Rand Co. in 2007, the acquired company launched a familiarization program for employees on both sides of the Pacific, even sending U.S. employees to Seoul to immerse themselves in Korean culture, says Bonnie Guttormson, SPHR, director of compensation and benefits at Doosan in West Fargo, N.D.

Bridging cultural differences is not the only challenge, according to Jay Warren, an attorney with Bryan Cave LLP in New York. During foreign takeovers, HR leaders must run on "a compliance track and business-culture track." One challenge on the compliance track: the need to "manage upward," which means not simply telling executives what they may want to hear but instead informing them if standard business operating procedures in their countries would lead to legal challenges in the United States.

After hearing bits and pieces about the at-will rule, owners of foreign companies may overestimate how much leeway U.S. employers have in dismissing employees, cautions Laurence Stuart, an attorney with Stuart & Associates PC in Houston and a member of the Society for Human Resource Management (SHRM) Labor Relations Special Expertise Panel. Stuart has come across a "cowboy mentality" among some new foreign owners of U.S. businesses—purchasers who assume that when an employee must be terminated, "anything goes."

Beginners' Mistakes

"There will be a huge difference" among foreign buyers that have US. operations and foreign buyers purchasing their first U.S. ventures, according to Donald Dowling Jr., an attorney with White & Case LLP in New York.

For HR professionals who already have been through mergers, much about foreign takeovers may seem the same as with new U.S. owners. Dowling says many urgent issues remain largely the same: post-merger integration, layoffs, internal restructuring, new reporting relationships, alignment of HR offerings and policies, and so forth.

That said, HR employees will face additional layers of complexity when purchasers are based abroad, Dowling says, noting that his wife works at a French-owned company. "When the foreign-based buyer has other existing U.S. operations, it will likely aim toward integrating this new operation with its other U.S. business lines," he says. "When the foreign-based buyer is taking its first steps into the U.S. via this acquisition, that is where the cultural and HR problems are likely to be most acute."

Stuart "has seen activity among foreign buyers looking for U.S. companies." He suspects this trend will intensify "if other economies get strong before us." In Texas, he sees the most activity among owners of international private equity firms based in Europe who are eyeing energy-related businesses.

Different Lens

Many foreign professionals have the "misconception that the U.S. employment market is not heavily regulated. That obviously is not correct," Stuart notes.

While the United States does not have the kinds of national and local severance and termination protection common in the European Union (EU), he says many U.S. laws protect classes of individuals from discrimination. That "makes the U.S. market more heavily regulated than Europe, but the risks aren't as obvious."

Foreign executives may be used to more-unionized settings but unfamiliar with laws such as the Americans with Disabilities Act and the Family and Medical Leave Act. Consequently, he cautions, sometimes "they don't understand the role documentation procedures and policies have in reducing risks."

> **Foreign executives may be used to more-unionized settings but unfamiliar with laws such as the Americans with Disabilities Act and the Family and Medical Leave Act.**

Stuart recommends employment law training to familiarize new owners with US. laws and their applications.

Dowling notes that "EU executives come from a culture that has complex and intrusive employment regulations—far more so than under U.S.-style employment at will." But, he says misunderstandings arise because the at-will rule has given rise to a highly evolved—to a European- disproportionate series of equal employment opportunity, discrimination and harassment regulations.

As a result, European executives purchasing U.S. businesses "need to reorient their thinking" about employment law compliance, according to Dowling. From the European perspective, "the good news is that the U.S. state and federal systems impose far fewer employment laws and rules than they are used to. The bad news is that Americans look at employment relationships through the lens of discrimination." And, he says, "To a European executive, Americans appear over-concerned with what the European might see as political correctness."

However, Dowling doesn't think foreign executives necessarily are surprised by the compliance risks in the United States: "European executives hear horror stories about U.S. court judgments—multimillion-dollar verdicts, runaway juries, class actions and unpredictable results," he notes. But they still "will need to be shown where the land mines lie."

Dowling adds that U.S. unionization laws constitute a separate issue, and he advises incoming businesses to develop a U.S. union strategy.

Stuart recalls several foreign-based clients that have unions in Europe and have been "pushed into signing global codes of conduct" that simply weren't practical for U.S. operations. For example, in global codes of conduct, foreign businesses may have provisions prohibiting mandatory overtime, even though mandatory overtime may be an industry norm in the United States and a feature many workers want. Or, global codes of conduct may specify the intervals for employees to have days off, even though seven-day workweeks while employees are offshore are common in the energy sector, he adds.

Stuart recommends that U.S. HR professionals and attorneys conduct due diligence and look into overseas policies that would be unlawful if applied in the United States. For example, mandatory retirement is common overseas.

HR professionals shouldn't be surprised if colleagues at acquiring companies do not understand the exempt/nonexempt distinctions under federal and state wage and hour laws, as well as other state-specific requirements, according to Baker & McKenzie attorneys Susan Eandi, Ute Krudewagen, John Raudabaugh and Carole Spink.

In addition, foreign employers often do not understand that employee benefits are provided at the employer's discretion in most circumstances, or that the amount and quality of benefits a company provides affects its ability to attract and retain employees, the Baker & McKenzie attorneys add.

Face to Face

There's much for U.S. employees to learn about the prevailing culture of an overseas purchasing company's C-suite.

At Bobcat, employees were used to having the C-suite overseas even before Doosan purchased it, since Bobcat was owned by Ingersoll Rand, a global construction equipment business based in Ireland. But, to help get employees on the right cultural track, some Bobcat employees were paid to travel to Seoul following Doosan's acquisition. Guttormson says the company started flying over top-level executives and is working its way down the organization. She is slated to be in the next group to visit.

Guttormson recommends familiarization training for employees in the United States as well as for those in the purchasing company, even if the purchaser seems to be a good match, as was the case with Doosan. Familiarization training might include an introduction to cultural differences. For example, Guttormson notes that Korean culture is "very hierarchical, so where here in the United States we're very free to talk with higher officials about differences, there the process is to go through the hierarchy."

To smooth the way for foreign travelers in the United States, Dowling recommends that employers start getting visas early.

Employees' Fears

Cultural differences intimidate some, according to Thomas Belker, SPHR, GPHR, managing director of HR for OBI—one of the world's largest home improvement companies, located in 15 countries—based near Cologne, Germany. "We say it is a global world, but nonetheless many line managers have never been exposed to dealing with cultural differences," he notes. "Nor do they necessarily understand anything about foreign laws and their impact on HR processes. There is quite normally a huge gap caused by resentment or a lack of understanding of foreign HR issues."

Belker, a member of the SHRM Global Special Expertise Panel, recommends starting with minor changes and paying close attention to employees' initial reactions.

Michelle Haste, an attorney with Crowell & Moring in London, recommends that HR leaders stay in "close contact with U.S. employees who may be fearful of acquisition by a foreign entity." She says HR executives from the purchaser and the seller should cultivate relationships that enable "full and frank communication on the differences."

Reset Expectations

One point of discussion should be the cultural work expectations, such as whether employees can speak freely or are expected to be subordinate to managers, advises Brenda Cossette, SPHR, HR director for the City of Fergus Falls, Minn., and a member of the SHRM Labor Relations Special Expertise Panel.

The foreign company can have very different values, and it may put a premium on running extremely efficient operations compared to some of our U.S. companies, Cossette says. "Employee loyalty to the new brand name or new company is a real difficult issue since many smaller companies are often bought up by foreign companies," she explains. "These small companies are proud of being a local company, and now a foreign company only sees them in terms of sales or diversification of their product lines."

According to Cossette, many Asian companies don't have big bonuses and stock plans for leaders, raising concerns among U.S. executives who depend on those plans—assuming these executives aren't laid off following the purchase.

Role Clarification

Stuart notes that in some jurisdictions, the HR function may even "be purely administrative as opposed to being strategic business partners."

HR leaders should be sure they understand what the decision-making process will be following the acquisition.

Will all decisions flow through headquarters abroad, or will the new C-suite choose not to get involved in day-to-day activities?

The answer affects liability in lawsuits, says Warren, explaining that if a foreign company acquires a publicly traded U.S. company through stock acquisition but does not get involved in decision-making, the parent company would have no legal liability.

However, if the foreign purchaser doesn't trust U.S. officers to make decisions and starts calling the shots, it would be treated as liable, he cautions. So, the acquiring company "may want to keep itself separate."

HR leaders should be sure they understand what the decision-making process will be following the acquisition.

Managing Upward

Managing upward always is a challenge, but particularly with officers based abroad—and when there are cultural and linguistic divides.

"Most of us try to listen to get to what the boss wants," Warren notes. But HR leaders should be quick to recognize when bosses overseas are inadvertently asking them to implement changes that would fly in the face of domestic law. Warren says that takes "active and patient listening."

The challenge, he notes, is to respond "in a way that does not lead to friction, not to say, 'That's not the way we do things here.'" He recommends that HR professionals make sure they understand what bosses are asking—and then, make sure it's legal stateside.

From *HR Magazine*, November 2009, pp. 49–52. Copyright © 2009 by Society for Human Resource Management (SHRM). Reprinted by permission of SHRM and via the Copyright Clearance Center.

A Material World

The growth of the global economy continues to change the landscape of the raw materials market. Realizing that the old rules no longer apply, manufacturers are looking inward for opportunities to drive costs back down without making their customers foot the bill.

NICK ZUBKO

How many times in the past year were you certain that what you were paying for raw materials couldn't possibly go any higher? It's probably more than you would care to admit. Having been proven wrong on that point on countless occasions, manufacturers have reached a level of acceptance to the instability of the commodities markets. They have stopped waiting for prices to peak, realizing that their production cycles will in all likelihood continue to grow more expensive every quarter, if not a little bit every week.

While that sounds like the bad news, it's really not—at least not completely. It means the novelty of those frequent and often vicious price spikes has finally started to wear off, and manufacturers can shift their attention to the question at hand: What do we do about it? But to fully understand where this issue is going, it's important to know how we got here. According to experts and manufacturers alike, there have been two key developments in the last year or two that share responsibility for the substantial hikes in raw material costs. The first one should be easy.

Driving Factors

You guessed it . . . oil. According to OPEC, the price tag on a barrel of oil was still around $70 as recently as a year ago, but has now skyrocketed over $140 a barrel as of late June. And that price affects everything. Not only does oil play a vital role in the production and transport of every product manufactured in the world today, but it's also a main ingredient in literally thousands of plastics, resins and other synthetic materials used in automotive, electronics, apparel and most industries in between. And what's more, the oil companies themselves are in the same boat as everyone else, spending nearly twice as much on energy and transportation as they did last year.

Rising oil prices have always been bad news for manufacturing, but adding recent trends in globalization to the mix has really launched prices into high gear. Demand for raw materials has grown enormously as markets in China, India and other Southeast

Asian countries continue to expand. According to Patrick Furey, senior category manager for spend management solutions provider Ariba Inc., until an unlikely scenario takes place in which those markets stop growing and stop demanding energy and raw materials, those prices are going to remain extremely volatile.

"Most manufacturers have learned that this isn't the same market anymore," Furey says. "The growth in China and India is slowing, but it's not going to slow to the point to where all of a sudden these markets drop off the face of the earth. They're still growing and their demand for raw materials—oil, energy, steel, copper—is going to continue to put stress on those markets. This issue is not going away any time soon."

Thus far, most manufacturers have been forced to push their rising material costs through to their customers. Dow Chemical Co., for example, announced in May a historic price increase of 20%, followed by another 25% in June, in response to the rising costs of oil, natural gas and hydrocarbon derivatives. Much like other manufacturers, Dow's chairman and CEO Andrew Liveris called the steps "extremely unwelcome but entirely unavoidable." Yet, these sorts of announcements seem to be made ever more frequently, with the increases growing more significant each time.

Obviously, passing on the costs to the customer isn't really a solution. So, to prevent this practice from escalating out of control, manufacturers are looking furiously for more innovative ways to cut costs throughout their operations. Not only are they getting lean in more aspects of production and working to strengthen relationships with key material suppliers, but they are also conducting intensive R&D efforts to explore cheaper alternative materials that can maintain the highest levels of quality while taking the pressure off themselves, their suppliers and ultimately their customers.

Constructive Relationships

Steel is of course a key material in manufacturing, and one that has been particularly vulnerable to the market's volatility. In fact, since the beginning of the year, steel prices have doubled—a combined effort of consistent demand and rising operating costs being absorbed by the steel mills, fabricators and even from the mines themselves.

Volatile steel prices are nothing new for construction equipment manufacturer Terex Corp., which purchases somewhere in the vicinity of 600,000 tons per year. But according to Tim Fiore, Terex's senior vice president of strategic sourcing, what makes this time different from previous run ups in the steel market is the recent consolidation that has taken place among the mills and their suppliers.

"There are fewer players and very little growth in capacity. Since there's such a consolidation of players now, the interest to cut prices as inventories start to grow is not going to be as great," Fiore says. "Coupled with that, the steel mills are having their own battles with the mining companies, who tend to command the market. And that has significantly driven up the price of coking coal and iron ore."

For Terex, some of the most important battles are being fought by second- and third-tier suppliers who consume two-thirds of the steel they buy. Traditionally, each of the company's 25 to 30 manufacturing plants around the world independently had purchased steel components such as castings, forgings and bearings from key fabricators. Two years ago a concerted effort was made to transition to a more consolidated approach to supply management.

When steel prices began shooting through the roof those efforts were thrust into high gear. In the space of a year, Fiore says the focus of the program evolved from simply achieving significant cost reductions to working to ensure that supplier performance and on-time delivery of those critical components could be maintained.

"Several key suppliers have had significant capacity constraints and struggled to keep up with demand. Generally those are the smaller, vertically integrated companies, and many of their components have fairly long lead times," explains Fiore. "So we're working closely with them to make sure they don't become economically unstable—and in the near-term, that they are able to acquire the steel we need to prevent major component shortages. Because, as you get deeper into the supply chain, the degree of flexibility you have gets to be a lot less."

"We're working closely with [key suppliers] to make sure they don't become economically unstable—and in the near-term, that they are able to acquire the steel we need to prevent major component shortages."

—Tim Fiore, senior vice president of strategic sourcing for Terex Corp.

One area manufacturers are exploring to create even more flexibility is substituting some of their more expensive materials for cheaper alternatives. In an ongoing effort to reduce the overall material content of their vehicles, Terex started swapping out the sheet metal covering on certain pieces of equipment with plastic or fiberglass replacements. These developments are collaborative efforts between the company's engineering, quality and supply-management segments, and in many cases have included marketing and sales because they are the ones who will have to sell their customers on whatever material changes are ultimately made.

"For example, if we change from a metal enclosure to a plastic enclosure, what's the reception and market going to be? Are they going to see that as a less-expensive, lower-quality approach, or a smart move to reduce weight? It really takes a number of different functions to make these changes," Fiore says.

Burning Rubber

Steel only makes up 10% of the raw materials purchased by Goodyear Tire & Rubber Co., but that doesn't make the current market situation any easier. In addition to natural rubber, Goodyear depends heavily on a steady supply of oil-based chemicals used to produce synthetic rubber and a material called carbon black, which is used as both a pigment and reinforcing agent. According to the Rubber Manufacturers Association, oil-based products account for about 60% of the cost to manufacture a tire, which amounts to approximately 7 gallons per tire. And these days, those costs add up quickly.

In fact, JPMorgan estimates that raw material prices for tire manufacturers have gone up 23.4% in 2008, adding to the 22.6% boost the market had already experienced in 2007. The cost of natural rubber, an agricultural commodity sourced from plantations in a variety of equatorial climates around the world, has also increased more than 20% since last year.

Before costs really started to take off, Goodyear embarked on an "Advantaged Supply Chain" program, which closely evaluates how the company focuses its efforts in purchasing, logistics and global sourcing. The process quickly helped Goodyear evaluate how much could be done to offset the rapid price increases, says Mark Purtilar, vice president of purchasing and CPO at Goodyear.

"Manufacturers can't control these prices, and they often aren't able to offset all of them, so they have to focus internally," Purtilar suggests. "This program was the best preparation we could have done to face these costs. But we definitely put a turbo charger on the process when they started to rise at such a dramatic rate. We put more effort and resources behind the program, broke everything down, and implemented systems capabilities to automate wherever possible. It made us push down on the accelerator."

"Manufacturers can't control these prices and they often aren't able to offset all of them, so they have to focus internally."

—Mark Purtilar, vice president of purchasing and CPO for Goodyear Tire & Rubber Co.

Even with the increased flexibility, high raw material costs still forced Goodyear to announce price increases of 7% to 9% this year. But further efforts are being made to reduce material costs through the exploration of other chemical-based alternatives. The company has technology in the works to increase its capability to substitute between synthetic rubber, and natural rubber, depending upon the cost of each material.

Since each type of rubber has different performance attributes, some can be substituted while others can't. Airplane tires, for example, have a predominance of natural rubber because of its inherent heat-dissipating capability. Consumer tires tend to have more flexibility. Goodyear is now capable of achieving a 20% substitution rate versus the industry average of about 7%, without impacting tire performance.

A large component of this success is that in addition to extensive R&D to determine suitable substitutions, Goodyear's procurement department often works in collaboration with product designers to help determine what possible alternative materials can be utilized.

"That is important because procurement is the eyes and ears to the outside world, continually scouring the supply base," explains Purtilar. "We discuss alternatives that R&D might be exploring to see if they mesh with alternatives we're exploring. Then we get our groups together to share best practices, innovation techniques and ideas to be able to develop those alternative materials."

Calculated Defense

In addition to being faced with the price of aluminum rising more than 20% this year, Lockheed Martin Aeronautics Co. has also been challenged by the availability of some key raw materials during production of its F-35 Joint Strike Fighter (JSF) aircraft. Recently the company started incorporating larger quantities of composite materials into its designs, which are strong, stable and can be integrated with sophisticated stealth technology and radar-absorbent materials.

However, the addition of these composites required a shift to titanium that has further challenged its supply chain, according to Mike Jones, Lockheed Martin's enterprise supply chain integrator of information systems technology.

"Titanium is expensive, it's rare and it's hard to work with," Jones explains. "There's a lot of it in Russia, but we work with the U.S. Department of Defense and we don't get to buy Russian titanium."

With foundries around the world running at capacity, Lockheed Martin was left struggling with short supplies. To support production of the F-35 the company developed a tool to assist in gathering data from various systems to generate a comprehensive, time-phased raw material forecast, dubbed the Forecasted Raw Materials application, or FoRM.

"We needed to come up with a raw material forecasting tool able to support both metallic and composite part manufacturing," says Jones. "And we needed to aggregate the totals by material type. Just saying titanium wasn't enough, because it comes in different forms, grades and classes. There are a

tremendous number of different types of materials and each one has different properties, so we needed to know how much we used each and every time."

The technology was designed to be able to adjust variables throughout production to drive forecast recalculation and maximize availability of titanium and various composites. Accurate forecasting was especially important for composites, which are time and temperature sensitive and have limited shelf lives. "You have to keep [composites] in freezers until you use them," Jones explains. "Otherwise you end up generating rolls and rolls of scrap."

Material forecasting also helps Lockheed Martin reduce scrap by preventing miscalculations in respect to part sizes and thicknesses, which is particularly important for titanium orders. If a part made of the high-strength metal comes in slightly larger than designed, machining off the extra titanium will waste a great deal of valuable time and can result in unwanted part wear.

And while the initial purpose of this endeavor was to ensure availability of materials and prevent parts shortages, additional benefits soon became clear as well. Now that purchasing agents have access to accurate material forecasts, price negotiations tend to go a little differently, according to Jones.

"They never had this kind of detailed information before," he says. "Now buyers can negotiate pricing not based on past performance, but on what's actually going to happen on the JSF program *this* time. In fact, on the composite side we negotiated a 28% reduction in composite raw materials—a little over $30 million in savings—immediately out of the box."

Seeing All Sides

While a manufacturer's ability to predict its own material needs can certainly help control its costs and improve production, its ability to do the same for commodities prices probably won't improve any time soon. But there are enough ways to improve internally to sufficiently offset rising prices by looking at all other aspects of the operation that can contain costs.

In the meantime, manufacturers will need to realize that they are not the only ones feeling the heat generated by the market's volatility. Ariba's Furey points out that many suppliers are now more reluctant to enter into long-term deals without some sort of adjustment clauses for raw materials. That means buyers might have to change the structure of their supply contracts to include these types of clauses—even in markets where they never had to before.

"Manufacturers need to remember that everyone is being faced with the same pressures on raw materials. A supplier in China isn't getting steel any cheaper than a supplier in the U.S. right now. If anything, it's probably more expensive," Furey says. "The companies who are going to come out on top are those who ultimately have gotten lean in their entire operation, can control costs and thereby remain the most competitive in the market."

Keynote Panel Session 1: Whose Income Is It? How Business Is Caught in the Global Competition and Controversy for Tax Revenues

This panel set the tone for the entire Symposium with a strategic discussion on the global race among countries to attract and retain business operations in their jurisdictions. In this increasingly competitive global environment, tax controversy across multiple jurisdictions is becoming a frequent occurrence in both developed and developing countries as well as in the 50 U.S. states.

Timothy M. McDonald et al.

Introduction

MS. OLSON: Thank you. We have a great group for this opening discussion which we have titled, *Whose Income is it?* First, to my immediate left is Michael Mundaca. Mike is the Deputy Assistant Treasury Secretary for International Tax Affairs. At this point, he is the most senior person in tax policy at the Treasury Department, and he is wearing a lot of different hats. Clearly, he is the Acting Assistant Secretary *de facto* if not *de jure*. We are really pleased, Mike, that you could take the time this morning to come over to be with us. Mike has been at Treasury for about a year and a half. This is his second stint at Treasury. In between those stints, he was with Ernst & Young in Washington, D.C. In his previous stint at Treasury, he served as the Deputy International Tax Counsel. I had the pleasure of working with him during that period of time, which spanned the late 1990s and early part of this decade. Mike's biography also includes his service as the Treasury senior advisor on electronic commerce.

Next to Michael is Tim McDonald. Tim is the Vice President for Finance and Accounting, Global Taxes, at the Procter & Gamble Company. Tim has been with Procter & Gamble since 2003. He is responsible for all matters pertaining to corporate income taxes globally including the tax policy positions that the company takes involving legislation, planning, compliance and audit defense. He has a staff of 200 people to keep up with P&G's global tax function, which is located in 32 different countries.

Next to Tim is Joel Walters, who is the Corporate Finance Director at Vodafone in London. Joel is a graduate of the University of Minnesota Law School, and also has an LLM from Georgetown. Before joining Vodafone, Joel worked for Diageo and Grand Met.

So, three great panelists. We are happy to have all three of them with us this morning.

We are going to start with some slides that will set the backdrop for our discussion. They help to illustrate the kinds of things that Grant Aldonas spoke about in the opening session that are important for us to bear in mind as we consider the question—whose income is it?

- Slide 1, *Growth in U.S. Exports and Imports, 1992–2007,* is a graphic depiction of the change in U.S. exports and imports from 1992 to 2007. The yellow bars on the left are 1992, and the gray bars on the right are 2007. What you see in the graph is a remarkable increase in the quantity of exports and imports on the part of the U.S. You can see over the course of the last 15 years how much more globally interconnected we have become, and the graph illustrates the importance of being globally interconnected.

- Slide 2, *Foreign Direct Investment Inflows,* is a graphic depiction of foreign direct investment flows from 1990 to 2000 to 2006. The yellow segments at the top of each of those bars are foreign direct investment flows into developing countries. The gray segments are flows into developed countries. You can see that there is a shift occurring with more foreign direct investment flows to the developing world relative to the developed world over the period from 1990 to 2006.

- Slide 3, *Top 20 Countries Ranked by GDP 1992 & 2007,* shows the top 20 countries ranked by GDP in 1992 and 2007. Focusing on the changes in the chart, China moved from number eight on this list in 1992 to number four in 2007. India moved from number 15 in 1992 to number 12 by 2007. Russia, which was not on the list at all in 1992, moved to number 11 in 2007. Perhaps with what is going on with petroleum markets, Russia will fall on the list

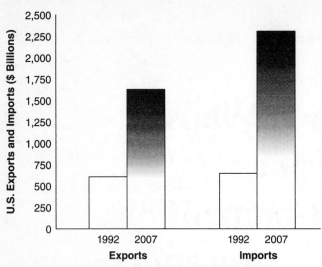

Growth in U.S. Exports and Imports, 1992–2007

Source: U.S. BEA International Economics Accounts.

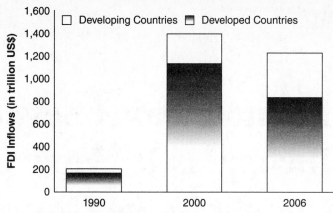

Foreign Direct Investment Inflows

Source: UNCTAD, World Investment Report 2007.

again in coming years. There are countries that were on the list in 1992 that have dropped off entirely by 2007. These represent remarkable shifts. What the changes illustrate is the importance of participation in the emerging world, as well as in the developed world because there is a lot of growth occurring in the developing world.

- Slide 4, *Relative Rates of Growth and Contributions to GDP between 1992 and 2007,* illustrates relative rates of growth and contributions to global gross domestic product between 1992 and 2007. The top part of the chart, which includes developed countries, has growth rates much less significant than the emerging market and developing countries in the bottom half of the chart, where the average growth rate was 287 percent during that period of time—three times as much as the growth rate among the advanced countries. We still see a significant contribution, 62 percent, to world growth on the part of the developed countries, but that is because of the size of the United States and European economies relative to the size of the economies of emerging market and developing countries. The key point is that emerging market and developing countries are becoming rapidly more important for economic growth.

The key point is that emerging market and developing countries are becoming rapidly more important for economic growth.

- Slide 5, *Future Population,* shows future projected population by mid-2050. Population growth is projected to be high in the developing world. India is at the top with one and three-quarter billion people, China is next with nearly a billion and a half, and the U.S. is in third place with 438 million. So, what we see is a rapidly growing population outside of the U.S. and the developed world. It is important to understand in considering why

there is so much investment outside the U.S. that we are only five percent of the world's population. So there are literally billions of reasons for businesses to invest in places other than the U.S.

- Slide 6, *Penetration Rates of New Technologies in Selected Countries, 2006,* is an interesting depiction of the penetration rates for new technologies. What the chart indicates is that there is a lot of room for growth in PC usage, in Internet usage, and in cellular subscription in the developing world.

Top 20 Countries Ranked by GDP 1992 & 2007

GDP Rank	1992	2007
1	United States	United States
2	Japan	Japan
3	Germany	Germany
4	France	China
5	Italy	United Kingdom
6	United Kingdom	France
7	Spain	Italy
8	Canada	Spain
9	China	Canada
10	Brazil	Brazil
11	Mexico	Russia
12	Netherlands	India
13	Korea	Mexico
14	Australia	Korea
15	India	Australia
16	Sweden	Netherlands
17	Switzerland	Turkey
18	Argentina	Sweden
19	Belgium	Belgium
20	Taiwan	Indonesia

Source: International Monetary Fund.

Relative Rates of Growth and Contributions to GDP between 1992 and 2007

	1992	2007	1992–2007	
	GDP	GDP	GDP Growth	Contribution to World Growth
United States	6,038	13,808	118%	25%
EU-15	2,990	15,728	97%	25%
Japan	3,770	4,382	16%	2%
Other	2,190	5,271	148%	10%
Advanced Countries	**20,227**	**39,188**	**94%**	**62%**
China	488	3,280	672%	9%
India	281	1,101	292%	3%
Other developing Asia	608	1,402	176%	3%
Western hemisphere	1,329	3,609	172%	7%
Middle East	448	1,400	212%	3%
Africa	410	1,107	170%	2%
Central & Eastern Europe	412	1,890	358%	5%
Other	123	1,696	1281%	5%
Emerging Market and Developing Countries	**3,998**	**15,484**	**287%**	**38%**
World	**24,226**	**54,673**	**125%**	**100%**

Source: International Monetary Fund.

Projected Population Mid–2050 (Millions)

Range : 0 – 1,755 Billion

India	1,755	
China	1,437	
United States	438	
Indonesia	343	
Pakistan	295	
Nigeria	282	
Brazil	260	
Bangladesh	215	
Congo De Rep of	189	
Phillippines	150	
Ethiopia	148	
Mexico	132	
Egypt	118	
Vietnam	113	
Russia	110	

Future Population

Source: Population Reference Bureau.

- Slide 7, *Economic Growth,* is a comparison of real growth and capital flows in the emerging world. Note that growth is headed off the charts in the emerging markets and developing world.
- Slide 8, *Corporate Tax Rates,* has two charts illustrating corporate tax rates. The chart on the left depicts the combined U.S. rate relative to non-U.S. OECD (Organisation for Economic Co-operation and Development) countries. Relative to the rest of the

OECD, we see the U.S. tax rate dropped in 1986 with the enactment of the Tax Reform Act of 1986, which was fully implemented by 1989. Then the rest of the world began to follow U.S. corporate rates down. Other countries have continued to cut their corporate rates, while we have stayed at about the same point for the last 20 years, resulting in a significant wedge between U.S. corporate tax rates and those of the rest of the OECD.

125

Penetration Rates of New Technologies in Selected Countries, 2006

	PC Usage	Internet Usage	Cellular Subscriptions
United States	80%	70%	80%
EU 15	60%	52%	108%
Brazil	20%	23%	53%
Russia	13%	18%	106%
India	3%	11%	15%
China	6%	10%	35%

Source: UN Stats, Millennium Development Goals Indicators.

Corporate Tax Rates

MR. MUNDACA: Thanks, Pam. These numbers are very interesting. I think what we are going to try to do here is link together some of what Grant Aldonas was talking about and what Pam was talking about to what is happening in globalization, what is happening in trade, what is happening in the international tax space, what is happening with corporate tax rates, with corporate tax audits, what is happening to multinationals and how they are treated around the world by the various tax authorities. The corporate tax rates I think are a good place to start. As Pam's slides indicate, only the U.S., Brazil and Sweden (countries in the top 20 by GDP) have not lowered their corporate tax statutory rates since 2000, and only the U.S. rate has gone up, because of some State tax changes. That is a stark statistic. Looking just at OECD countries, the U.S. statutory rate is now about 50 percent higher than the average OECD rate. The average OECD rate now is about 25 percent. So even amongst the 30 countries of the OECD, the U.S. is an outlier.

A couple of other facts to keep in mind, though. The U.S. marginal corporate tax rate, the tax rate applied to the last dollar earned by a corporation, is about average amongst other large economies due to the fact that we have a narrower corporate tax base (because of accelerated depreciation and treatment of interest payments) relative to other countries. And that is again a trend that the U.S. has not yet taken up—broadening the corporate tax base and lowering the corporate tax rate. That is, the U.S. still has a fairly narrow corporate tax base.

Another thing to keep in mind is that the U.S. collects less revenue as a share of GDP from its corporate tax than other major trading partners do.

So how do you pull all this together, how do you make sense of all this? How do we have a high corporate tax rate and yet collect less corporate tax than our major trading partners as a percentage of GDP.

A couple of facts make us unique: The amount of business income earned by corporations in the U.S. is less than 50 percent of the total business income earned, which is an important factor to keep in mind as we talk about what we are doing on corporate taxes. For us, corporate tax reform is only half or even less than half of the story of business tax reform, and that has to be taken into account especially as we consider the effects on competitiveness both domestically and internationally. Changes we make to the corporate tax system don't necessarily spread across business income evenly.

We must keep all these facts in mind as we talk about the future of the corporate tax system in this country. And as Pam alluded to, there is going to be a lot of pressure in the United States to do some reform.

Now, a lot of the talk has been about health care, and that is going to be the legislative focus, I think, for the rest of this year. Some tax reform may be part of that, but I think, in the short term—potentially not this year, but certainly early in this administration—tax reform is going to be a focus, and corporate tax reform in particular. We are going to see soon the release of an outline of the President's first budget, and there will be, as you have seen in the press and as was alluded to last night in the President's address to Congress, some corporate tax matters addressed in that budget.

Taxation of Foreign Source Income

Another trend I think we need to keep in mind. What about the taxation of a foreign source income? We have talked about how the U.S. is an outlier on corporate tax rates generally. What about the taxation of foreign source income?

Most of our major trading partners have moved over the last couple of years—while they have moved to lower their corporate tax rates and broaden their corporate tax base, by eliminating preferences, such as accelerated depreciation, for example—they have moved to narrow the base by excluding large chunks of foreign source income, especially dividends from controlled foreign corporations.

We, the U.K. and Japan are the primary large economies with worldwide systems at this point, but as you all know, Japan and the U.K. appear now to be moving toward significant territorial reforms, which will leave us, of the large economies, with Ireland, Mexico and Korea, as the last standing that have a worldwide tax system.

Again, I think as we look at what reform is coming down and what we need to do, we have to be cognizant of our place in the global community and how our tax rules may be out of sync at this point with those of some of our major trading partners.

A larger question to consider as you look at this is, if the trend is to drop corporate tax rates, and narrow the corporate tax base to domestic income by excluding foreign income, is the corporate tax a dying animal, is it something that countries are moving away from entirely?

Enforcement

Having said that, looking at enforcement, we see the real oddity of what is developing. While countries have been lowering their rates and in essence foregoing their tax on foreign source income, they have upped their enforcement of the laws that remain in place. They have been—and I think we will hear about this from Tim and Joel—more aggressive in trying to collect the revenues under these new systems that they have put in place. Again, it's a tension I think we are going to see very starkly over the next couple of years: the need for countries to continue to create jobs and grow countered by the need for revenue. There is also obviously a political element to this, that the loss of jobs to countries overseas and the shrinking of corporate tax base are very hot political issues, and countries have to address that. But again, as I see it from where I sit, there are these tensions countries are going to have to resolve. Every country recognizes, especially now, the need to grow, the need to create jobs, but they also recognize that the revenue needs of their countries are growing and they need sources of revenue for those revenue needs.

While countries have been lowering their rates and in essence foregoing their tax on foreign source income, they have upped their enforcement of the laws that remain in place.

With that, I will turn to the business colleagues to see if they are seeing the same sort of trends that I am seeing, that even as corporate tax rules are changing and potentially becoming more favorable to corporations, the enforcement of those rules is becoming quite tight.

Business Perspective

MR. WALTERS: I will kick off on the business perspective. There will be lot of consistencies in the things I say, to previous comments. There is a lot of overlap from my perspective. I think my role in this panel is to set the stage and begin the business aspect of the view of where we are today and what we are seeing out there.

I had an interesting conversation last night with someone. We were talking about the tension that is out there that was just being described. The comment was correctly made that it is always going to be the case, isn't it, that you are always going to have business moving at a dramatic speed and government always a bit chasing behind trying to sort out how to deal with the new world and how to tax and protect their revenue base. But I think this is more than that now. I think that it is probably indeed fair to say that this is always true. But in my view, and what I see day to day, the acceleration and the dramatic pace is a seismic change in how business operates in a global way and how governments need to deal with this. When you come to sessions like this people are always saying we are at a crossroads. Today is the day it has become dramatic. But I do honestly believe at this moment the changes are seismic, we are in a very different world, and that is what we are dealing with.

Tim is going to get more into the detail of what we are seeing out there and what's happening in the governments as they are trying to deal with some of this. So I will just kind of set the stage in a general way.

I guess the first thing I would say is that my perspective isn't as somebody who spends a lot of time thinking about capital import or export neutrality. I am not a policy guy, so I don't spend as much time thinking about how rates or basis of taxation compare to other governments from a policy perspective. I am just a guy who, on a day-to-day basis, makes decisions about where Vodafone is going to operate its business. We are out making choices on a daily basis. What is the environment in which we want to operate? That's the perspective I come from. I do care about the policy and administration in the countries that we operate, so these questions are of interest to me, and I do think about them. But the bigger policy questions are not what I do. We make decisions. Where should we put this business activity? That is the perspective I come at it from.

Seismic Change

In terms of the pace of change, let me just give you a little bit of background, because I think it is important. When you think about Vodafone in particular, you can really see what I mean by seismic change. The first mobile phone call made by a Vodafone executive in the U.K. was in 1985, so 24 years ago was the start of our business. This year we will produce about $70 billion of revenue, and that is in a market that some people estimate to be $1 trillion in terms of telecommunications globally. So that is what has changed in our business in just 24 years.

We started out in Newbury, England, and we began as a U.K.-based business. This year about four percent of our global profits will be generated in the U.K., so 96 percent of our business is in countries outside of the U.K. where we are competing with a whole variety of competitors. Everybody from 02 to T Mobile in terms of global competitors, local mobile virtual network operators (MVNOs) who are buying and selling air time locally, traditional government-owned telecommunications companies, and, increasingly, the Googles and the Microsofts of the world who are all trying to get into the space.

So, we are out dealing with a very global environment, very fast-changing business, spending 96 percent of our time competing in a true global marketplace, and that is our business. I think that it is very important to have that in mind. We are not a domestic U.S. company or U.K. company who is interested in global taxation. We are a global company that competes all around the world.

While that is happening, the attention and focus on business performance, as most of the people in the room know, has dramatically increased as well. One example I can give of that. Last June we released some of our KPIs (Key Performance Indicators), which we do, because we only do half-year and full-year results in the U.K., so the other two quarters we do KPI results with some broad indicators of how we are performing. We came out and basically said that we were performing well all across our sectors, but we said we are starting to see some softness in specific places. We got really punished for that in terms of the analyst's view and the market reaction. I think the moral of that is that in the world we live in, where it used to be the case if you could perform on a portfolio basis, or perform in 96 out of 100 markets, the markets would give you credit for that.

Tax in the Boardroom

Today there is just no sympathy for failing to deliver on every line, in every market, every day, and there is no opportunity to err in that. And what does that mean? That means on every line of the Profit and Loss Statement, cash flow, balance sheet, everything we do, we are looking for a competitive advantage and complete certainty. That is our objective as a business. That is what we are out pursuing, and the tax lines are no different in that.

That means, on every line of the Profit and Loss Statement, cash flow, balance sheet, everything we do, we are looking for a competitive advantage and complete certainty.

I am usually surprised when I get the reaction, yes, but, you know, people shouldn't be out competing on the tax line, should they, they shouldn't be trying to drive down their tax burden on a global basis. But tax is no different in business—trying to drive that down when living in a very difficult global competitive environment.

There was some discussion a few years back in the U.K. about bringing tax into the board room, and I was always skeptical that tax wasn't already in the board room and that the boards of big companies weren't considering tax on a detailed basis. Even if I am wrong and there was a gap here, there no longer is a gap because tax is front and center, certainly in our board room. I think I could safely say that the boards of other big companies are focused on this as well. I have to deliver every year an effective tax rate for the market. I have to deliver every year the cash flow. We have committed to the market that we are going to produce between five and six billion pounds of free cash flow on an annual basis, and tax is a big contributor to that. I also have to deliver as much certainty as I can in a very uncertain world and what the next couple of days are going to be talking about on the tax controversy. For example, you can see by looking at our annual report, we have about two billion pounds of tax at stake in some litigation in the U.K.

Most everybody, because they always come up and talk to me about it when they see me, know that we are in litigation in India on a \$2 billion issue. We have to try to manage that kind of controversy, that kind of difficulty and again be creating a competitive advantage and certainty. I don't think it's just in the board room where we perceive that this is important. It is really important,

I will give you a couple of examples. In November of 2005, when we did our results, one of the things that we announced was that we had five billion pounds of provisions for tax disputes on the balance sheet that would be rolling out over the next three years, and our share price just got punished for that over the next couple of days. All the newspapers in the U.K. jumped on it. One of the headlines I can remember was "Vodafone reveals 5 billion pound tax hole." So they were paying attention and tax was important.

Another story. I was on a bus at the Milan airport going out to get on a plane, and somebody walked up to me and said, "I know who you are. I am an analyst, and we just took the Vodafone outlook up on the back of your outlook on tax, and I just wanted to come up and tell you that we are going to be announcing that today."

So this has a real impact. People are paying attention to tax, so it is not just the board that is telling me we need to produce certainty and competitiveness in the tax lines. It is real and it's getting reflected in the share price, and you can see that. So, therefore, it is simply a fact that business is going to look to seek those things out and it is going to locate its business activities and it is going to operate in a way in which it can achieve them.

Again, I mention that sometimes I am surprised that people act like, why should you be doing that with tax? I can understand that with labor costs, transportation costs, energy costs, but tax isn't a cost that you should be pursuing opportunities to maximize efficiency. In my view, it is absolutely what we should be doing.

The reason I feel like we can be doing that is at Vodafone we have a code of conduct in tax, which dictates the decisions we make and how we operate. We have worked out with many tax authorities—including HMRC (Her Majesty's Revenue and Customs) in the U.K.—principles of working, which are about openness and transparency. And Vodafone has values, and with the Tax Department that I lead, we talk about being proud of what we do. In my view, as long as we do all of those things, and we operate in that way, it is perfectly legitimate for us to seek competitiveness and certainty on all the tax lines and drive performance to the bottom line. So, we are out doing that even if some people may be surprised or even uncomfortable.

With that said, then, we are therefore seeing businesses really pushing to try to create maximum performance.

As was mentioned, that is coming at the exact same time governments are seeing unprecedented need for cash, unprecedented need for revenue, and tremendous tension on their bottom line. And we are absolutely seeing that, and this is the topic for the next couple of days. We are absolutely seeing that in debates over who gets to tax what in this global environment. Ninety-six percent of my profits are outside the U.K. The discussion is very much front and center. Who gets to tax that, and everyone is focused on trying to do that.

Who Gets to Tax It Today and Tomorrow?

First, is what I call who gets it today. This is the operational tax aspect, transfer pricing, VAT (Value Added Tax), those kinds of things. As I said, we have got lots of litigation, we have got lots of controversy, we have got lots of issues with virtually every tax authority in every country we operate, all focused on who gets to tax it today, because of these operational issues.

We are also seeing it on the policy side. Who gets to tax it tomorrow. The U.K., as was mentioned, had a lot of discussion last year about how it would tax foreign profits. In my view, the U.K. did the right thing and stepped back from the direction it was going about a year or so ago in terms of taxing worldwide income on certain kinds of businesses, instead, looking to develop a more focused territorial structure with anti-avoidance rules. Again I think this is right, but a lot of debate and discussion around that is yet to come.

I think all that says is that as we continue to pursue performance, governments are seeking who can tax it today and who can tax it tomorrow strategies. The level of controversy, the level of difficulty is absolutely growing and I think fundamentally changing, and not just as a natural evolution but something more dramatic and important.

Again, Tim is going to go into that a little bit more fully in terms of administration and policy. I think the one thing I would say, which I have heard I think a couple of times already this morning, and as long as I have got the microphone I will take the opportunity to throw it out, because I may not have it again for a while. For me, this comment is fundamentally focused on emerged economies. Having an approach of tax administration and development of their policies which is designed principally to track down and drag back income generating activities when they leave is out dated. It's a very defensive strategy that focuses on when a company or a business sets up operations somewhere for a whole variety of reasons, what are the rules we need to go out and claw back, so we can tax it?

The fundamental change in my mind, which will deal with the seismic shift with global companies and trying to deal with government's appetite and need for revenues in this kind of environment, is when those emerged economies start saying instead

Real growth and capital flows

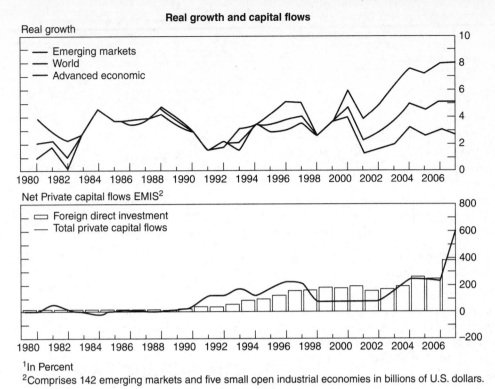

Real growth

- Emerging markets
- World
- Advanced economic

Net Private capital flows EMIS[2]

- Foreign direct investment
- Total private capital flows

[1]In Percent
[2]Comprises 142 emerging markets and five small open industrial economies in billions of U.S. dollars.

Source: IMF World Economic Outlook Database, October 2008

Economic Growth

Source: Bank for International Settlements, CGFS Paper No 33/ at 23.

how do I create a policy of administration that plays offense and invites those businesses to put their operations in my country and attracts and retains those businesses. That will fundamentally change this. Then these governments will go to companies and businesses and say you are looking for competitiveness, you are looking for certainty, we are going to provide that to you. Operate here. That will change the dynamic, and I think that's really where we need to go with all of this. Tim?

Cash Flow Matters

MR. McDONALD: Thanks. I am from Procter & Gamble and I guess Joel and I have a lot of similarities and some differences. My company is much older than Vodafone. P&G is now 172 years old. And yet we are both very global. P&G now has over 60 percent of its sales outside the U.S., and we are focused on making that percentage more significant, because over 95 percent of the world's consumers do not live in the U.S.

We do see a lot of the same things that Joel describes, and I think the one difference I would emphasize probably more is the cash flow aspects of tax policy. I think what has been externally validated as more important than perhaps most believed in the last 12 months is that cash flow truly matters. The current global financial crisis painfully proves the point. Cash flow is how companies survive, it is how they fund growth, it is how they pay their workers, and whether they can pay their workers more, and tax policies directly affect not only a company's P&L performance but also its competitiveness due to the cash flow impacts of tax policy.

So, as much as I care about the P&L, and I care about my company's stock price, it is the cash flow that determines a business

decision's true economics. We at P&G have a very robust culture talking about building the company for the next generation of management, the next generation of shareholders and how does the company prosper for an additional 100 years. In that longer run horizon, cash flow is everything. It's whether your company survives or not, and so to that extent, our tax policy choices in the context of a global economy may be about something much bigger than their narrowly conceived tax technical point or about any one company and whether their stock is up or not. These policy choices may be much more about the U.S. economy's long-term level of prosperity. So, I think the tax policies being discussed today are critically important so that we get the potentially big policy choices correct. I think we are at an inflection point in the U.S. of either becoming more similar and competitive with the other economies of the world or more isolationists, dissimilar and noncompetitive with the rest of the globe, ultimately, our choices will dramatically affect our children's standard of living.

Global Multinationals

This panel is charged to set up the entire conference to discuss globalization, international tax policies and their effect on competitiveness. The title to our panel "Whose income is it?" is kind of interesting. It has two prongs. Superficially, this is just a question about transfer pricing. There is however a much more basic issue being discussed at the root cause. The tax audit challenges are now much more contentious and occurring even where the transfer pricing has clearly been correctly done. Fundamentally, there is often an unstated question about why the company operates in a different and more global manner than in the past? The modern

129

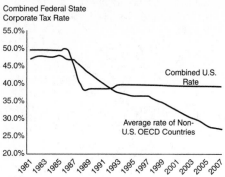

Corporate Tax Rates

GOP Rank	Country	2000 Statutory Corporate Tax Rate	2009 Statutory Corporate Tax Rate	Change from 2000 to 2009
1	United States	39.4	39.5	0.1
2	Japan	43.3	41.3	2.0
3	Germany	52.0	33.0	10.1
4	China	33.0	25.0	8.0
5	United Kingdom	30.0	28.0	2.0
6	France	32.0	34.4	3.3
7	Italy	39.5	30.3	0.2
8	Spain	35.0	30.0	5.0
9	Canada	44.0	35.0	0.0
10	Brazil	34.0	34.0	0.0
11	Russian Ferderation	35.0	22.0	13.0
12	India	45.0	41.8	3.2
13	Korea Rep	30.0	25.0	5.8
14	Mexico	35.0	28.0	7.0
15	Australia	34.0	30.0	4.0
16	Netherland	35.0	25.5	9.5
17	Turkey	33.0	20.0	13.0
18	Belgium	40.2	34.0	6.2
19	Sweden	28.0	28.0	0.0
20	Indonesia	30.0	28.0	2.0

2009 International Corporate Income Tax Rates

business management structures often focus on a concentration of intellectual property rights and management in either a regional or global entrepreneurial company. This has tax revenue implications to the other countries in the region who are not chosen to be the regional entrepreneur location.

The audit question is often, is this business description real and substantive from a business perspective or an artificial tax gimmick? Why did the tax revenue drop and apparently should we attempt to stop the tax base from moving out of that tax authority's country? To understand these tax questions, I think you have to step back and understand that business, as Grant Aldonas described in our opening Keynote speech, is operating very differently, in irreversible ways, as compared to even 15 or 20 years ago. Most companies operated in many countries (*i.e.,* as multinationals) 20 years ago, but they weren't operating as integrated global multinationals. They operated like, as we at P&G did, as small copies of the global parent company in each of their foreign countries. They had fully staffed corporate functions and a largely autonomous management structure in every country. So, in most countries, the byproduct was a tax audit environment that was stable. The tax authorities in each country got their shot at taxing all of the manufacturing and sales activity in their country on a full local entrepreneurial basis as less probably as a royalty back to the country of the parent company.

There might have been a controversy if you had sustained losses in a country, which maybe was explainable. You might have had some contested discussion, if you predominantly imported goods to their country at resale minus, or predominantly sourced out of that country as a manufacturing source at cost plus.

But an interesting dynamic occurred when all the multinational companies were on the locally autonomous "country by country" management structure, what I will hereafter call the "same country" structure. The tax authorities were constrained and couldn't get too aggressive on a transfer pricing theory or method selection because often they would be defending the opposite side of the argument in their next unrelated Competent authority case. Using aggressive transfer pricing theory would actually hinder their revenue collection efforts somewhere else because they had to be theoretically consistent. So, for example, if they wanted to aggressively go after manufacturing income and over emphasize a manufacturer's appropriate return, they may be creating a problem

for themselves auditing a taxpayer whose transactions involve imported goods using resale minus, and *vice versa.*

Globalization and Specialization

What has really changed is that businesses are now global, and they have to be global. Those that are not operating globally are probably not long for this world if their competitors become effective global multinationals, at least for most business models.

> **What has really changed is that businesses are now global, and they have to be global, and, in fact, those that are not operating globally are probably not long for this world if their competitors become effective global multinationals, at least for most business models.**

The globalization point is worth developing. In Grant's keynote speech, he talked about the reduction of various barriers to global trade. I think the reduction in many barriers, customs duties, the currency control restrictions, the WTO trade barrier rules, have all promoted globalization and to some extent tax competition.

P&G is a consumer products company, for us globalization is also about the consumer tastes. What we observe is a homogenization of consumer base beyond country borders. Basically, our consumers are looking more and more the same by region and even globally, and, in fact, we tell the street, for the last eight or nine years that we are focused on our 23 global billion dollar brands. We have moved away from regional brands, and for the most part we have divested or are questioning local-only brands, because they are not as relevant to us, and they are not part of our strategic advantage. So, these regional and globalizing trends take us away from a geographic country focus. That change leads P&G and companies like us to a different management structure and different way of doing business. This is not a fad. Thinking and acting globally is actually a survival issue. If you can achieve a more efficient business model, you must, because others will. For many companies, like P&G, globalization is closely linked to specialization and scale. Achieving scale and specialization whenever you can becomes an imperative. Purchasing for example is no longer done on a country-by-country basis; it has to be done strategically with global price, quality and replenishment standards under competitive volume-based bidding.

Specialization for my company also impacted our main expertise: marketing. Under our prior "same country" local model the country president had very high levels of authority in deciding how her country was managed. The country president would commit to annual sales, net income and cash flow growth objectives and as a result were given wide range of authority in how to deliver these commitments. Our "same country" management structure produced some crazy behavior from a marketing perspective. Sometimes a country president would position a premium tiered product as mid-tier to generate more country sales. In places in Europe where advertisement and image/product placement spills over into neighboring countries this level of lack of coordination is destructive to the greater marketing strategy. It created confusion in branding and image and wasted advertising. We had to evolve away from that type of decentralized marketing. We also had brand-new innovative products launched in our home country. It took us three or four years to launch it in other countries, because the country structure left local management the prerogative to say when they were going to go forward with that large and expensive new product launch campaign, and if they couldn't meet their numbers that year, they held back, they delayed the new product launch. What happened? Our competitors did copy-cat products and they launched their imitator product in other markets ahead of us. In those markets, the copy cat competitor was viewed as the innovator. As a branded company, we can't let that happen, so we had to become more global.

Tax Auditor Expectation Gap

The globalization trend and the evolution of modern global business models are creating a new tax audit paradigm which appears to have drastically reduced the constraint on aggressive audit theory consistency previously described. Now, places that previously were more reasonable and balanced in their audit approach are becoming extremely aggressive and revenue result orientated. These same locations tend to be high-tax countries that are rarely selected as regional entrepreneurial locations. So, what does that mean for the tax revenues? Well, the authorities have a revenue expectation, and this business dynamic has drastically disrupted that historic revenue expectation that they had. They don't have the same entrepreneurial business activity and as a result the same type of revenue sources. Instead they have generally a reduced but more stable tax revenue stream. So, their first reaction is that they don't like it. They don't like the lost revenue, they don't believe the business model works of that real business risk and management activity have been transferred out of their country. They really don't want to ordinarily be a routine low-risk country (unless losses are involved). Unfortunately, we can't have every country as an entrepreneur. The model is, at a minimum, a regional model or possibly global model, but it can't be a per-country model.

So, that leads us to expectation gaps. Interestingly, the theoretical acceptance of the regional entrepreneurial model has recently been accepted in the U.S. After a long discussion on the contract manufacturing regulations, I think, more or less, the U.S. got it right. I think there are some people that are disappointed. There is perhaps a heavy dependence on personal activity on individuals and whether they do substantial contribution, but I think there is at least some overall recognition, for the first time, that this model actually can work without triggering a likely Subpart F inclusion. I think the foreign tax audit environments are catching up with this acceptance of these new business models, but our experience is that it is expensive and somewhat painful. Our experience is all over the map. We have some countries that have actually readily accepted the explanation, audit it aggressively, but the audit produced no change in audit results. We often followed up with an APA (Advance Pricing Agreements) request which was granted and some have expired and been actually renewed without difficulty. In contrast, we have had one country where we went in, got a pre-ruling before the business converted to the regional entrepreneurial structure. They were all fine with it. Administrations changed. The next administration wholly repudiates the rulings. They sued themselves (the government) in court to invalidate the ruling.

They said that the former administration was incompetent, immoral and whatever else they could come up with. They actually asserted a PE (Permanent Establishment) and 100-percent attribution of profits without a profit or return for the 3,000-person headquarters that actually managed that country. In fact, they said it was impossible for us to run our business outside that country. The government official talked in terms of the business as theirs, possessive plural, and I actually said to them, this income is not yours, in fact, the last time I checked your government doesn't own a single share of my parent company or our subsidiaries.

But there was an assertion that they had a stake in our business and its historic income levels, and they weren't willing to let it change. Their theory overrode their treaty obligations with the country where the regional entrepreneur was located as well as our understanding of their domestic law. They also had an alternative theory that there was a deemed sale of the entire business at its "fair market value" *based on its historic cash flows*. This local affiliate was a licensee who had no local intangibles in that country to speak of and yet they said they want to tax in perpetuity the income stream of the former business model, and they want it as an upfront cash payment. Fortunately, things did settle down. Two administrations later, five years of audits, an additional year and a half of competent authority and a bilateral APA application, and we finally got an acceptance of routine returns and a transition payment that was modest and that recognized our transfer pricing view of the business. This was an extremely difficult audit and it was an OECD country.

MS. OLSON: But not an OECD country that is here today.

MR. McDONALD: That's true; it was a different country. In another country, I will call this audit "a theory in search of facts," the auditors constantly were trying to find facts that would disprove our description of the business and prove their hypothesis. At one point they actually visited our regional headquarters, and as they walked away said, "I wish my boss was here. He doesn't believe this place exists." After a total of five years of audit, two additional years of competent authority negotiations, we finally resolved 12 years once again with routine profits and a respecting of the conversion and obtained a five-year bilateral APA. Smaller countries are a little less predictable. We have got one that is espousing a Philip Morris-Italian PE theory that we are still working, but overall, we have been making pretty good progress. We have got eight OECD countries with APAs and four non-OECD jurisdiction APAs. We are trying to expand our ruling coverage and have more APA rulings pending. But what we do see is there is a tremendous amount of cost, energy and hostility to the idea that the world changed. P&G is regularly audited in probably at least 40 countries. Fortunately for P&G, we operate a similar business model around the world. Our goal is therefore to continue to expand our APA footprint. We are probably going to head towards obtaining and then maintaining rulings in 30 countries. Our intention is to use the moral authority of 30 governments all accepting the transfer pricing theory and results to convince the 31st, the 32nd, and 33rd country that they need to be relatively similar.

The World Is a Single Market

So, what does this mean beyond P&G? Well, as I stated initially, the bigger policy implications of not embracing a company's need to evolve and to effectively compete globally are stark. This is related to the larger debate about maintaining deferral in the U.S. international tax rules. In both cases, there are asserted challenges about whether the business rationale and competitiveness policy claims are real. In the deferral debate, we risk being labeled unfairly as unpatriotic for developing our foreign market potential. There is a confusion that assumes that if you investing in the foreign markets it is to the detriment of domestic investment, as if it is an "either-or choice." The truth is we invest everywhere we have a return. We are not capital constrained, so if there are opportunities to invest in the U.S., and there are, we are investing and we are expanding in the U.S., but we are also investing and expanding abroad. Ninety-five percent of the world's consumers live outside the U.S.A lot of our future growth is outside the U.S. because our market share and household penetration rates are much lower there. If we don't grow outside the U.S., and our non-U.S. competitors prosper there, we will eventually die here. Some believe that the arm's-length transfer pricing rules are flawed or dead, as I think some have said, and that businesses as a conclusion should not be allowed to evolve or restructure without tax.

I think these beliefs are misplaced. I think, number one, the business reality is the world is a single market or will evolve into a single market. You need to be efficient, and you need to be competitive with all the global players not just those from the U.S. The reason is not an esoteric P&L reason. It is because if you don't have competitive cash flows; you will not be competitive long term, and you will lose the survival race. The old business model designs need to evolve. You cannot have policy that freezes a business structure, and the reason is simple. New companies will not be constrained by a historic inefficient design pre-tax. They will be allowed to optimize from a clean slate unencumbered by history in a much more rational way that globally runs a global enterprise more efficiently on a pre-tax basis. If you don't let existing/historic competing companies have the same type of opportunity to evolve globally in an efficient pre-tax structure, then you have pre-ordained all existing/historic businesses to slowly die or be acquired. And by the way, those global designs also have an opportunity to be more efficient on a tax basis as well.

The U.S. should not make our U.S.-based multinational any more noncompetitive given our existing worldwide system with its difficult foreign tax credit methodology, and a tax rate that is almost 15 percentage points above the norm. The pressure is acute. If you have 15 to 20 percent cash flow disadvantage as compared to your non-U.S. competitors, the outcome is known, it is just a question of how long it will take for them to win the race. Those that have that kind of structural cash flow disadvantage cannot win. To say otherwise is to think that you are immune from these market realities. It is implicitly an arrogant belief to think that there are to be no competitiveness consequences, Americans would need to be uniquely brilliant versus the rest of the world. They implicitly would have to out-think the foreign competitor on every other line of P&L to compensate for this cash flow disadvantage on tax policy. I do not think that anyone informed in tax policy actually believes that Americans have a unique monopoly on great ideas to win the race despite an uncompetitive tax policy.

It is important to note that a unilateral uncompetitive tax policy precludes a level playing field for U.S. multinationals as compared to their foreign competitors, because the U.S. is the only major economy with global multinationals that still has a worldwide taxation system. The U.S. does not have jurisdiction to impose our policies globally on non-U.S. multinationals. The same is true for any country as compared to the foreign multinationals of that country. The U.S. also does not have unique insight to dictate policy either by edict or by moral persuasion.

We have jurisdictional constraints on whether we can impose the theory. First, for almost 100 years, income tax treaties have allocated taxation rights for corporate income taxation based on source and residency principles. Even where you don't have a treaty, we have a national interest in trying to preserve treaty-like policies and respect that same type of allocation rights. It also probably often overlooked, the trade rules have drastically curtailed the ability to equalize the playing field for U.S. multinationals because it is impermissible under trade rules to have a border adjustment for income tax or any other direct tax. Ironically, probably not thought of at the time, indirect taxes like VAT are permissibly adjusted at the border, and as a result they are probably our future.

So, if we cannot compel consistent global tax policies on the foreign multinational, where does that take us? Well, I think some are arguing we just need to get the rest of the world back on the right page and this tax policy "crisis" of harmful tax competition and global multinationals unpatriotic behavior of "shipping jobs offshore" is solved. Essentially it is a belief that even if we cannot compel the other governments to adopt tax policies strongly similar to ours, they will be convinced to do so once they understand that all governments will be better off and, what some economists call "global welfare" will be achieved, if we end tax competition. Everyone should therefore adopt a pure worldwide system without deferral, or maybe just a U.S. hybrid system and possibly with the same rates we have, or a territorial system, but in a theoretically pure design that raises more revenue than repeal of deferral. The truth is, these options are all theoretically possible, but practically, they are *not at all realistic,* because no government will actually pursue policies that are not in its national interest. They don't actually pursue global welfare as the theory might suggest.

This is not just assertion or hypothesis, the experiment has been run. For the last 20 years, governments have been cutting their tax rates, meanwhile encouraging discussions about stopping harmful tax competition. It is kind of ironic that they have lulled the U.S. to sleep with their rhetoric while they cut their home country tax rates. Their behavior speaks louder than their words. We just haven't followed suit. I think if you look at the EU experience in particular, it is fascinating. The larger countries of the EU for 15 years tried to discuss, threaten and attempted to cajole Ireland and more recently the new entrants to not have a low tax rate for corporations. They even threatened to curtail their infrastructure expenditures to the new EU entrants, but what did the governments there do? They politely listened but didn't change their policies. It was because they viewed it was in their national self-interest to help promote the growth of their multinationals and the foreign multinationals that operate in their country, and they exploited their competitive advantages including tax competition, because their job is to promote the national welfare of their citizens.

Ironically, across the EU now, the idea of stopping tax competition in practice has waned. Even the countries that were the most vocal against tax competition such as Germany and France have cut their rates rather dramatically over the last couple of years.

So, where do we go broadly from a corporate income tax policy? We have two choices. We can almost unilaterally continue our historic worldwide tax policy with high rates. It has implicit assumptions that there are no competitiveness consequences for U.S. multinationals because there are no real foreign competitors' effects to worry about. There is an implicit belief that the U.S.-centric leadership role, both economically and as a policy matter, will carry the day and that others will follow. I think behavior suggests not. The world has in effect moved away from our international tax policies and theory.

We, in effect, can choose to just maintain or modify slightly our current system despite the rest of the world having a very competitive corporate tax landscape, or we pursue an alternative described below, which in my personal view is a more appealing new policy choice. I think we should pursue the predominant international norm on tax policies and design. We would need to adopt a competitive definition of a tax base, a competitive tax rate at or below the OECD average, and we need to maintain the competitiveness of rate. So if other countries cut their rates further, as I predict they will, we cut our rate appropriately to remain competitive as part of the norm of international design. The U.S. would also adopt a territorial system like all of our major trading partners that is realistic, and does not have wholesale disallowance of domestic expenses. It also follows that we do what other countries have done to address the revenue shortfall that these first two policies create by also adopting a legally permissible indirect tax such as a VAT. The advantage of a VAT is that equitably, taxes identical domestic and nondomestic goods equally and therefore it eliminates a dramatic distortion in competitiveness and trade. If you do these three things, you will also politically need to address progressive concerns, and there are tools to deal with that.

We probably have to think about a more progressive income tax, we probably have to deal with our payroll tax system, and we probably have to think about a VAT rebate mechanism for at least poverty level and below household income levels, so that we don't inadvertently shift the tax burden to those that can't afford it. But the advantage of the cluster of these three or four policies is that we probably have a system that is much more immune from distortions of globalization and yet still raises revenue and, if designed right, probably can do it on a quite progressive basis.

I think the second choice gives us stronger long-term GDP growth, at least according to Treasury, implicitly, that would also give us more tax revenue if there is more growth. It would

probably produce higher real wage growth. There is plenty of academic research that analyzes corporate tax rates and real wages which suggests, if corporate income tax rates are above the norm, real wage growth is suppressed. In fact, separately, there is robust research that shows that global multinationals in the U.S. pay their employees significantly higher salaries for similar jobs compared to domestic-only companies. Part of that is because they are more successful enterprises. I think that is a desirable thing. If we, instead of cursing the global multinationals, embrace them and try to help them grow, we actually have a strategy that probably promotes greater job growth and retention of the most valuable jobs in the economy. Our historic policy choices unfortunately probably cannot achieve these same objectives as efficiently.

Another Look at Corporate Tax Rates

MS. OLSON: Thank you, Tim. Slide 8 shows the OECD average corporate tax rate being slightly above 25 percent. Senator Grassley said we ought to get our corporate rate down to 25 percent. Chairman Rangel's bill from the last session of Congress took rates down to 30 1/2 percent with some fairly significant base broadening—though Mr. Rangel's staff has said that they got to a 30 1/2-percent rate without breaking a sweat—and Mr. Rangel has said that he wants to bring that rate down a little bit further. I am not sure whether Mr. Rangel plans to go quite as far as Senator Grassley's 25 percent. We are looking at a large need for revenue based on the projected budget deficit, including the enactment of the stimulus bill last week. So we face a need for more revenue.

Other countries around the globe face a need for more revenue, as well. Mike, we would be interested in your thoughts about whether we can get the additional revenue we need out of the income tax base or whether we have to turn to a VAT as Tim suggests. The press pool comments from the fiscal responsibility summit on Monday indicated that there was some discussion about a VAT in the tax session. Mike, we are also interested in your observations, based on your engagement with international organizations and other countries during the year and a half that you have been back at Treasury, on what other countries are thinking about taxes, trying to tax income on a global basis or on a local basis, and where things are going.

MR. MUNDACA: I think what Tim talked about is not only what companies are facing, but what governments are facing as well, which is they both are recognizing that the business landscape has shifted, which is why you have seen such developments as the dropping of the corporate tax rate and the move toward a territorial system. On the other hand, our governments know, as Joel mentioned, that companies are competing on taxes as well, that they are looking to drive down their tax costs just like they are looking to drive down all sorts of other costs, and therefore, governments, because of the need for revenue, because of their knowledge of company behavior, and because of their experience of looking at their tax collections over the last couple of years from multinational corporations, have started to increase their enforcement and have started to come up with some new and novel theories of how to tax under current law. So, even as they are driving down rates, and even as they are in essence giving up taxing a big chunk of foreign source income, we have seen international organizations and other countries, posit expanded theories of jurisdiction to tax, thus expanding the tax base even as they give up on taxing foreign source income, that is by considering a narrower slice of income as foreign. So, therefore, we are seeing countries expand what they consider to be domestic source income. We have seen countries as well try to mold the treaties and transfer pricing rules that they have agreed to implement in a way that looks at business restructuring as an opportunity to either continue to tax what has left, or to impose an exit task on what is leaving. Again, countries are realizing that business is mobile, but many have not yet come to the realization that when they leave, the country loses their rights to tax if they have moved toward a territorial system.

So, we have seen in the OECD and elsewhere again some novel theories on how countries that do see operations leaving, that do see so-called supply chain management structures coming in with respect to their multinationals may hold on to more of the tax base than perhaps their domestic rules would otherwise allow without these overlays of some more novel theories of jurisdiction to tax. I think that is going to continue. I don't think it is an overstatement, as Ed Kleinbard's article on territoriality[1] points out, that territoriality increases to an extraordinary degree the pressure on transfer pricing rules, and that is already an area that already is under a good deal of pressure. So we have seen countries again moving toward more enforcement, more again novel theories of tax jurisdiction and transfer pricing to try to keep some of the tax base they see leaving because of their move to territoriality and because of business' moves of personnel, investment, etc., to other jurisdictions. As Tim mentioned, and this is I think something else to consider, back in the 1960s when our international tax rules were formed, many of the assumptions underlying those rules was that income was being deflected to jurisdictions in which there was no economic activity, and that what we really had to do was try to match the economics with the tax, and that is a lot of what Subpart F was about. But again, as Tim mentioned, investment is what is shifting now, it is not a mere income shift; it is an investment shift. And that creates a new problem: You don't want your tax rules to say, in essence, well, what we would like you to do is not shift investment and assets overseas, but if you do, you are outside our tax net, and if you don't, then, you will be, because we know what the response is going to be. Investment and assets will be shifted overseas, and jobs are going to follow. And the tax rules, pushed them offshore. So again I think that is part of what countries are struggling with, that they have made these changes to their tax rules and are now having to live with the consequences. We will see, especially as countries like Japan and the U.K. and others get more experience with territoriality and its implications, what the next generation of tax changes is going to be. I think for the U.S., and if we have this conference on Friday as opposed to today, there might be a little bit more to tell on what some of the President's plans might be, after the budget outline is released tomorrow, but I don't think it will be any surprise to anyone who listened to the President's address last night, that he will not be proposing a territorial system, that when he talked about closing the loopholes that allow corporations to send jobs overseas, he wasn't previewing a move toward a territorial system. We will have, as we move forward, two different world views. We will have the U.S. worldwide tax system and then we will have all of our major trading partners having moved toward a territorial system, and we will see how the tensions between those views play out.

Question & Answer

MS. OLSON: We have a few questions here from the audience. The first one says, "It is interesting to look at the differences between the way other countries have gone and the way the U.S. is going. Is there anything that you have seen in the discussions with other countries that is pointing them in a different direction than the direction it appears we may be taking in the budget?"

MR. MUNDACA: It would be interesting if you have a chance to ask anyone from the U.K., their experience, and the Japanese, the ones moving the most recently toward a territorial system, what motivated them. But we have seen in discussions with other countries that the motivation is twofold. It is their experience in trying to tax foreign source income and their economic analysis of the effects of moving toward a territorial system. I think many of these countries have become convinced that it is the best way for them to maintain the investment that comes into their countries and maintain the health of their multinationals.

Again, we will see if that is the right choice or not. The counter to that is that a lot of these countries are now seeing, that having moved to a territorial system, their multinationals are seeking to lower their local corporate taxes by moving investment and jobs outside of that country. Again, there are two ways to respond to that. You can (1) move back to a worldwide system or increase enforcement and come up with broader views of your jurisdiction to tax, or (2) you can drive your rates down further. I think a lot of countries are having to face that now, that having moved to a territorial system, what their next move is going to be. It seems the initial response is this enforcement response, this moving toward a broader view of jurisdiction. We have seen coming out of Europe this week a lot of noise from France and from Germany and others on anti-tax haven initiatives, because they think tax havens are sucking out their, not just individual, but corporate tax base, as well. So, I think the initial response has been on that front, the enforcement and broadening of jurisdiction front. We will see if that is successful and if countries may then have to move toward either rethinking the move to territoriality or perhaps to further drive down rates.

MS. OLSON: How do we define "tax haven" for purposes of the exercise that is underway? If you have rates under 20 percent, are you a tax haven?

MR. MUNDACA: A couple of bills use a list, and I think there are a couple of important co-sponsors on some of those bills, but—not speaking for the administration—in forming any list, you have to be very careful as a general, so-called "tax haven" list probably isn't going to be much help to anybody. You need to know why you are forming this list: The list of countries that may be used by individuals, for example, to hide money in banks is very different from a list where corporations might use low tax rates in order to generate better returns on their investments, and no one list is going to serve all the different purposes people want to put these lists to.

It might be better if we were going to go this route to have different sorts of initiatives that focus on individuals, that focus on evasion as opposed to avoidance, that focus on the different uses to which tax havens are put. But at least in the rhetoric coming out of Europe, I haven't seen that subtlety in the analysis. I think they are looking to a very broad definition, that is, a country that has any one of the criteria that were set way back in the late 1990s, the low tax rate, the lack of transparency, the so-called ring fencing—giving special rates for foreign investment. Again, a list that includes all countries that do all of those things, it is going to be, not only quite long, but I think quite unwieldy and ineffective in addressing the problems tax havens present.

MS. OLSON: We have a question from the audience for Joel. The question is whether you can provide some more details about the arrangements with HMRC regarding openness and transparency.

MR. WALTERS: I am happy to do that. I see Dave Hartnett (Permanent Secretary for Tax, Her Majesty's Revenue & Customs) is here, and he can comment if he would like to, as well. The history is actually quite simple. There have been discussions in the U.K. for quite a while as to whether should there be a contract between business and HMRC in terms of how we operate together.

I didn't think that there could be such a thing as a contract, because I am not in a position to bind my shareholders to do anything that I am not required to do by law or regulation, and therefore, it felt to me like that was going too far. But what did feel to me was right is I want an organization that operates in an open and transparent way.

We only do tax planning if we think (1) the law supports us; (2) we think the law is intended to support us, we are not just slipping through a hole in the law; (3) that it is consistent with our values and we are satisfied that it is something we would want to do. If all those things are true, then, there is no reason we shouldn't be open and transparent and deal with tax authorities in a respectful way and communicate in the right way with each other.

So, we sat down with HMRC and we said, let's put together some principles on how we act, how we operate with each other, and on a quarterly basis we will give each other 360° feedback as to how we are doing. And we do that, and I think it has been a great thing, because I think it has moved the level of trust up. I think it has moved the level of communication up. And I think that in my view it reinforces the values that I want in the team, because the team knows whatever it is we do from a planning perspective or however we act today, we are going to openly discuss that with HMRC someday in the future. It reinforces the ways of working that I want from the team. So, it is really just a set of principles that we sat down and we agreed we would operate under and we would test each other on how we are doing. I think it has been a really positive thing from my perspective.

MS. OLSON: Terrific. Any closing comments from any of the three of you? Thanks everyone.

End Notes

1. This panel discussion took place at the 10th Annual Tax Policy and Practice Symposium, *Certainty in an Uncertain World? Revolving Cross-Border Tax Controversies,* held on February 25–26, 2009. The panelists' comments were edited, annotated and augmented prior to publication.

2. Edward D. Kleinbard, *Throw Territorial Taxation From the Train,* Tax Notes, Feb. 5, 2007.

TIMOTHY M. MCDONALD, Vice President—Finance & Accounting, Global Taxes, Procter & Gamble MICHAEL MUNDACA, Deputy Assistant Secretary (International Tax Affairs), U.S. Department of the Treasury JOEL WALTERS, Corporate Finance Director, Vodafone PAMELA F. OLSON, Partner, Skadden, Arps, Slate, Meagher & Flom LLP (Moderator)

Exploiting the Global Supply Chain

What changes when your sourcing and markets go international? Everything!

JEREMY N. SMITH

The difference between an international and purely domestic supply chain strategy? "Everything!"

So says Greg Lehmkuhl vice president, global automotive, for Menlo Worldwide Logistics, one of five veteran executives World Trade asked to advise companies going global for the first time or expanding existing international operations. Doing business abroad introduces vast new variables to a preexisting, mostly domestic supply chain.

"If I looked back five years ago, probably five percent of the requests for transportation solutions were international," says Erv Bluemner, vice president, product marketing transportation solutions, RedPrairie. "Now the numbers are between thirty and thirty-five percent. Most of that shift has occurred in just the last twenty-four months."

Lehmkuhl tells the same story. Five years ago, the automotive suppliers he served might have seen 'going global' as a choice. Now, however, competitors have set up shop in Asia or South America or Eastern Europe. "Clients aren't asking if you have an international strategy anymore," he says. "They're asking you to demonstrate it. It's becoming the ante instead of the differentiator."

Take the example of an automotive components manufacturer operating primarily out of Mexico. When a major U.S. automaker representing half their business ordered them to shift some of their sourcing to China, management balked, asking Menlo to perform a total landed cost comparison. "It took us four weeks," Lehmkuhl says. "We did studies of sixty percent of their procured parts. We came back with the opinion, given all the risks and all the costs, that it did make sense in most cases for them to move their sourcing to China."

Yet the company wasn't convinced. They decided to wait and see. Within a year, Lehmkuhl says, they lost forty percent of their business.

Granted, making the change from a North America-based to a global supply chain is no slam-dunk.

"The complexity of managing the supply chain increases exponentially when you move offshore," Greg Lehmkuhl says. "You have to have a defined, well-articulated, and proven strategy."

According to the experts, companies must be willing to examine and rethink every aspect of their existing business model. That means looking inward before expanding outward and revising P&Ls to focus on total landed cost.

"It's often the C-level executives who make these decisions, but when they go international, companies need a coordinated strategy across their procurement, operations, sales, marketing, and logistics groups," says Jeff Scovill, vice president, global forwarding, C.H. Robinson. "All those entities need to be involved."

Here, as ever, logistics is the tie that binds. "You can be reactionary and still be successful domestically because the logistics team can come in at the last moment and take in the slack," says Scovill. But that doesn't work internationally. Start to finish, he says, "Logistics has to make sure, at every step of the supply chain, you're moving goods through, you're tracking of inventory, and you're keeping customers happy."

As firms go global, for example, Scovill says, they should understand their long-standing channels may become obsolete. "Often customers will just assume they can feed inventory from overseas supply channels into their existing domestic supply channels," he says, "rather than evaluating total landed costs of ownership."

A C. H Robinson customer sourced products from Asia and Europe and shipped them to the Midwest simply because that's where existing distribution centers—remnants of domestic manufacturing operations—existed. But eighty percent of their customers were located close to the East or West Coast. "They incurred costs moving the products from the East or West Coasts to the Midwest facilities, and then they incurred costs shipping them back to the coasts," Scovill recalls. "Of course, one of the first things we did was change their distribution channels, so when they were bringing product in, they could keep them on the coasts and avoid having to go through that additional expense."

The promise of lower total landed cost—and, with it, higher market share—lures American companies offshore. Delivering fully on that promise, however, calls for optimal end-to-end supply chain visibility.

The promise of lower total landed cost lures American companies offshore but delivering on that promise calls for optimal supply chain visibility.

Supply chain software solutions provider RedPrairie sees more and more middle-tier customers engaging in global supply chain networks for the first time, Erv Bluemner says. Not all understand the trade-offs. "You can't save fifty cents per widget and then pay an extra sixty cents for transport—especially if it doesn't get through customs. Purchase and transportation management systems need to be connected."

Jim Ritchie, president and chief executive officer of YRC Logistics, agrees. "The current supply chain process for a lot of clients is that the product gets sourced in a foreign country, loaded in a container, put on an ocean vessel that moves to the U.S., gets offloaded, clears customs, and then somebody breaks open the container." But opening a container should never be the first real confirmation companies have that what they ordered was what was shipped. If so, mistakes and miscommunication will take months rather than days to discover.

"If you don't have good visibilities, you can have product that can arrive at port and sit there for an extended period of time, with no knowledge that they are there," says Jeff Scovill. "We have customers who have had their products sit for 60, 90, 100 days without knowing it. By the time they figure out what's happening they've incurred thousands of dollars in detention and demurrage fees before they even get access to their products."

C.H. Robinson served a consumer products company whose earlier efforts at overseas sourcing ended in an even worse situation. As flow of goods increased from China to the U.S. West Coast, the buyer found itself with significant gaps in supply chain visibility. "They needed a set of four or five SKUs for fulfillment of their customers and didn't know where they were located, when they were arriving, or when they would be available," Jeff Scovill says.

The solution: assert control and get visibility, either with your own custom transportation management system (smaller companies can subscribe to hosted solutions at affordable cost) or through service providers like 3PLs,

Rule Number One: Take Your Time!

The top mistake executives make in going global is being unrealistic about their timelines.

"They expect to have a Chinese partner up and running in a year, but the partner wants to gain friendship and get to know you," says Greg Lehmkuhl, vice president, global automotive, for Menlo Worldwide Logistics. Time and again, he's seen American executives fly in, interview suppliers, and want to start buying six to ten weeks later. Every time they've failed.

STEP ONE is devoting sufficient time up front to your partnerships, be they with overseas suppliers or third-party supply chain providers. In every case, what matters for success is that the partner offers sufficient presence and expertise in the target region.

STEP TWO is executing slowly. No company's first overseas subcontract should be for any of its five most critical components. Instead, firms should start outsourcing with low-volume, low-impact, multi-sourced products that they can easily replace domestically. That way if expected shipments don't arrive on time—or product quality isn't up to par—business life goes on as usual.

STEP THREE is strategizing risk. This can be as easy as asking a simple question: How fast could you change your supply chain if something bad happens? Make sure the answer is one you can live with. Otherwise, Lehmkuhl says, a single missed shipment may devastate the company.

freight forwarders and ocean carriers. If you choose the second option, Erv Bluemner warns, buyer beware. "Any number of times I've gone into customers and they've said that they use one specific freight forwarder for everything and they don't have any basis for cost comparison," he says. "Often you can do better if you have a system that allows you to connect to multiple ocean providers and multiple freight forwarders, where you can consider multiple ports of exit and entry."

An international supply chain entails a new approach to financing. Mike Bellardine, director of global trade and international payment services, KeyBank, suggests hiring an experienced cash manager. "Working capital is hard to forecast. One size doesn't fit all."

New sets of risks comes into play. "It's possible that the seller may have the goods on the boat and delivered before the financial papers clear," says Bellardine, offering the example of a KeyBank client purchasing internationally in an Asian country for the first time: "The inventory was time-sensitive and they wanted to make sure it fit their sales window. What happened was physically the goods arrived in port ahead of the documents

Know Your Terms

Negotiating an international sales contract? "Both parties need to pay as much attention to the terms of sale as to the sales price," reminds the International Business Institute.

Between consignees and consignors on each international transaction, so-called INCOTERMS dictate every aspect of the purchase: when title to goods changes hands, where risk is involved, who is responsible for various costs and charges that occur in the supply chain. "What will happen a lot of time is that people get into global supply chains and they go overseas on an import basis," says Jeff Scovill. "They make the mistake of getting things from point A to point B without knowing the terms."

In short, Scovill says, importers purchase goods under one of four INCOTERMS:

- CIF—cost insurance and freight
- CFR—cost and freight (no insurance)
- DDU—delivered, duty unpaid
- DDP—delivered, duty paid

In either of the first two cases, the seller of the goods is responsible for all the costs of moving the goods to a named location—for example, a port or container yard or warehouse in the United States. Only in the second two cases, however, is the seller also responsible for performing customs clearance. Whether DDU or DDP, says Scovill, "they're acting as the importer of record, and either they or the buyer pay the duties."

Customs, duties, taxes, and delivery—clearly, the costs add up. Read international contracts carefully and consult an expert before signing on the bottom line.

---

necessary to clear customs." No documents, no deliveries. No deliveries, no sales.

Tricky as it may be, coordinating international inventory and paperwork can seem simple by comparison with the task of foreign currency calculations. "As soon as a customer crosses the border, they face the same cash management issues they did domestically—but now on steroids," says Bellardine.

Or consider the more complicated case of a domestic grain seller distributing in Eastern Europe. A surging euro made such export sales attractive, but what guaranteed each new buyer would pay as promised? "Normally, if you have a new domestic client, you can set internal house or credit limits," Bellardine says. "In this case there were two problems. One, they're in Eastern Europe—how do I get a view on the buyer? Two, even if the buyer's good, how do they get the currency to pay me?"

Answering those questions required the buyer to get a letter of credit from a Russian bank, then the seller to get a confirmation from KeyBank of the Russian bank's reliability. "Of course it costs a fee, but it's almost like buying insurance on the receivable."

The physical supply chain carries additional risks when it goes global. Containers take an average of 11 to 23 days to travel from foreign suppliers to the United States. What happens in the case of delay or error?

"If you have only a one-week float to meet your customer's lead time and you're shipping by sea, a blip is going to devastate you," says Menlo's Greg Lehmkuhl.

He speaks from experience. An automotive component manufacturer turned to Menlo for help after betting big on Asian outsourcing without properly calculating the risks to inventory. "They were going to save $4 or $5 million a year, but there was port congestion in Los Angeles-Long Beach," Lehmkuhl says. Instead of paying $20,000 for a chartered aircraft from Mexico to the United States, the company paid $750,000 for aircrafts originating from Asia. Just like that, an anticipated $5 million savings became a $20 million loss.

Whether moving goods by land, sea, or air, going global means a company or its partners must adapt to existing physical infrastructure, supply channels, and foreign regulation.

Europe, for example, has a well-developed transportation infrastructure and short distance between ports, but an emerging market like Vietnam—where an increasing number of American companies are sourcing—often lacks direct ocean or air freight links to the United States. That creates opportunity for delay, damage, and other risk factors. Even in fast-modernizing China, standard business practices may ignore what can be taken for granted in the U.S. Pallets, for example are costly compared to labor in China, so goods move manually, taking extra time to load and unload as well as increasing the frequency of damage. Paperwork, meanwhile, literally changes hands, passing from driver to driver, truck to truck, all to align with different regional regulations.

"There's no slick Internet system that's going to manage that process in China or any other country," says Greg Lehmkuhl. "It's about real, on-the-ground operations."

Last on the going global checklist: read the fine print.

Changing international regulations may challenge even the best expansion plan and execution. "It's shocking—if you don't pay attention to regulatory events in targeted emerging markets—how fast your business case can dissolve," says Greg Lehmkuhl. He cites the case of an automotive parts distribution center moving from Southeast Asia to China's Guangxo province. "In this province, hazardous material regulations changed. They had to warehouse all hazardous materials offsite in a separate and contained hazardous material warehouse."

Existing U.S. trade agreements and customs laws are no less important. Time and again, return on investment may disappear with a single duty rate or classification change.

Remember, too, work-in-progress inventories may enjoy lower duties than finished products.

A concurrent trend—often called pre-mixing—is siting distribution centers outside the United States. Rather than by individual item or manufacturer, shipments are grouped by ultimate destination—regions, cities, and even single stores. Total transit time shrinks, domestic labor and infrastructure costs decline, and orders are verified before they leave the foreign country; nor do overseas mixing centers show up on a company's working capital balance sheet.

"You eliminate your risk based on what was ordered versus what was shipped and you accelerate your time to final destination," says Jim Ritchie, calling it one of today's strongest international supply chain trends.

From *World Trade,* May 2008, pp. 32–34, 36. Copyright © 2008 by BNP Media. Reprinted by permission.

UNIT 4

Issues in International Business

Unit Selections

Key Points to Ponder

- The developing world is changing and taking a more active role in the global marketplace. Where do you think this is headed? Do you think there are countries in the developing world that will soon compete with the developed world?

- How do you see the way people are treated in the developing world different from how they are treated in the developed world? Should American or European standards be applied to different cultures? Why or why not? Do global corporations have a right to do that? Do they have a responsibility? Do their customers have the obligation to hold them to their social codes?

- How important are green policies? Should they be applied to developing countries? How can corporations best implement green programs? What are the dangers for green organizations when dealing with corporate organizations?

Student Website
www.mhhe.com/cls

Internet References

China.org
http://china.org.cn/english/index.htm
Green Peace
www.greenpeace.org/usa/
Private Sector Development Blog of the World Bank
http://psdblog.worldbank.org
The Development Gateway
www.developmentgateway.org/
The Economic Times
www.theeconomictimes.com
Further information regarding these websites may be found in this book's preface or online.

Over half of the world's population lives in the developing world. Three of the four largest countries in terms of population are among the developing world countries: China, India and Indonesia. China and India alone account for 2.4 billion people, more than twice the entire population of Europe, Canada, Japan, Australia, New Zealand, and the United States combined. The fate of what happens in the developing world will be the fate of what happens in the global economy. India and China, as well as many of the other developing countries are the ones that are coming out of the global recession much faster than the developed countries, and the game in international trade and development would appear to be changing.

Companies from China and India would appear to be investing in some of the lesser developed parts of the world and especially Africa. For years, both Chinese and Indian companies have been off-shoring highly labor intensive, low skilled work to lower cost venues. The "Flip-flop" business was off-shored long ago. Today, much of that investment is focused on countries in Africa where economic development has not occurred on the scale that it has in Asia. There are many opportunities in Africa for investment and Chinese and Indian organizations are aggressively pursuing those opportunities. Today, African trade with China and India roughly equals that with Africa's traditional trading partners in Europe and the United States.

Foreign aid has been a way for developed countries to attempt to assist lesser and least developed countries. But, that foreign aid has often come with strings attached to it. Often the money must be used to purchase items from the donating country, often specific items. This is not the best use for the foreign aid money. The receiving country's main need may be for farm equipment, but the foreign aid money may require them to purchase military equipment. The countries will take the money and buy the equipment, but what they really needed were tractors, not tanks.

The way organizations are operated outside the developed world can, at times, be very ethically challenging. Many countries outside the developed world have no rules or regulations on how the employees of corporations should be treated or if they do have rules, those rules are either loosely enforced or not enforced at all. The safety of the workers is sometimes compromised in an effort to squeeze the last nickel of profit out of the operation with no regard for the safety of the workers. Long-term health considerations are tossed aside in the knowledge that the workers will have little recourse against their employer when they become ill. This is happening on the very doorstep of the United States as seen in "International: Through the Looking Glass of the Global Economy OHS."

Global corporate citizenship goes beyond just being a good neighbor. Global corporate citizenship means taking an active role in the important issues facing the international environment including climate change, water shortage, infectious diseases, and terrorism. Global corporate citizenship means being an active player in the development of the future of the world's international environment. It goes beyond the traditional concept of simply writing a check for a good cause and

© glowimages/Getty Images RF

walking away from the problem for someone else to spend the money. It means getting involved, and the company actively spending the money itself to see that it is appropriately utilized and that the firm gets its money's worth. Companies will be criticized for taking this approach, for taking too active a role in how their resources are spent. But, history has shown that too much of corporate philanthropy has been wasted, especially in the developing world, so organizations owe it to themselves, the recipients, and their stockholders to make certain that the money and investments they make are utilized more effectively. "Global Corporate Citizenship: Working with Governments and Civil Society," explains this and how corporations can best help to solve some of the problems facing the global society.

The greening of the economy has been a major factor in both the domestic and the international agenda. President Obama has made the green economy a major part of the agenda of his administration. The same can be said in the international environment. Everywhere, organizations are seeking to become more "green" in the way they do business. This benefits the company from several perspectives. First, from the perspective of costs, becoming green, generally means using less carbon-based energy, and as the price of carbon-based energy is almost certain to climb in the long-run, going green will help to keep costs down. The second is from a marketing perspective. Greener products are generally viewed more favorably by consumers, giving the company a better image overall. Finally, the third reason is that more and more countries are demanding that companies produce products that are "green" as opposed to the old formulas for producing those products. This includes automobiles that get better gas mileage to laundry products that produce less environmental pollutants. Going green simply makes sense for any corporation.

There is, however, one aspect of the green economy that "Green Organizations" need to be careful of. Corporate sponsorship can be very dangerous for green organizations to either seek or accept. While these corporate organizations may want to affiliate themselves with particular environmental groups as a part of their corporate strategy of becoming "green" it may not be in the best interests of the green organization for them to accept the affiliation. Accepting money from a large corporation generally means that the large corporation will list the fact that they support "X" group on their website and in their corporate literature. They have, after all, donated money to the organization, usually on an annual basis. The money the company has donated is probably relatively small in terms of the corporation, but likely to be large in terms of the green organization. Money, it should be remembered can be like a drug and after a few years the green organization can become dependent on that money from the corporate source. The removal of those funds, or even the threat of removal of those funds can place the mission of the organization in jeopardy. Green organizations would do well to be cautious in dealing with large corporations and keep them at arms length.

There are many issues in the international business environment. More issues will be coming to the forefront every day. Terrorism, another oil crisis, war, ethnic cleansing, another economic crisis may all be on the horizon. But good news can also be there too. Wars eventually do end, tyrants are eventually toppled, an economic crisis is eventually resolved, and since the start of the industrial revolution, about 250 years ago, technology has found a way to resolve many of the problems that plagued the human race for centuries. There have been much darker times than the ones we live in today. There is hope. Whatever the crisis, this, too, shall pass.

What One Hand Gives, the Other Takes

Industrial Countries' Policy Coherence for Development

Rich countries' policies in areas such as trade, the environment, investment, migration, security, and technology could either bolster or blunt the effectiveness of their own aid policies to poor countries, depending on whether and to what extent all these policies are coherent or contradictory. Too often they are not coherent. But the main message of this author is that policy coherence for development cannot be determined by the rich industrial countries alone. Meaningful developing-country participation is essential in forming coherent, constructive policies.

RONALD MENDOZA

Rich countries' foreign aid policies are intended to help poor countries develop. But their policies in other areas—spanning trade, the environment, investment, migration, security, and technology—could be just as (if not more) important in attaining that goal. If these other policies are contradictory to foreign aid, they could blunt the latter's effectiveness and hinder development in poor countries. Rich countries' policy contradictions are myriad, and a number of them could have serious implications for poor countries' development prospects.[1]

"Tying" foreign aid is one case in point. Essentially, this policy requires that part of the aid is spent to purchase inputs from the donor country. Designed to generate economic benefits for the donor by promoting its domestic commercial and trade interests, this policy often comes at the cost of aid effectiveness—tying aid could contradict aid itself. Studies suggest that "tying" could raise aid project costs by about 15–30 percent, effectively reducing aid value by 15 percent or over, and it could also result in a misallocation of resources and the use of inappropriate technologies (Jepma 1994). At present, only about 42 percent of official development assistance by rich countries is untied (OECD 2006).

Some trade promotion policies of rich countries could also prove contradictory to their own development assistance efforts and detrimental to development. A specific example is the Norwegian Ship Export Campaign of 1976–1980, which resulted in the export of vessels and equipment to a number of developing countries. Financed through the Norwegian Guarantee Institute for Export Credits (GIEK), these projects proved to be economically unsustainable, so that government counter-guarantees on the part of the developing countries were triggered, and the Norwegian government became a creditor. A subsequent evaluation of the program by the Norwegian government concluded that there was a lack of needs analyses and risk assessments that would have revealed how this project was contradictory to the development of the countries participating in it. In October 2006, Norway took what many in the development community saw as a groundbreaking step: unilaterally declaring as "illegitimate" about $80 million in debt related to the ship export campaign that was owed to it by Egypt, Ecuador, Peru, Jamaica, and Sierra Leone. As a way of sharing responsibility for this failure, Norway canceled this debt and, taking a further step, chose not to declare this move as a contribution to Official Development Assistance (ODA).[2]

Norway's debt cancellation is but one of many fairly recent examples of industrial countries' recognizing and acting on instances of their own policy incoherence vis-à-vis their broader efforts to contribute to development. This paper seeks to shed light on this issue and its growing importance. "Policy coherence" is defined herein as the mutual consistency of policies, and it could be viewed either proactively, requiring coherent policies to be mutually supportive, or as a minimum condition, requiring that policies at least not be contradictory. Thus there are two main levels of coherence: one where the policies are reinforcing in their effects (i.e., a strong form of coherence) and another where "at least no harm is done" (i.e., a weak form of coherence). Understanding this issue in these terms is especially useful when policies with different objectives are analyzed. The hierarchy of policy objectives is not always well defined nationally, let alone internationally. And there is often no easy way to prioritize among myriad, often competing, policy objectives and their beneficiaries.[3] Under these circumstances, "weak form coherence" is often the best that policymakers can aim for.

Why raise this issue now? Increasing emphasis on aid effectiveness, growing recognition that aid alone is insufficient for development, and increasing globalization and its resulting policy externalities are some of the principal reasons that enhancing rich countries' policy coherence for development is emerging as one of the key challenges for public policy today. The present discussions on this topic, however, have been largely rich-country–centric. This paper briefly scans some of the key ideas on policy coherence for development, and it argues that, in addition, it would be important to examine its distributional and regime aspects. The point made here is that policy coherence for development cannot simply be "supplied" by industrial countries. Proactive developing-country participation is essential to forging agreement on in what forms and to what extent policy coherence for development will take shape.

Why the Growing Interest in Policy Coherence?

Increasing interest in industrial countries' policy coherence for development results from perhaps three main factors: increasing emphasis on aid effectiveness; growing recognition that aid alone is insufficient for development; and increasing globalization and its resulting policy externalities.

More Bang for the Foreign Aid Buck

Growing interest in policy coherence could be traced in part to donor countries' heightened efforts to increase aid effectiveness and accomplish more with their aid. Even as many donor countries face their own domestic challenges that could tighten the fiscal purse strings further, they are nevertheless expected to live up to their aid commitments and contribute to internationally agreed policy objectives in part embodied in the Millennium Development Goals (MDGs).[4] Significant resources are required to achieve these goals—the United Nations Millennium Project (2005, 240) estimates that about $73 billion in 2006, rising to $135 billion in 2015, would be required to meet the MDGs in all poor countries. Yet, increases in ODA in recent years have been modest when compared to the needed resources, and part of these flows has been focused mostly on only certain countries.[5] This places even more emphasis on aid effectiveness—that no aid is wasted and that available resources are put to best use for development.

Trade, Not Aid

There is also stronger recognition of the fact that development assistance or aid alone is insufficient in achieving development—echoing, in part, the decades-old call for "trade, not aid" in many parts of the developing world. This is reflected in part in Millennium Development Goal 8, which calls for a global partnership for development, including taking steps such as further developing an open trading and financial system and dealing comprehensively with developing countries' debt problems. Growing attention is given to ensuring "development friendliness" in other areas to reinforce aid. For instance, Birdsall et al. (2005, 150) note that a scheme for temporary work visas amounting to no more than 3 percent of the rich countries' total labor force could easily yield $200 billion annually for the citizens of developing countries. Furthermore, liberalization of industrial

countries' markets as well as investments in trade facilitation in developing countries[6] could create welfare gains for low- and middle-income countries of about another $150 billion per year (Hertel 2004, 23–24). Hence, it has been argued that policies in international trade and migration as well as in other areas, such as investment, environment, security, and technology, could be critical in improving the development prospects of poor countries. Within, as well as across, each of these areas, policy coherence could bolster development objectives.

Your Policy, My Backyard

The preponderance of policy externalities—policy effects stretching across borders—has also placed the onus on more coherent policymaking. Externalities emerge as a by-product of many economic activities that in certain cases are directly facilitated (or condoned) by public policy. This outcome could, of course, be true for any country; however, by virtue of their (individual and collective) economic size, the industrial countries are often among the primary generators of many of these externalities. From a development perspective, one could judge these externalities as being positive (promoting development) or negative (obstructing development). For instance, positive worldwide externalities could emerge from sound monetary policies and robust financial regulations in industrial countries—home to some of the largest financial centers in the world.

However, some of their domestic policies also produce border-transgressing negative externalities. Domestic agricultural protection policies in these countries, for example, tend to depress world prices and limit the revenue opportunities for many developing-country farmers (Baffes 2006), as well as create possible inefficiencies in the subsidizing country itself (see Box 1). In 2004, tariff and budget-based support to agriculture in Organization for Economic Cooperation and Development (OECD) countries reached about $350 billion, with about $280 billion going directly to producers. Developing-country farmers are at a significant disadvantage, as illustrated, for example, in the case of the sugar sector, where total support in OECD countries of about $6.4 billion per annum is roughly equal to the entire annual sugar exports of developing countries (Newfarmer 2006, 17). Hence, enhanced policy coherence is often required in order to promote more activities that generate positive externalities and to mitigate incidences of negative externalities.

Policy Coherence from an Industrial Country Viewpoint

An industrial country perspective on policy coherence reveals important insights, particularly as these countries' individual and collective policies often have widespread and relatively larger effects across borders and on the developing world. A growing number of studies have been undertaken on the topic (see, for instance, Forster and Stokke 1999; OECD 2004a). The policies examined in these coherence-related studies could be roughly categorized into two broad types: external policies (i.e., those explicitly directed across borders) and domestic policies that have cross-border consequences (i.e., international

Box 1
On U.S. Agricultural Policy

"[C]urrent agriculture policies are not sufficient for addressing the challenges facing farmers and the nation as a whole. Federal farm programs, while remaining popular with many producers, are not serving U.S. agriculture as well as in the past and are having unintended consequences. These programs have traditionally been justified as a way to provide insulation against market fluctuations and keep more small farms in business. Current programs do, in fact, increase incomes and provide some protection against sharp market changes. But rather than keep smaller farmers on the land, they have contributed to farm consolidation and higher land prices. This, in turn, makes it more difficult for younger farmers to enter farming. In many cases the programs also discourage producers of program commodities from switching crops as markets change and undermine the incentive to innovate and develop the specialty products today's consumers want.

Continued U.S. backing of our current farm programs is also one of the major reasons for the recent collapse of the World Trade Organization's (WTO) Doha Round of negotiations. The view of this as a positive development by some U.S. farm groups is shortsighted. If it can be restarted, the Doha Round could be a catalyst for expanding markets for U.S. food and agricultural products. Additionally, our current farm programs are vulnerable to WTO litigation for breaking current international trade rules. We run the risk of losing these programs through litigation without receiving the benefits that a negotiated Doha Round agreement would provide. Farm programs that serve a smaller and smaller portion of farmers may also be vulnerable to Congressional budget-cutting because of their continuing high cost and perceived inequity at a time of historic deficits. To be efficient and environmentally sustainable, agricultural production must be flexible and responsive to market opportunities. The biggest opportunity for American farmers today is in the new markets created by dramatically changing patterns of demand: Economic growth in developing countries; population growth and evolving consumption patterns in both the United States and developing countries; the expanding role of agriculture in energy production. To secure these new markets, farm production must reorient itself to today's changing world, and public policy must support this goal."

Source: Bertini et al. (2006, 4–5).

externalities). Examples of the former include official development assistance and international trade and financial policies, whereas examples of the latter include studies of domestic agricultural support policies and domestic environmental policies. Each of these policies affects the developing world in distinct ways, and understanding their possible interactions and effectiveness are clearly among industrial country policymakers' concerns.

Assessments of policy coherence for development could determine whether and to what extent policies reinforce (or contradict) each other. Ideally, these conclusions could be reached by assessing policy impact and then comparing the results directly against the various stated goals of development, such as the Millennium Development Goals. However, given the measurement difficulties, present discussions on this topic have generally not focused on the final development impact of industrial-country policies. For practical and pragmatic reasons, alternative approaches have been taken, and proxies for "impact" have been used. These include assessing resource flows, policy effort, and institutional reforms implemented. One could think of these factors simply as different possible "units of measure" that could help indicate the extent to which policy coherence is being (or can be) enhanced.

Resource Flows

Estimating resource flows is one alternative to evaluating policy impact. Capital scarcity is seen as one of the most critical impediments to growth and development in poor countries. Increasing resource flows to the developing world is therefore a critical policy objective that feeds into final development outcomes like poverty reduction, increased education, and better health. Policies that, explicitly or inadvertently, shrink resources in the developing world could be deemed incoherent with the policies that seek to facilitate these resource flows in support of development. Resource flows are obviously rough indicators, given that there are myriad other factors that jointly determine how these flows affect development.[7]

Various studies, notably a few on aid and trade, have tried to assess net resource flows into developing countries. Some juxtapose aid to certain countries with the unrealized export revenues due to agricultural support policies in industrial countries (see Table 1). Here, aid is intended to benefit developing countries by increasing resource flows to them; on the other hand, agricultural support policies are intended to benefit domestic producers, and in the process diminish trade revenues in developing countries. Using resource flows as a "unit of measure" for policy coherence, it often appears that "What One Hand Gives, the Other Takes."

However, trade revenues are not equivalent to foreign aid flows. The nature and motivations behind these two flows are inherently different. Development assistance, or foreign aid, is ideally a form of "giving" where the development of the recipient is the primary objective. Trade revenues, on the other hand, are the result of a mutually beneficial exchange, or a *quid pro quo*. Hence, these assessments often attempt to suggest—but in fact do not necessarily measure—some notion of "net benefit" by showing the opposing direction of these flows. At an intuitive level, the figures in Table 1 nevertheless underscore possible contradictory policies.

Policy Effort

A relatively more direct alternative could be to assess the policies themselves—to examine the "policy effort" that countries individually undertake toward enhanced policy coherence. That is, one could "grade" industrial countries on the presence,

Table 1   What One Hand Gives, the Other Takes

- In 2001, Mali received $38 million in U.S. aid . . .
  . . . but lost $43 million in cotton export earnings due to U.S. subsidies.
- Burkina Faso received $27 million in heavily indebted poor countries (HIPC) debt relief . . .
  . . . but lost $28 million in cotton export earnings due to U.S. subsidies.
- Mozambique received $136 million in EU aid . . .
  . . . but lost $106 million in sugar export earnings due to EU subsidies.
- In 2002, EU aid to Brazil, Thailand, South Africa, and India were $10 million, $14.6 million, $121.8 million, and $13 million respectively[a] . . .
  . . . but that same year, EU sugar policies cost Brazil $494 million, Thailand $151 million, and South Africa and India around $60 million each.
- In 2003, U.S. subsidies to its cotton growers totaled $2.3 billion—about 1.5 times higher than its foreign aid to Africa that year. These subsidies contribute to depressing world prices, leading to income losses for near-subsistence cotton farmers in West Africa and Central and South Asia. In West Africa alone, rich-country subsidies lead to income losses in excess of about $150 million per year.[b]
- In 2004, for every $3 of EU aid to Mozambique, the EU "takes back" $1 through restrictions on access to the EU sugar market.
- In 2004, U.S. tariffs on imports from India, Indonesia, Sri Lanka, and Thailand brought in $1.87 billion in revenues—twice the amount the U.S. committed for tsunami relief to these same countries.[c]

Sources: Unless otherwise stated, data are from OXFAM International (2002a; 2002b; 2004).
a. External aid financed from the general budget of the Commission and the European Development Fund (in euros) taken from EC (2002, 177–80). Dollar values calculated using the 2002 average exchange rate of €1.06 = $1.
b. Baffes (2006, 121–24).
c. Roodman (2005a, 3).

extent, and quality of their policies in areas that are deemed crucial to development. The Commitment to Development Index (CDI) of the Center for Global Development and *Foreign Policy* magazine has pioneered this approach.[8]

Intended to generate widespread interest and debate on industrial countries' policies and their effects on development, the CDI is an annual index calculated for each of twenty-one OECD Development Assistance Committee (DAC) member countries (except Luxembourg). The CDI is composed of indicators in seven policy areas (called "policy domains"): official development assistance or aid, trade, investment, migration, environment, security, and technology. One of the main rationales behind the CDI is that foreign aid policies need to be complemented and reinforced by policies in these other areas to achieve development, thus alluding to the need for *strong form* policy coherence (i.e., policies that reinforce each other in support of development in poor countries). Table 2 summarizes the components of the indicators in each area and notes some of the key features in the construction of the CDI.

The index is so far a unique attempt to evaluate and rank the industrial countries on the "development friendliness" of their policies. All twenty-one countries are given scores based on indicators in each of the seven policy areas. These indicators are based partly on the availability of data and the extent to which they represent the key policies within each area. To illustrate, the index score on aid is based first on aid totals with principal and interest payments on debt netted out in order to more closely reflect net transfers to recipients (akin to the resource-flows approach discussed earlier). A penalty is applied to the score if the country has policies that tend to diminish the impact of aid, such as through "tying" and the tendency to

fund many small projects or "project proliferation." Thus, these specific forms of policy incoherence are penalized, and result in a lower score.[9]

On the other hand, strong form coherence is also rewarded. The score is increased by accounting for the private giving to developing countries caused by fiscal policy (e.g., tax incentives). Furthermore, a "selectivity weight" is applied to reflect the recipient country's appropriateness for aid, based on its quality of governance and need. Thus, a donor country that gives aid to better governed and poorer countries (instead of using aid for nondevelopment—i.e., geopolitical—purposes) will tend to get a higher score on the aid policy area.

Thus, the final score is meant to reflect the "quality adjusted aid quantity" (Roodman 2005b). All these features of the index provide a fuller picture of not just the level of resources channeled to poor countries, but also the ways these resources are channeled, which could be equally important in ensuring strong development outcomes.

Because the scores in aid (and in the other areas where necessary) are weighted for differences in country size (e.g., wealth), countries could be ranked within each policy area. For instance, the United States with income roughly twenty times that of Spain could give a greater volume of aid than the latter. However, based on the methodology of the CDI, the measured "efforts" of these two countries in pursuing coherent development assistance policies are presently not dramatically different, after scaling for size and discounting for contradictory policies.[10] Furthermore, across policy areas, countries could rank very differently. Denmark, for example, ranks first in aid in 2005, but only fifth in trade (tied with four other countries) and ninth in investment (tied with three others). Ranking therefore depends

Table 2 Summary Description of the Commitment to Development Index

Policy Domain	Components	Some Key Features
Aid	Index based on gross aid totals with the following adjustments: • Debt service from developing countries on concessional loans deducted. • Three aspects of "aid quality" factored in as discounts or penalties: tying, (lack of) selectivity, and the tendency to fund many small projects. • Portion of private charitable giving is credited to government tax policies.	"Selectivity weight" is intended to reflect the recipient country's appropriateness for aid, based on a combination of governance (i.e., aid is more effective where there is good governance) and poverty (i.e., need). Emergency aid is exempted from selectivity weighting to reflect that some types of aid may be more valuable in countries with very poor governance.
Trade	Index based on measure of barriers to goods exports from developing countries, composed of: • Index measuring combined effect of tariffs, nontariff measures, and domestic subsidies. • Indicator of "revealed openness" (i.e., imports from developing countries as a share of importer's GDP).	• The indicator of "revealed openness" was included in order to take account of unmeasured (tacit) barriers. • The tariff data refer to upper bound rates committed in the WTO and do not factor in the preferences granted to poor countries, such as through the U.S. Africa Growth and Opportunity Act and the European Everything But Arms Initiative.
Investment	Index based on qualitative survey of government policies in the following areas: • Provision of quasi-political risk insurance. • Procedures to prevent double taxation. • Actions to prevent bribery and other corruption. • Measures to support foreign investors moving to developing countries. • Policies that affect portfolio flows (e.g., restrictions on pension fund investment in developing countries).	Improves on 2003 index, which used foreign direct investment (i.e., an outcome rather than a policy).
Migration	Index based on weighted indicators of: • Immigrant flows, i.e., gross non-DAC immigrant inflow/total immigrant inflow multiplied by net immigrant inflow over five years/receiving country population. • Share of foreign students that are from non-DAC countries. • Index measuring countries' contributions to aiding refugees and asylum seekers.	• The original migration index contained two additional indicators that were dropped. The ratio of gross non-DAC immigrant inflow to receiving-country population was dropped due to overlap with two other indicators (i.e., the first two). The difference between the unemployment rates of natives and of immigrants was also dropped as an indicator due to possible ambiguity in its beneficiality (i.e., high unemployment among immigrants could be a good sign of more openness to immigration). • This policy area suffers from lack of disaggregated data on remittances and still very little understanding of the linkages between policies and actual migration flows. Furthermore, illegal migration remains largely unresearched.
Environment	Index based on weighted measures of: • Depletion of shared commons. • Contributions to international efforts and government cooperation.	Some proportion of the index weight goes to outcome measures with non-policy elements.
Security	Index based on contributions to international peacekeeping and forcible human interventions (e.g., Australian-led intervention in East Timor in 1999).	The index is different from the 2003 version due to: • Expansion in scope to include forcible human interventions. • Expansion of timeframe from 2 to 10 years, in recognition that interventions do not occur often.
Technology	Index based on government financial support for research and development, counting government funding and tax incentives.	• The index reflects only technology generation, but not technology diffusion. • The current system of intellectual property rights protection based on the Agreement on Trade Related Aspects of Intellectual Property Rights (TRIPS) is not reflected by the index.

Note: The interested reader may wish to refer to Roodman (2004; 2005b) for further details on the construction of the CDI.

Box 2
Are Rich-Country Policies in Aid and Trade Becoming Less Coherent?

The components of the Commitment to Development Index could be used to monitor trends in policy areas over time, indicating whether policy efforts are progressing positively and in unison (mutually supportive), regressing (both becoming worse), or might be contradictory (one improving and the other regressing). One way to do this would be to estimate the changes in the components of the index—say for aid and trade—and then construct a cross-plot each year. Each index component is constructed so that increases reflect greater development friendliness; thus positive changes in each component (and in the overall index) over time reflect improvement.

To illustrate, comparing changes in the aid[a] and trade[b] components, for example, policy efforts in these areas were generally moving in a coherent—mutually supportive—direction in 2004 for a few countries (see Figure 1, quadrant 1). However, a caveat to consider is that the aid and trade policies of a number of countries were moving in unison, but in a regressive (non-development-friendly) direction (quadrant 3). That year, about seven countries' aid and trade policies may have moved in contradictory directions (quadrants 2 and 4).

For 2005, changes in the aid and trade components of several rich countries seem to suggest more pronounced contradictions in their policies, compared to the year before, as indicated by the more negative slope in the scatter plot as well as the presence of a dozen countries in Figure 2, quadrant 2 (where there is progress in the trade component but regress in the aid component). This seems to have grown worse in 2006, with even fewer countries located in quadrant 1 (only two in 2006, as compared with eight in 2005, and seven in 2004). The trend for 2006 (see Figure 3) also seems to indicate that most rich countries' aid and trade policies are either moving in generally opposite directions (quadrants 2 and 4), or are *simultaneously* regressing (quadrant 3).

Source: Author's calculations based on data from the Center for Global Development's Commitment to Development Index, www.cgdev.org/section/initiatives/_active/cdi/.

a. The aid component is primarily based on the quantity of aid governments give, factoring in quality indicators such as penalizing donors for giving aid to rich or corrupt governments, for overburdening recipients with lots of small aid projects, or for "tying" aid, which forces recipients to spend it on the donor country's own goods rather than shopping around for the lowest price. A higher aid index score suggests that the country's aid policies are more development friendly.

b. The trade component essentially reflects how open rich countries are to trading with poor countries. It uses data on main types of barriers: tariffs on imports and agricultural subsidies. It rewards tax deductions and credits that support private charity and penalizes countries for erecting barriers to imports of crops, clothing, and other goods from poor nations. A higher trade index score suggests that the country's trade policies are more development friendly.

on how a country compares with its peers within each of these policy areas. Finally, the country's scores in each area are then aggregated (using equal weights for each score) to arrive at the final index, which again lends itself to a cross-country ranking. In 2006, for example, the Netherlands ranked only fourth in aid but placed in the top half of ranked countries in all seven components of the CDI so that it received the highest overall ranking for commitment to development that year.

While the CDI is clearly still a work in progress,[11] its approach offers certain benefits. The index focuses on the policies themselves, which are relatively easier to measure and update, allowing the index to be reported every year. Policies are also the most pragmatic starting point for discussions on enhancing policy coherence, making "policy effort" a useful bellwether indicator of what policy actions have been (or can be) taken. The CDI also provides an "across-policy-area scorecard" that is comparable across countries and across years. Drawing from our definition earlier, we could view this scorecard as an indicator for how actively an industrial country pursues *strong form* coherence compared to its peers. Changes in the components of the index—for instance, for aid and trade—could also be monitored, revealing whether rich countries are moving in the direction of greater or lesser coherence (see Box 2). Over time, this index could possibly serve as an effective incentive, particularly for countries on both ends of the ranking—leaders would want to stay on top, and laggards would want to improve their ranking. In fact, the Netherlands has already taken the lead by

adopting the CDI as a performance indicator for its own policy coherence for development (Van Ardenne 2003).

Institutional Reforms

The lack of cooperation, coordination, and discussion across different government agencies and entities in the policy design and implementation stages could also clearly produce incoherent policies. Hence, another "unit of measure" for policy coherence could try to reflect the organizational, legal, and political dimensions of facilitating coherence. Some studies have assessed the extent to which coherence-enhancing institutional reforms and innovations have been undertaken. One should take note that these reforms need not focus on policy coherence for development alone—that is, they could simply be part of broader efforts to improve policy coherence in general within countries. These reforms could take the form of laws enacted or international agreements signed in order to bind countries to policy coherence objectives, specific coordinating functions or agencies created to ensure coherence across different line ministries, or the development of analytical capacity to evaluate policy impact.[12] Focusing more specifically on policy coherence for development, Table 3 lists some of the institutional reforms tailored for this purpose. Sweden, for example, is the first nation in the world to pass a law on an integrated global development policy—requiring its agriculture, environment, migration, trade, and other policies to align to fight poverty and promote sustainable development.

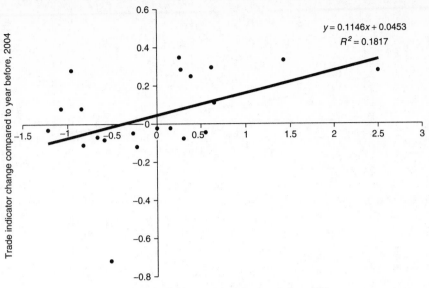

Figure 1   Changes in Aid and Trade Policy Indicators, 2004

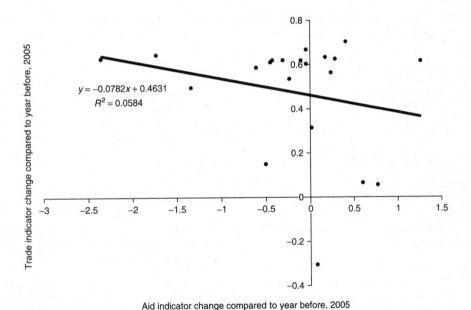

Figure 2   Changes in Aid and Trade Policy Indicators, 2005

Assessments that focus on institutional reforms are, for the most part, qualitative.[13] Incoherence could be the result of "missing" policy inputs, which in this case are embodied in institutional reforms. Various agencies and institutions of government have their specific function, mandate, and policy objectives. For very obvious reasons, if these agencies do not discuss or coordinate policies, they are unlikely to achieve policy coherence, particularly when faced with multiple, and possibly competing, objectives. For instance, how would the Agriculture Ministry know that some of its projects and policies to help domestic farmers could in fact counteract some of the projects and policies of the Aid Ministry? More importantly, once such policy incoherence is discovered, what would be the process to resolve it? The analytical tools and the institutional and organizational

framework for discussion, as well as the legal mandate for such coordination to take place, are therefore critical in weeding out institutional and organizational causes of incoherence. Critics could note that these elements might not necessarily ensure policy coherence, but at the very least they are probably necessary preconditions.

Policy Coherence from a Developing-Country Viewpoint

While resource flows, policy effort, and institutional reforms are important dimensions of policy coherence, notably from an industrial country perspective, additional important dimensions

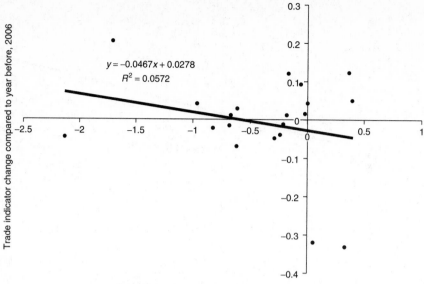

Figure 3   Changes in Aid and Trade Policy Indicators, 2006

Table 3   Examples of Institutional Reforms for Enhanced Policy Coherence

Country (or group of countries)	Reform	Function
European Union	Maastricht Treaty	The 1992 treaty stipulates in Article C that the external policies of the Union should be consistent with each other; and in Article 130V it requires that the European Community (EC) take into account development policy objectives in its other policies.
	Interservice Quality Support Group	Established since 2001, and serving under the Development Commissioner, the IQSG contributes to policy coherence by acting as a single monitoring entity for all Country Strategy Papers (CSPs) for EC aid recipient countries.
Germany	Extended Right of Review by the BMZ of all legislation	Since 2000 as part of the Joint Standing Orders (GGO) of the Federal Ministries, this regulation requires all legislation to be reviewed by the Ministry of Economic Cooperation and Development (BMZ).
Netherlands	Policy Coherence Unit Within the Ministry of Foreign Affairs	Created in 2002 and directly positioned under the Director-General for International Cooperation, this unit ensures coherence across government agencies and operates in project teams with key players from other divisions in the ministry and other departments.
Spain	Law on International Development Cooperation	Passed in 1998, this law states that the principles and objectives of Spanish development cooperation should be reflected in all other policies affecting developing countries.
Sweden	Bill on Integrated Development Policy	Passed in 2003, the bill calls for the alignment of aid, trade, agriculture, environment, migration, security, and other policies with the objectives of reducing poverty and promoting sustainable development.
Over 100 countries and organizations	Paris Declaration on Aid Effectiveness	Endorsed in March 2005, the Paris Declaration is an international agreement to which over 100 ministers, heads of agencies, and other senior officials adhered and committed their countries and organizations to continue to increase efforts in harmonization, alignment, and managing aid for results with a set of monitorable actions and indicators.

Sources: Ministry of Foreign Affairs of the Netherlands (2004); Ministry of Foreign Affairs of Sweden (2003); OECD (2004a); and the Paris Declaration on Aid Effectiveness (see www.oecd.org/dataoecd/11/41/34428351.pdf).

could be revealed by taking a developing-country perspective on the topic—notably the distributional and regime aspects of policy coherence for development. Each reveals how policy coherence in many respects is not only an industrial-country issue to be handled internally or in industrial-country forums—developing countries can and should play a crucial role.

Distributional Aspects

One important additional aspect of policy impact pertains to its distributional dimension. Industrial countries could work toward enhanced policy coherence in various areas of critical interest to the developing world, but how would different developing countries be affected by these efforts? Would countries in Africa, for instance, benefit from further trade liberalization in industrial countries? The evidence suggests uneven country performance, as low-income countries have had meager success in penetrating global markets. Between 1990 and 2003, low-income countries managed only a 0.5 percent increase in their share of global non-oil trade, while middle-income countries snapped up a hefty 14 percent (Newfarmer and Nowak 2006, 373). In addition, various scholars have argued that some countries in Africa could actually be harmed (Panagariya 2004; Polaski 2006). Further liberalization in industrial countries is expected to erode the trade preferences given to some of the least developed countries (LDCs), a number of which are in that region. A few net food-importing LDCs could stand to lose from the elimination of Northern agricultural subsidies, since this would tend to drive up world agricultural prices.

Assessing the distributional dimension of policy coherence for development in any one policy area is therefore of critical interest to all developing countries since not all of them will necessarily benefit (nor benefit to the same degree). A more disaggregated analysis could better reveal how different countries—and different sectors within these countries—stand to lose or gain from enhanced policy coherence. Indeed such an analysis could also enable a closer approximation of the impact on development, since it could often be country and/or sector specific.

In addition, enhanced policy coherence is not always good for all. Drawing still from the example of eliminating agricultural subsidies, if some net-food-importing developing countries could actually be harmed, then more insight on the distribution dimension would allow policymakers to consider and more systematically evaluate the appropriateness of additional policies, such as possible compensating arrangements, in order to ensure, as a minimum condition, weak-form coherence (i.e., "at least no harm is done").

Regime Dimension

Increasingly, industrial country policies are becoming embedded in international regimes. In such cases, it would also be critical to assess policy coherence for development for these policies. Should they be found to be incoherent, then the appropriate entry point for reform might no longer be at the industrial-country level but at the regime level. This signals the growing importance of various international regimes that are taking shape as a result of international agreement on certain policies. Analyses of the design or "architecture" of various international (i.e., bilateral or multilateral) regimes have in fact been undertaken quite extensively across various disciplines, including environmental economics, international finance and trade, and international relations, to name a few.[14] The underlying logic behind many of these studies is also one of coherence: Are the various rules or components of a regime coherent with respect to its objectives, and are those objectives coherent with development?

For instance, Bradford and Lawrence (2004) examined policy options that could be unilaterally considered by each of the eight industrialized countries they studied. They found that Japan, for example, could decide to further liberalize its domestic markets in its own—as well as the developing world's—interest.[15] Such policy reforms would therefore be within its discretion. However, broader liberalization policies could be the result of further negotiations at the World Trade Organization (WTO).

From another angle, regimes could also have a direct impact on development that is distinct from industrial country policies. The WTO Agreement on Trade Related Aspects of Intellectual Property Rights (TRIPS) is an example. By triggering the enforcement of stronger intellectual property rights (IPRs) laws across countries, TRIPS could benefit predominantly technology-exporting countries at the expense of predominantly technology-importing countries. Here, it is not industrial country policies per se, but the international harmonization of certain rules that could harm developing countries, which largely fall under the latter technology-importing group. This would therefore not be captured by assessments of industrial country policies.

One way to evaluate this regime would be to again assess its effect on resource flows to the developing world. In terms of net transfers, Maskus (2000) used an index of patent rights for a sample of countries to measure the possible effects on patent values of harmonizing these rights. The forecasted effects on net transfers are illustrated in Figure 4.[16]

With the implementation of stronger laws on IPRs, the United States, Germany, and France are expected to gain substantially from net transfers—sourced mainly from some industrial and many developing countries that are net consumers of patented products and technologies. Note that the United States alone is projected to gain some $6 billion, while Brazil is expected to experience negative net transfers of roughly $2 billion. Regimes such as TRIPS could trigger government policy actions as well as responses among various market actors, which in turn could affect resource flows, welfare, and, more broadly, development in poor countries. Hence, possibilities for enhanced policy coherence for development could sometimes require an entry point for reforms within regimes. Developing countries should, ideally, play a proactive role in pressing for these regime reforms, when and where those are necessary.

Quo Vadis?

This paper, no doubt, only scratches the surface of the issue of policy coherence for development. However, based on the foregoing discussion, several concrete steps could already be considered in moving forward.

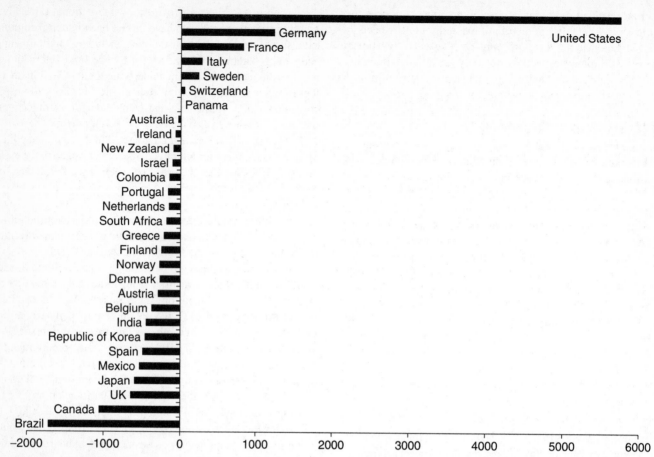

Figure 4   Estimated Net Rent Transfers from TRIPS-Induced Strengthening of 1988 Patent Laws in Selected Countries
Source: Maskus (2000, 184, table 6.1).
Note: Figures in 1995 $ millions.

First, assessments of policy impact, while crucial and necessary, are also quite likely to be insufficient and need to be complemented. This paper suggests that assessing the distributional aspect is also important, because enhanced policy coherence across different policy areas affects various developing countries in different ways. To highlight this distributional dimension, it could be useful to undertake analyses of industrial countries' policy coherence for development not only from their perspective (e.g., Forster and Stokke 1999; OECD 2004a), but also from the perspective of specific developing countries. For example, recent studies by the OECD examined the role of industrial countries' policies notably from the 1960s to the 1990s in the development takeoff of a number of East Asian countries (see Fukusaku et al. 2005). Such studies therefore offer a useful lens to clarify factors that might be specific to only some developing countries and regions (also perhaps certain time periods). In addition to taking a developing-country perspective, it could be useful to undertake more distribution-sensitive analyses of the expected spillover effects from various industrial country policies.

Assessing the coherence of policies already embedded in regimes could also provide important insights. In these assessments, it would be useful to differentiate the policies that are subject to each country's discretion from those policies that are embedded in international regimes. For instance, in the absence of an international migration regime, policies in this area are still largely within the discretion of industrial countries. Thus they could be "graded" as the Commitment to Development Index does on how "development friendly" they are in this policy area. However, in the case of international rules on IPRs, it would not be appropriate to follow this approach. Reforms in this policy area require specific focus on the TRIPS regime and the World Trade Organization. Here, the entry point for policy reforms would no longer be within the discretion of industrial countries. International collective agreement, rather than the actions of any one industrial country, would be crucial in facilitating any reforms thought to be necessary.

Some consensus on policy coherence therefore deserves examination, since establishing an agreed-upon target for it is also critical. As noted earlier, policy coherence is also a matter of degree. Incremental steps toward enhanced policy coherence could be taken, but how would one judge whether those would be enough? There is an urgent need to develop joint North-South, consensus-driven goalposts of policy coherence for development. Policy coherence, at the end of the day, is about managing different objectives. The outcomes from this "management" depend crucially on how balance is struck across different objectives and, most likely, also different beneficiary groups. Achieving enhanced coherence therefore requires that developing countries also exert their views in policy discussions and debate.

Notes

1. This is not to say that poor countries do not themselves have policy contradictions, many of which hamper their own development. These have been analyzed extensively in the literature on economic reforms and development policy and will not be the focus of this paper. Instead, the main interest here is on rich countries' other policies—in addition to foreign aid—in an effort to contribute to the still nascent literature in this area.

2. For further information, see EURODAD (2006) and Royal Norwegian Ministry of Foreign Affairs (2006).

3. In addition, in some cases the exact direction and degree of impact of some policies may be impossible to predict ex ante. Policy coherence also thus tends to follow an incremental process. There is an extensive literature in organizational theory and notably on incrementalism, which becomes relevant when considering the complex issues here. It is beyond the scope of this paper to treat this aspect, but it is flagged here for the interested reader.

4. For further information on the MDGs, see www.un.org/millenniumgoals/.

5. Net ODA in 2003 increased by 3.9 percent in real terms from the year-before level. Of the $2.3 billion net increase, $2 billion was focused on the start of reconstruction in Iraq. In 2004, net ODA rose by about $7.7 billion, and about a third of this went to Afghanistan and Iraq. In 2005 and 2006, a temporary spike in aid levels was expected because of major debt relief for Iraq and Nigeria (i.e., $19 billion in 2005 and $11 billion in 2006). Preliminary data for 2006 suggest that development aid from Organization for Economic Cooperation and Development (OECD) countries fell by about 5 percent in 2006. See OECD (2004b; 2005; 2006; 2007).

6. For instance, investments in port efficiency, customs environments, regulatory environment, and electronic commerce.

7. For instance, in terms of aid flows, different ways and channels of giving aid could also have an impact on its effectiveness. Some of these features are addressed by the Commitment to Development Index (CDI), a policy-coherence indicator that focuses on "policy effort" and is discussed in the next subsection.

8. See www.cgdev.org/rankingtherich/home.html.

9. When and where available and appropriate, the method of discounting draws on empirical evidence on the countereffects of these other policies. For instance, "tying" is expected to raise aid project costs by about 15–30 percent, reducing aid value by some 15–23 percent (Jepma 1994). The CDI scores for aid therefore discounts "tied" aid by 20 percent.

10. The 2005 scores on aid policy were 1.9 and 2.6 for the United States and Spain respectively. In 2006, the scores were 2.2 for the United States and 2.5 for Spain. See www.cgdev.org/section/initiatives/_active/cdi.

11. Some methodological issues in the CDI remain, including the method of scaling and weighting within and across the various policy areas. At present, across-policy-area scores are equally weighted in the CDI, yet some policy areas (such as that of international trade or labor migration) may have a potentially much larger impact and therefore might merit greater weight. There is no straightforward way to deal with this issue, however. In addition, with the availability of more data, each of the indicators could be further improved. As a final point, "policy effort" as a unit of measure also does not reflect whether the steps toward enhanced policy coherence are "sufficient." That is, the index does not reflect whether development objectives are achieved, or how much different countries benefit from enhanced policy coherence. The implicit assumption is simply that more "coherence" (in more policy areas) is better for development (and developing countries in general) than less. The interested reader may wish to turn to Roodman (2004; 2005b) and Sawada et al. (2004) for a discussion of further possible improvements in the CDI methodology.

12. More broadly, Hilker (2004) expands on past work by the OECD and develops an analytical framework specifically for institutional mechanisms to promote policy coherence for development. She examines several elements: (a) government/institutional structures; (b) political context, commitment, and leadership; (c) policy frameworks/statements; (d) stakeholder analysis/consultation; (e) analytical capacity and knowledge management; (f) policy coordination mechanisms; (g) working practices and policymaking processes; and (h) monitoring, accountability, and lesson learning.

13. For some examples, the interested reader may wish to refer to the country case studies contained in the edited volume of Forster and Stokke (1999), *Policy Coherence in Development Co-operation.* The peer reviews of the Organization for Economic Cooperation and Development also include a section on policy coherence that contains detailed discussion on institutional reforms. See OECD (2004a).

14. It is beyond the scope of this paper to discuss these; the interested reader may wish to refer to the studies of international regimes in Hasenclever et al. (1997).

15. If Japan alone were to take steps toward enhanced policy coherence for development by removing its barriers to trade, Bradford and Lawrence (2004, 11–12) estimate that it could generate about $41 billion in welfare gains for the developing world, not to mention about $135 billion for itself. Such a reform would enhance policy coherence in two ways. First it would enhance coherence within Japan's policies to promote its own welfare. In addition, it would enhance coherence between Japan's trade and development (i.e., official development assistance) policies.

16. The counterfactual in this exercise was to evaluate what the additional net present value of patents would have been in 1988 had each country in the sample satisfied its TRIPS commitments. Innovation and patent rights were held constant, thus resulting in a static calculation of how rents would be shifted. This builds on earlier work on this topic by McCalman (1999).

References

Baffes, John. 2006. "Cotton and the Developing Countries: Implications for Development." In *Trade, Doha and Development: A Window into the Issues*, ed. Richard Newfarmer. Washington, DC: World Bank.

Bertini, Catherine, August Schumacher, and Robert Thompson. 2006. *Modernizing America's Farm and Food Policy: Vision for a New Direction.* Report of the Task Force on U.S.

Agriculture Policy. Chicago: Chicago Council on Global Affairs. Available at www.thechicagocouncil.org/UserFiles/File/Task%20Force%20Reports/Agriculture%20Task%20Force%20report.pdf.

Birdsall, Nancy, Dani Rodrik, and Arvind Subramanian. 2005. "How to Help Poor Countries." *Foreign Affairs* 84, no. 4: 136–52.

Bradford, Scott C., and Robert Lawrence. 2004. *Has Globalization Gone Far Enough? The Costs of Fragmented Markets.* Washington, DC: Institute for International Economics.

EURODAD (European Network on Debt and Development). 2006. "Norway Makes Groundbreaking Decision to Cancel Illegitimate Debt." October 3, 2006. Brussels. Available at www.eurodad.org/articles/default.aspx?id=737/.

Forster, Jacques, and Olav Stokke, ed. 1999. *Policy Coherence in Development Co-operation.* European Association of Development Research and Training Institutes (EADI) Book Series 22. London: Frank Cass.

Fukusaku, Kiichiro, Masahiro Kawai, Michael G. Plummer, and Alexandra TrzeciakDuval. 2005. *Policy Coherence Towards East Asia: Development Challenges for OECD Countries.* Paris: OECD.

Hasenclever, Andreas, Peter Mayer, and Volker Rittberger. 1997. *Theories of International Regimes.* Cambridge: Cambridge University Press.

Hertel, Thomas. 2004. "Assessing the Provision of International Trade as a Global Public Good." Background paper for *The New Public Finance: Responding to Global Challenges.* Available at www.thenewpublicfinance.org/background/hertel.pdf.

Hilker, Lyndsay McLean. 2004. "A Comparative Analysis of Institutional Mechanisms to Promote Coherence for Development: Case Study Synthesis of the EU, US, and Japan." Paper presented at the OECD Policy Workshop on Institutional Approaches to Policy Coherence for Development, May 18–19, Paris. Available at www.oecd.org/dataoecd/0/31/31659769.pdf.

Jepma, Catrinus J. 1994. Inter-Nation Policy Co-Ordination and Untying of Aid. Brookfield, VT: Ashgate.

Maskus, Keith. 2000. *Intellectual Property Rights in the Global Economy.* Washington, DC: Institute for International Economics.

McCalman, Phillip. 1999. "Reaping What You Sow: An Empirical Analysis of International Patent Harmonization." Working Paper in Economics and Econometrics 374. Canberra: Australian National University.

Ministry of Foreign Affairs of the Netherlands. 2004. "Millennium Development Goal 8: Developing a Global Partnership for Development, Progress Report by the Netherlands." The Hague: Ministry of Foreign Affairs. Available at www.minbuza.nl/default.asp?CMS_ITEM=6625AAAB61534816875BD52E1E0117F9X3X50352X73/.

Ministry of Foreign Affairs of Sweden. 2003. "Sweden, First in the World with Cohesive Development Policy." Ministry of Foreign Affairs, Stockholm. Available at www.sweden.se/templates/News_7578.asp.

Newfarmer, Richard. 2006. "Through the Window: Beacons for a Pro-Poor World Trading System." In *Trade, Doha and Development: A Window into the Issues*, ed. Richard Newfarmer, pp. 15–26. Washington, DC: World Bank.

Newfarmer, Richard, and Dorota Nowak. 2006. "The World Bank in Trade: The New Trade Agenda." In *Trade, Doha and Development,* pp. 371–82.

Organization for Economic Cooperation and Development (OECD). 2004a. "Extracts from the Development Cooperation Review Series Concerning Policy Coherence." Paris. Available at www.oecd.org/dataoecd/23/16/25497010.pdf.

———. 2004b. "Modest Increase in Development Aid in 2003." Paris: OECD. Available at www.oecd.org/document/22/0,2340,en_2649_33721_31504022_1_1_1_1,00.html.

———. 2005. "Aid Rising Sharply, According to Final ODA Figures for 2004." Paris. Available at www.oecd.org/dataoecd/0/41/35842562.pdf.

———. 2006. OECD DAC Development Co-operation Report 2005. Paris.

———. 2007. "Development Aid from OECD Countries Fell 5.1% in 2006." Available at www.oecd.org/document/17/0,2340,en_2649_33721_38341265_1_1_1_1,00.html.

OXFAM. 2002a. "The Great EU Sugar Scam: How Europe's Sugar Regime Is Devastating Livelihoods in the Developing World." OXFAM Briefing Paper 27. Available at www.oxfam.org/eng/pdfs/pr022508_eu_sugar_scam.pdf.

———. 2002b. "Cultivating Poverty: The Impact of US Cotton Subsidies on Africa." OXFAM Briefing Paper 30. Available at www.oxfam.org/eng/pdfs/pp020925_cotton.pdf.

———. 2004. "Dumping on the World: How EU Sugar Policies Hurt Poor Countries." OXFAM Briefing Paper 61. Available at www.oxfam.org.uk/what_we_do/issues/trade/bp61_sugar_dumping.htm.

Panagariya, Arvind. 2004. "Tide of Free Trade Will Not Lift All Boats." *Financial Times*, August 2, 2004.

Polaski, Sandra. 2006. "Winners and Losers: Impact of the Doha Round on Developing Countries." Carnegie Endowment for International Peace, New York. Available at www.carnegieendowment.org/files/Winners.Losers.fina12.pdf.

Roodman, David. 2004. "The Commitment to Development Index: 2004 Edition." Center for Global Development, Washington, DC. Available at www.cgdev.org/rankingtherich/docs/Technical_description_2004.pdf.

———. 2005a. "The 2005 Commitment to Development Index: Components and Results." Center for Global Development, Washington, DC. Available at www.cgdev.org/files/3647_file_Commitment_to_Development_Index_Brief.pdf.

———. 2005b. "The Commitment to Development Index: 2005 Edition." Center for Global Development, Washington, DC. Available at www.cgdev.org/doc/cdi/technicaldescrip05.pdf.

Royal Norwegian Ministry of Foreign Affairs. 2006. "Cancellation of Debts Incurred as a Result of the Norwegian Ship Export Campaign (1976–1980)." Available at www.regjeringen.no/en/dep/ud/Documents/Reports-programmes-of-action-and-plans/Reports/2006/Cancellation-of-debts-incurred-as-a-result-of-the-Norwegian-Ship-Export-Campaign-1976–80.html?id=420457/.

Sawada, Yasuyuki, Hirohisa Kohama, Hisaki Kono, and Munenobu Ikegami. 2004. "Commitment to Development Index (CDI): Critical Comments." FASID Discussion Paper on Development Assistance no. 1. Tokyo. Available at www.fasid.or.jp/english/publication/discussion/pdf/DP_1_E.pdf.

United Nations Millennium Project. 2005. *Investing in Development: A Practical Plan to Achieve the Millennium Development Goals.* New York: United Nations Development Programme. Available at www.unmillenniumproject.org/documents/MainReportComplete-lowres.pdf.

Van Ardenne, Agnes. 2003. "Statement by the Minister for Development Co-operation of The Netherlands, representing the constituency consisting of Armenia, Bosnia and Herzegovina, Bulgaria, Croatia, Cyprus, Georgia, Israel, Republic of Macedonia, Moldova, The Netherlands, Romania, and Ukraine." 68th Meeting of the Development Committee, Dubai, September 22, World Bank, Washington, DC. Available at http://siteresources.worldbank.org/DEVCOMMINT/ Documentation/20128823/DCS2003–0052-vanArdenne.pdf.

RONALD MENDOZA is a policy analyst and economist with the Office of Development Studies, United Nations Development Programme (UNDP). The views expressed herein do not necessarily reflect the views and policies of the UNDP. The author thanks Chandrika Bahadur, Pedro Conceição, Paola Deles, and Inge Kaul for very helpful discussions on the topic, and Jeff Madrick, David Roodman, and Yanchun Zhang for their comments on an earlier draft. All remaining errors are his.

Unequal Access

India's lower castes are seeking a toehold in the global job market.

EMILY WAX

As a Dalit, Pratibha Valmik Kamble is part of the poorest and most ostracized community in this subcontinent's ancient caste system, a group of people so shunned that they are still known as untouchables. Her mother is a maid, her father a day laborer.

Yet here in this prospering city, Kamble, 24, was recently applying to an Indian firm called Temp Solutions to go to Philadelphia for a well-paying social service job there. During the interview, she twisted her hands nervously in her lap, knowing that if she landed the position, she would not only make more money than both of her parents combined, she would enhance their social status, and her own.

India has long had an affirmative action program for federal government jobs, setting aside 23 percent of positions for the most oppressed castes. Now, activists are campaigning to open the private sector to them as well, whether the employer is Indian or multinational. Prime Minister Manmohan Singh recently said he favors that goal.

So does Temp Solutions co-owner Michael Thevar, himself a member of a low-ranking caste. He gave Kamble the job. "I'm so proud of you," he told her after delivering the good news. "I know so well how much you struggled. That's why I am that much more impressed."

Kamble's eyes went wet as she straightened her mustard-colored outfit and smiled, appearing to be almost embarrassed by his praise.

Recruiting drives aimed at hiring members of India's underprivileged castes, who make up 70 percent of the population, remain rare in the subcontinent's booming service sector. But as India hurtles into world markets, such hiring has touched off a larger debate over the country's 3,000-year-old caste system.

In much of India, the system organizes people into a rigid social order by accident of birth, determining everything from professions to marriage partners.

While the caste system is outlawed by the constitution, low-caste Indians still experience severe discrimination. Dalits are regarded as so low that they are not even part of the system. To this day, they are not allowed to enter many Hindu temples or to drink water from sources used by higher castes.

So far, only two major companies—Bharti Enterprises and Infosys—have announced they would set aside jobs for Dalits and other oppressed castes.

Ramesh Bajpai, executive director of the New Delhi-based American Chamber of Commerce in India, says the issue of affirmative action for oppressed castes has not been raised among his members—an indication, some Indian workers contend, that many U.S. companies are not fully aware of the caste system and its complex legacy of discrimination.

India-based executives for IBM and Microsoft, which are among the top foreign employers in this country, declined to comment for this article.

"Things are changing in India and, I believe, changing for the good," says Bajpai. "As far as we know, our member companies try to hire across the spectrum of Indian society. But since the government has started talking about this issue, we in the industry will follow. It is a complex and interesting discussion."

An estimated 86 percent of technology workers at multinationals and large Indian outsourcing firms come from upper castes or wealthy middle castes, according to a study released in August 2006 by the government and activist groups.

At the same time, the vast majority of Indians living in the United States and Britain come from upper castes, partly because they have better access to work and education visas and can afford expensive plane tickets.

"Caste should not be globalized, and as India rises economically, that is the real fear," says Thevar. "I think this is the moment in India for us all to stand up and tell the world that we are capable. There is no longer such a thing as untouchable in the world."

Thevar and Dalit activists have even lobbied the U.S. Congressional Black Caucus, with whom they see common cause and a shared experience in discrimination.

Congress has taken notice, and in July passed a resolution calling for the United States to work with India to address the problem of untouchability by "encouraging U.S. businesses and other U.S. organizations working in India to take every possible measure to ensure Dalits are included and are not discriminated against in their programming."

"It is now time for this Congress to speak out about this ancient and particularly abhorrent form of persecution and segregation—even if it is occurring in a country considered to be one of America's closest allies," Republican Rep. Trent Franks of Arizona said during a speech last spring on the House floor. Franks went on to call Dalits "one of the most oppressed peoples on Earth."

The 2006 study found that public health workers refuse to visit 33 percent of Dalit villages, while mail is not delivered to the homes of 24 percent of Dalits.

The reason for the neglect, the study said, is that some in the upper castes believe lower-caste people are dirty and lack dignity in their labor as latrine cleaners, rickshaw drivers, butchers, herders and barbers.

The debate on affirmative action in India is similar to the one in the United States in terms of discrimination and ways to end it. But in India, those who experience discrimination, especially in rural areas, are the majority and are ruled by an elite.

The issue here is complicated by India's turbulent history of race, class and caste. Centuries-old customs of arranged marriages and inherited professions perpetuate caste divisions, which are further reinforced by some interpretations of Hinduism, India's dominant religion, which sanctions the caste system.

The country's education system also hardens caste. Lower castes largely attend public schools, which teach local languages, while private schools attended by upper castes teach English—the most important criterion to be hired at a call center, where young employees spend their nights helping customers phoning from the United States.

Opponents of affirmative action argue that government set-asides should have lasted only 10 years after independence in 1947, not the six decades that they have. In the workplace and in colleges, affirmative action programs breed resentment, the critics say, because they dilute merit-based hiring that should, in theory, reward the most qualified job candidates, regardless of caste.

Creating quotas for the private sector would be a "disaster," says Shiv Khera, an author who opposes set-asides on the grounds that they call too much attention to caste. "We shouldn't even be asking what caste people are."

He also says that affirmative action will not fix what he sees as the roots of caste divisions: deeply impoverished public schools that don't teach English or even have enough funding for up-to-date books. The government should fix those schools, Khera says, "not worry about the private sector," a view echoed by others.

Still, affirmative action has helped pull tens of thousands of people out of abject poverty and into universities and government jobs, while creating a small Dalit middle class that many hope will expand along with India's economy. It also has given rise to a new kind of struggle, as other low-ranking groups known here as the "backward castes" protest that their government designation isn't "low-caste enough" to make them eligible for job set-asides, Khera says.

"That just shows you that set-asides don't work," Khera adds. "It just makes the people more aware of caste and who's getting what job and why."

But inside the interview room, the young professionals applying for jobs with Temp Solutions said they would have never gotten an education without set-asides. The interviews were held at the Manuski Center, part of a Buddhist monastery. Hundreds of thousands of Dalits have converted to Buddhism in an attempt to escape the caste system.

Sitting in a circle as they waited to hear whether they would get jobs, Kamble and the other students talked about the often harrowing discrimination they faced.

"I knew there was hatred in the world and in India, when as a child I watched some upper castes refuse to sell my mother lentils and rice in the nicer part of the market because we were 'dirty,' and from a backward caste," said Vivek Kumar Katara, 22, who has a master's degree in social work focusing on helping the mentally ill. Without quotas, Katara said, "I honestly don't know if professors would have even let me sit in the same class as upper castes."

After awarding jobs to Kamble, Katara and others, Thevar said they would be expected to return to India once their visas expired and to help hire from their own communities.

"It will be our responsibility to tell the world about caste and fight it," Kamble said as a group of chosen candidates raced downstairs to call or tell their parents, who were anxiously waiting. She is to work for a child social services agency in Philadelphia.

Pacing downstairs, Kamble's gray-haired father, Valmik, put his thick, callused hands over his eyes and wept when he found out his daughter would be working for a major company. "I'm so happy and so proud," he said, hugging her. "I never dreamt of such a thing for our family."

China and India Go to Africa
New Deals in the Developing World

Harry G. Broadman

Economic activity between Africa and Asia is booming like never before. Business between the two continents is not new: India's trade with Africa's eastern and southern regions dates back to at least the days of the Silk Road, and China has been involved on the continent since it started investing there, mostly in infrastructure, during the postcolonial era. But today, partly as a result of accelerating commerce between developing countries throughout the world, the scale and pace of trade and investment flows between Africa and India and China are exceptional. (Throughout, Africa is used as a shorthand for sub-Saharan Africa.) Africa's exports to China increased at an annual rate of 48 percent between 2000 and 2005, two and half times as fast as the rate of the region's exports to the United States and four times as fast as the rate of its exports to the European Union (EU) over the same period.

Much of this activity is concentrated in a handful of African countries and in the extractive industries, such as oil and mining. But increasingly, businesses from China and India are also pursuing strategies in Africa that are about far more than natural resources: in addition to rapidly modernizing industries, both countries have burgeoning middle classes with rising incomes and purchasing power whose members are increasingly buying Africa's light manufactured products, household consumer goods, and processed foods and using its back-office services, tourism facilities, and telecommunications.

Fundamental differences in the resource, labor, and capital endowments of Africa and Asia make them complementary business partners—meaning that the trend will likely be sustained. This is good news, because the boom is a potentially pivotal opportunity for African countries to move beyond their traditional reliance on single-commodity exports and move up from the bottom of the international production chain, especially if growth-enhancing opportunities for trade and investment with the North continue to be as limited as they have been historically.

To be sure, there are several complications and obstacles. Africa's exports to and investment in Asia remain limited in scale and scope, Chinese and Indian companies in Africa sometimes displace African companies in local markets while creating few jobs there and sometimes even taking some away, and certain of these companies' activities are perceived to complicate already difficult political situations on the ground. What is more, fully realizing the prospects created by Chinese and Indian business is contingent on the implementation of demanding reforms. African governments must adopt policies that enhance African companies' international competitiveness, foster better governance, improve their countries' financial and labor markets, and attract investment in infrastructure. China and India, for their part, must eliminate their protectionist trade policies and allow the import of competitive high-value-added goods and services from Africa.

But if all sides do their share, China's and India's dramatically expanding commercial interest in Africa—home to 300 million of the world's poorest people and a region that presents the world's most formidable development challenge—could be an unprecedented opportunity for the region's growth and for its integration into the global economy.

Out of Africa

Since 1990, both Africa's exports to Asia and its imports from Asia have grown more rapidly than either its exports to or its imports from any other region of the world. Exports grew by 15 percent annually between 1990 and 1995 and by 20 percent between 2000 and 2005; imports grew by 13 percent annually between 1990 and 1995 and by 18 percent between 2000 and 2005. Meanwhile, between 2000 and 2005, the EU's share of exports from Africa dropped by half—so that Asia now buys about the same size share of Africa's exports as does the United States or the EU, Africa's traditional trading partners.

This recent burst in trade stems from a sharp upturn in the appetite of Asia's emerging economic giants, China and India, for African products—the result, in turn, of those two countries' booming economies. China and India have eclipsed Japan and South Korea as the most important Asian markets for African goods. Africa's exports to China and India have grown almost twice as fast as the region's total exports. China and India now buy ten percent and three percent, respectively, of all of Africa's exports.

The pattern of China's and India's trade with Africa is concentrated geographically. Eighty-five percent of the continent's exports to China come from five countries, the oil-exporting nations of Angola, Equatorial Guinea, Nigeria, the Republic of Congo, and Sudan. South Africa alone accounts for 68 percent of the region's exports to India, most of which are in minerals, precious stones, metals and alloys, and chemicals. Reflecting the broader profile of Africa's export patterns worldwide, a few unprocessed goods—namely oil, ore, metals, and raw agricultural commodities—dominate, accounting for 86 percent of total trade flows to China and India. Value-added manufactured exports make up a small share of Africa's exports—only eight percent of total exports to China, for example.

But this is changing, because the boom, driven until now by the growing demand for supplies for China's and India's expanding industries, is increasingly propelled by the incipient consumption of those countries' middle classes. China and India are beginning to import from Africa far more than fuels and minerals and metal products; their imports now include commodities (such as cotton or food products) that have undergone some labor-intensive processing in Africa and will be further processed in Asia in preparation for industrial or consumer use. To be sure, China and India export far more manufactured goods, machinery, electronics, and medical supplies to Africa than Africa does to China and India, and the imbalance exposes Africa to some risks: a sizable number of consumer goods from China and India directly compete against Africa's domestic products. But imports from China and India increasingly include capital goods, and those are helping to bolster the competitiveness of Africa's manufacturing sector by providing intermediate inputs for products that are assembled or processed in Africa and then shipped to the EU, the United States, and other markets.

The rapid increase in foreign direct investment (FDI) flows between Asia and Africa, even though much more modest than the increase in trade, is also noteworthy. India's cumulative FDI in Africa was $1.8 billion as of the end of 2004; China's was $1.3 billion as of the end of 2005. Over the past decade, much of this investment, too, has been concentrated in a few countries and in the extractive industries: for example, 50 percent of the FDI from China went to the oil- or mineral-rich countries of Nigeria, Sudan, and Zambia. But in the last few years, China's and India's FDI flows to Africa have begun to reach many other sectors (including apparel, agroprocessing, power generation, road construction, tourism, and telecommunications) and many more countries (including Botswana, Ethiopia, Kenya, Madagascar, Mauritius, Mozambique, Senegal, South Africa, and Uganda).

South by Southeast

Owing to differences in China's and India's cultures, political systems, and economic policies, there are significant variations between the operations of Chinese and Indian firms in Africa. Whereas most Chinese businesses on the continent are medium-sized or large state-owned or state-controlled enterprises, Indian companies vary more in size and are typically either privately owned or under mixed private-public ownership. As a result, the two sets of firms perceive commercial risks differently, which colors their business strategies in a variety of ways. Chinese firms tend to enter new markets in Africa by building new facilities, creating business entities that are vertically integrated, buying supplies from China rather than local markets, and selling in Africa mostly to government entities. They rarely facilitate the integration of their workers into the African socioeconomic fabric. Knowing that they can rely on Beijing's deep pockets, they are often able to outbid competitors for procurement contracts from local governments. On the other hand, most Indian firms in Africa acquire established businesses, are less vertically integrated, prefer to procure supplies locally or from international markets (rather than from Indian suppliers), engage in far more sales to private African entities, and encourage the local integration of their workers. In a 2006 survey of 450 business owners in Africa, almost half of the respondents who were ethnically Indian had taken on African nationalities (with most of the other half retaining their Indian nationality), compared with only four percent of firm owners who were ethnically Chinese (the other 96 percent had retained their Chinese nationality). This finding suggests that Indian immigrants are substantially more integrated into the African business community than are Chinese immigrants, who are relative newcomers.

The commercial activity of Chinese and Indian companies in Africa has been significantly aided by Beijing's and New Delhi's public programs for trade and investment finance. The Chinese government, largely through the Export-Import Bank of China and more recently through the China Development Bank, provides export credits, loans, and investment guarantees to Chinese investors. At the end of 2005, its concessional loans to all of Africa reached $800 million and covered 55 projects in 22 countries. In 2006, Beijing issued "China's African Policy," which set out core principles to guide future cooperation with the continent, and hosted a widely heralded summit with 48 African leaders, at which President Hu Jintao announced that China would double its assistance to African countries by 2009, provide them with $5 billion in concessional loans and credits, establish a $5 billion fund to encourage Chinese investment in Africa, and cancel the interest-free debt it was owed by 33 African states. Likewise, the Export-Import Bank of India facilitates trade and investment between India and African countries. Its activities have historically been concentrated in eastern and southern Africa, where, thanks to a long tradition of commerce and immigration, an Indian diaspora is already well established. But the bank recently launched the Focus Africa Program to identify new priority areas for bilateral trade and investment. In 2006, it extended to African countries a line of credit totaling $558 million, about half of which went to the Bank for Investment and Development of the Economic Community of West African States.

Such government backing has sometimes led to the perception that the overseas activities of Chinese and Indian companies are an extension of the two countries' foreign policies (much as support from the U.S. government and the EU for similar programs has caused similar perceptions). That can be a public-relations headache for Beijing and New Delhi given some of the downsides of these activities for Africans. Indeed, there are significant problems and imbalances. Whereas Asia buys almost one-quarter of Africa's total exports, Africa's exports to Asia represent little more than one percent of the world's exports to Asia. African FDI in Asia is extremely small, in both absolute and relative terms. Typical Chinese and Indian investments in Africa, such as large-scale oil or mineral exploration projects, are capital intensive and so create few new jobs. Furthermore, as Chinese and Indian entrepreneurs bring consumer goods from home into Africa, they sometimes displace African producers in domestic sales and exports, for example, in the textile and apparel sectors. Competition can spur African firms to become more efficient, but it can also create unemployment and inflict other social costs. Where African workers have been displaced, such as in Zambia, there have been sharp reactions and public demonstrations. Worse, some governments, nongovernmental organizations, and media outlets have recently criticized Chinese firms for the political implications of their activities—for example, for the conflict in Darfur. Beijing is increasingly aware that the overseas activities of Chinese companies can be a liability and that it needs to mitigate the costs to

its reputation. It has begun to take steps to do so by, for example, recently issuing "good corporate citizen" guidelines to govern the operations of Chinese multinationals in Africa.

Nevertheless, on balance, China's and India's rapidly growing commerce with Africa presents a major development opportunity for the continent. In recent years, the international marketplace has witnessed a big change: production chains have been divided into discrete functions, each of which can be performed by a separate entity, such as a foreign subsidiary or supplier. This development has boosted trade in intermediate goods and components and enabled corporations worldwide to become more footloose. The advent of data systems that provide real-time information on the international movement of goods up and down the production chain has allowed for the more efficient and ever cheaper shipping over long distances not only of assembled durable goods but also of components for just-in-time manufacturing products and—an important point for the fertile countries of Africa—of perishable goods. The result has been the rapid growth of trade within related industries, also known as network trade, in which, for example, a country imports cotton in order to produce garments and then exports those garments to third countries. This is true especially relative to the more traditional trade of final goods from different industries, such as the export of bananas or the import of machinery.

Such global value chains offer African countries a chance to increase the volume, diversity, and worth of their exports. African companies in several industries—for instance, the automobile industry (in South Africa), the fresh-cut-flower industry (in Uganda), and apparel manufacturing (in Kenya)—either have already engaged in or have strong prospects for engaging in network trade. And because many of the Chinese and Indian firms active in Africa are part of multinational corporations integrated into global value chains, doing business with them can help African companies expand their own engagement in network trade. This expansion is already evident in the areas of food processing (in Tanzania), textiles (in Ghana), fishing (in Senegal), and back-office services (in Tanzania).

Chinese and Indian firms in Africa are at the vanguard of the integration of Africa's economies.

As a result of their integrated corporate structures, moreover, Chinese and Indian multinationals engaged in Africa have played a significant role in facilitating links between trade and FDI. This is important because in some sectors, such as the extractive industries, the flow of investment from these firms to Africa increases the volume of African exports by offering markets not only to those firms' home countries but also to countries outside of Asia. These links between trade and FDI offer important opportunities to African firms, and in order to exploit them, more and more of these companies are entering into joint ventures with Chinese and Indian investors. By virtue of their integration in global corporate structures, Chinese and Indian businesses in Africa are also able to run larger operations and thus achieve greater economies of scale than their African counterparts. Thus, they can export a wider array of higher-value goods than can African firms in the same sectors. They also are more extensively integrated into both Africa's own regional trade networks and a geographically wider set of markets outside of Africa. In other words, Chinese and Indian firms in Africa are at the vanguard of the integration of African economies across the continent and into the global marketplace.

Holding Back

Unfortunately, various constraints are preventing such benefits from spreading across more economic sectors and to more countries in Africa. For one thing, tariffs in many African states, as well as in China and India, still limit trade, even though as members of the World Trade Organization (WTO), these countries have relatively liberalized trade policy regimes and have set tariffs on a nondiscriminatory basis, at "most favored nation" levels. The average tariff rates that most of Africa's leading exports face in Asia, including in China and India, are higher than those they face in the United States and the EU. This is particularly the case with agricultural commodities, and especially in India. Matters are better and improving in China: as part of its 2006 economic-assistance package, Beijing unilaterally eliminated tariffs on 190 commodities from Africa's 25 least-developed countries, and in 2007 it began to increase the number of exempted commodities to 440. But in China and India, African products continue to face the far more serious problem of escalating tariff-rate structures, under which more processed imports are subject to higher tariffs. This rule has discouraged the import of high-value-added processed products from Africa, such as ground coffee, cocoa powder, and roasted cashews. African states, for their part, have lowered many of their import tariff rates significantly in recent times, and major imports from China and India, including electronics, machinery, and transportation equipment, generally face relatively modest tariffs. But African states maintain many high tariffs against the Asian goods they import the most, such as textiles, yarn, apparel, footwear, and light manufactured goods. This has a pernicious effect: high import tariffs on textiles and yarn, for instance, raise production costs for African apparel manufacturers and thus limit the competitiveness of their products.

Another set of problems arises from the current network of trade agreements that African countries have been fashioning to foster regional integration, a critical goal on a continent with so many small and landlocked countries. Africa has not been immune to the worldwide proliferation of regional free-trade agreements that has occurred, along with multilateral trade liberalization, over the past 30 years. Every African country is now a member of at least four different agreements, and there are eight formal "regional economic communities" (or customs unions) and eight other types of regional integration entities or initiatives on the continent. The resulting "spaghetti bowl" of overlapping agreements has complicated customs administration and processing, driving up the cost of trade and deterring investment. The 2006 survey of 450 business owners operating in Africa suggested that most of them—be they Chinese, Indian, or African—find these arrangements ineffective at best and at worst an impediment to trade within Africa.

To be sure, these traditional trade-policy-related factors are critical constraints on the ability of African businesses (and governments) to make the most of the activities of Chinese and Indian companies. But perhaps more important are the constraints resulting from domestic economic factors not usually thought of as connected to international commerce. Most African nations, like other developing countries, have a thin base of internationally competitive domestic enterprises, nascent market institutions, and underdeveloped national infrastructure—all of which prevent local businesses from engaging significantly in sustainable and profitable international transactions. There has been increasing diversity in the performance of African governments trying to deal with these problems in recent years, with several countries making significant improvements, such as Burkina Faso, Ghana, Madagascar, Mauritius, and Mozambique. But in many states, poor governance and regulatory burdens remain serious limitations to trade and investment. These countries have seriously deficient judicial systems due to inadequate resources and human capital, weak institutions, and a lack of transparency. Business disputes tend to be costly, in terms of both time and fees. And inefficiency is sometimes compounded by corruption, with insidious effects: smaller African companies carry a disproportionately large burden when it comes to making unofficial payments, and exporters and large firms tend to be inspected more often, which seriously constrains their ability to conduct business.

All of this is unfortunate because vigorous competition in African markets could help increase the local benefits of trade with and investment from China and India. African countries with more intense competition among domestic firms (such as Mauritius and South Africa) make better exporters. Likewise, the African sectors that face more internal competition not only attract more FDI from China and India but also eventually become more effective at penetrating Asian and other markets. There is also a positive consequence for African companies in Africa: in African markets that face tougher competition because of imports from Asia, the barriers for African start-ups to enter the market generally drop. In other words, domestic competition and international integration reinforce each other over time; success at home breeds success abroad, and vice versa.

But such benefits are often impeded by prosaic problems such as poorly functioning capital markets, limited skilled labor, and lack of infrastructure. Restricted access to finance is one of the most significant constraints on business development and expansion in Africa. Acute shortages of skilled labor, coupled with restrictive domestic labor regulations that limit the mobility and flexibility of workers, increase the costs of running a business. Business costs in Africa are also high because the quality of the power supply is poor, telephone service is erratic, and Internet access is limited. In Senegal and Tanzania, for example, there are interruptions in electric power during 20-25 percent of production time. Telecommunications networks, especially those geared toward business services, are still woefully underdeveloped in Africa, even though a surge of private providers of mobile telephony is helping greatly by providing higher-quality service at lower cost. Inefficient transport systems and ports and problems with other basic logistics create serious bottlenecks that slow the movement of goods within Africa and to outside markets: it can be as expensive to transport products from Angola to South Africa as it is to ship them from Angola to China.

Such obstacles, in turn, increase the costs to businesses—even those of African origin—of conducting cross-border transactions with the continent. Foreign companies hunting for deals in Africa are often constrained by inadequate information about how to spot new market opportunities, search for new trading or investment partners, establish marketing channels, transfer personnel and technology, or determine how best to utilize logistical, transport, and communications systems. For example, African firms rarely adhere to internationally recognized technical standards and accreditation schemes, such as those governed by the International Organization for Standardization. That limits the ability of potential importers in China and India to compare the quality of African products with that of similar goods produced elsewhere.

A Lever for Growth

Market opportunities for trade with and investment from international actors will no doubt continue to grow for Africa. But as the world economy globalizes further, competition from other regions in the South will become stronger. Thus, African policymakers must make better use of Asia's current involvement as a lever for growth. China's and India's rapidly growing activities in Africa are a major opportunity for the continent's economies to move away from an excessive reliance on a few raw commodities and toward greater production of labor-intensive light manufactured goods and services. This engagement could also help African companies become more efficient by exposing them to more competition, advances in technology, and modern labor skills. And it could lead to greater integration of African countries not only with other regions of the world but, perhaps most important, on the continent itself, where most domestic markets are too small and too shallow to sustain the large-scale production of internationally competitive exports.

Devising and implementing an agenda for reform is thus critical. Experiences elsewhere—the East Asian economic miracle, the recent accession of several central and eastern European countries to the EU—have shown that reform tends to be most successful when it involves a combination of actions. Three lessons stand out in particular for African governments and their prospective partners and investors from China and India. First, it is important to implement sound policies regarding tariffs and trade agreements and, even more so—especially in African states—to reform fundamental features of domestic economies. Second, policies should facilitate linkages between investment and trade flows in order to create opportunities for African firms to engage in modern network trade. Third, there should be a clear division of labor among the various stakeholders—Africans, Chinese, Indians, and the international community, including multilateral and bilateral development agencies.

Both African and Asian countries must lower their overall tariffs, including those set at most-favored-nation levels, ideally within the context of the Doha Round of WTO negotiations but unilaterally, if necessary. Beijing's recent decision to lift all import tariffs on hundreds of commodities from some of Africa's least-developed countries is a good start. But China and India should also eliminate their escalating tariff structures, which prevent Africa's leading high-valued-added processed goods from entering their markets at competitive prices. Africa, for its part, must rationalize and harmonize its confusing and inefficient network of overlapping regional trade agreements. This is a tall order since the regional entities overseeing the agreements have strong vested interests in maintaining them. Yet it is absolutely essential for Africa's development to accelerate regional integration—which is the underlying objective of these agreements anyway. Other regions of the world, such as southeastern Europe, have begun to simplify their trade agreements, sometimes with the help of expertise from the WTO, the World Bank, and other international organizations.

Once the flow of commerce between Africa and Asia is encouraged, it must be translated into greater growth in Africa. Such growth will come only when Africa's domestic markets are more fully reformed so as to increase competition, ensure sound governance, develop infrastructure, and generally foster a hospitable investment climate. To this end, African governments should further eliminate administrative and policy barriers that prevent new businesses from entering the market and commercially nonviable firms from exiting it. The competition policies of most African countries are still underdeveloped; they must be institutionalized in order to build and maintain vigorously competitive industries and guard against restrictive business practices. This will require not only enacting competition laws based on global best practices and establishing enforcement agencies with regulatory authority, well-trained staffs, and political clout but also educating the public to understand that market competition plays a pivotal role in economic development by driving the costs of products and services down and improving choice, quality, and innovation.

Such reforms should be implemented in tandem with two closely related sets of policies. First, it is important to facilitate the growth of private African businesses through reforms that reduce rigidities in the continent's labor markets (by lowering the costs of hiring and firing personnel), further develop its financial markets (by increasing the availability of credit and lowering its cost to productive enterprises), and strengthen workers' skills (by offering them training and secondary and postsecondary education). Second, it is essential to increase the institutional capacity of African states to develop and enforce social, environmental, and product-safety standards that conform to international norms and apply to all investors, domestic or foreign.

Strengthening governance by improving the quality of basic market institutions, establishing more effective systems of checks and balances, and reducing incentives for corruption is also critical to the international economic integration of Africa. As it is in other developing regions of the world, achieving progress in governance in Africa will be a formidable task. But in recent years, a growing number of Africa's leaders have established or started participating in major regional initiatives to deal with the continent's governance problems, such as the African Peer Review Mechanism of the New Partnership

for Africa's Development and the Extractive Industries Transparency Initiative. However, more extensive measures at the national level are still needed to increase transparency and accountability in the conduct of public officials: the implementation of effective systems to manage public finances, the establishment of ombudsmen and competitive public-procurement practices, and the reform of public administration to align pay with performance would be good first steps. Improving governance will also require strengthening the enforcement of commercial contracts. The settlement of international business disputes in Africa is generally impaired by lengthy procedures, the lack of qualified and independent judges, and weak enforcement mechanisms. Policies that simplify (and so reduce the costs of) formal legal procedures would fortify the sanctity of contract and property rights, thus improving businesses' confidence in Africa's investment climate. In recent years, several countries, such as Ghana, Mauritius, Mozambique, Namibia, Rwanda, South Africa, and Tanzania, have already made promising advances in implementing such reforms.

Finally, it is essential to develop and improve the infrastructure in most African countries, especially those that have small markets or are landlocked. A clear priority should be to improve and modernize these countries' road and rail transport systems, ports, and telecommunications and information technology capacities. Meeting this challenge will require continued privatization or private-public partnerships to entice new investments. Customs procedures must be simplified. The focus should be on improving coordination among border-related agencies; making customs codes and associated regulations rule-based, transparent, and commercially oriented; and introducing customs authorities to information technology. The development experiences of other regions with contiguous landlocked countries, such as the Balkans or Central Asia, can provide practical lessons for African reformers.

Against this backdrop, African governments should also implement measures specifically intended to encourage Chinese and Indian businesses operating in Africa to forge linkages between their investments on the continent and trade flows out of it. African countries that bring their FDI policy regimes in line with international best practices in order to attract world-class investors—including sophisticated Chinese and Indian multinationals—will increase their national firms' chances to participate in the international marketplace. Indeed, the formation of such linkages is critical to enabling African actors to take advantage of the continent's vast natural-resource wealth, extract more value from the processing of these resources, and increase the participation of African firms in modern network trade. Creating world-class FDI policy regimes means, among other things, treating foreign investors like national investors, ensuring that all trade-related investment measures are consistent with WTO rules, providing for binding international arbitration for disputes between states and private investors, and abiding by international legal standards for expropriation and compensation.

This reform agenda will, of course, take years—if not decades—to implement: hence the importance of explicitly acknowledging who needs to do what. Inevitably, the lion's share of the effort will fall to the parties with the most to gain from reform—in this case, primarily African states and to a lesser extent China and India. African states, which must implement wide systemic reforms, have the most daunting tasks. One especially difficult job facing China and India is eliminating their escalating tariff rates. The international development agencies will have to share some of the burden, not only through traditional budgetary support but also by supporting institutional capacity building in African countries (especially in competition policy and governance), the development of infrastructure and the financial sector, the harmonization of trade agreements and technical standards, and the improvement of customs regimes and secondary education. They can also play a key role in encouraging international companies to respect fiduciary, social, and environmental safeguards in overseas investments in Africa.

African leaders must take advantage of China's and India's commerce by pursuing bold reforms that serve Africa's self-interest.

As the global marketplace becomes increasingly integrated, much is at stake for the economic welfare of Africa. After years of stop-and-go economic growth, many African countries now appear to be advancing at a sustainable pace. Over the past decade, Africa grew at an average rate of 5.4 percent, on par with the rest of the world. The dramatic increase in commerce recently between Africa and Asia's emerging giants—China and India—is a major contributor to this growth. Africans cannot afford to be left behind in the newest phase of globalization—the maturation of South-South commerce, which China and India are leading. African leaders must be proactive and take advantage of the opportunities created by China's and India's commercial interest in Africa by pursuing bold reforms that serve Africa's self-interest. And the rest of the world must work to ensure that Africans can benefit from these new patterns of international commerce.

HARRY G. BROADMAN, Economic Adviser for the Africa Region at the World Bank, is the author of *Africa's Silk Road: China and India's New Economic Frontier* (World Bank, 2007), from which this essay is drawn. The views expressed here are his own.

From *Foreign Affairs,* vol. 87, no. 2, March/April 2008, pp. 95–109. Copyright © 2008 by Council on Foreign Relations, Inc. Reprinted by permission of Foreign Affairs. www.ForeignAffairs.org

International OHS

Through the Looking Glass of the Global Economy

In late 2007, a multinational group of EHS professionals traveled to Mexico to observe working conditions at a giant open-pit copper mine in Cananea. What they found shocked them.

GARRETT BROWN

The occupational health and safety conditions at the giant open-pit copper mine in Cananea, Mexico displayed how workplace safety in the global economy can best be understood through the intersection of transnational corporations, a "race to the bottom" in working conditions and growing labor internationalism.

The historic, open-pit mine and processing plants in Cananea, Mexico are operated by the family-owned, transnational conglomerate Grupo Mexico, which acquired the mine for pennies on the dollar during the privatization of Mexico's state enterprises in the 1990s. Grupo Mexico also ended up owning several of Mexico's railroads, as well as copper mines in Peru, and it recently bought the bankrupt ASARCO (American Smelting and Refining Co.), which has mine and smelter properties in Arizona. Cananea is just 30 miles south of the Arizona border.

Like other transnational corporations in the global economy, Grupo Mexico has been on a relentless drive to reduce production costs, including weakening or eliminating labor unions, to boost corporate profits. Two years ago, Grupo Mexico began sustained attempts to replace unionized mine workers in Cananea with lower-cost, non-union contractor employees.

When Local 65 of the Mexican Miners union—one of the oldest and strongest in Mexico—refused to allow non-union maintenance and housekeeping contract employees into the mine, Grupo Mexico literally disassembled the dust collectors in the multi-building Concentrator Department and piled the duct work on the ground next to Area 23, one of the enclosed buildings processing the copper coming from the open-pit mine.

From that time forward, there has been a contest of wills between Grupo Mexico and the miners over how much silica-containing ore dust the mine workers are willing to breathe—given that the company disconnected the local ventilation

systems—and how important it is to the miners to prevent their union from being steadily eaten away by increasing numbers of non-union contract employees. Some 400 contract workers already are on the job along with 1,200 unionized mine workers.

Over the last 2 years, the mine's concentrator buildings have been filled with dense clouds of rock dust, forming snowdrift-sized piles of settled dust two to three feet high through the plants. A bulk sample of the accumulated dust taken in October 2007 and sent to an AIHA-accredited laboratory in the United States found the dust was 23 percent crystalline silica, with 50 percent of particles in the respirable range of less than 10 microns in diameter.

Finally, in July 2007, the miners union struck the Cananea mine over health and safety issues, foremost among them being hazardous exposures to silica, a known human carcinogen and the cause of debilitating and usually fatal silicosis. The union miners also were reacting to an attempt by Grupo Mexico to establish a rival, company-friendly union (with only 85 members compared to the historic union's 1,200 members) as the sole legal union on site.

When the Cananea miners went on strike on July 30, the United Steel Workers (USW) union in the United States launched a solidarity campaign. The USW represents copper miners in Arizona working for ASARCO, now owned by Grupo Mexico, and, "thinking globally," has tried to build bridges to both the Mexican and Peruvian miners unions as all three unions have members employed by Grupo Mexico.

The Peruvian miners union also has conducted several strikes at Grupo Mexico-owned facilities over the last year, in part in response to Grupo Mexico's attempt to impose 12-hour shifts, instead of 8-hour days, on the mines. The unions consider 12-hour shifts in mining operations to be a serious safety hazard due to accidents caused by worker fatigue.

Reaching Out for Help

In September 2007, USW passed along to the all-volunteer Maquiladora Health & Safety Support Network (MHSSN) a request from Local 65 of the Mexican Miners union for an independent evaluation of the working conditions in the Cananea mine and the health status of the mine workers.

In 2 weeks, the MHSSN pulled together a volunteer team of eight occupational professionals to go to Cananea to conduct extensive interviews with 70 miners, perform lung function tests (spirometry) on the miners and spend 4 hours touring both the open-pit mine and the processing plants.

The OHS survey team consisted of three Mexicans (two occupational physicians and an industrial hygienist), four U.S. citizens (an occupational doctor, a registered nurse, an industrial hygienist and a Mexican-American pulmonary technician) and a third industrial hygienist from Colombia. A Southern California local union of the USW put up the $3,500 needed for travel expenses and all the professionals donated their time.

The OHS survey team spent a day and half interviewing and testing mine workers, who were recruited to participate by Local 65 of the Mexican Miners union, at the miners union hall in downtown Cananea. The afternoon of the second day was spent driving through the giant open-pit mine and walking through the multiple processing plants, where the bulk samples of settled rock dust were collected.

The multi-national OHS survey team was shocked at the level of disrepair and non-existent housekeeping in such a large facility operated by a major transnational corporation. The team concluded the Cananea mine and processing plants were being "deliberately run into the ground," according to the report issued by the survey team in November. Among the team's other findings, based on the worker interviews and spirometry test results, were:

- Semi-quantitative calculations indicate workers in the concentrator area are exposed to dust levels of at least 10 milligrams per cubic meter of air (mg/m3). The respirable quartz silica component of this dust would be at least 1.2 mg/m3, or 10 times greater than the Mexican Maximum Permissible Exposure Limit (LMPE) of 0.1 mg/m3;

- There are substantial elevations in the prevalence of respiratory symptoms in a population that should be healthier than the general, non-industrial worker population. These symptoms include shortness of breath, wheezing, cough and sputum production, which appears to be related to dust exposure estimates. These symptoms reflect past exposures, and likely underestimate the burden of disease that will occur in this population if the current exposures continue;

The group found that Grupo Mexico, in violation of existing Mexican workplace safety regulations, failed to:

- Conduct sufficient industrial hygiene monitoring to identify, evaluate and later control health hazards to miners including exposure to mineral dusts (including silica), acid mists, airborne solvents, high noise levels, high vibration levels and hot and cold conditions;

- Install effective ventilation and source pollution controls for silica-containing dust in the concentrator buildings and in the two ESDE plants to prevent hazardous exposures to sulfuric acid mists. The presence of high levels of acid mist is indicated by the fact that the floors and structural steel frame of ESDE II building have been eaten away;

- Conduct a comprehensive medical surveillance program to determine the health status of workers exposed to airborne contaminants (silica, heavy metals like lead, acid mists, solvents) and physical hazards such as noise and vibration;

- Provide the training required by Mexican law to workers with hazardous exposures that trigger the training requirement. Despite high noise levels, exposure to chemicals and exposures to energized machines, 91 percent of the interviewed miners had not received noise training, 58 percent had not received chemical hazards training, 70 percent had not received electrical hazards training and 75 percent had not received training on lockout/tagout procedures for operating and repairing energized equipment; and

- Correct serious electrical, machine-guarding and other safety hazards created by industrial-scale mining, crushing and pulverizing, acid leaching and electro-plating and milling operations to produce fine powder copper ore from refrigerator-sized rocks blasted out of an open-pit mine.

The OHS survey team could not verify the exact circumstances of the 50 separate accidents reported at the site in the past 12 months. The anecdotal reports of broken limbs, amputations, electrocutions, falls, burns and at least one fatality suggest these incidents were the result of unsafe working conditions, poorly maintained machinery and equipment and inadequate safety procedures. The investigators also found the enterprise's required Joint Management-Labor Safety Committee is small—six members total—and unable to conduct or oversee effective safety inspections, hazard corrections, accident investigations and employee training.

In April 2007, before the strike closed the facility, two inspectors from the Mexican Department of Labor (STPS) also inspected the mine and processing plants over 2 days. At the end of the site visit, the inspectors issued a report ordering Grupo Mexico to implement 72 separate corrective actions. The STPS findings confirm the reports of unsafe working conditions made by workers interviewed in October by the MHSSN team.

Among the 72 corrective actions prescribed by the STPS include orders to: 1) re-assemble and use dust collectors in the concentrator buildings; 2) repair the malfunctioning brakes on a 10-ton and a 15-ton crane in Area 30 of the concentrator; 3) install guards on moving parts and energized equipment; 4) correct numerous electrical hazards; 5) repair or replace damaged or missing wall and roof panels; and 6) implement a major housekeeping effort to clean up accumulated dusts throughout the plant.

Report Issued

In November 2007, the MHSSN team publicly issued its report at a press conference in Mexico City with miners from Local 65 in Cananea, representatives of the national office of the Mexican Miners union and USW members from the Arizona ASARCO mines and USW's Pittsburgh headquarters. (English and Spanish language versions of the MHSSN report, and photographs from the Cananea mine, are posted at www.igc.org/mhssn.)

Following the press conference, the joint MHSSN-union delegation met with STPS officials to request the creation of a tripartite (government-management-labor) commission to verify working conditions at the Cananea mine. Grupo Mexico, for its part, denied there were any unsafe conditions or worker illnesses at the mine.

A day later, the STPS responded by stating that the MHSSN study was not "legally valid," but refused to either follow up its own April 2007 inspection or establish a special fact-finding commission to resolve conflicting reports of actual conditions in the mine and processing plants.

The next step of this international OHS project will likely include filing a complaint under the labor side agreement of the North American Free Trade Agreement (NAFTA) in January 2008 by MHSSN and interested unions and labor rights organizations in Mexico and the United States. Efforts also are being made to raise funds for a more comprehensive health study of active and retired mines to determine the prevalence of respiratory diseases like silicosis.

The "new world order" of occupational safety and health in the globalized economy is evident even in this small project. A transnational corporation operates facilities in three countries, and, as many other transnationals do, exerts downward pressure in each country to maximize operating revenues and profits. The mine workers in the three countries are building bridges of solidarity and working toward "coordinated bargaining" with their common employer. And at the same time, occupational health professionals from three countries are volunteering their time and expertise to prevent a "race to the bottom" in workplace safety from undermining working conditions and workers' health throughout the global economy.

GARRETT BROWN, MPH, CIH, is coordinator of the Maquiladora Health & Safety Support Network and was a member of the OHS survey team in Cananea. The Cananea report and photos are posted at www.igc.org/mhssn.

Deadly Business in Moscow

An American lawyer's experience underscores the lawlessness outsiders operating in Russia can face.

TOM CAHILL

J amison Firestone was at his desk when the commotion began. On the morning of June 4, 2007, the American attorney heard loud voices coming from the reception area of his law firm, Firestone Duncan, on Krasnoproletarskaya Street in Moscow. He went out to investigate and was greeted by two dozen officers from the Russian Interior Ministry.

Over the next seven hours, he says, the security forces corralled Firestone and his staff in a conference room, ransacked the offices, and confiscated computers and documents. When one of Firestone's employees objected, he was beaten so severely he required hospitalization for three weeks.

On the same day, Russian police raided the Moscow headquarters of one of Firestone's clients, the prominent foreign investment firm Hermitage Capital Management. Its founder, the American-born financier William Browder, had become a strong critic of the state-controlled energy conglomerate Gazprom and has been barred from reentering Russia since 2005. The searches of the offices marked a major escalation in Hermitage's conflict with the Russian government. And Firestone, 44, who had spent 18 years helping Western companies navigate the murky waters of Russia's legal system, knew what it could mean. "Corrupt law enforcement is the single biggest risk to business in Russia," he says. He braced for the worst.

His fears came true within months, when records confiscated during the June 2007 raids allegedly were used in an elaborate $230 million fraud that exploited three Hermitage funds to extract phony tax refunds from the Russian government. In 2008 an attorney from Firestone's firm who helped represent Hermitage was imprisoned on tax charges; he died behind bars last November after being denied medical treatment, creating a furor in Moscow. Finally, last year two unsuccessful attempts were made to steal $21 million in taxes paid to the Russian government by a company for which Firestone served as general director, he says. The people behind these attempts used his forged signature to seek rebates, a method similar to that used in the Hermitage case, he adds.

"Stealing the Country"

Now Firestone, a former board member of the American Chamber of Commerce in Russia, has fled to London, fearing that he, too, could end up in jail. "Police [in Russia] have to stop being the Mafia," he says. "These people are stealing the country."

The alleged victimization of Browder and Hermitage is well known. In interviews with Bloomberg News, however, Firestone for the first time is alleging government-sponsored fraud aimed at him personally. His account underscores the arm-twisting and lawlessness that can afflict outsiders doing business in Russia. As widely reported, oil giants British Petroleum and Royal Dutch Shell have suffered politically backed attempts to wrest control of aspects of their Russian operations. The French carmaker Renault likewise has come under government pressure to assist a Russian manufacturer in which it had invested.

The risk of being targeted for abuse by government officials—sometimes operating in league with Russian businesses—is a central reason the country has attracted less than one-fifth the foreign investment in China and Brazil and half of what's invested in India, according to three years of data compiled by fund tracker EPFR Global.

Corruption is a central reason Russia has attracted far less investment than China or Brazil.

In the wake of the death of Firestone's colleague, Sergei Magnitsky, the heads of the Moscow police's tax crimes department and the city's prison division were both fired. That's not enough, says Browder, 45, who has been based in London for the past five years. "We've written well-documented complaints to the top law enforcement officers in the country that a number of police officers, judges, organized criminals, and businessmen have been involved in the theft of almost $500 million from the state and were involved in imprisoning Sergei Magnitsky," he says.

In October 2008, Magnitsky complained about the Hermitage case to Russia's State Investigative Committee, the equivalent of the U.S. Federal Bureau of Investigation. He said the officers involved in the raid on the law firm may have been linked to the Hermitage fraud, according to a transcript of his testimony.

A little more than a month later, on Nov. 24, 2008, five officers arrived at Magnitsky's home at 7 A.M. and took him in for questioning. He was accused of involvement in an alleged tax fraud perpetrated by Hermitage and was pressured to withdraw his complaint and implicate Browder, according to petitions Magnitsky filed with the Interior Ministry's Investigative Committee. "When I repeatedly rejected these propositions by the investigators pushing me to commit such a base act, the conditions of my detention become worse and worse," Magnitsky wrote in a Sept. 11, 2009, filing. Two months later, on Nov. 17, the 37-year-old father of two died from toxic shock and heart failure after being held in pretrial detention for 358 days.

Some of the records taken from Firestone's office in the 2007 raid involved an investing company called OOO Anrider. The documents showed that Anrider had paid $21.6 million in taxes in 2006, according to Firestone. A filing with Russian tax authorities dated Apr. 24, 2009, claimed that Anrider overpaid taxes by $21 million and deserved a refund. Firestone says he learned of the filing after the claim was rejected and copies of the papers were sent to him. The documents included what Firestone alleges were forgeries of his signature and Anrider's corporate seal. Someone, he says, was trying to use his identity to steal tax revenue and, in the process, possibly implicate him.

The lawyer, a native New Yorker who began studying Russian in high school and speaks it fluently, alerted tax authorities last August that the claim was bogus, documents show. The tax office didn't respond, and the police declined to open an investigation.

The Russian Interior Ministry's Investigative Committee declined to comment about Firestone or Magnitsky; it would only confirm that it is investigating Browder for alleged tax fraud. "He's screaming that they stole his companies, but he's not talking about the tax he didn't pay," spokeswoman Irina Dudukina says. "If he thinks he's innocent, then he should give evidence."

Browder, who has been placed on the Interior Ministry's wanted list, says his companies were all audited and that no tax claims have been filed against them. "They're trying to cover an enormous crime against the budget with fabricated allegations," he says.

Firestone agrees. "When you see corruption on this scale at the same time as the President is demanding investigations and cracking down, it's brazen," he says. He left his apartment in Moscow before Christmas, as if going away for the holiday, and hasn't been back.

Global Corporate Citizenship
Working with Governments and Civil Society

KLAUS SCHWAB

Compared to just a decade ago, it is now common for business-people to talk about social responsibility and the importance of being good corporate citizens. Many business leaders today consider it critical to engage with shareholders, the communities in which their companies operate, and others affected by and interested in what they do. The diverse activities needed to respond to these expanded duties are widely referred to by the catchall phrase "corporate social responsibility." It incorporates a host of concepts and practices, including the necessity for adequate corporate governance structures, the implementation of workplace safety standards, the adoption of environmentally sustainable procedures, and philanthropy.

Blanketing these various responsibilities with the single term "corporate social responsibility" is an oversimplification that has led to a great deal of confusion. It is necessary to distinguish between the different types of corporate activities, so that the work companies do to engage in society is fairly recognized and appreciated and companies are better able to benchmark themselves against the performance of different enterprises and learn from example. A better understanding of engagement requires separate definitions for corporate governance, corporate philanthropy, and corporate social responsibility as well as for an emerging element: corporate social entrepreneurship, that is, the transformation of socially responsible principles and ideas into commercial value.

Above all, a new imperative for business, best described as "global corporate citizenship," must be recognized. It expresses the conviction that companies not only must be engaged with their stakeholders but are themselves stakeholders alongside governments and civil society. International business leaders must fully commit to sustainable development and address paramount global challenges, including climate change, the provision of public health care, energy conservation, and the management of resources, particularly water. Because these global issues increasingly impact business, not to engage with them can hurt the bottom line. Because global citizenship is in a corporation's enlightened self-interest, it is sustainable. Addressing global issues can be good both for the corporation and for society at a time of increasing globalization and diminishing state influence.

The Factors at Play

Today's corporate engagement in society is the inevitable result of a number of factors. First, the role of the nation-state has diminished. In early modern Europe, the church's power over people was undermined by the emergence of the sovereign state; in the contemporary world, no single government can do everything. Even the military might of most states depends in large part on the supplies and support provided by private industry.

The intensified pace of globalization due to advances in technology is the most significant factor in the weakening influence of the state. Fast transportation links and the speedy flow of information have negated the relevance of geographic borders. Whether it is poverty in Africa or the haze over Southeast Asia, an increasing number of problems require bilateral, regional, or global solutions and, in many cases, the mobilization of more resources than any single government can marshal.

The limits of political power are increasingly evident. The lack of global leadership is glaring, not least because the existing global governance institutions are hampered by archaic conventions and procedures devised, in some instances, at the end of World War II. Sovereign power still rests with national governments, but authentic and effective global leadership has yet to emerge. Meanwhile, public governance at the local, national, regional, and international levels has weakened. Even the best leaders cannot operate successfully in a failed system.

As state power has shrunk, the sphere of influence of business has widened. Companies get involved in the health of workers, the education of employees and their children, and the pensions that sustain them in retirement. Corporations have an impact on everything from air quality to the availability of life-saving drugs. They have become integral to the survival of governments and the political stability of nations and regions. The ranks of transnational and global companies are increasing. Even small and medium-size high-growth enterprises, many of them from developing countries, have become global in approach. Consequently, at the same time as state power has declined, the influence of corporations on communities, on the lives of citizens, and on the environment has sharply increased. This fundamental shift in the global power equation means that just as communities and citizens look to government for answers and leadership, so now they target corporations with both requests for help and criticism for wrongdoing.

The deepening engagement of business must also be seen in the context of the emergence of a more active civil society. Civil society has taken on a more prominent role in international media since the 1992 UN Conference on Environment and Development in Rio de Janeiro. There has been a proliferation of nongovernmental organizations (NGOS), including several that are global in scope and presence. The focus of much of the civic action of NGOS has naturally been corporations. After an initial confrontational approach, some of the toughest critics have come to appreciate that many business leaders—of small and large corporations, in developed and developing economies—are sincerely engaged in society. Many civil-society organizations now focus on working with business instead of confronting it.

A Framework for Engagement

The case for corporate engagement in society is compelling, and business leaders must look carefully at how their companies are engaged, consider what more they can do, and act. The World Economic Forum has developed a framework to help business leaders in this task. It grew out of three decades of providing a platform for companies to engage in society. In 1971, the forum first identified the stakeholder concept—the idea that a company has a clear responsibility to the community beyond its shareholders. Two years later, at the annual forum meeting, the stakeholder concept became the cornerstone of the Davos Declaration, which articulated the fundamental principles of a corporation's social and environmental responsibility. Since then, the forum has actively promoted these ideals and further developed the concept of corporate engagement.

Businesses frequently miss the true benefits of an integrated strategy for effective corporate engagement. Sharpening definitions of the concept of corporate engagement is critical to making the business sector understand and practice it better. Clarification is also important to ensure that the general public better appreciates the complex challenges companies face and can assess how effectively or not they address them.

Five core concepts—corporate governance, corporate philanthropy, corporate social responsibility, corporate social entrepreneurship, and global corporate citizenship—define the different types of business engagement. Corporate governance is more than the way in which a company is run. It means that a company complies with local and international laws, transparency and accountability requirements, ethical norms, and environmental and social codes of conduct. Every company is subject to some form of governance; otherwise, it would not have the basic licence to operate. The central issue is the quality of this governance. An enterprise either complies or does not comply with the laws and standards that apply to it. Good corporate governance means that the company's conduct meets or exceeds what is required on paper—not doing any harm because it is following the rules and possibly even doing good by going beyond the mandated minimum. Corporate governance is how a company behaves when nobody is looking.

Without good corporate governance, no other form of corporate engagement is credible.

Good corporate governance means that a company's conduct exceeds what is required.

A key part of corporate governance is the development and implementation of internal programs to promote ethics, moral standards, and socially acceptable practices. These should include respect for human rights and adherence to labor standards, as well as in-house efforts to prevent bribery and corruption. This can be especially difficult for companies in jurisdictions where the rule of law is weak and what is acceptable may not be clear. Many companies now publish standards of business conduct that guide their decision-making and set the parameters for their professional relationships worldwide.

More than 3,000 companies in about 120 countries have signed on to the UN Global Compact, a framework of ten core principles to guide business behavior in areas such as human rights, the environment, labor practices, and corruption. Launched at the forum in 1999 by then UN Secretary-General Kofi Annan, the UNGC has become a powerful force for promoting good corporate governance, even though it is strictly voluntary and based on self-assessment. Companies that lag in reporting their progress are delisted; last year, 500 were cut. Another example of good corporate governance is subscribing to the Global Reporting Initiative, a program to institute international guidelines for sustainability reporting, the publishing of an organization's economic, environmental, and social performance and impact. The GRI was launched in 1997 by NGOS in the United States with the support of the UN Environment Program. Today, over 1,000 organizations, including many corporations, use the GRI guidelines to assess their sustainability practices.

Good corporate governance should not be seen as only a compliance issue. Companies should be actively involved in the development of standards and practices, adapting them continuously to the requirements of global markets and public expectations. New areas calling for tighter governance rules include executive compensation and the transparency of new financial instruments such as hedge funds and private equity funds.

Reaching Out

Corporations are moving beyond the mandatory requirements of corporate governance. Corporate philanthropy has been on the rise in many countries in recent years. It includes cash contributions; grants; donations, including salary-sacrifice programs and the giving of products; services; and investments. Outright corporate donations to global initiatives, such as Médecins Sans Frontières, or money provided for relief operations after natural disasters also qualify. In determining what is corporate philanthropy, intention and context are key factors. Corporate philanthropy is engagement that does not go beyond writing a check or handing out donated goods. Social investing is a special form of corporate philanthropy, in which a company invests in organizations or programs that have broad social appeal, such as inner-city housing projects or funds for student loans. Instances of corporate philanthropy and social investing can also be instances of global corporate citizenship. If a cash contribution is linked to a company's active engagement in a global effort to address climate change, for example, then the charitable act is also an act of global corporate citizenship. And if a corporation takes an active part in the management of an inner-city housing project in which it has invested, then it is practicing both social investing and global corporate citizenship.

In the past, corporate philanthropy was the preferred way for corporations to give back to society. Today, business leaders recognize that companies can make more efficient contributions through active engagement. The framework developed by the forum encourages the stakeholder approach to corporate engagement and refers to this as "corporate social responsibility." This involves how a corporation responds to the expectations of its stakeholders—the wide community of all the organizations and individuals that are in any way affected by or interested in its actions: shareholders, owners, investors, employees, suppliers, clients, consumers—while trying to increase the company's value. Corporate social responsibility means addressing the wider financial, environmental, and social impact of all that a company does. It entails minimizing the negative effects of the actions of a company and maximizing the positive ones on stakeholders as well as on the communities in which the enterprise operates and the governments with which it must work.

Corporate social responsibility is measured through so-called triple bottom-line accountability, according to which a company reports not only on its financial results but also on what it is doing and what it is not doing in meeting stakeholder expectations of its environmental and social responsibilities. Nike, for example, has committed to achieving or exceeding its published baseline requirements for sustainability—from design to manufacturing—for all its footwear by 2011, apparel by 2015, and equipment by 2020.

Today, corporate social responsibility extends along the whole chain of value creation. For example, corporations must provide the necessary information, education, and training to suppliers and clients to ensure that a product or service can be effectively and safely used. In that regard, the global insurance group AIG offers customers financial-education programs to help them learn how to make the right investment decisions to meet their needs. Some business leaders will point to their corporation's engagement in a number of corporate social responsibility projects around the world, which, they argue, make the corporation a global citizen. But the sum of acts of local citizenship does not make a globally involved citizen; global issues must be addressed on a global scale.

Corporate social entrepreneurship is strictly defined as the transformation of socially and environmentally responsible ideas into products or services. The last decade has seen many individuals come up with innovative ideas to address the specific social and environmental needs of the communities in which they are living. The role model of these social entrepreneurs, Muhammad Yunus, the inventor of microcredit, received the Nobel Peace Prize in 2006. Today, pioneering enterprises integrate social entrepreneurship into their core activities by actively channeling their research-and-development capabilities in the direction of socially innovative products and services. Examples of corporate social entrepreneurship include Deutsche Bank offering innovative microfinance schemes or socially responsible investment products, the Toyota Motor Corporation producing a hybrid car, or Unilever empowering women to become entrepreneurs in rural India while at the same time raising awareness on the importance of hygiene and nutrition.

Citizens of the World

Global corporate citizenship goes beyond the concepts of corporate philanthropy, including social investing; corporate social responsibility; and corporate social entrepreneurship in that it entails focusing on "the global space," which is increasingly shaped by forces beyond the control of nation-states. Global corporations have not only a license to operate in this arena but also a civic duty to contribute to sustaining the world's well-being in cooperation with governments and civil society. Global corporate citizenship means engagement at the macro level on issues of importance to the world: it contributes to enhancing the sustainability of the global marketplace.

Global corporate citizenship refers to a company's role in addressing issues that have a dramatic impact on the future of the globe, such as climate change, water shortages, infectious diseases, and terrorism. Other challenges include providing access to food, education, and information technology; extreme poverty; transnational crime; corruption; failed states; and disaster response and relief. Each of these problems is global in scope, even if the solutions may be locally focused.

When engaging in global corporate citizenship, companies should get involved in areas and in ways in which they can contribute meaningfully. The primary responsibility for meeting these global challenges still rests with governments and international organizations. But companies can contribute in an appropriately balanced partnership with the public sector and relevant civil-society groups. The right balance should be found among all the actors involved so that there is agreement on who should lead and so that progress is not stymied by infighting or a lack of direction. Business should not feel the need to overstep its boundaries or take on responsibilities that belong to the state.

Companies that practice global corporate citizenship do so either through thought leadership, that is, by providing the knowledge and technology essential to addressing a particular global problem, or through concrete action, that is, through the execution of a coordinated plan—or they do both. The Gleneagles Dialogue on Climate Change, Clean Energy, and Sustainability, a partnership led by governments in the G-8 (the group of highly industrialized states) and the -20 (the group of developing countries with a special interest in agriculture) and involving the world's biggest energy-producing and energy-consuming countries, is an example of companies practicing global corporate citizenship through thought leadership. Microsoft's Unlimited Potential initiative, which aims to bring the benefits of technology to five billion people yet to experience the opportunities that computers offer is a notable action-oriented example. Microsoft's project is a multi-stakeholder effort to bridge the global digital divide by fostering innovation in business and education and raising the skill levels of individuals to improve their employment prospects and the growth of enterprises. Yet another action-oriented program is the World Economic Forum's Global Education Initiative, which assembles partners from business, government, and civil society to support critical reforms in education. The success of initial programs in Egypt, Jordan, and the Indian state of Rajasthan has inspired the forum to form an alliance with UNESCO in developing a joint program, Partnerships for Education, which is meant to promote multi-stakeholder approaches within the global education community with the goal of achieving education for all.

Since companies depend on global development, it is in their interest to help improve the state of the world.

Global corporate citizenship is an extension of the stakeholder concept and involves the corporation acting as a stakeholder in global society, together with government and civil society. Global corporate citizenship can be considered a long-term investment. Since companies depend on global development, which in turn relies on stability and increased prosperity, it is in their direct interest to help improve the state of the world.

When a company creates a coordinated strategy for corporate engagement in society, it is likely to practice different types of engagement at the same time. And a particular act by an enterprise may not fit just one of the concepts. Nestlé voluntarily takes measures to reduce the water it uses in its operations. Since these measures are intended to benefit the water supply and the water-management needs of the communities in which the company operates, they qualify as acts of corporate social responsibility. As Nestlé engages with governments and NGOS to reduce water use in a broader way, it also offers an example of global corporate citizenship. If the company gave free water to a community, it would be engaging in corporate philanthropy. And if it sold recycled water in biodegradable bottles, that would be an act of corporate social entrepreneurship.

The Right Mindset

Enterprises should proactively mobilize a range of partners to effectively address global challenges. Lamentably, however, many business leaders are reluctant to accept that role. A study conducted by the global consulting group McKinsey & Company in 2007 found that fewer than half of the senior executives surveyed in the United States believed that they or their peers should take the lead in shaping the debate on major issues such as education, health care, and foreign policy. Only one-seventh of the respondents believed that they were playing that role, and the majority of them said that they were motivated primarily by personal reasons and were acting as private citizens.

There are not only motivational but also practical reasons why business leaders shy away from social engagement. The proliferation of Websites on the Internet and new media channels such as blogs and the rise of shareholder activism may prompt some business leaders to refrain from thinking beyond the next financial quarter. The "short-termism" these developments promote could lead some CEOS to assume that engaging in society is not worthwhile because the value of corporate engagement is typically realized only in the medium or long term. Moreover, fast-changing conditions in the market may result in "zapping," or indiscriminate decision-making, in the same way that political leaders might zigzag on a policy in response to poll results.

Short-termism and zapping, as well as the growing challenges thrown up by the often painful economic transformations of globalization, can blur corporate vision. They may lead to paralytic management or a kind of corporate attention deficit disorder, whereby companies lose focus on the big picture. In such cases, companies may lose their motivation or willingness to engage in society. Corporate leaders may also be overwhelmed by the sheer magnitude and complexity of global challenges and the expectations of the public for them to assume partial responsibility for all the deficiencies of the global system.

This mindset must be changed. Corporations must engage on global issues while understanding that the business community cannot on its own solve global problems such as poverty, poor education, and inadequate health care. Governments and multilateral organizations cannot be discharged from their responsibilities to deliver such public goods. "Corporations are not responsible for all the world's problems, nor do they have the resources to solve them all," Michael Porter, a Harvard Business School professor, and Mark Kramer, the managing director of FSG Social Impact Advisors, wrote in the *Harvard Business Review* in December 2006. "Each company can identify the particular set of societal problems that it is best equipped to help resolve and from which it can gain the greatest competitive benefit," Porter and Kramer added. "When a well-run business applies its vast resources, expertise and management talent to problems that it understands and in which it has a stake, it can have a greater impact on social good than any other institution or philanthropic organization."

The examples of Microsoft's information technology skills training and Nestlé's water management, and many others as well, offer several conclusions about the practice of global corporate citizenship. First, global corporate citizenship must be a multi-stakeholder endeavor. The ultimate responsibility for addressing global issues lies with states and international organizations. Many governments recognize their limitations and are eagerly promoting public-private partnerships. Corporations should put aside any reservations they may have about partnering with governments and civil society as long as the initiatives in which they want to participate can be run properly and efficiently.

Second, for global corporate citizenship to be meaningful, effective, and sustainable, it must align with a company's specific capabilities and with its business model and profit motive. This also requires the active involvement of CEOS and should reflect their vision of what is good for the corporation and society. If this happens, it is more likely that the enterprise will find ways of engaging that are compatible with its business objectives and beneficial for society as well. Corporations should, however, beware of being parties to grand declarations or general commitments to solve global issues, since such commitments can blur people's perceptions of the distinct roles of the public and private sectors. The legitimacy of a corporation engaged in global corporate citizenship comes not from declarations but from results.

Third, global corporate citizenship should never be undertaken from a defensive or apologetic position. The ultimate role of business in society remains to do business. Global corporate citizenship should not develop from a bad conscience or a feeling that one must give back to society; it should be a feature of this globalizing world that stretches traditional boundaries. Global corporate citizenship is a logical extension of corporations' search for a consistent and sustainable framework for global engagement—and one that adds value for both the companies and the global space in which they engage. It is a form of corporate engagement that can reinforce the positive role of business in society and enhance profitability in the long term. Indeed, global corporate citizenship integrates both the rights and the responsibilities that corporations have as global citizens. And in relying on a multi-stakeholder approach to tackling global problems, it can point out the way to new models of effective global governance that integrate business as a key stakeholder.

From *Foreign Affairs,* vol. 87, no. 1, January/February 2008, pp. 107–118. Copyright © 2008 by Council on Foreign Relations, Inc. Reprinted by permission of Foreign Affairs. www.ForeignAffairs.org

Going Green: The Challenges and the Solutions

KEVIN KELLY

> "The conservation of natural resources is the fundamental problem. Unless we solve that problem it will avail us little to solve all others."
>
> —Theodore Roosevelt

Roosevelt's words are a perfect summary of the problems facing automakers in relation to balancing the survival of their business and protecting the global environment. Lawmakers, scientists and activists around the globe are demanding automakers become more environmentally-conscious. Rising global temperatures, skyrocketing fuel costs and changing weather patterns are all held up as the payback for years of neglecting the environment and of the production and use of inefficient vehicles that are designed to stoke egos more than the ecosystem. While the auto industry itself is not solely to blame for the world's changing environment—livestock emit more dangerous greenhouse gas emissions than all of the vehicles on the planet and commercial buildings and homes are notorious energy wasters—the massive visibility of the automobile and ever-clogging roadways make it an easy target.

Driving Forces

Automakers are not known for their responsiveness when it comes to meeting the demands of environmentalists. This resistance has resulted in lawmakers and regulators forcing the hand of the industry to become more conscious of the impacts the automobile poses on the environment.

In the U.S., pressure has been placed on the industry by both state and federal governments. California is leading the way on when it comes to state action. The California Air Resources Board (CARB), established in 1967, has taken up the mantle by passing regulations to reduce automobile carbon dioxide (CO_2) emission levels by 22% from the 2002 fleet average by the '09 model year—equal to 323 g/mi. The regulation further requires

vehicles to achieve a more stringent 205 g/mi average by 2016—a 30% reduction from the '09 levels. Taking a page from California's rule book, New York, Rhode Island, Massachusetts, Connecticut, New Jersey, and Maine have all decided to adopt similar requirements. On the national level, Congress has finalized plans to increase the Corporate Average Fuel Economy (CAFE) standard to 35 mpg by 2020, from the current 27.5 mpg average for passenger cars and 20.7 mpg for light-trucks.

Similarly, European regulators are addressing vehicle emissions with Euro 5 standards, which go into effect in 2009 for vehicles on sale in the '11 model year. The regulation calls for diesel vehicles—which account for more than 50% of the European light-duty vehicle market—to achieve carbon monoxide (CO) output levels of 500 mg/km, along with NOx emission levels of 60 mg/km—a 24% reduction from current Euro 4 standards—with particulate matter output (diesels produce soot and aerosols including ash and metallic abrasion particulates, as well as sulfates and silicates) limited to 5 mg/km—an 80% reduction from Euro 4 standards. Gasoline-powered vehicles must achieve CO targets of 1,000 mg/km, with total hydrocarbon outputs set at 100 mg/km and NOx output capped at 60 mg/km—a 25% reduction from Euro 4. The European Commission is currently drafting rules for Euro 6, slated to take effect in the '15 model year, which is likely to include a 50% reduction in passenger vehicle emissions from Euro 5, along with diesel NOx and hydrocarbon emissions capped at 170 kg/km. Beyond just looking at tailpipe emission, European regulators will require automakers to design their vehicles to support a target of 95% recyclability by weight by 2015.

Social Pressures Build

The auto industry is feeling pressure from consumers to develop higher-mileage vehicles, particularly in light of rising gas prices. According to the Bureau of Labor Statistics, the average U.S. consumer is expected to shell out an additional 12% for gasoline in 2007, while average hourly earnings are increasing at a rate of only 3.5%, meaning, consumers are finding a bigger portion of their budget going out the tailpipe. The situation does not bode well for automakers, especially those relying on big trucks and SUVs to support their bottom lines. It's not only pocket book pressures influencing consumers. From news reports about seemingly aberrant weather patterns to films like An Inconvenient Truth and Happy Feet, people are learning more about the environment than ever before. Scientists are also taking their message directly to the public as the latest report from the United Nations Intergovernmental Panel on Climate Change—declaring the temperature of the Earth has increased by 0.74°C from 1906 to 2005, along with a 1.8 mm/yr. rise in sea levels from 1961 to present—has been debated in print, on television and radio. Former U.S. Vice President Al Gore has become household celebrity through his relentless raising of concern over global warming. "There's a growing awareness of climate change and the rapid availability of information is driving this change in mindset," says Jacquelyn Ottman, who has been advising the U.S. Government and Fortune 500 companies on responding to the environmental movement for more than 20 year as the president of J. Ottman Consulting (www.greenmarketing.com).

Environment = Massive Commitment[2]

Although the U.S. auto industry—which has lost more than $20 billion since 2005—is developing alternative-fuel vehicles and improving the efficiency of plants and building operations, there is a general failure in developing a holistic commitment to sustainability throughout entire organizations, from the most senior executives down to the plant floor. The necessity to improve the image and performance of the auto industry in the area of sustainability cannot be accomplished in the short term, nor can it be the responsibility of engineering, manufacturing or design alone. It's time to embrace sustainable innovation as a core competency, aimed at changing the mindset toward improving the environmental impact of the entire industry. Suppliers also must become responsive to the needs of OEMs when it comes to sustainability, making sure their own operations are energy and resource efficient. If the industry fails to meet the challenge, the pressures will only get more pronounced. A recent study from McKinsey & Co. (www.mckinsey.com) projects annual greenhouse gas emissions in the U.S. will rise 35% by 2030 to 9.7 gigatons. Of that, the transportation sector, which contributes 2.1 gigatons each year, is expected to grow by 1.3% to 2.8 gigatons.

When thinking along the lines of sustainable innovation, automakers must change the way they balance "green" with the bottom line. The auto industry seems to lack the financial foresight to take advantage of long-term savings and goodwill that comes with being green. "We need to have a one-year payback," Tom Neelands, director of GM's Worldwide Facilities Group, Energy and Utility Services, responds when asked how GM weighs investment decisions in green technology at the plant and facility level. That short-term outlook, unfortunately, is not uncommon in the industry, and it is something that needs to be addressed. Andrew Hobbs, director of the Environmental Quality office at Ford, says his company is trying to change the way financing of green technologies are handled: "One of the

things we're trying to convince the financial community to do is look at the long-term liability. We find we can make a great business case for some technologies when we think about the potential liability of not having them five, ten, or fifteen years from now."

Little Things Mean a Lot

The answers to solving the complexities of sustainability will not be solved by a silver bullet. Most progress will be made in incremental steps across all facets of each organization. Simple things, like switching to the use of compact fluorescent or LED lighting systems in office buildings, or turning off all computers and electronic equipment at the end of the workday, can make notable differences when they are added up. On the engineering side, close scrutiny of vehicle and component weight, powertrain and transmission optimization along with development of hydrogen and electric drive systems, all play critical roles in helping the auto industry gain regulatory compliance and share of consumer mind when it comes to sustainability.

Vehicle design is playing an increasingly vital role in the development of green vehicles. Designers must not only develop exteriors that look jaw-dropping, but they must also pay attention to the aerodynamic performance of their designs, particularly as the industry tries to squeeze every minute mile per gallon gain out of each vehicle. Designers will also have to utilize new materials in an effort to reduce the overall weight of the vehicle, again a key demand when it comes to improving overall efficiency. One of the materials that will find more application is aluminum, due to its inherent strength and reduced weight compared to traditional steel. Aluminum's formability is another benefit. In order to fully optimize the benefits of aluminum, however, designers and engineers will have to look beyond the skin of the vehicle for maximum optimization. According to a study by the Massachusetts Institute of Technology, the body-in-white accounts for 27% of the total weight of the vehicle, providing enormous potential when it comes to improved weight efficiency. Moving from a traditional unibody to a space frame design could help optimize weight reduction and vehicle rigidity. Space frame designs have been used in low volume, niche applications for several years—Audi is the most notable proponent of the technology. Making complex rails that maximize the benefits of improved aerodynamics can be better accomplished through space frame construction. Aluminum has failed to gain mass acceptance because of its higher raw material cost compared to traditional steel, but looking at material selection through the approach of sustainable innovation and a holistic systems approach could change the perception of its total cost in the near future. However, steel producers have developed a range of strong, lightweight materials, so the hurdles for aluminum will continue to be set high.

The use of natural materials is likely to expand in design studios as vehicle recyclability pressures build. Ford currently uses soy-based foam in the seats of its Mustang and plans to expand use of the material into other areas of its vehicle, including structural applications in A-pillars. Likewise, the company is studying ways to use natural fiber materials, such as coconut

Ford's Environmental Focus

Ford is taking a step-by-step approach to meeting the green challenge. And unlike other automakers that are taking a "moon shot" approach to trying to create environmental technologies, Ford is working toward making the millions of cars and trucks it builds more fuel efficient through cost-effective, common sense approaches. "We're on this path for a long time and it's a long-term commitment and it is a commitment that is best served not by technologies that you can provide in the tens or twenties or even thousands; we need plans that work on millions of vehicles and that means these plans need to be affordable and the infrastructure needs to be in place to support them," says Derrick Kuzak, Ford's group vice president of global product development.

In the near-term—from 2008 through 2012—Ford intends to improve the efficiency of its internal combustion engines through the addition of direct-injection and turbocharging technologies, resulting in a 10% to 20% improvement in fuel economy and better performance. "Fuel economy is at the top of the list for our consumers in terms of purchase considerations, and we have to respond to that quickly," Kuzak says, adding Ford also plans to launch a family of dual-clutch transmissions to support its new engine strategy and install electric power steering systems in nearly 90% of all vehicles. Once that's complete, Ford will concentrate on reducing the average weight of its vehicles anywhere from 250 to 750 lb. by doing things like using more lightweight materials, including high-strength steels, aluminum and composites. Kuzak predicts if Ford reaches its weight savings goals and can install smaller displacement engines in its vehicles with turbo technology, fuel economy can be improved as much as 50%. Beyond weight savings, Ford will improve battery and vehicle electrical systems management, along with improving vehicle aerodynamic performance. "At the same time we will continue to progress on hybrids. We have already committed to a plug-in hybrid," Kuzak says. Further down the road—beyond 2020—Ford plans to increase electric drive systems in its vehicle. Kuzak suggests that by then, the nature of powertrains will be different: "Now the high volume becomes plug-in hybrids, or fuel cells or hydrogen-powered internal-combustion engines. We don't know which of them will win, but they will all play a role." And at that point in time, Ford will make its high-volume moves.

All of these technologies will help boost Ford's green status, but it still remains critical the company develop products that customers demand. "If our products are not relevant, we are not supporting sustainability from an economic standpoint. The most important part of sustainability is having relevant products going forward and as customers needs change we realize we need to change," says Nancy Gioia, director of Ford's sustainable mobility technology and hybrid vehicle programs group. Building green products that customers aren't interested in is possibly less environmental than not having them at all.

---

fiber, for bumper supports and interior trim pieces. These materials are easier to recycle and take less energy to produce than petroleum-based plastics. Besides recyclability benefits, using green materials as visual cues on vehicle interior and exterior applications can help boost the "environmental" image of a particular model. Chrysler, for example, is studying using bamboo and cork materials in future interiors. "If the appearance is a positive and the cost is a positive, there is no reason we shouldn't use those materials," says Brandon Faurote, head of Chrysler's advance exterior and interior design group.

Being Green Italian Style

Improved fuel efficiency is hardly something you'd expect to see on the radar at one of the most famous high-performance car brands, but Ferrari isn't taking a backseat to the high-volume producers. The company plans to improve the efficiency of its future cars with a target of reducing fuel consumption by 40% by 2012 and reducing vehicle CO_2 emissions from 400g/km to 280–300 g/km. The Mille Chili (Italian for 1,000 kg—the target weight of the vehicle) concept provides a glimpse into plans for making its cars more efficient, complete with active aerodynamics via openings in the underbody that change size and shape, depending on vehicle speed. The chassis and bodywork are constructed from carbon fiber and composite materials; low rolling resistance tires provide added efficiency.

Beyond just looking at the vehicle, there are other approaches. Ferrari's owner, Fiat, has tasked its engineers with changing the way consumers interpret how their driving impacts the environment. The automaker has developed EcoDrive, a computer software program developed by Microsoft that records vehicle CO_2 emissions output and fuel economy on a USB key. The key can be plugged into a PC where the software will analyze the performance of the driver and provide useful tips on how to improve fuel economy and lower harmful emissions by minor changes to driving behavior.

Green Factories

Manufacturing's role is probably most crucial in helping to improve the environmental performance of the industry. The hundreds of millions of dollars spent retrofitting and upgrading assembly, stamping and powertrain facilities provide more than ample opportunity for the industry to achieve significant financial gains when it comes to being green. Clay Nesler, vice president of Global Energy and Sustainability at Johnson Controls Building Efficiency division (www.jci.com), says it's critical for the auto industry to include sustainability as part of plant upgrade expenditures. But even on-going operations can provide advantages: "We find that the highest return on investment when it comes to building efficiencies is looking at maintenance of equipment and this requires little capital outlay, but provides

Green Beyond Automotive

The lengthy product development timeframes automakers face tends to put them behind other industries when it comes to designing products that take advantage of consumer eco-friendliness concerns. Here's what some other companies are doing:

- IBM (www.ibm.com) changed the way it applies acoustic foam to its computer panels by discontinuing the use of chemical-based adhesives and replacing them with dart-shaped connectors that hold the foam in place. This change not only helped IBM reduce the amount of greenhouse gas emissions in the production process through the elimination of the adhesive, it also provided for ease in recycling when the product reached the end of its lifecycle.
- Steelcase's (www.steelcase.com) Think office chair was designed with a focus on recycling. It can be disassembled with the use of a few hand tools in 5 minutes with 99% of its overall content able to head to the recycling heap.
- Intel's (www.intel.com) Haifa, Israel, server facility uses water to chill the room to keep the computer systems running at peak performance. Traditional practice would route the heated water at the end of the process to cooling towers to evaporate, but Intel uses the hot water to heat the adjacent buildings in the winter and provide hot water to the showers in the facility's gym.
- Sun Microsystems (www.sun.com) decided to take the LEED building concept one step further by eliminating office space altogether. As part of its Open Work program, employees can work from home if they choose. The program cut Sun's real estate costs by $67.8 million and prevented nearly 29,000 tons of CO_2 in 2006, alone.
- Otis Elevator's (www.otis.com) Gen2 lift replaces the outmoded steel cables used to lift the passenger cars with polyurethane-coated steel belts, resulting in a lubrication-free system that does not require an expensive machine room to operate. The technology also provides for regenerative drive, which returns electricity to the building when the elevator travels downward, resulting in an elevator that is 75% more efficient than traditional systems.
- Key Tech's (www.locknpop.com) Lock n' Pop water-based adhesive can be sprayed onto the bottom and top of boxes to secure them in place on top of pallets during shipping. Once they arrive at their destination, the boxes can be removed from the stacks without any damage. Lock n' Pop reduces harmful gas emissions emitted when producing or using traditional adhesives.

marked savings," he says, noting lighting is one area that provides quick returns with little outlay. According to the McKinsey study, lighting accounts for more than 19% of greenhouse gas emissions associated with buildings and retrofitting incandescent lighting systems with compact fluorescent or LED lighting systems can cut power consumption by as much as 12%.

The biggest area of potential benefit from a cost savings and emissions reduction perspective are paint shops, which represent 60 to 75% of total assembly facility operating costs, according to Gordon Harbison, Services and Solutions manager at Dürr Systems (www.durr.com/en/). Since paint shops use massive amounts of air to keep spray booths clean and compliant with tight climate control requirements, it's vital to find ways to reduce the amount of natural gas used to heat the air entering the booths. Dürr developed a system it installed at a few GM facilities using a process called "building-2-booth" where general shop ventilation, which is already climate controlled, is routed to the spray booth using the building itself as the duct work. The program is expected to result in saving an average of $4 per vehicle over traditional spray booth control processes with a reduction in harmful greenhouse gas emissions. Dürr is also working to promote the use of energy-curable coatings, which use ultraviolet light or electron beams to cure vehicle paint on bodies. Several pilots are being tested for use on spot repairs at the end of the assembly line and the results are promising, with less paint being discarded due to the fact that the paint does not begin to dry until it is hit with the light or beams. Using the process on full vehicle bodies has proven challenging because complex surfaces found on many vehicles cause light bending problems and uneven cures.

Providing power to the plant itself holds ample promise for reducing cost and improving efficiency. Johnson Controls' Nesler says automakers should look at using cogeneration for plant operations. Currently, most power plants vent the heat produced during electricity production through cooling towers directly into the atmosphere. Through cogeneration, the heat generated is used for climate control of the facility being powered, thus reducing the need for separate heating equipment that uses natural gas or other resources. Cogeneration plants can use multiple feedstocks to provide heat and electricity, including waste woodchips, straw or various biomass materials. "This becomes a very attractive option when you look at the rising costs of natural gas and other resources," Nesler says. Beyond cogeneration, automakers can also turn to the sun to power their facilities. While solar panels have been available for decades, the technology used to produce them is becoming more cost-effective. The cost of photovoltaic technology is expected to drop from $300 to $350 per megawatt-hour in 2005 to $90 per megawatt-hour in 2030, moving solar power penetration from a 0.5-gigawatt capacity in 2005 to 148 gigawatts in 2030, according to the McKinsey study. GM has installed photovoltaic panels on two of its parts warehouses in California under a unique business partnership with Constellation Energy (www.constellation.com), which designed, built and owns the arrays. GM agreed to a long-term contract to buy electricity generated from the solar systems, while any excess power is sent directly to the general power grid, where Constellation earns money from the state utility.

A holistic approach to green building has been developed by the U.S. Green Building Council (www.usgbc.org). Its Leadership in Energy and Environmental Design (LEED) building certification program awards points for satisfying specific building criteria in several categories: sustainable sites, water efficiency, energy & atmosphere, materials & resources, indoor environmental quality and innovation in design. Buildings are awarded either a certified, silver, gold or platinum certification level, depending on the points earned. LEED certification can be granted for existing facilities, with a focus on improved maintenance and upgrading of equipment over a set timeline. LEED has become vogue of late, with Toyota, GM, Honda and Ford being some of the biggest proponents of the program. Honda already certified two of its U.S. facilities—the Honda R&D central plant facility in Raymond, OH, and its Northwest Regional Center in Gresham, OR, at the Gold LEED level—and has plans to expand to two more facilities in 2008.

Unfamiliar Territory

Being green isn't rocket science, but it does require a significant change in thinking. Automakers should look beyond the dealer lots to see how they can truly reshape the image of the industry going forward because the pressures from environmental groups and regulators will not abate. "In the early 1990s we went through a period of 'green washing' where if you came out with one product you were green. Now, consumers know better," says green marketing expert Ottman. She suggests that auto execs may have to think as former IBM CEO Lou Gerstner did, when he changed the model from computer-maker to technology solution-provider. As urban centers get more densely populated, it may be time for the auto industry to look at itself as transportation solution providers. With more than 645 cities around the globe offering car sharing services to their residents, it may be beneficial for automakers to look at partnering with the companies that provide the shared vehicle services. What about the dealers and market share? No doubt they will shrink, but if one automaker takes the lead, there will likely be fast followers. Speaking of the automakers, Ottman says, "They have to be looking at these things in order to stay in the game long term—if they see the writing on the wall." The writing can no longer be ignored by those companies that want to survive.

From *Automotive Design and Production*, January 2008. Copyright © Gardner Publications, Inc., Cincinnati, Ohio. Reprinted by permission.

UNIT 5

The Future and International Business

Unit Selections

Key Points to Consider

- How do you think the evolving global demographics will change world trade? How do you think these changes will affect society? What is likely to be the impact on the developing world and the developed world?

- What do you think of the concept of the BRIC countries? Do you think Russia should be included? What about the N-11?

- What kind of companies and industries do you think will survive and prosper in the next 20, 30 or 50 years? What is likely to be their major characteristics?

- What kind of job do you think you will be doing and where do you think you will be working in the future? What do you think the chances are that you will be working outside your home country during your career? Would you be willing to work in another country if the pay was lower, but your standard of living was about equal because of price purchase parity?

Student Website
www.mhhe.com/cls

Internet References

Commission on the future of Worker-Management Relations
    www.dol.gov/sec/media/reports/dunllop/dunlop.htm
The Futurist
    www.wfs.org/futurist.htm
The Economist
    http://theeconomist.com
Virtual Library Demography and Population Studies
    http://vlib.org/development
Further information regarding these Websites may be found in this book's preface or online.

The world has changed. But, the question is where does the world go from here and how is that going to impact world trade. There are certainly trends that can be identified for the future. The first is the ascendancy of countries from the third world. People have identified the BRIC (Brazil, Russia, India and China) countries as the ones to watch in the future, but it would seem that one of the countries, Russia, may not be one of the ones to watch for the future. Russia is loosing population at the rate of about 1 million people per year and male life expectancy is on a par with many third-world countries. Rather than being on the ascent, Russia's fate would seem to be tied to the price of oil, and the political situation in the country remains unclear.

There are, however, countries that do bear watching in addition to Brazil, India and China, sometimes referred to as the N-11 (Bangladesh, Egypt, Indonesia, Iran, Korea, Mexico, Nigeria, Pakistan, the Philippines, Turkey and Vietnam). Indonesia, the largest Muslim country in the world and the forth largest country in terms of population, seems to have overcome decades of political corruption and strife and would now seem to be on the path to economic prosperity. Vietnam is now one of the fastest growing economies in the world, although from a very small base. In South America, Chile while not a member of the "N-11", has reconciled a recent history of political turmoil and appears to be on the way toward economic prosperity. All three of these countries have one thing in common in that they recently overcame periods of turmoil whether political, military or both. They are now coming out of that period and are on their way to developing mixed capitalist economies where individual effort is rewarded and economic growth is being experienced.

A definite trend in society that will certainly affect international business is the "The New Population Bomb: The Four Megatrents That Will Change the World". World demographics are certain to change over the next 50 years. In the developed world of the United States, Europe, and Japan, the percentage of the world's population is almost certain to decline and the actual number of people in many of the countries may also decline.

Probably, the most obvious example is Japan which has the highest life expectancy of almost any country in the world. It also has one of the lowest birth rates of any of the developed countries. This causes what demographers call an inverted pyramid where there are more people in the more senior age brackets than there are people in the younger age brackets. Seniors require more in the way of services, such as medical, and social than do healthy younger people. Unfortunately, it is the healthy younger people who have to pay for the services as the seniors have retired and are now living off their pensions and whatever social security like programs the government has in place. This is a problem faced to varying degrees by every developed country.

Conversely, in the developing world, while life expectancy is increasing, it still does not match that of the developed world, and the fertility rate (number of live births per woman of child bearing age), in some instances is as high as five, while in the developed world, in some countries, it is as low as 1.1. It means that, in some countries, in the developing world, the population

© Comstock/PunchStock RF

will triple in the next fifty years, while in the developed world, in some countries, the population could drop by half.

The population bomb will create problems for both the developed world and the developing world. For the developed world, the question is how will the promises that have been made to all of the citizens be kept? How will Social Security like programs and medical care be paid for as more and more people require more and more services that will have to be paid for by fewer and fewer people? As these programs start to take a larger share of the gross domestic product of the society, how much will be left over for the rest of the economy? How much will productivity in the society have to increase to cover these increases in cost just to stay even or expand the economy?

In the developing world, population explosion means that attempting to spread resources over a population pool that is expanding faster than the available resources is only going to lead to poverty and unrest. It means that these countries may never catch-up with the developed world. The only way that the developed world and the developing world can possibly deal with their respective problems is for people from the developing world to immigrate to the developed world. This will solve the problem of not having enough people to support the aging populations of the developed world and it will relieve the stress in the developing world of too many people attempting to live off too few resources. But, it also means that there will be significant changes in the developed world. Significant minorities will exist in societies that were once extremely homogeneous. Learning to deal with these new "citizens" is certain to stress the developed world.

Companies that are able to deal with this new developing future are the ones that will be investing in that future. Industries that will survive will be the ones that invest in research and development. As Mark Hennessy discusses in "The Enterprise of the Future," the industries that invest in research and development will be the ones that will probably be around for the foreseeable future. The ones that do not are likely to go the way of the buggy-whip.

Finally, learning to deal with the future global economy means learning. Education and training are not a once and done experience anymore and flexibility is the key to career success. It is a global economy and it is a global workforce. That means, to be successful, individuals must learn to be mobile and to be able to go where the work is, and where the work is may not necessarily be in their hometown, their home state or even their home country. For the past several hundred years people have come to North America in search of work. In the not too distant future, people may be leaving North America in search of work as discussed in "Finding a Job in the 21st Century."

The world has certainly changed. Dealing with these changes will be the challenge that will face everyone in the 21st Century. It is a new world: one with many challenges, many opportunities and many changes yet to come.

The New Population Bomb: The Four Megatrends That Will Change the World

JACK A. GOLDSTONE

Forty-two years ago, the biologist Paul Ehrlich warned in The Population Bomb that mass starvation would strike in the 1970s and 1980s, with the world's population growth outpacing the production of food and other critical resources. Thanks to innovations and efforts such as the "green revolution" in farming and the widespread adoption of family planning, Ehrlich's worst fears did not come to pass. In fact, since the 1970s, global economic output has increased and fertility has fallen dramatically, especially in developing countries.

The United Nations Population Division now projects that global population growth will nearly halt by 2050. By that date, the world's population will have stabilized at 9.15 billion people, according to the "medium growth" variant of the UN's authoritative population database World Population Prospects: The 2008 Revision. (Today's global population is 6.83 billion.) Barring a cataclysmic climate crisis or a complete failure to recover from the current economic malaise, global economic output is expected to increase by two to three percent per year, meaning that global income will increase far more than population over the next four decades.

But twenty-first-century international security will depend less on how many people inhabit the world than on how the global population is composed and distributed: where populations are declining and where they are growing, which countries are relatively older and which are more youthful, and how demographics will influence population movements across regions.

These elements are not well recognized or widely understood. A recent article in The Economist, for example, cheered the decline in global fertility without noting other vital demographic developments. Indeed, the same UN data cited by The Economist reveal four historic shifts that will fundamentally alter the world's population over the next four decades: the relative demographic weight of the world's developed countries will drop by nearly 25 percent, shifting economic power to the developing nations; the developed countries' labor forces will substantially age and decline, constraining economic growth in the developed world and raising the demand for immigrant workers; most of the world's expected population growth will increasingly be concentrated in today's poorest, youngest, and most heavily Muslim countries, which have a dangerous lack of quality education, capital, and employment opportunities; and, for the first time in history, most of the world's population will become urbanized, with the largest urban centers being in the world's poorest countries, where policing, sanitation, and health care are often scarce. Taken together, these trends will pose challenges every bit as alarming as those noted by Ehrlich. Coping with them will require nothing less than a major reconsideration of the world's basic global governance structures.

Europe's Reversal of Fortunes

At the beginning of the eighteenth century, approximately 20 percent of the world's inhabitants lived in Europe (including Russia). Then, with the Industrial Revolution, Europe's population boomed, and streams of European emigrants set off for the Americas. By the eve of World War I, Europe's population had more than quadrupled. In 1913, Europe had more people than China, and the proportion of the world's population living in Europe and the former European colonies of North America had risen to over 33 percent. But this trend reversed after World War I, as basic health care and sanitation began to spread to poorer countries. In Asia, Africa, and Latin America, people began to live longer, and birthrates remained high or fell only slowly. By 2003, the combined populations of Europe, the United States, and Canada accounted for just 17 percent of the global population. In 2050, this figure is expected to be just 12 percent—far less than it was in 1700. (These projections, moreover, might even understate the reality because they reflect the "medium growth" projection of the UN forecasts, which assumes that the fertility rates of developing countries will decline while those of developed countries will increase. In fact, many developed countries show no evidence of increasing fertility rates.) The West's relative decline is even more dramatic if one also considers changes in income. The Industrial Revolution made Europeans not only more numerous than they had been but also considerably richer per capita than others worldwide. According to the economic historian Angus Maddison, Europe, the United States, and Canada together produced about 32 percent of the world's GDP at the beginning of the nineteenth century. By 1950, that proportion had increased to a remarkable 68 percent of the world's total output (adjusted to reflect purchasing power parity).

This trend, too, is headed for a sharp reversal. The proportion of global GDP produced by Europe, the United States, and Canada fell from 68 percent in 1950 to 47 percent in 2003 and will decline even more steeply in the future. If the growth rate of per capita income (again, adjusted for purchasing power parity) between 2003 and 2050 remains as it was between 1973 and 2003—averaging 1.68 percent annually in Europe, the United States, and Canada and 2.47 percent annually in the rest of the world—then the combined GDP of Europe, the United States, and Canada will roughly double by 2050, whereas the GDP of the rest of the world will grow by a factor of five. The portion of global GDP produced by Europe, the United States, and Canada in 2050 will then be less than 30 percent—smaller than it was in 1820.

These figures also imply that an overwhelming proportion of the world's GDP growth between 2003 and 2050—nearly 80 percent—will occur outside of Europe, the United States, and Canada. By the middle of this century, the global middle class—those capable of purchasing durable consumer products, such as cars, appliances, and electronics—will increasingly be found in what is now considered the developing world. The World Bank has predicted that by 2030 the number of middle-class people in the developing world will be 1.2 billion—a rise of 200 percent since 2005. This means that the developing world's middle class alone will be larger than the total populations of Europe, Japan, and the United States combined. From now on, therefore, the main driver of global economic expansion will be the economic growth of newly industrialized countries, such as Brazil, China, India, Indonesia, Mexico, and Turkey.

Aging Pains

Part of the reason developed countries will be less economically dynamic in the coming decades is that their populations will become substantially older. The European countries, Canada, the United States, Japan, South Korea, and even China are aging at unprecedented rates. Today, the proportion of people aged 60 or older in China and South Korea is 12–15 percent. It is 15–22 percent in the European Union, Canada, and the United States and 30 percent in Japan. With baby boomers aging and life expectancy increasing, these numbers will increase dramatically. In 2050, approximately 30 percent of Americans, Canadians, Chinese, and Europeans will be over 60, as will more than 40 percent of Japanese and South Koreans.

Over the next decades, therefore, these countries will have increasingly large proportions of retirees and increasingly small proportions of workers. As workers born during the baby boom of 1945–65 are retiring, they are not being replaced by a new cohort of citizens of prime working age (15–59 years old).

Industrialized countries are experiencing a drop in their working-age populations that is even more severe than the overall slowdown in their population growth. South Korea represents the most extreme example. Even as its total population is projected to decline by almost 9 percent by 2050 (from 48.3

million to 44.1 million), the population of working-age South Koreans is expected to drop by 36 percent (from 32.9 million to 21.1 million), and the number of South Koreans aged 60 and older will increase by almost 150 percent (from 7.3 million to 18 million). By 2050, in other words, the entire working-age population will barely exceed the 60-and-older population. Although South Korea's case is extreme, it represents an increasingly common fate for developed countries. Europe is expected to lose 24 percent of its prime working-age population (about 120 million workers) by 2050, and its 60-and-older population is expected to increase by 47 percent. In the United States, where higher fertility and more immigration are expected than in Europe, the working-age population will grow by 15 percent over the next four decades—a steep decline from its growth of 62 percent between 1950 and 2010. And by 2050, the United States' 60-and-older population is expected to double.

All this will have a dramatic impact on economic growth, health care, and military strength in the developed world. The forces that fueled economic growth in industrialized countries during the second half of the twentieth century—increased productivity due to better education, the movement of women into the labor force, and innovations in technology—will all likely weaken in the coming decades. College enrollment boomed after World War II, a trend that is not likely to recur in the twenty-first century; the extensive movement of women into the labor force also was a one-time social change; and the technological change of the time resulted from innovators who created new products and leading-edge consumers who were willing to try them out—two groups that are thinning out as the industrialized world's population ages.

Overall economic growth will also be hampered by a decline in the number of new consumers and new households. When developed countries' labor forces were growing by 0.5–1.0 percent per year, as they did until 2005, even annual increases in real output per worker of just 1.7 percent meant that annual economic growth totaled 2.2–2.7 percent per year. But with the labor forces of many developed countries (such as Germany, Hungary, Japan, Russia, and the Baltic states) now shrinking by 0.2 percent per year and those of other countries (including Austria, the Czech Republic, Denmark, Greece, and Italy) growing by less than 0.2 percent per year, the same 1.7 percent increase in real output per worker yields only 1.5–1.9 percent annual overall growth. Moreover, developed countries will be lucky to keep productivity growth at even that level; in many developed countries, productivity is more likely to decline as the population ages.

A further strain on industrialized economies will be rising medical costs: as populations age, they will demand more health care for longer periods of time. Public pension schemes for aging populations are already being reformed in various industrialized countries—often prompting heated debate. In theory, at least, pensions might be kept solvent by increasing the retirement age, raising taxes modestly, and phasing out benefits for the wealthy. Regardless, the number of 80- and 90-year-olds—who are unlikely to work and highly likely to require nursing-home and other expensive care—will rise dramatically. And even if 60- and 70-year-olds remain active and employed, they will require procedures and medications—hip replacements, kidney transplants, blood-pressure treatments—to sustain their health in old age.

All this means that just as aging developed countries will have proportionally fewer workers, innovators, and consumerist young households, a large portion of those countries' remaining economic growth will have to be diverted to pay for the medical bills and pensions of their growing elderly populations. Basic services, meanwhile, will be increasingly costly because fewer young workers will be available for strenuous and labor-intensive jobs. Unfortunately, policymakers seldom reckon with these potentially disruptive effects of otherwise welcome developments, such as higher life expectancy.

Youth and Islam in the Developing World

Even as the industrialized countries of Europe, North America, and Northeast Asia will experience unprecedented aging this century, fast-growing countries in Africa, Latin America, the Middle East, and Southeast Asia will have exceptionally youthful populations. Today, roughly nine out of ten children under the age of 15 live in developing countries. And these are the countries that will continue to have the world's highest birthrates. Indeed, over 70 percent of the world's population growth between now and 2050 will occur in 24 countries, all of which are classified by the World Bank as low income or lower-middle income, with an average per capita income of under $3,855 in 2008.

Many developing countries have few ways of providing employment to their young, fast-growing populations. Would-be laborers, therefore, will be increasingly attracted to the labor markets of the aging developed countries of Europe, North America, and Northeast Asia. Youthful immigrants from nearby regions with high unemployment—Central America, North Africa, and Southeast Asia, for example—will be drawn to those vital entry-level and manual-labor jobs that sustain advanced economies: janitors, nursing-home aides, bus drivers, plumbers, security guards, farm workers, and the like. Current levels of immigration from developing to developed countries are paltry compared to those that the forces of supply and demand might soon create across the world.

These forces will act strongly on the Muslim world, where many economically weak countries will continue to experience dramatic population growth in the decades ahead. In 1950, Bangladesh, Egypt, Indonesia, Nigeria, Pakistan, and Turkey had a combined population of 242 million. By 2009, those six countries were the world's most populous Muslim-majority countries and had a combined population of 886 million. Their populations are continuing to grow and indeed are expected to increase by 475 million between now and 2050—during which time, by comparison, the six most populous developed countries are projected to gain only 44 million inhabitants. Worldwide, of the 48 fastest-growing countries today—those with annual population growth of two percent or more—28 are majority Muslim or have Muslim minorities of 33 percent or more.

It is therefore imperative to improve relations between Muslim and Western societies. This will be difficult given that many Muslims live in poor communities vulnerable to radical appeals and many see the West as antagonistic and militaristic. In the 2009 Pew Global Attitudes Project survey, for example, whereas 69 percent of those Indonesians and Nigerians surveyed reported viewing the United States favorably, just 18 percent of those polled in Egypt, Jordan, Pakistan, and Turkey (all U.S. allies) did. And in 2006, when the Pew survey last asked detailed questions about Muslim-Western relations, more than half of the respondents in Muslim countries characterized those relations as bad and blamed the West for this state of affairs.

But improving relations is all the more important because of the growing demographic weight of poor Muslim countries and the attendant increase in Muslim immigration, especially to Europe from North Africa and the Middle East. (To be sure, forecasts that Muslims will soon dominate Europe are outlandish: Muslims compose just three to ten percent of the population in the major European countries today, and this proportion will at most double by midcentury.) Strategists worldwide must consider that the world's young are becoming concentrated in those countries least prepared to educate and employ them, including some Muslim states. Any resulting poverty, social tension, or ideological radicalization could have disruptive effects in many corners of the world. But this need not be the case; the healthy immigration of workers to the developed world and the movement of capital to the developing world, among other things, could lead to better results.

Urban Sprawl

Exacerbating twenty-first-century risks will be the fact that the world is urbanizing to an unprecedented degree. The year 2010 will likely be the first time in history that a majority of the world's people live in cities rather than in the countryside. Whereas less than 30 percent of the world's population was urban in 1950, according to UN projections, more than 70 percent will be by 2050.

Lower-income countries in Asia and Africa are urbanizing especially rapidly, as agriculture becomes less labor intensive and as employment opportunities shift to the industrial and service sectors. Already, most of the world's urban agglomerations—Mumbai (population 20.1 million), Mexico City (19.5 million), New Delhi (17 million), Shanghai (15.8 million), Calcutta (15.6 million), Karachi (13.1 million), Cairo (12.5 million), Manila (11.7 million), Lagos (10.6 million), Jakarta (9.7 million)—are found in low-income countries. Many of these countries have multiple cities with over one million residents each: Pakistan has eight, Mexico 12, and China more than 100. The UN projects that the urbanized proportion of sub-Saharan Africa will nearly double between 2005 and 2050, from 35 percent (300 million people) to over 67 percent (1 billion). China, which is roughly 40 percent urbanized today, is expected to be 73 percent urbanized by 2050; India, which is less than 30 percent urbanized today, is expected to be 55 percent urbanized by 2050. Overall, the world's urban population is expected to grow by 3 billion people by 2050.

This urbanization may prove destabilizing. Developing countries that urbanize in the twenty-first century will have far lower per capita incomes than did many industrial countries when they first urbanized. The United States, for example, did not reach 65 percent urbanization until 1950, when per capita income was nearly $13,000 (in 2005 dollars). By contrast, Nigeria, Pakistan, and the Philippines, which are approaching similar levels of urbanization, currently have per capita incomes of just $1,800–$4,000 (in 2005 dollars).

According to the research of Richard Cincotta and other political demographers, countries with younger populations are especially prone to civil unrest and are less able to create or sustain democratic institutions. And the more heavily urbanized, the more such countries are likely to experience Dickensian poverty and anarchic violence. In good times, a thriving economy might keep urban residents employed and governments flush with sufficient resources to meet their needs. More often, however, sprawling and impoverished cities are vulnerable to crime lords, gangs, and petty rebellions. Thus, the rapid urbanization of the developing world in the decades ahead might bring, in exaggerated form, problems similar to those that urbanization brought to nineteenth-century Europe. Back then, cyclical employment, inadequate policing, and limited sanitation and education often spawned widespread labor strife, periodic violence, and sometimes—as in the 1820s, the 1830s, and 1848—even revolutions.

International terrorism might also originate in fast-urbanizing developing countries (even more than it already does). With their neighborhood networks, access to the Internet and digital communications technology, and concentration of valuable targets, sprawling cities offer excellent opportunities for recruiting, maintaining, and hiding terrorist networks.

Defusing the Bomb

Averting this century's potential dangers will require sweeping measures. Three major global efforts defused the population bomb of Ehrlich's day: a commitment by governments and nongovernmental organizations to control reproduction rates; agricultural advances, such as the green revolution and the spread of new technology; and a vast increase in international trade, which globalized markets and thus allowed developing countries to export foodstuffs in exchange for seeds, fertilizers, and machinery, which in turn helped them boost production. But today's population bomb is the product less of absolute growth in the world's population than of changes in its age and distribution. Policymakers must therefore adapt today's global governance institutions to the new realities of the aging of the industrialized world, the concentration of the world's economic and population growth in developing countries, and the increase in international immigration.

During the Cold War, Western strategists divided the world into a "First World," of democratic industrialized countries; a "Second World," of communist industrialized countries; and a "Third World," of developing countries. These strategists focused chiefly on deterring or managing conflict between the First and the Second Worlds and on launching proxy wars and diplomatic initiatives to attract Third World countries into the First World's camp. Since the end of the Cold War, strategists have largely abandoned this three-group division and have tended to believe either that the United States, as the sole superpower, would maintain a Pax Americana or that the world would become multipolar, with the United States, Europe, and China playing major roles.

Unfortunately, because they ignore current global demographic trends, these views will be obsolete within a few decades. A better approach would be to consider a different three-world order, with a new First World of the aging industrialized nations of North America, Europe, and Asia's Pacific Rim (including Japan, Singapore, South Korea, and Taiwan, as well as China after 2030, by which point the one-child policy will have produced significant aging); a Second World comprising fast-growing and economically dynamic countries with a healthy mix of young and old inhabitants (such as Brazil, Iran, Mexico, Thailand, Turkey, and Vietnam, as well as China until 2030); and a Third World of fast-growing, very young, and increasingly urbanized countries with poorer economies and often weak governments. To cope with the instability that will likely arise from the new Third World's urbanization, economic strife, lawlessness, and potential terrorist activity, the aging industrialized nations of the new First World must build effective alliances with the growing powers of the new Second World and together reach out to Third World nations. Second World powers will be pivotal in the twenty-first century not just because they will drive economic growth and consume technologies and other products engineered in the First World; they will also be central to international security and cooperation. The realities of religion, culture, and geographic proximity mean that any peaceful and productive engagement by the First World of Third World countries will have to include the open cooperation of Second World countries.

Strategists, therefore, must fundamentally reconsider the structure of various current global institutions. The G-8, for example, will likely become obsolete as a body for making global economic policy. The G-20 is already becoming increasingly important, and this is less a short-term consequence of the ongoing global financial crisis than the beginning of the necessary recognition that Brazil, China, India, Indonesia, Mexico, Turkey, and others are becoming global economic powers. International institutions will not retain their legitimacy if they exclude the world's fastest-growing and most economically dynamic countries. It is essential, therefore, despite European concerns about the potential effects on immigration, to take steps such as admitting Turkey into the European Union. This would add youth and economic dynamism to the EU—and would prove that Muslims are welcome to join Europeans as equals in shaping a free and prosperous future. On the other hand, excluding Turkey from the EU could lead to hostility not only on the part of Turkish citizens, who are expected to number 100 million by 2050, but also on the part of Muslim populations worldwide.

NATO must also adapt. The alliance today is composed almost entirely of countries with aging, shrinking populations and relatively slow-growing economies. It is oriented toward the Northern Hemisphere and holds on to a Cold War structure that cannot adequately respond to contemporary threats. The young and increasingly populous countries of Africa, the Middle East, Central Asia, and South Asia could mobilize insurgents much more easily than NATO could mobilize the troops it would need if it were called on to stabilize those countries. Long-standing NATO members should, therefore—although it would require atypical creativity and flexibility—consider the logistical and demographic advantages of inviting into the alliance countries such as Brazil and Morocco, rather than countries such as Albania. That this seems far-fetched does not minimize the imperative that First World countries begin including large and strategic Second and Third World powers in formal international alliances.

The case of Afghanistan—a country whose population is growing fast and where NATO is currently engaged—illustrates the importance of building effective global institutions. Today, there are 28 million Afghans; by 2025, there will be 45 million; and by 2050, there will be close to 75 million. As nearly 20 million additional Afghans are born over the next 15 years, NATO will have an opportunity to help Afghanistan become reasonably stable, self-governing, and prosperous. If NATO's efforts fail and the Afghans judge that NATO intervention harmed their interests, tens of millions of young Afghans will become more hostile to the West. But if they come to think that NATO's involvement benefited their society, the West will have tens of millions of new friends. The example might then motivate the approximately one billion other young Muslims growing up in low-income countries over the next four decades to look more kindly on relations between their countries and the countries of the industrialized West.

Creative Reforms at Home

The aging industrialized countries can also take various steps at home to promote stability in light of the coming demographic trends. First, they should encourage families to have more children. France and Sweden have had success providing child care, generous leave time, and financial allowances to families with young children. Yet there is no consensus among policymakers—and certainly not among demographers—about what policies best encourage fertility.

More important than unproven tactics for increasing family size is immigration. Correctly managed, population movement can benefit developed and developing countries alike. Given the dangers of young, underemployed, and unstable populations in developing countries, immigration to developed countries can provide economic opportunities for the ambitious and serve as a safety valve for all. Countries that embrace immigrants, such as the United States, gain economically by having willing laborers and greater entrepreneurial spirit. And countries with high levels of emigration (but not so much that they experience so-called brain drains) also benefit because emigrants often send remittances home or return to their native countries with valuable education and work experience.

One somewhat daring approach to immigration would be to encourage a reverse flow of older immigrants from developed to developing countries. If older residents of developed countries took their retirements along the southern coast of the Mediterranean or in Latin America or Africa, it would greatly reduce the strain on their home countries' public entitlement systems. The developing countries involved, meanwhile, would benefit because caring for the elderly and providing retirement and leisure services is highly labor intensive. Relocating a portion of these activities to developing countries would provide employment and valuable training to the young, growing populations of the Second and Third Worlds.

This would require developing residential and medical facilities of First World quality in Second and Third World countries. Yet even this difficult task would be preferable to the status quo, by which low wages and poor facilities lead to a steady drain of medical and nursing talent from developing to developed countries. Many residents of developed countries who desire cheaper medical procedures already practice medical tourism today, with India, Singapore, and Thailand being the most common destinations. (For example, the international consulting firm Deloitte estimated that 750,000 Americans traveled abroad for care in 2008.)

Never since 1800 has a majority of the world's economic growth occurred outside of Europe, the United States, and Canada. Never have so many people in those regions been over 60 years old. And never have low-income countries' populations been so young and so urbanized. But such will be the world's demography in the twenty-first century. The strategic and economic policies of the twentieth century are obsolete, and it is time to find new ones.

References

Goldstone, Jack A. "The new population bomb: the four megatrends that will change the world." *Foreign Affairs* 89.1 (2010): 31. *General OneFile*. Web. 23 Jan. 2010. <http://0-find.galegroup.com.www.consuls.org/gps/start.do?prodId=IPS&userGroupName=a30wc>.

The Man Who Named the Future

GILLIAN TETT

On the desk of Jim O'Neill, chief economist for Goldman Sachs, stand four filmsy flags. They look out of place among the expensive computer terminals of the investment bank's plush London office, like leftovers of a child's geography homework or cheap mementos from backpacking trips to exotic parts of the world. But these flags hint at a more interesting story—of the latest way in which money and ideas are reshaping the world. The small scraps of fabric are pennants for big countries: Brazil, Russia, India and China. And a decade ago, O'Neill decided to start thinking of them as a group—which he gave the acronym Bric.

It was a simple mental prop. The bolder move was to predict–publicly, and in Goldman's name—that by 2041 (later revised to 2039, then 2032) the Brics would overtake the six largest western economies in terms of economic might. The four flags would come to represent the pillars of the 21st-century economy.

At the time, many scoffed at this idea. The predictions turned conventional western wisdom on its head; and O'Neill hardly seemed an obvious champion of the concept. A large man with working-class Manchester roots, he does not exude the aura of any globetrotting elite. His office is decorated with splashes of cherry red memorabilia from Manchester United Football Club, and he still speaks with the thick, flattened vowels of his childhood. Indeed, when O'Neill coined the term Bric in 2001, he had never properly visited three of the four countries (the exception was China), and spoke none of their languages. Yet, notwithstanding those unlikely beginnings, in the past decade, Bric has become a near ubiquitous financial term, shaping how a generation of investors, financiers and policymakers view the emerging markets: companies ranging from Nissan to media group WPP have developed Brics business strategies; several dozen financial institutions now run Brics funds; business schools have launched Brics courses; and this April Phillips de Pury will be holding a Brics-themed auction. "The Brics concept . . . that O'Neill created . . . has become such a strong brand," says Felipe Goes, adviser to the mayor of Rio de Janeiro, who is organising the first Brics think-tank.

O'Neill speaks in smaller spheres for a moment: "It has transformed my life," he says.

To some critics, the fuss about Brics is overblown. The term is hype, spin, from a bank and banking industry accustomed to disguising such guff as genuinely new ideas and concepts—the better to profit from them. "Brics is really just marketing—it's nonsense!" says Charles Dumas, a London-based economist who disputes many elements of the Brics concept, such as the idea that these countries will keep growing inexorably into the future. Others are more cynical still, arguing that Goldmans Sachs has used the concept to extend its global power, and thus turbo-charge its formidable profit-making machine. O'Neill denies this latter accusation. "I really believe in this idea of Brics, that this idea can make the world a better place—it's what drives me," he says.

But even if Brics is self-interested spin, such spin—an idea in itself, really—can sometimes take on a life of its own, beyond what its creators expect or even hope for. By creating the word Brics, O'Neill has redrawn powerbrokers' cognitive map, helping them to articulate a fundamental shift of influence away from the western world. And if you believe that the way humans think and speak not only reflects reality, but can shape its future path too, then this Brics tag has itself come both to reflect and drive the change—albeit from some unlikely beginnings.

The way O'Neill, 52, tells the tale of how he developed the Brics—and he is a born raconteur—starts, a touch melodramatically, on the day terrorists flew aircraft into the World Trade Centre and Pentagon, killing thousands of people.

The son of a postman, O'Neill grew up in south Manchester, where he studied at the local comprehensive (Oasis's Noel and Liam Gallagher were pupils there too, albeit later) and spent much of his time playing football. After school, he decided to study at Sheffield University, partly because it offered easy access to watch Manchester United. (Today, he has season tickets at Old Trafford, and leaves spare tickets behind the bar at a local pub, for childhood friends to use.) During his time there, between "getting drunk and playing football", O'Neill discovered a passion for economics. And after completing a doctorate in the subject, he worked as a foreign exchange analyst at a series of City banks, eventually joining Goldman in 1995 as co-head of economics. In the summer of 2001, Gavyn Davies, O'Neill's highly respected co-chief, announced his departure–leaving O'Neill the sole leader, and under huge pressure to perform. "I thought: 'Oh my god, I have got to put my imprint on this department,' he recalls. 'I was searching for a theme and a new idea.'"

Inspiration came—a bittersweet gift. On September 11, as the first aircraft approached the Twin Towers, where he had delivered a lecture a few days earlier, O'Neill was hosting a global video conference call. Halfway through, the New York faces vanished from the screen. O'Neill later learnt the staff had been safely evacuated from their offices, but he still reeled in shock at the events. In the days that followed, his mind began to whir. As a foreign exchange analyst, O'Neill had always been a passionate advocate of globalisation, and was fascinated by the rising power of Asia. And to him, the horror in Manhattan was a powerful demonstration of exactly why the non-western world was starting to matter more and more—albeit in a negative way. However, O'Neill also believed—or hoped—that this shift in power could be seen in a more positive sense, too. "What 9/11 told me was that there was no way that globalisation was going to be Americanisation in the future—nor should it be," he says. "In order for globalisation to advance, it had to be accepted by more people . . . but not by imposing the dominant American social and philosophical beliefs and structures."

In practical terms, O'Neill decided, that meant economists had to look more closely at how non-western economies could wield more power in the future. As he scoured the globe, he became increasingly fascinated by four countries: Brazil, India, Russia and China. In one sense, the four seemed disparate, separated geographically and culturally; they had never acted as a bloc in any way, never conceived of themselves as a unit. Yet what they all shared in 2001 were large populations, underdeveloped economies and governments that appeared willing to embrace global markets and some elements of globalisation. To O'Neill, these characteristics made them natural sisters: they all had the potential for rapid future growth.

Excited, he tried to work out how to label this bunch. Since China was easily the largest, it made sense to put its name first. "Lloyd Blankfein [Goldman Sachs's chief executive] always teases me about it—he says I should have called the group the Cribs," O'Neill recalls. But O'Neill thought that a word linked to babies would seem patronising. So on November 30 2001, he launched his Big Idea: Goldman Sachs's Global Economic Paper?#66, "Building Better Global Economic Brics". He predicted, soberly, that "over the next 10 years, the weight of the Brics and especially China in world GDP will grow"—and warned, perhaps a little less soberly, that "in line with these prospects, world policymaking forums should be reorganised" to give more power to the group he had now dubbed Brics.

The paper immediately sparked interest among Goldman Sachs's corporate clients, particularly those already selling—or trying to sell—consumer products to the emerging markets. "I found the Bric thing fascinating right from the start," says Martin Sorrell, chief executive of WPP. "It tapped into what we had been already discussing." But to many investors and bankers—including some inside Goldman Sachs—it all seemed rather fanciful, particularly given that countries such as Brazil had recently experienced hyperinflation. "When I first spoke at a big group in Rio [after the paper was published], it was to around 1,000 investors from all of Latin America," recalls

O'Neill. "The guy who was introducing me whispered in my ear as he went to the podium, 'we all know that the only reason the B is there is because without it there is no acronym.'"

But O'Neill kept discussing the concept with colleagues and in 2003 his team produced the next offering: a paper called "Dreaming with Brics: The Path to 2050". It boldly declared that by 2039 the Brics group could overtake the largest western economies in scale. "The list of the world's 10 largest economies may look quite different in 2050," it said. That prediction launched O'Neill's team into what he calls Briclife. Within days, Goldman economists were flooded with e-mails from executives at companies ranging from mobile telecoms group Vodafone to miner BHP Billiton to Ikea and Nissan. By luck—or insight—O'Neill had produced this tag just as many western businesses were trying to hone their strategies to sell products to the non-western world, or to use regions such as China as a manufacturing base. And in a world where corporate boards face information overload, Brics suddenly provided executives with a snappy way of discussing strategy. Better still, unlike phrases such as "emerging markets" or "developing world", Brics did not sound patronising, or unpromising; it was neutral, strong, politically correct.

Soon rivals, such as HSBC and Deutsche Bank fund unit DWS, were launching dedicated investment funds marketed under the label of Brics. "We asked our lawyers if we could trademark the word Brics, but they said not—apparently it's not a product," O'Neill recalls. Steadily, the brand spread, taking on a life beyond Goldman. Initially, most hedge funds ignored the concept as marketing hype. But as investors began to purchase assets specifically linked to the rise of Brics, the hedge-funders recognised that the way that China, say, was making cars could affect demand for Brazilian copper. New correlations were developing in asset prices, amid strong investment flows (since 2003, the Brics stock markets have risen from 2 to 9 per cent of global market capitalisation, and O'Neill forecasts they will represent almost 50 per cent of global market capitalisation in 2050).

Unsurprisingly, O'Neill's rivals started to snipe. Some economists said it was ridiculous to make forecasts as far out as 2050, particularly since many of O'Neill's projections seemed to involve extrapolating current growth on a straight line. Others took issue with the idea that the four Bric countries could–or should–be described as a group. "Economically, financially and politically, China overshadows and will continue to overshadow the other Brics," analysts at Deutsche Bank argued. Some banks tried to ban their employees from using the B word. "Why the hell should we do Goldman's marketing for it?" says the chief executive of one of the world's biggest investment banks. Meanwhile, out in the market, some investors suggested it would be better to talk about Bricks (with Korea included), or Brimck (with Mexico as well) or even Abrimcks (chucking in the Arab region and South Africa). One market wag joked that somebody should start trading the Cement bloc (Countries Excluded from the Emerging New Terminology).

O'Neill fought back. The Goldman team started to crank out Bric research, looking at everything from the future size of the Indian middle class to car use in Brazil. In an effort to soothe some ruffled feathers, in 2005 O'Neill tried to explain why Korea and Mexico had not been included in his big idea (the rather arbitrary-sounding reason was that they were members of the Organisation for Economic Co-operation and Development). He also tried to placate some of the non-Brics by offering a new term: the "N-11", or Next Eleven nations on the list to emerge as powers. This was a confusingly broad club, encompassing Bangladesh, Egypt, Indonesia, Iran, Korea, Mexico, Nigeria, Pakistan, the Philippines, Turkey and Vietnam, but within months companies such as Nissan and WPP were bandying "N-11" around their boardrooms. Another marketing tag—or boundary on a cognitive map—had been born.

Nor was it just the corporate world getting excited. O'Neill heard that politicians in Nigeria were slapping the term on their internal propaganda campaigns, redefining some of the slogans for their own ends; it was uncannily reminiscent of how 19th-century Nigerians once transposed the language of the Anglican Church to their own cultural traditions.

Perhaps the most remarkable aspect of O'Neill's golden child is what it didn't do: collapse under scrutiny as the credit crisis hit. Over the past two years, many of Wall Street's big ideas have been exposed as woefully ill-conceived at best, utterly fallacious at worst. However, during the great re-reckoning, the Brics concept has flourished. Most of the Brics and N-11 emerged from the crisis well, relative to the economies of the western world. Their banking systems are intact, and their economies are growing at breakneck speed. "As a result," wrote O'Neill in a recent paper, "we think our long-term 2050 Bric 'dream' projections are more, rather than less, likely to materialise." More specifically, Goldman now predicts that China's economy will become as big as the US's by 2027, while the total Brics group will eclipse the big western economies by 2032—almost a decade sooner than first thought.

That, O'Neill argues, will overturn many western assumptions about how the world works. These days, Goldman aggressively recommends that investors decide which western companies to invest in based on whether they are selling to the Brics and N11, rather than just western consumers. (In another piece of neat cultural transposition, Goldman recently dubbed this strategy "investment in the Brics Nifty 50" [companies which sell to the Brics region]—a reference to the "nifty 50" of big western companies that were beloved by investors back in the 1970s, when it was presumed that the US and Europe would provide the engines of growth.) "We estimate that two billion people could join the global middle-class by 2030, mainly from Brics," Goldman's latest research note trills.

The argument is beloved by some investors. "Had you heeded O'Neill's work and gotten invested in the stock markets of those four nations [back in 2001], you'd have made more money this past decade than by doing virtually anything else conceivable," declared Joshua Brown, an influential investment commentator, on his Wall Street blog last month. (O'Neill brushes off the praise as "somewhat embarrassing".) Others fear it is the next big bubble. To some, the exclusion of countries such as South Africa—or even Indonesia—looks increasingly odd. And the inclusion of Russia is presenting an ever-greater headache, given that the Russian economy was the one Bric to take a real fall in the credit crisis—so severe, in fact, that some investors (and even a few bankers inside Goldman) suspect it is now time to kick Russia out of the group.

Unsurprisingly, O'Neill is reluctant to undermine Goldman's relations with Moscow by doing that. Although he admits that Russia has "disappointed", he also insists that if the country "recovers strongly and quickly in 2010 and 2011, as we expect, we believe it will deserve its Bric status."

But now another Brics-related phenomenon is emerging. In the early years of Bric-dom, the four countries chosen by O'Neill had different reactions to the designation. There was delight in Russia, bafflement in China, cynicism in Brazil and indifference in India. Now, the countries are using the idea to forge tentative links in reality—not just the world of investment ideas. In May 2008, Russia hosted the first formal Bric summit, a meeting of Bric foreign ministers in Yekaterinburg. In July 2009, it followed this with a formal gathering of all four Bric heads of state.

As meetings go, these were symbolic, not substantive. Although the four countries discussed how they could better co-ordinate their affairs to gain greater influence—and seek alternatives to the dollar—they did not agree on any tangible steps. But this year in the early summer, the four countries will meet again, this time in Brazil. In anticipation, the Brazilian authorities are establishing a group of academics and a formal think-tank to brainstorm how to develop the Brics agenda. As part of that, they plan to host a conference next month in Rio—with the participation of O'Neill himself. McKinsey, which has used a version of the Brics concept in its consulting strategy, will also be involved.

It might seem ironic that the four countries would choose a term created by an American bank to define themselves but it is not unprecedented. When countries such as India first developed their sense of national identity and rebelled against the British—or when Soviet republics such as Uzbekistan developed a similar nationalism–they did so using the borders that had also been imposed, artificially and arbitrarily, by an outside power. When the cognitive map is redrawn by a dominant power—even in the world of marketing and investment bank "spin"—it tends not to be erased so much as appropriated.

"Is there much evidence that the Brics countries are collaborating today in practical terms?" O'Neill asks. "Not really, no. But that could change in the future—you look at how Brazil supplies commodities which China needs . . . or the fact that they all have quite similar ideas about how to manage their economies."

Or as Felipe Goes, the Brazilian official in Rio charged with setting up the world's first Brics think-tank, says: "It is somewhat ironic [that we use the word Brics] . . . but that reflects the fact that in the modern world it is people like Goldman Sachs and McKinsey who have the resources and minds to develop ideas." Indeed, what makes a large institution such as Goldman so influential these days is not simply its trading acumen and political connections, but also its ability to invest heavily in what bankers sometimes call "thought-leadership", by funding analysis and ensuring it is read around the world.

Back in New York, some of Goldman's older managers are aware of the cultural ironies of the Brics boom. During the first 120 years of its history, Goldman made most of its profits from American markets, and today the firm is often viewed as the most politically well-connected of the US banks. If you step into the office of its headquarters at 85 Broad Street, in downtown Manhattan, the first thing that you see is a vast American flag, looming over the dull brown marble lobby. Yet appearances can deceive. While O'Neill has spent the past decade trying to carve out his own intellectual niche by promoting the Brics, so too—far more discreetly—Goldman has been remaking itself, building activities outside the American heartland to capture the growth that O'Neill forecasts. In the past decade, the bank has opened more offices across the world than in the whole of its previous history, and while revenues from the Americas accounted for 60 per cent of its earnings 10 years ago, they now represent about half (and far less if Latin America is excluded). Indeed, senior Goldman executives expect that within a few years, profits that are "made in America" will be a minority of total earnings.

That pattern is certainly not unique to Goldman Sachs: most other western banks have also been expanding across the globe in the past few years. Deutsche Bank, for example, has been deftly building an emerging markets derivatives franchise, while HSBC is now so convinced that its future lies in Asia that Michael Geoghegan, chief executive, recently relocated to Hong Kong from London.

Still, the swing is particularly striking at Goldman, given its all-American past. These days, one of the buzzwords at 85 Broad Street is "domestification", or the idea that the bank must build businesses around the world that provide local clients not simply with international services, but also with services in their local markets. Rather than treating non-western countries as far-flung frontiers or pawns in a trading game, the new corporate rhetoric insists that the Brics (and other non-western countries) are markets in their own rights. Thus in Brazil, Goldman recently started selling Brazilian investment funds to Brazilians. In Japan, there are staff who barely speak a word of English. And in China—where Goldman Sachs most certainly does not fly a big US flag—the bank is sponsoring a Chinese business school, to ensure access to a stream of authentically local Chinese students.

This drive is going hand in hand with a complex process of cultural engineering. As the bank acquires more non-western staff, it is devising programmes to rotate its locally hired employees through headquarters, to ensure that they learn "Goldman values". It also takes care to send staff from New York and London out to the regions, and to shuffle different ethnic groups between different regions.

As its sponsorship of Chinese business schools shows, Goldman is trying to raise a new generation of local leaders. "If you look at the history of the London office of Goldman, you can see how over a decade or two, you can have locals rise to the top," says one top executive. "That is our goal across the world. The idea is to get embedded, to show that we are there for the long term . . . but also to ensure that our Goldman values are everywhere in the world."

It all might sound reminiscent of the way the British empire operated in the 19th century—or the way the Russian Communist party once tried to knit the diverse peoples of the Soviet Union into a single ideologically based nation. Only this time, it is MBA programmes and Goldman training courses, rather than British public schools or communist training camps, that provide the cultural glue. And—perhaps most important of all—Goldman Sachs (unlike earlier empires) is not overtly acting with a nationalist or political agenda; insofar as it has a real loyalty, it is to its own bottom line and its ability to make profits.

Put it another way: Goldman will keep flying Old Glory only as long as it believes that there is profit to be made under that banner. No wonder a senior member of the US government remarked a couple of years ago, partly in jest, that sooner or later, Goldman "is going to have to choose whether it wants to really be American or not". If O'Neill is even half-right in his predictions, it may not be a straightforward choice.

Gillian Tett is the FT's capital markets editor. Her last piece for the magazine was about the JP Morgan bankers who invented the "credit derivative"—and their reactions to the derivatives-induced financial crisis. Read it at www.ft.com/foolsgold

On Monday, the FT begins a five-part series on Bric consumers–who they are, what they buy, who is selling to them and what their rise means for the global economy.

The Enterprise of the Future

MARK HENNESSY

Last May, IBM unveiled results from its 2008 Global CEO survey where we asked more than 1,000 CEOs around the world how their organizations were addressing new and changing customers, global integration, and business model innovation. Not surprisingly, our analysis found there is a clear difference in how successful organizations are addressing the future compared to the approach taken by underperformers. We also learned that CEOs are looking to the CIO as a crucial leader in determining an organization's success, with the support of the CTO.

Today, a CIO has power unimaginable only 10 years ago. In the past, success was based on technical expertise. But today, CIOs don't just keep the organization running, they are also a catalyst of change—and in charge of moving their organizations forward. CIOs can transform the IT structure of the organization and rely on CTOs to extend that transformation into a company's products and research initiatives.

The vision for the future as shaped by our CEO survey that unveiled the "Enterprise of the Future" will be: hungry for change, innovative beyond customer imagination, globally integrated, disruptive by nature, and, in terms of social responsibility, not just generous, but genuine in all of its actions and decisions. I believe that by identifying the five characteristics CEOs see as the future enterprise, there are five strategies CIOs need to adopt to attain success in this new era.

1. *Use IT infrastructures that can respond to rapid, and constant, change, while also mitigating risk.*

CEOs have said that their organizations are bombarded by change, and many are struggling to keep up. CIOs have a unique vision across the enterprise and an understanding of the core processes and information that make the organization tick. CIOs should look for approaches like Service Oriented Architecture (SOA), open standards, virtualization and consolidation, converged communications, multi-sourcing and shared services—which all gain new appeal in this environment.

Change also brings risk—and our jobs are all about managing and minimizing risks—so enhanced risk mitigation, business resiliency, security and service management initiatives will be key to success.

2. *Provide and invest in technology that encourages collaboration with the empowered customer.*

The enterprise of the future is also one that is innovative beyond customer imagination. The rise of the Internet and connectivity has produced a more informed, demanding customer—capable of influencing peers on buying decisions. It's therefore important to find ways to cultivate these influencers through the development of collaborative relationships. A major capability to develop and exploit is providing customers ready access to information and interaction. We need to deliver better, more convenient ways to transact business, and better, real-time collaboration. This requires the application of new technologies like Web 2.0, SOA, social networking, and 24 × 7 access to self-help portals. The CTO can look at social networking with demanding customers as a way to gain insight for new research projects and products. The empowered consumers are no longer a threat, but provide an opportunity to differentiate.

3. *Use IT to integrate global data and information.*

Nearly all CEOs are adapting their business models and moving aggressively toward global business designs. The third key to the Enterprise of the Future is global integration, and that's something that technology is ideally suited to support. Technology can help shrink the world via global integration of applications and common data strategies, improved communications and access—from anywhere, via any device, at any time. With CEOs moving to global business models and embracing global partnerships and integration, information must flow seamlessly around the world. This requires an infrastructure that removes barriers to integration by adopting common standards and collaborative tools and techniques.

However, getting there requires an investment in expanded IT and bandwidth—and integrating people, processes and information is challenging. I know that first-hand, since we've been on our own journey toward becoming a globally integrated enterprise.

The Enterprise of the Future is also going to be disruptive by nature. What does that mean for CIOs? Well, we know that flexible, adaptable IT systems can remove obstacles to business-model changes and help meet the accelerating pace of change—including integrating acquisitions into the fabric of the enterprise. So, it is essential that the CIO be able to engage and lead the right level of discussion to ensure successful support of business model transformation. This approach requires leading the discussion on business, not technology,

20 Largest R&D Spending Industries in 2008 and 2009 (by SIC Group)

Industry	SIC No.	R&D Spending (Millions $)		R&D $ as % Sales	R&D $ as % Margin	Annual R&D % Growth (3)
		2008 (1)	2009 (2)			
Aircraft	3721	7549	8253	6.1	30.6	9.8
Biological pds, ex diagnostics	2836	10283	11506	20.5	27.4	15.7
Chemicals and allied products	2800	6476	6505	3.5	9.1	0.5
CMP programming, data process	7370	19281	20733	8.8	19.1	7.9
Computer and office equipment	3570	8971	9492	3.5	13.4	6.0
Computer communication equip	3576	7805	8643	14.1	22.1	11.4
Conglomerate	9997	8491	8591	1.9	4.7	1.5
Electr, other elec eq, ex CMP	3600	10350	9970	4.4	13.5	−3.8
Electronic computers	3571	7503	7998	5.1	15.3	6.8
Household audio and video eq	3651	4996	5022	6.1	48.5	0.5
Motor vehicle parts, accessory	3714	6729	6801	4.4	28.8	1.9
Motor vehicles and car bodies	3711	47618	49869	3.8	16.4	−1.5
Petroleum refining	2911	10271	11609	0.3	1.4	14.0
Pharmaceutical preparations	2834	96468	105577	17.3	22.5	9.9
Phone comm ex radiotelephone	4813	6562	7030	0.8	1.7	4.7
Prepackaged software	7372	27989	30821	4.6	20.7	10.7
Radio, TV broadcast, comm eq	3663	25544	28712	10.7	31.0	13.2
Radiotelephone communication	4812	9646	10082	2.7	4.8	5.7
Semiconductor, related device	3674	32478	34935	13.1	27.9	8.5
Tele and telegraph apparatus	3661	8223	9083	14.8	36.9	10.2

R&D Ratios & Budgets. June 2008 Edition. Published by Schonfeld & Associates, Inc., Libertyville, Illinois, www.saiBooks.com. *(1)* Estimate, *(2)* Forecast, *(3)* Annual growth rate is relative to 2007.

terms. It's calculating ROI on systems and applications that support new models, not merely requesting the expense to plan and build them.

4. *Look for IT that leverages social responsibility initiatives.*

We learned that CEOs are embracing social responsibility initiatives, and both CIOs and CTOs can play a leadership role here, too.

CTOs can work with engineers, developers and designers to create sustainable and environmentally friendly products. These must have longer product life cycles, require little or no replacement of parts, and can be recycled or disposed of with minimal environmental impact.

CIOs can implement technologies that make the business more sustainable as well. For example, major energy and money savings are possible through consolidation and virtualization of data centers. IT plays a major role in enabling workforce mobility, too. Greater mobility enables alternate work locations, which can cut down on commuter mileage and energy use, while lowering business expense and increasing worker productivity and satisfaction.

At IBM, 40 percent of our workforce across the world is now mobile—and we see that trend toward mobility accelerating as the number of mobile devices accessing data over networks doubles every 2.5 years. This requires a resilient IT infrastructure and an even greater emphasis on data and communications security. We anticipate more change in this area with the introduction of innovative new enterprise mobile technologies and applications.

5. *Be bold!*

Finally, we learned that financial outperformers are making bolder plays than the organizations that are lagging. Both CTOs and CIOs are in a unique position to explain the strategic business value to IT investments and move the business forward. Remember, the CEO is looking to the CIO to be a catalyst of change, and the CTO is integral to that effort.

From *Research-Technology Management*, September/October 2008, pp. 7–8. Copyright © 2008 by Industrial Research Institute, Inc. Reprinted by permission.

Finding a Job in the 21st Century

Seek training, be flexible, and get hired in the fast-moving working world of the future.

JOHN A. CHALLENGER

The current recession, expected to be the worst economic crisis since the Great Depression, will surely put to rest those old concerns about looming labor shortages, right? Probably not. In fact, immigration, globalization, outsourcing, and other trends affecting employment and the workplace will evolve over the next five, 10, and 20 years to change the workplace completely, and well-trained and flexible workers will be at a premium.

More than 5 million layoffs have been announced in the United States since the beginning of 2008. Economists are projecting that U.S. unemployment may top out at 10.5% or over 11% by the middle of 2010.

At Challenger, Gray & Christmas, we look at official unemployment, but we also track job-cut announcements. These provide an indication of where the job market is going in the short term.

We observed in April that the rate of layoffs, while still high, was slowing. The global economy was not entering a roaring recovery, but we were hearing faint signals that the worst of the worst was over. On the one hand, manufacturing jobs in the United States continued to vanish. On the other hand, the layoff rate in the financial sector seemed to have stabilized.

At our firm, we talk to human-resources people around the country on a casual, anecdotal basis; the people we're speaking with are taking whatever measures they can to avoid making further layoffs. They don't want to be short-staffed in the event of a turnaround. The current cycle will surely go down in history as the worst in most people's memory. Fortunately, the future of work looks completely different.

Key Piece of Advice for Job Seekers

As unemployment continues to rise, more people are seeking help to improve their employability. My key piece of advice for job seekers is to get a fast start. Don't let your résumé gather dust. If you've been laid off, use contacts as quickly as possible to uncover new positions and opportunities.

The second piece of advice I offer is to consider changing industries. Look outside your normal boundaries, but look within your job function. You'll want to pursue jobs that correspond to your core competency and that lets you do what you do best. Your skills are your best asset; they're what you're selling. Be ready to make the potential customer list for those skills as long as possible. What many people don't realize is the variety of jobs in different fields that may be open in a single industry, requiring people with all sorts of talents and abilities.

Let me give an example: Health care is commonly touted as an industry forever in need of workers. Conversely, the personal computer (PC) market in the United States has been weak of late. Our firm counted layoffs in the computer industry up 75% in 2008 from the year before, and analysts expect PC sales to fall an additional 10% by the end of 2009.

For a qualified IT worker or computer programmer seeking employment, one strategy is to wait for the global PC market to recover. Another strategy is to sell your technical skills to a growing industry like health care.

Most of us assume that growth in health care translates into more competition among employers to find qualified nurses and doctors. Surely, the doctor and nurse shortage will continue and favor qualified candidates for those jobs in the future. But in the years ahead, as baby boomers and the United States spend more money on medical care, the industry will need more computer scientists and database technicians to streamline operations and create new systems.

The coming innovation leap that will sweep the health-care field will extend well beyond simply digitizing medical records. If the industry is to meet rising demands for service from an aging population and contain costs, it will become

U.S. Employment Ups and Downs, 2006–2016

The Five Largest Employment increases

Job	Employees, 2006	Employees, 2016	Percentage Change
Network Systems and Data Communications Analyst	262,000	402,000	53.4%
Personal and Home Care Aide	767,000	1.16 million	50.6%
Home Health Aide	787,000	1.17 million	48.7%
Computer Software Engineer	507,000	733,000	44.6%
Veterinary Technologist/Technician	71,000	100,000	41.0%

The Five Largest Employment Declines

Job	Employees, 2006	Employees, 2016	Percentage Change
Photographic Processing Machine Operator	49,000	25,000	− 49.8%
File Clerk	234,000	137,000	− 41.3%
Sewing Machine Operator	233,000	170,000	− 27.2%
Electrical and Electronic Equipment Assembler	213,000	156,000	− 26.8%
Computer Operator	130,000	98,000	− 24.7%

Source: "Employment Projections: 2006–2016." U.S. Bureau of Labor Statistics. Website, www.bls.gov

much more reliant on information technology. The industry will need to reach and train qualified workers wherever they may be through e-learning technologies. Health-care providers will want to automate the delivery of health care as much as possible; they'll want to detect symptoms and diagnose patients remotely through advanced sensing technologies.

This is only one example among many. The health-care industry also needs therapists of all types, business managers, human resource professionals, and even journalists and communications workers to track new developments and medical breakthroughs and publicize good work or medical research to the public (and to potential hospital donors). The world still needs journalists, but the information gathering and refinement process that is journalism will, more and more, happen at communications offices or niche-specific publications as opposed to regional or local newspapers. Finding opportunity in the future may mean sacrificing the dream of working for a particular cherished employer or even for a particular type of company. Many industrial titans of the twentieth century won't exist five years from now. That doesn't mean skills won't still be in demand.

The Globalized Workforce

Another question I'm asked frequently is, where are the jobs *going?* Many American workers fret about their jobs moving overseas to China and India. Outsourcing and even immigration have become convenient punching bags for pundits looking to blame someone or something for rising unemployment. But the argument that we can protect jobs by "keeping them at home" or "not hiring immigrant labor" doesn't reflect the realities of globalization or labor in the twenty-first century.

The global labor market is not a zero-sum game. If U.S. firms are going to reach new customers in China and India—and they will have to in order to grow and be relevant in the twentyfirst century—then they will have to hire workers in those countries. More people in these countries finding work will create bigger markets for U.S. goods. China will continue to build factories and operations in order to put its large population to work; India will grow as a mathematics and engineering center. In the Philippines, a great accounting and health-care center exists; in South Korea, a manufacturing base is flourishing and will continue to do so.

All of these countries will experience employment growth, and yes, some of the growth will be from American firms hiring in those countries partly to better secure access to the Chinese and Indian consumers. There's no getting around it: U.S. companies need to be able to compete in these international markets if they are to expand in the United States.

However, companies from around the world will also have plenty of reasons to hire in the United States, which has a highly skilled labor force and the most diverse population of any country. The United States is uniquely suited to reach out to a global population.

The strength of the U.S. economy lies in its ability to capture global growth and to collaborate with economies around the planet. In the years ahead, the way that growth occurs will be very different from the past. From the middle of the twentieth century onward, U.S. companies began expanding aggressively into other countries; the pursuit of global growth translated into large U.S. firms cajoling foreign officials for special treatment or special contracts to set up shop. For U.S. employees overseas, a corporate expansion meant higher salaries and more money to live apart from the local community. I call this the colonial corporate expansion model.

IBM is one of the first big companies to transition out of that mode of overseas expansion and into a more community-focused strategy. In February 2009, IBM gave 4,000 laid-off workers the opportunity to move to other countries where the company had positions open (India and Brazil, for example) through a program called Project Match. IBM was willing to pay for the move and help with visa procurement. The catch? The company told the employees that they would be paid local wages; the employees would live among the population.

Naturally, not every IBMer took to the idea. As originally reported in *Information Week,* one employee group called the Alliance@IBM was furious, complaining that the company was asking employees to "offshore themselves." They had a point; wages in India even for highly skilled IT workers are often a quarter of what they are in the United States.

But many of the employees—those with fewer commitments, who didn't have to worry about paying down a mortgage because they were young and just starting out, or who were looking to do something other than play shuffleboard in retirement—were intrigued by the idea and took the company up on the offer. Arrangements like Project Match may be a wave of the future, exciting and increasingly *de rigueur.* It reminds me of something I heard Larry Summers remark at a Harvard alumni event not long ago. When he was a student, he said, the final requirement to graduate was to swim a lap around the pool. In the future, it will be having spent a semester overseas.

Mobility, Flexibility, and the Workforce of the Future

IBM's Perfect Match program showcases one of the biggest trends to affect the future of work: increased mobility and flexibility. The information-technology revolution, which began with widespread adoption of PCs in the workplace in the 1980s, has changed virtually every aspect of doing business. In the next decade, that trend will accelerate and obliterate many long-held notions of work.

For many, the office of the future will not be an office at all. The mobile workforce will carry their office in their pocket; they'll work when it's most convenient for them or for the client. The U.S. Bureau of Labor Statistics reports that the number of Americans who worked from home or remotely at least one day per month for their employer rose from 12.4 million in 2006 to 17.2 million in 2008. (The trend may slow slightly in 2009.) Telecommuting is an easy way for employers facing tight budgets to give employees something that more and more of them say they want: time. Enhanced mobile flexibility will be a boon to the employers that take advantage of it as well. This will better enable smart companies to place employees where they can be most useful—namely, where customers and clients are located.

Contrary to a lot of popular opinion, face time is still important, but it may be less important within companies than between companies and customers.

Imagine, for instance, a customer walking into a car dealership and being greeted not by a salesperson but by an actual car designer, available to answer any and every technical query a consumer might have, or even design specifications on the spot (for a premium, of course). Many Ferrari buyers already get something like this royal treatment when they buy a new car directly from the factory in Maranello, Italy. For about $3.1 million, wealthy car enthusiasts can, in essence, design their own F430, 612 Scaglietti, or Enzo. What does the famously hobbled U.S. car industry look like when Chevrolet buyers can have the same personalized car-buying experience as someone buying a Ferrari Enzo?

Getting to that future from where we are now doesn't require a tremendous amount of technical IT innovation. What's needed is a little imagination and, again, flexibility. The twenty-somethings will lead this change. Today's younger workers will be the ones who help U.S. companies succeed abroad in the new era of globalization and mobility.

Hopefully, we'll continue to see more examples of the Project Match phenomenon playing with more people from more countries, coming to the United States to work as elements of the economy and to take advantage of U.S. educational opportunities. America's ability to attract these people is one of its key assets.

The U.S. economy will need these highly skilled workers desperately, a fact that underscores why immigration reform is so vital to the future of U.S. business. If the United States cannot remain an attractive destination for talented and well-trained workers from around the world, the country won't grow economically as it did in the past. Also, the U.S. government must find ways to support lifelong education. As new fields grow, education must become a permanent part of every worker's career.

Immigration reform and lifelong learning are critical if the United States is to overcome the looming talent shortage. In the years ahead, it will pay dividends not just economically, but also in terms of more-effective foreign policy.

The more people from more places who feel they have a connection to America—either because someone they know has gone to America on a work or student visa or because they had a positive experience with a U.S. worker locally—the more effective the U.S. government will be in marketing its policies abroad. My hope is that people from around the world still want to take part in the U.S. educational experience. But American educational institutions will also expand as global brands with campuses in China, India, Europe, Africa, and Latin America.

The opportunities of the future will go to the best-trained, most-flexible candidates, and they will be spread globally. But opportunity exists and will increase; of that you can be certain.

JOHN A. CHALLENGER, chief executive officer of Challenger, Gray & Christmas, is one of the most quoted labor and employment experts in America. He's become a regular fixture on CNN, CBS, and a host of other networks and is a featured speaker at WorldFuture 2009, the annual conference of the World Future Society. Website www.challengergray.com.

Test-Your-Knowledge Form

We encourage you to photocopy and use this page as a tool to assess how the articles in *Annual Editions* expand on the information in your textbook. By reflecting on the articles you will gain enhanced text information. You can also access this useful form on a product's book support website at www.mhhe.com/cls

NAME: DATE:

_____

TITLE AND NUMBER OF ARTICLE:

_____

BRIEFLY STATE THE MAIN IDEA OF THIS ARTICLE:

_____

LIST THREE IMPORTANT FACTS THAT THE AUTHOR USES TO SUPPORT THE MAIN IDEA:

_____

WHAT INFORMATION OR IDEAS DISCUSSED IN THIS ARTICLE ARE ALSO DISCUSSED IN YOUR TEXTBOOK OR OTHER READINGS THAT YOU HAVE DONE? LIST THE TEXTBOOK CHAPTERS AND PAGE NUMBERS:

_____

LIST ANY EXAMPLES OF BIAS OR FAULTY REASONING THAT YOU FOUND IN THE ARTICLE:

_____

LIST ANY NEW TERMS/CONCEPTS THAT WERE DISCUSSED IN THE ARTICLE, AND WRITE A SHORT DEFINITION:

We Want Your Advice

ANNUAL EDITIONS revisions depend on two major opinion sources: one is our Advisory Board, listed in the front of this volume, which works with us in scanning the thousands of articles published in the public press each year; the other is you—the person actually using the book. Please help us and the users of the next edition by completing the prepaid article rating form on this page and returning it to us. Thank you for your help!

ANNUAL EDITIONS: International Business 16/e

ARTICLE RATING FORM

Here is an opportunity for you to have direct input into the next revision of this volume.
We would like you to rate each of the articles listed below, using the following scale:

1. **Excellent: should definitely be retained**
2. **Above average: should probably be retained**
3. **Below average: should probably be deleted**
4. **Poor: should definitely be deleted**

Your ratings will play a vital part in the next revision.
Please mail this prepaid form to us as soon as possible.
Thanks for your help!

RATING	ARTICLE	RATING	ARTICLE
	1. Globalization: Where Do We Go from Here?		22. Expanding Opportunity at the Base of the Pyramid
	2. China Must Carry the World		23. Hailun Piano and the Quest for Quality
	3. The World Is Not Flat		24. Distant Dilemmas
	4. Is Global Trade a Threat or Opportunity?		25. Jobs on Another Shore
	5. Economists Rethink Free Trade		26. Offshored Headquarters
	6. Globalization with a Human Face		27. A Material World
	7. The Global Debt Bomb		28. Keynote Panel Session 1: Whose Income Is It? How Business Is Caught in the Global Competition and Controversy for Tax Revenues
	8. The World Economy: The Global Financial Crisis and Collapse in World Trade		
	9. International Special Report: A Financial Crisis to the West—a Fundamental Crisis to the East		29. Exploiting the Global Supply Chain
	10. "Everyone Needs to Rethink Everything": Reflections from the IMF's Former Chief Economist		30. What One Hand Gives, the Other Takes: Industrial Countries' Policy Coherence for Development
			31. Unequal Access
	11. The Balance of Payments: Office for National Statistics		32. China and India Go to Africa: New Deals in the Developing World
	12. Potential Future Functions of the World Trade Organization		33. International OHS: Through the Looking Glass of the Global Economy
	13. The Wicked Problem of Good Financial Markets		34. Deadly Business in Moscow
	14. Engaging China: Strategies for the Small Internationalizing Firm		35. Global Corporate Citizenship: Working with Governments and Civil Society
	15. Planning Ahead for IFRS 1: Initial Adoption of IFRS by U.S. Companies		36. Going Green: The Challenges and the Solutions
	16. The Global Financial Crisis: What Went Wrong?		37. The New Population Bomb: The Four Megatrends That Will Change the World
	17. The Work Left Undone: Perspectives on Small Business Opportunities in International Trade		38. The Man Who Named the Future
	18. Brazil's Iron Giant Reaches for the Top		39. The Enterprise of the Future
	19. NanoTech Firm Takes Passage to India		40. Finding a Job in the 21st Century
	20. Tata: Master of the Gentle Approach		
	21. Rethinking Globalization: Does "Think Global, Act Local" Still Apply?		

ANNUAL EDITIONS: INTERNATIONAL BUSINESS 16/e

NO POSTAGE
NECESSARY
IF MAILED
IN THE
UNITED STATES

BUSINESS REPLY MAIL
FIRST CLASS MAIL PERMIT NO. 551 DUBUQUE IA

POSTAGE WILL BE PAID BY ADDRESSEE

McGraw-Hill Contemporary Learning Series
501 BELL STREET
DUBUQUE, IA 52001

ABOUT YOU

Name

Date

_____

Are you a teacher? ❏ A student? ❏
Your school's name

_____

Department

_____

Address   City   State   Zip

_____

School telephone #

_____

YOUR COMMENTS ARE IMPORTANT TO US!

Please fill in the following information:
For which course did you use this book?

_____

Did you use a text with this ANNUAL EDITION? ❏ yes ❏ no
What was the title of the text?

_____

What are your general reactions to the Annual Editions concept?

_____

Have you read any pertinent articles recently that you think should be included in the next edition? Explain.

_____

Are there any articles that you feel should be replaced in the next edition? Why?

_____

Are there any World Wide Websites that you feel should be included in the next edition? Please annotate.

_____

May we contact you for editorial input? ❏ yes ❏ no
May we quote your comments? ❏ yes ❏ no